DUNCAN REGEHR

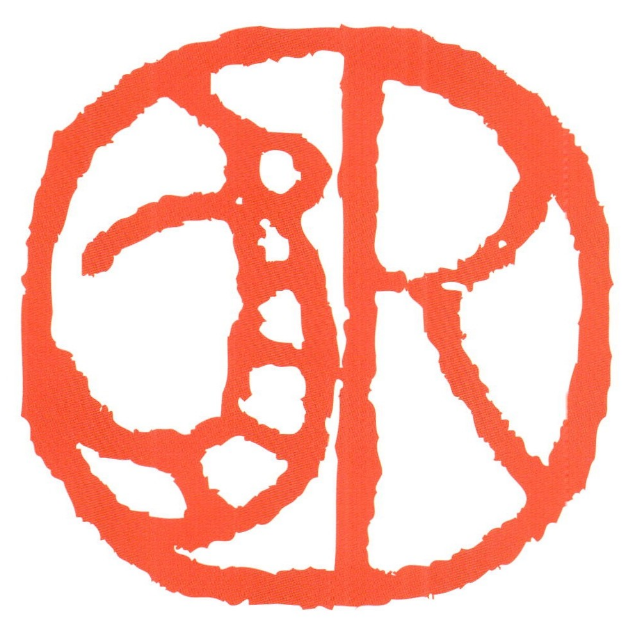

THE DRAGON'S EYE

An Artist's View

DUNCAN REGEHR

THE DRAGON'S EYE

An Artist's View

To Jonathan,
You have a great eye my friend.
With every good wish,
Duncan R.

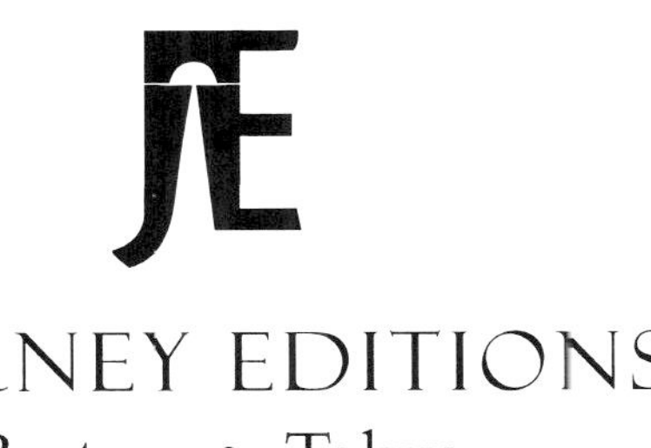

JOURNEY EDITIONS
Boston • Tokyo

For Catherine

First published in 1994 by
JOURNEY EDITIONS
153 Milk Street
Boston, Massachusetts, 02109

Library of Congress Cataloging-in-Publication Data
Regehr, Duncan,
The dragon's eye : an artist view / Duncan regehr.
p. cm.
1. Regehr, Duncan--Catalogs. I. title.
ND237.R277A4 1994
759.13--dc20 94-20866
CIP

ISBN 1-885203-03-9

Designed by Cynthia Patterson
Edited by Kathryn Leigh Scott

First Edition

3 5 7 9 10 8 6 4 2

Printed in Hong Kong

ACKNOWLEDGMENTS

I am greatly indebted to my dear friend, Jim McMullan for instigating the making of this book and to Peter Ackroyd for publishing it; to Cynthia Patterson who spent long hours with me designing this volume (and for her excellent midnight meals of Korean yams and vegetarian dumplings); to Kathryn Leigh Scott for her clarity; to Kevin and Joanna Connor for allowing me to stay in their lovely Los Angeles home while editing the final draft; to Baron and Baroness Devere-Austin of Delvin, Lord and Lady of Bradwell, for their counsel and insight; to my parents and family for their blessings; and to Roberta Scimone, Kathryn Sky-Peck, and the entire Journey Editions staff.

I give special thanks to the Los Angeles art agent, Donald Fonger, his wife Jan Dorian Whitney, and their crew at Museum Classics for retrieving so many of my works; and to "Q" Siebenthal, Simon Des Roches, and C. J. Campion for their photography.

My gratitude extends to all the collectors and contributors who sent slides and original work for image reproduction.

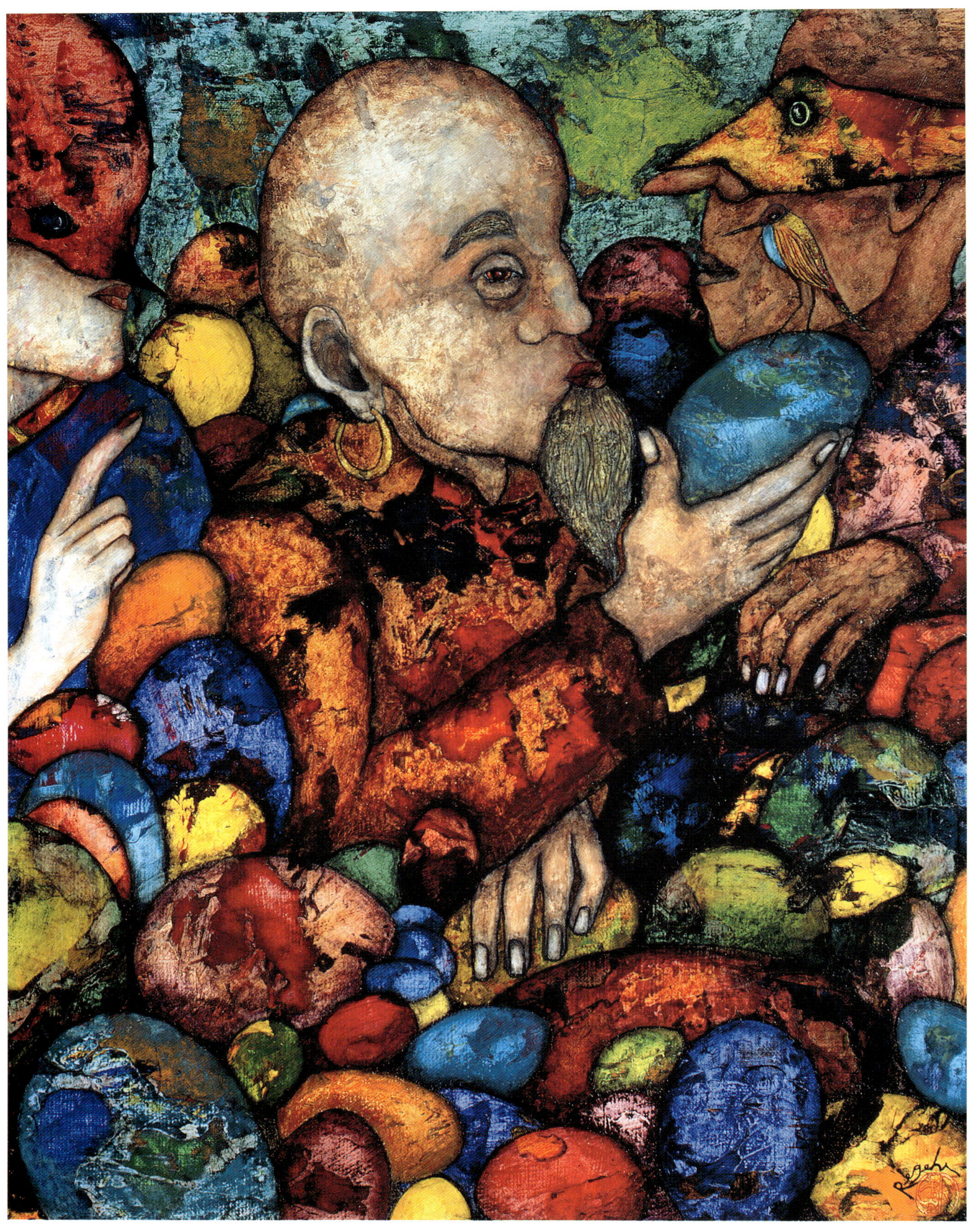

Miracle Minders OIL 24" x 18" 1992

CONTENTS

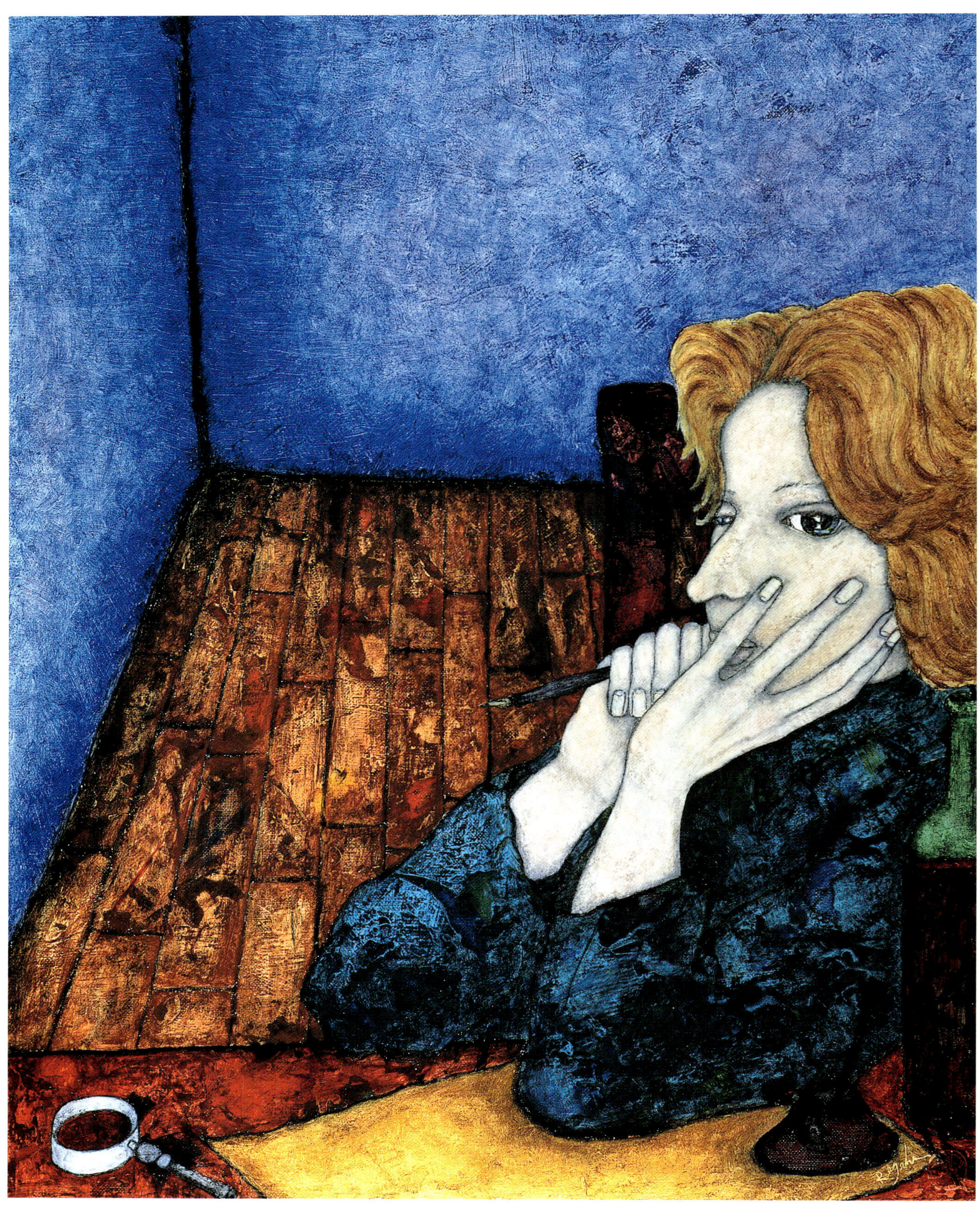

The Poet Oil 24" x 19" 1992

PREFACE

I am the sum of my art.
Therein lies my life.

THIS BOOK COULD BE described as an automonograph. Auto, in that it was written by the self, of the self. Monograph, since it focuses on a single category—the creation of art—as it relates to specific episodes of my life.

Apart from the first few pages which address early development and childhood, the chapters concentrate on the time between 1973 and 1993, and cover eight areas, or series, of my work.

The last twenty years of my paintings, prose, and verse reveal much more than this text or the small collection of plates enclosed with it; but the text does provide glimpses of experience and thought which may help to illuminate the growth of my work. The full range of influence is impossible to grasp, least of all by me.

Painting, acting, and writing monopolize my creative time, so it makes sense to speak of them as my life, rather than to refer to them as separate careers.

There are many artistic contributors who share in the development of an actor's performance, i.e., the director, the cinematographer, the editor, and the other actors. Writing can be influenced by a literary editor. But painting is a solo art medium, whereby I am the producer, director, performer. In that sense it could be viewed as a pure form of creative expression. However, each of these mediums does not outweigh another in its importance. Together, they support and influence each other to create a single voice through my life.

Michelangelo is famous for his work in the realms of sculpture, painting, and architecture. He is less known for his splendid creations as a poet. The merit of his literary reflections easily rivals that of his Renaissance contemporaries, some of whom chose writing as their only form of expression. Celebrity blinds as often as it blesses acknowledgment of the various mediums that make up an artist's life. But celebrity does not an artist make, talent does.

That precious art in which one time I was
Of so much reputation, now has made me
A poor old man, a slave in other's hands
I am undone, unless I perish soon.
—MICHELANGELO

For my own part, I have been blessed with a small measure of fame in recent years through acting in television and films. I can quite honestly state that my best work as an actor has been presented on the stage, in performances that have come and gone, unseen by most of the populace. For better or worse, television and film have had the advantage of offering global exposure via satellite broadcasting and cinematic publicity.

If the prominence I retain from the Silver Screen outweighs my recognition in the theatre, then it has certainly overwhelmed my presence as a painter and as a writer. Each of those two mediums has been a compelling force throughout my life.

Nor fame I slight, nor for her favors call;
She comes unlooked for, if she comes at all.
—ALEXANDER POPE

It is of little artistic importance that this book might adjust the scales of renown. Even less, if I consider the penniless life of that great letter-writing painter, Vincent Van Gogh, who neither welcomed nor received much attention until very near his death. Many contend that fame itself pushed poor Vincent to suicide. What is important is that the work represented on these pages will speak for itself, regardless of my status in other fields.

Along with my thanks to Charles E. Tuttle for asking me to write and compile this automonograph, I am equally grateful to celebrity for helping to promote the launch of it. My deepest appreciation is reserved for the publishers and exhibitors who supported my written and painted work long before they became aware of me as a thespian, and especially to those who continue their encouragement of all artists who choose to express themselves through more than one discipline of art.

The Muses speak as nine from one,
That when all is said and done,
The fruitful voice,
Through word and vision,
Bids art from each must come.
—DR

PROLOGUE

the story of the title

I WAS FILMING IN TORONTO during the Chinese New Year of 1988 (the Year of the Dragon). On a day off work I stopped by a small art supply shop in Chinatown and asked the proprietor where I could have a "chop" made. A chop is an engraved seal or ink-crest used mainly in the Orient as a signature by artists, officials and merchants to indicate the authenticity of drawings, goods, and manuscripts.

From the back room came a muffled voice. "I make. What you want for?"

The proprietor waved me through a curtained opening behind the counter. A small, elderly Chinese gentleman sat at a low desk lined with carving tools and various bits of soapstone.

"I'm an artist," I said, gesturing to the portfolio under my arm. "I was hoping to find someone who could make me a chop so that I can seal my work with it."

"I am also artist. Show me," he said, indicating my portfolio.

I spread my work out on a side counter. Most of the pieces were pen and ink line drawings, with a few black and white lithographs.

He took his time, studying the lines and details of each piece, at one point pausing to write my initials on a pad beside him. Finally, he held up a lithograph of "Brother Dragon and His Companion."

"You see through eye of the dragon," he smiled. "You give me this, I will make chop for you."

"O.K." I agreed. "But we should decide on a design."

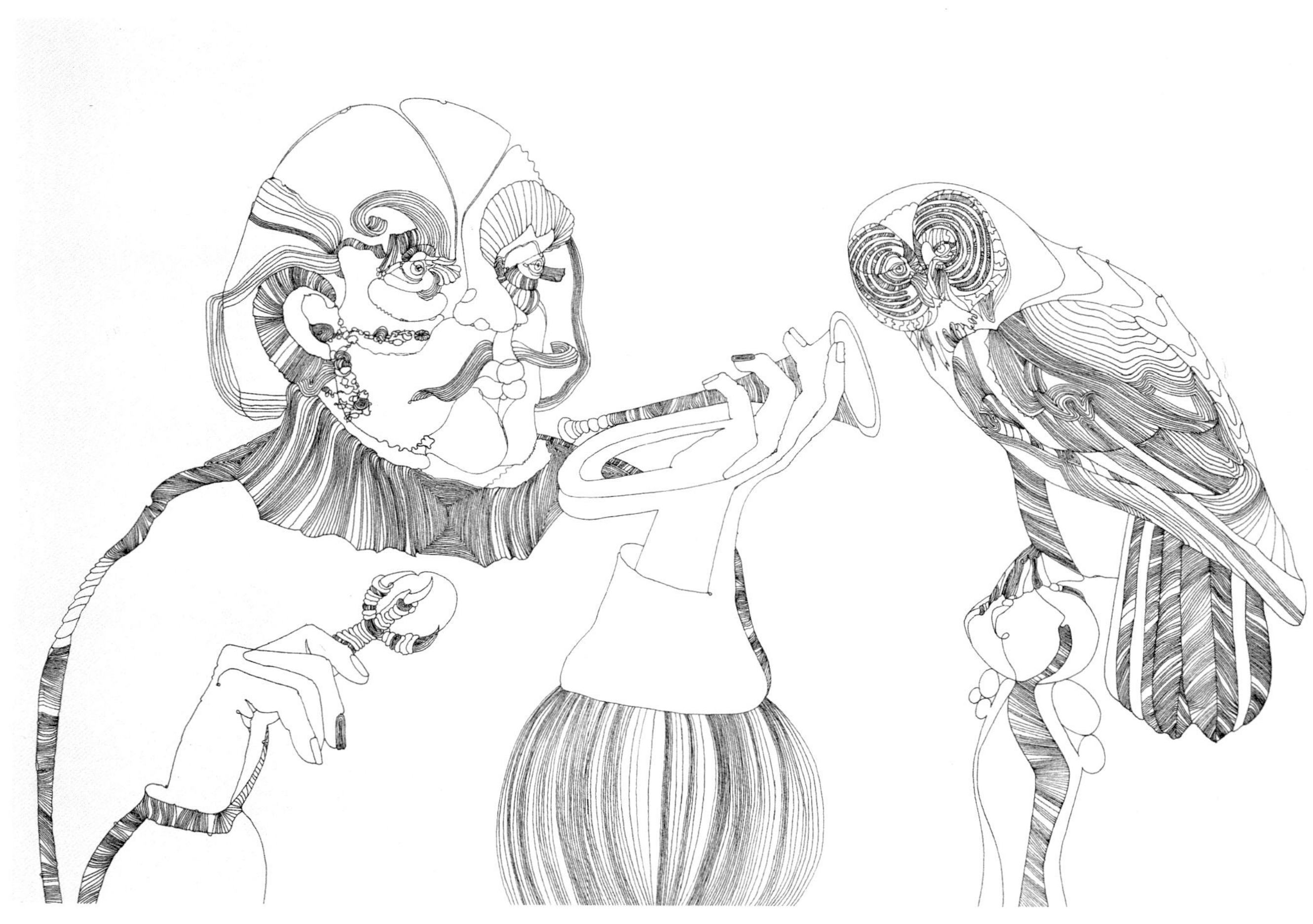

Brother Dragon and His Companion PEN AND INK 18" x 24"

He opened a drawer and pulled out a news article from the *Toronto Star* about the Year of the Dragon and a symbol that was believed to be the oldest written sign (well over ten thousand years old) of a Chinese dragon.

He carefully copied the dragon image, drawing beside it the initials of my name:

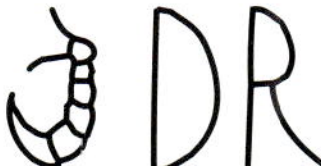

"You go now, come back maybe two hours. I make good chop for you. Dragon's eye." He chuckled.

A few hours later, I was embossing "Brother Dragon and His Companion" with my new chop. The old fellow had cleverly combined and carved the three images into a circular shape, not unlike an eye.

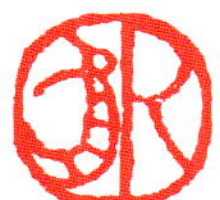

I have used the "Dragon's Eye" ever since, applying it to drawings, oil paintings, watercolors, and also to pieces that predate my chop's creation. I remained puzzled by the old man's comment, "You see through eye of the dragon," until the New Year of 1993 (the Year of the Rooster).

While I was writing this book and looking for an appropriate title, I became aware of an ancient Zen parable.

> *A master artist was summoned to the Emperor's court to paint an enormous mural of a dragon. He sent word that he was involved with other work of great importance and that he would be unable to do the painting.*
>
> *A royal aide arrived on the artist's doorstep with imperial orders to begin the mural at once. Again the artist explained that he was too involved with other work.*
>
> *The royal guards then seized the artist and dragged him to the Emperor's palace, where he was told that if he did not start painting immediately he would be put to death.*
>
> *The artist did as he was told. In a single day, he painted a most glorious multi-colored dragon, limned in gold.*
>
> *That evening the royal aide came to look upon the finished work and proclaimed it a masterpiece. The artist was paid a commission and told that the Emperor and his court would view the painting in the morning.*
>
> *The artist waited until everyone in the palace had gone to bed before applying two glowing white dots to the deep centers of the dragon's eyes. After collecting his materials, he covered the mural with a veil. Then he disappeared into the night and the far-off forest.*
>
> *Early the next day, the mural was unveiled before the Emperor and his court. All were enchanted by its exquisite beauty and lifelike features. As words of praise were voiced, the dragon's eyes flickered. His body slowly turned and he rose into the air, circling above the court before flying out of a window, leaving only his intricate outline on the white palace wall, and the red chop of the artist.*

I

SECRETS OF AN AUTODIDACT

Early Work and Portraits

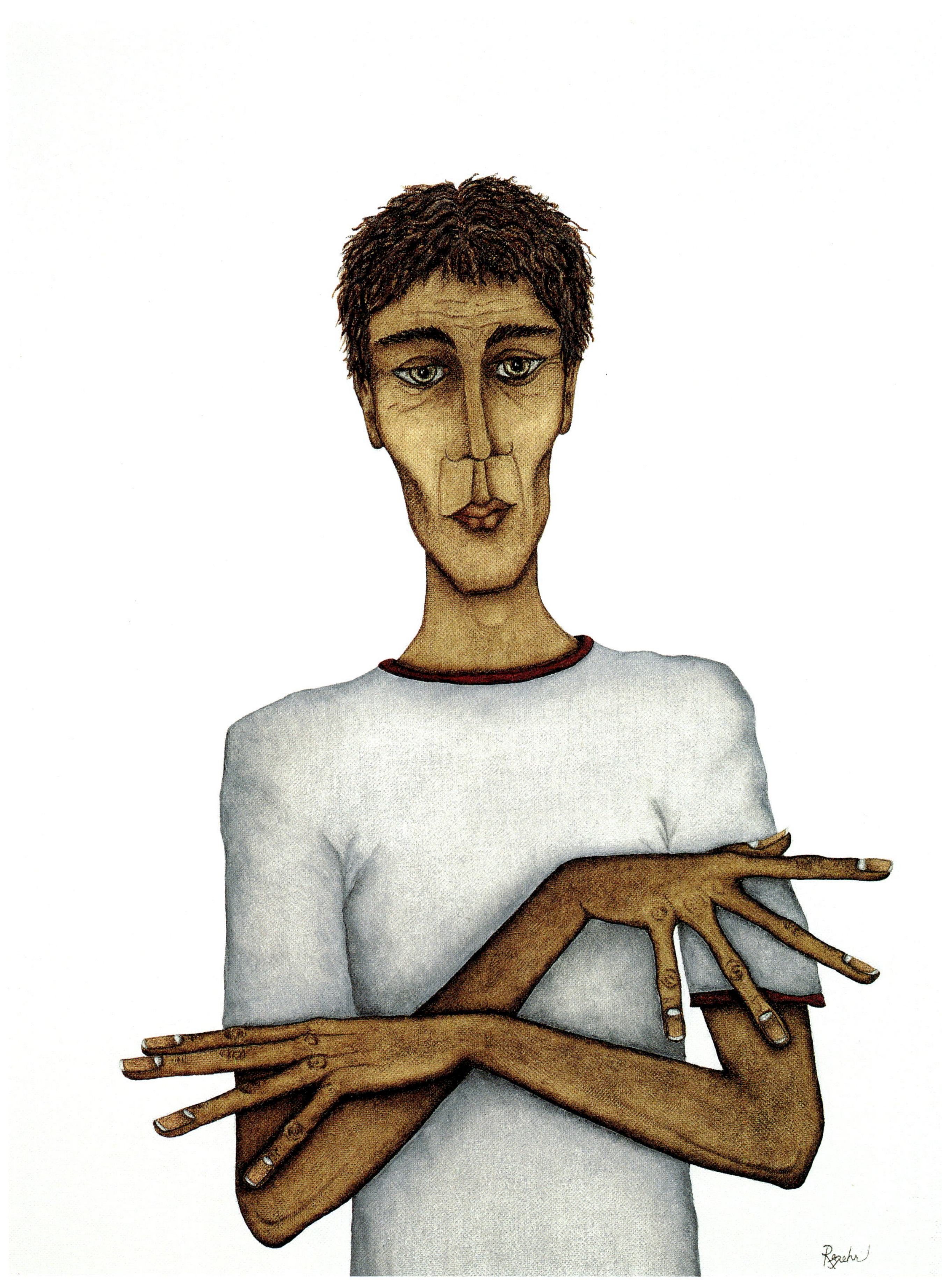

The Magician Oil 24" x 18"

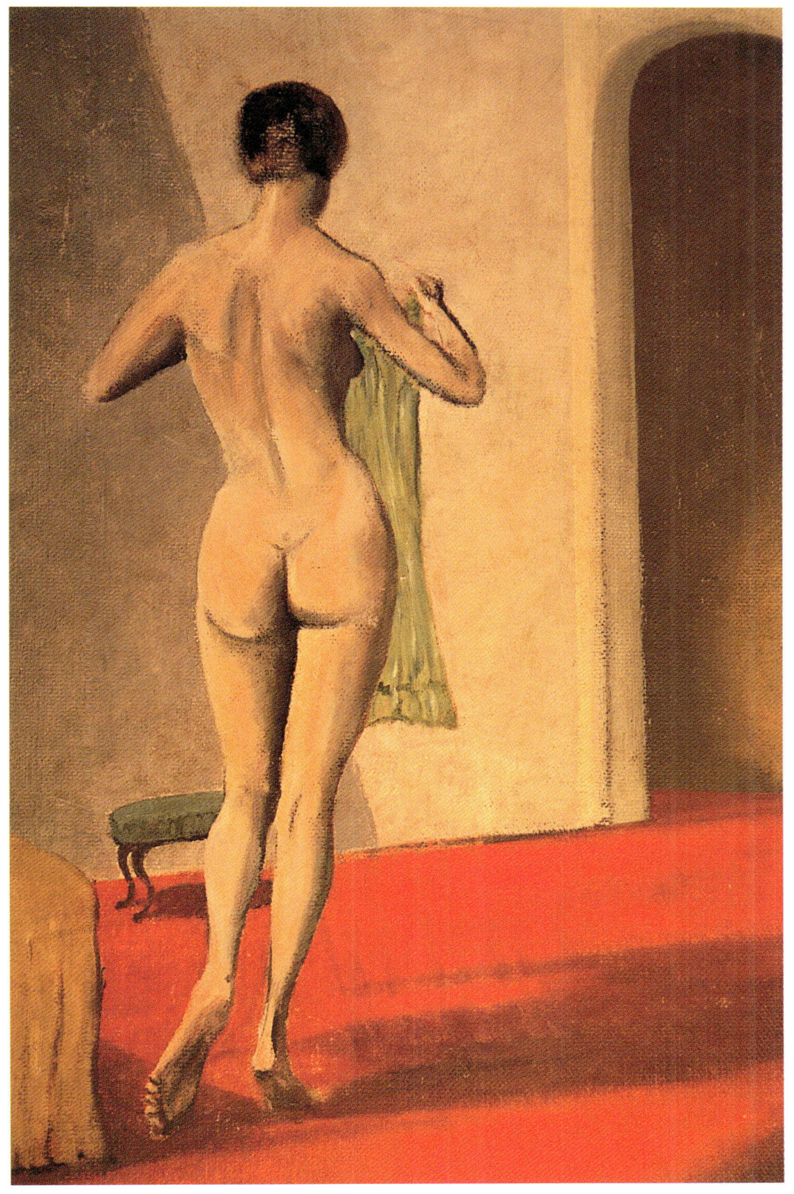

PETER REGEHR *The Red Carpet* OIL ON MASONITE 29" x 24"

As a youngster, the idea of growing up to be an artist did not occur to me. Art was a steady, ongoing process from the beginning. I never looked upon it as a career or a job. It was a way of life.

As an adult, not much has changed except that I am more aware of art-making as a constant state of becoming—a way of life where the *growing up* never ends.

Since early childhood I have been making work. My father's painting studio was in the house. Pencils, paper, ink and paint were always available. As far as I was concerned, art was as important to life as eating or breathing.

My attitude was not shared by other children, as I soon learned in elementary school in Victoria, Canada.

My teacher asked Rhonda Williams, the prettiest girl in the Primary Division to model for art class. She was wearing a dark sweater, tartan skirt, white ankle socks, and oxfords. Fairly standard attire for the early 1960s, but not very interesting I thought.

I mentally removed Rhonda's clothing and proceeded to draw the little girl in the nude. I saw nothing wrong with this. My father was painting a nude at home. I wanted Rhonda to appear as a goddess of nature, like T. Hart Benton's *Persephone,* a copy of which I had seen in my father's book on American painting.

My ink drawings progressed and Rhonda grew breasts, hips, and long flowing hair. Suddenly the teacher loomed over my shoulder. She was horrified. Rhonda was mortified. I was tongue-tied. The drawings were confiscated, and I was caned across the backside in front of the class.

Pride swallowed humiliation. I knew my drawings were special. Even though my draftsmanship was never considered to be any good (I was told often enough that it looked like scribbling), it somehow seemed "right" to me. They were part of me. The episode gave me an early sense that my art work was growing up to be my life. Later, I discovered that acting and writing would also be a part of this life.

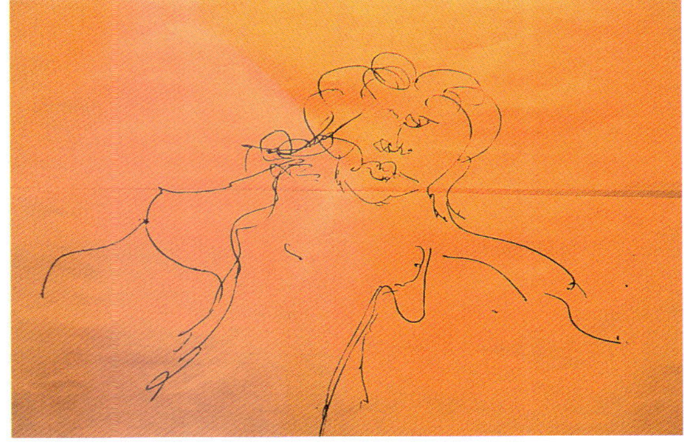

Rhonda INK ON PAPER

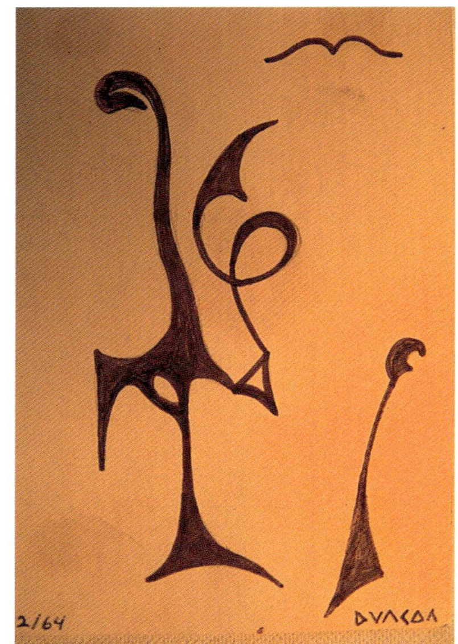

Crane
"PRETTY" WORK

Perhaps one negative result of the incident was that it drove me to work in secret. To this day, my process remains very private. I certainly stopped drawing nudes for many years.

I developed two types of material. "Pretty" work for school, which kept everyone else happy, and "special" work for myself, which dealt with my true feelings and ideas. I hid everything in the space where I slept behind the basement stairs.

I showed a little of my work to another teacher, Miss Pottinger, a gifted art instructor, who encouraged me to develop my colors. She would speak of color as though it were something rich and secret to eat, like dark chocolates, and referred to my paint box as "a treasure trove of jewels."

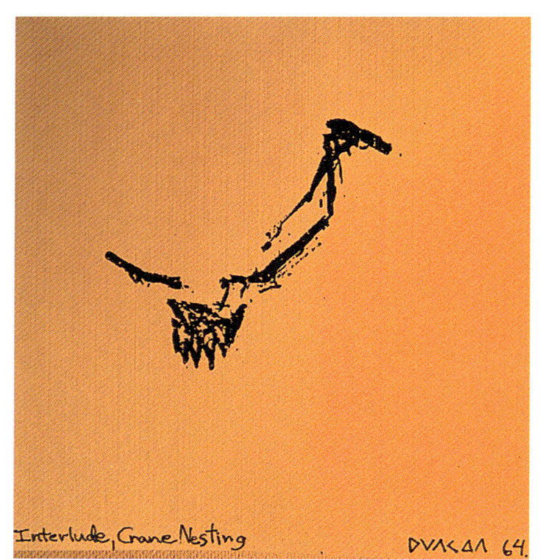

Crane "SPECIAL" WORK

She tried unsuccessfully to cure my habit of working with both hands. I had been trained to write the (supposed) right way, but I saw no reason why I had to apply the rule to art. I saw no reason for applying it to writing either, but I was told that I would always smear my own scribbles. I frequently and automatically changed hands whilst painting and was equally good at smearing with both. She called this ambidextrous switching "fidgeting."

Miss Pottinger felt that my assignments were messy and lopsided (a kind understatement) and that fidgeting was due to poor concentration. She was correct, but only halfway. My creations were terribly confused, but only because I had not trained my hands to act harmoniously upon one subject, like those of a pianist. One hand thinks and feels differently from the other, hence it was not lack of concentration, but split concentration that caused my problems.

This syndrome threads its way through most of my life. I am of two minds about nearly everything (sexuality being an exception); having a compulsion to seek contrast, analogy, and balance in everything I experience.

Today, all of my painted efforts are the result of fidgeting, but my line drawings are formed singularly by one hand or the other (smears and all).

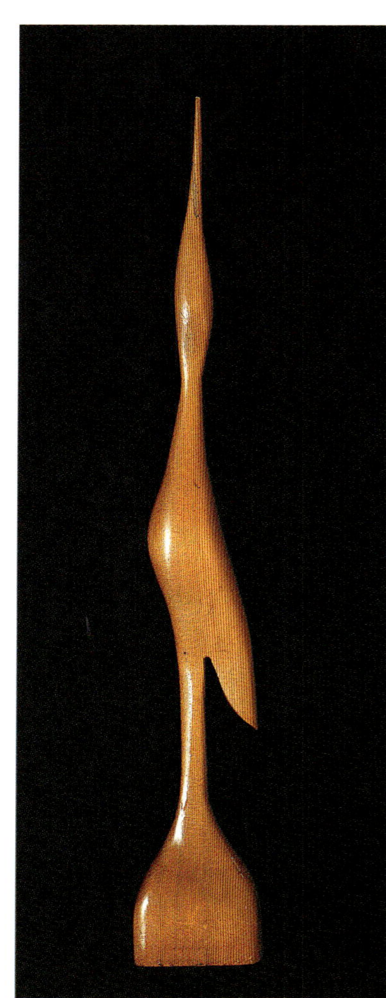

Crane "PRETTY" WORK

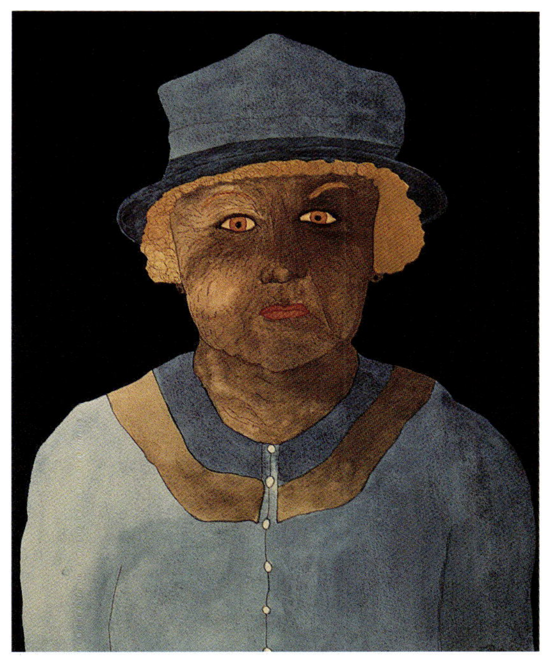

Miss P. WATERCOLOR 20" x 16"

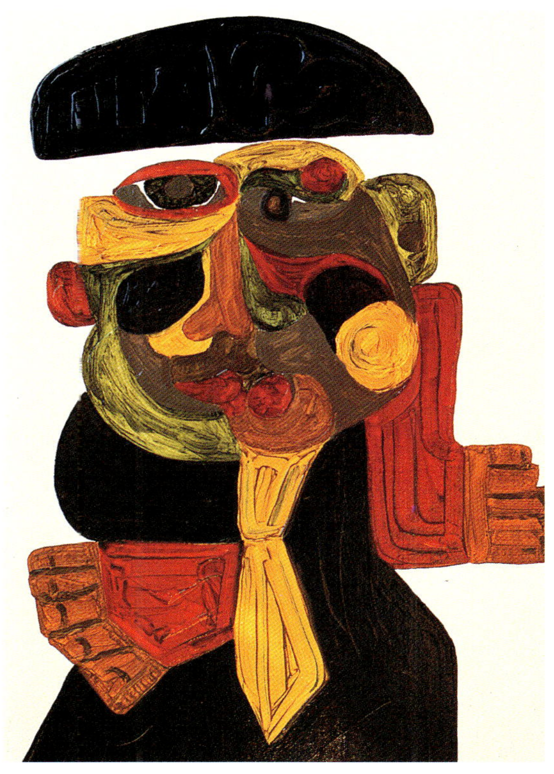

Picasso OIL 30" x 24"

Self Portrait (LINE DRAWING SERIES) PEN AND INK 18" x 24" 1989

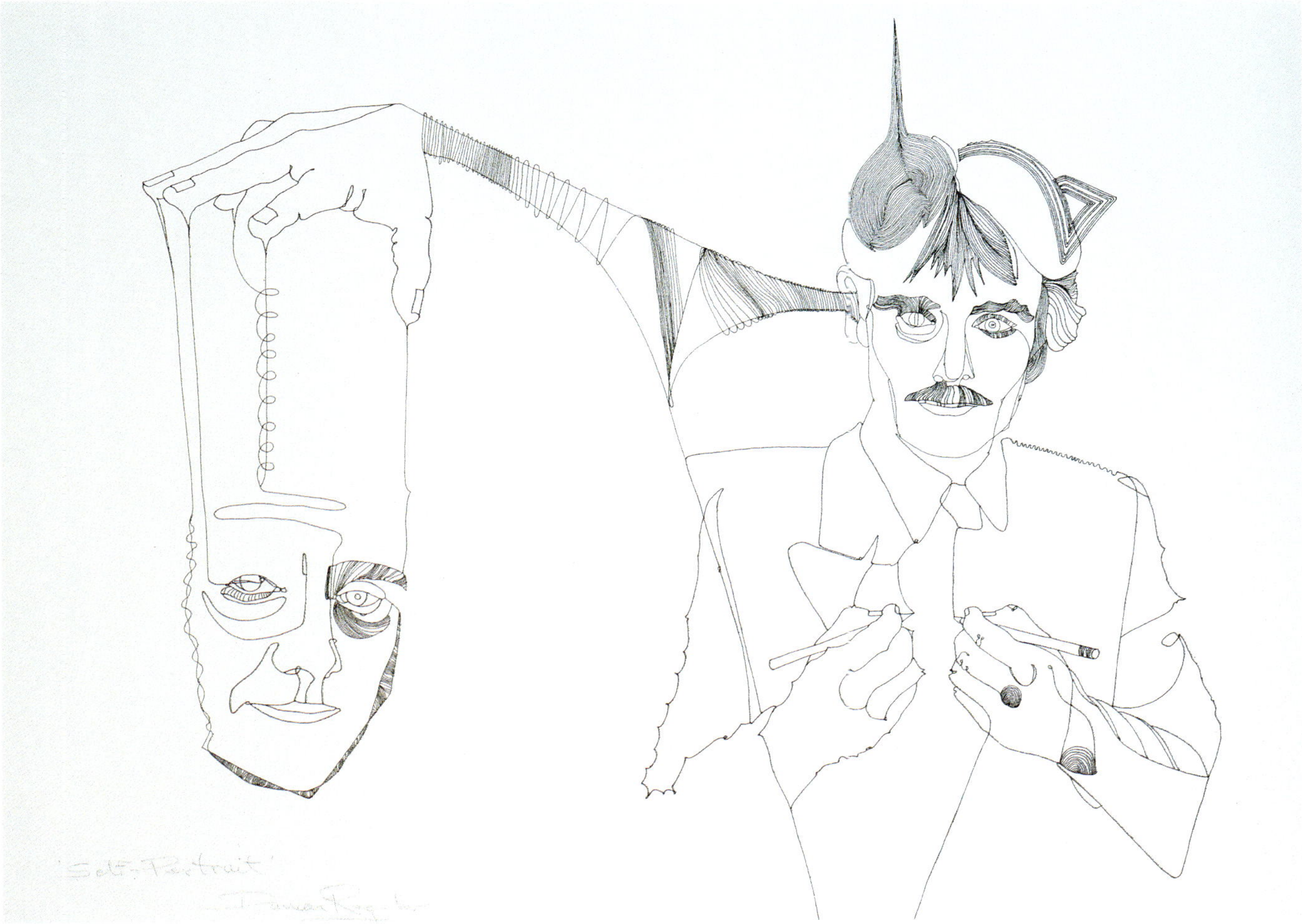

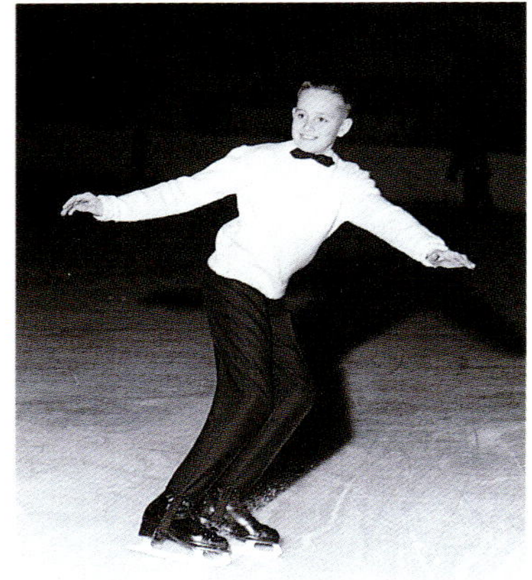

Skating, ten years old

Throughout the 1960s, my parents were taken with the idea that I might grow up to be a successful figure skater. Although I had other plans for myself, I pursued this artistic sport mostly to please them. They could ill afford the lessons. While I enjoyed freestyle skating, I resented the long hours of patch (precise lines, repeatedly etched one on top of the other and contained within a small rectangle of ice) which required my mind and body to focus on variations of the figure eight. During these sessions my imagination spiraled far away from those frozen patterns.

Skating was a backhanded gift. It taught me discipline and gave me an understanding of the moving body as an art form.

When I look at details of my pen and ink drawings and some of my earlier paintings, I see in their lines the swirling edges carved by a skate blade.

I was in awe of my father's paintings. Peter Regehr emigrated from Russia in 1926. As one-tenth of a Mennonite family, he grew up in the cradle of poverty on a farm in southern Alberta. Prairie landscapes and animals often dominate his subject matter.

I envy his solid draftsmanship. His creations are powerfully connected to the earth. My strongest childhood memories of him always include the garden where we grew vegetables . . . and built stone walls.

My father tried to give me pointers from time to time, but I was far too intimidated to show him any of my "special" work. I was an elusive pupil and I kept much of myself hidden from my family. Admittedly, I was attracted to the romance of keeping secrets, but I was convinced that I, my work and the way in which I worked, would never be accepted. I withdrew to develop on my own. In time, I grew more skillful and became comfortable enough to come out of hiding. I left home as the 1960s ended.

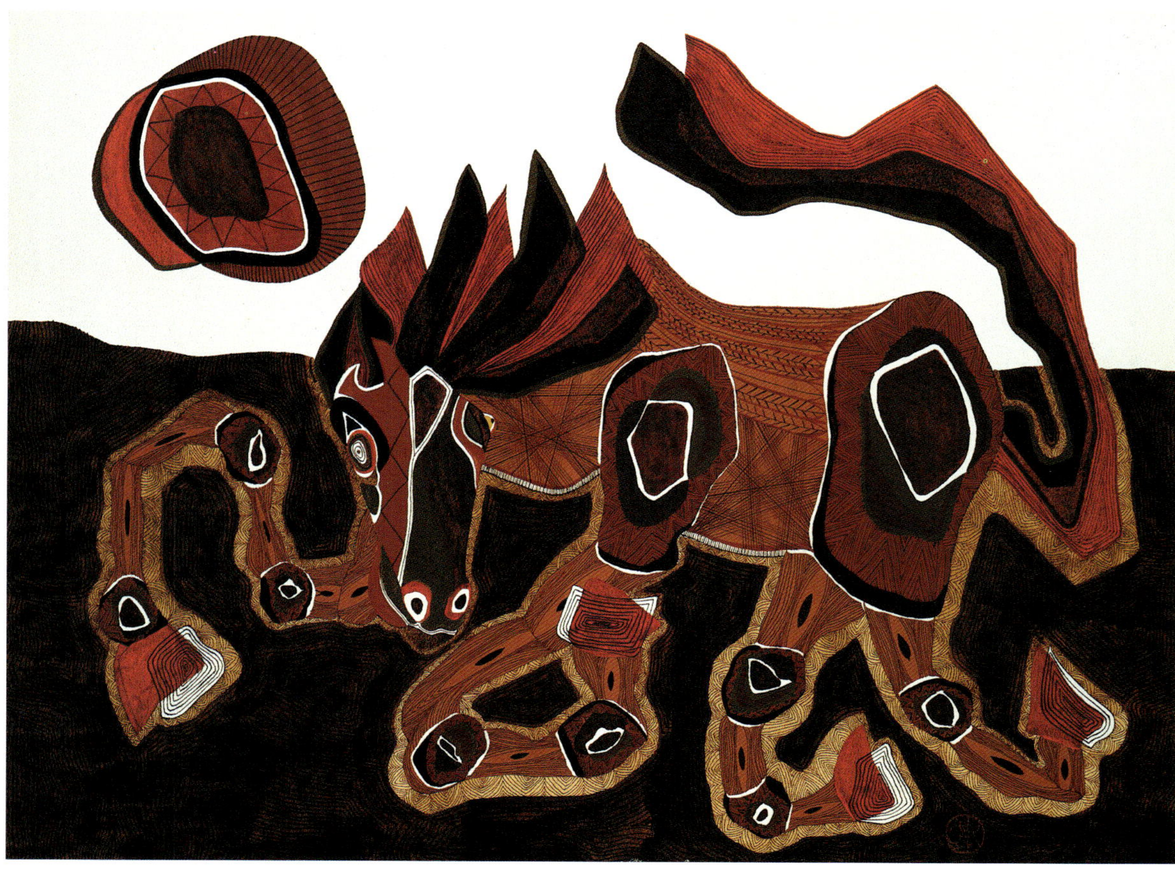

Nag's Flight-Equus
Ink and Watercolor
18" x 24" 1972

Peter the Rock – for my father

My father's hands are seventy-five,
With gorges and lattice fissures,
Where oceans and prairie swept
An iron darkness in stained knuckles.
Shale-sheathed palms challenge gravel
Winds and tenderness.
Cobbling in fingers and callouses, inlaid
With sea shells, petroglyphs and lava
Is the need to never tire.

But never a changer
Or strip-miner bound by Midas' gloves.
This rearranger heaves gravity
Delicate like a child.
And shifts granite by dainty fulcrum
To caress a flower's bed.

—DR

PETER REGEHR *Stone Horse* CASEIN ON MASONITE 16" x 21"

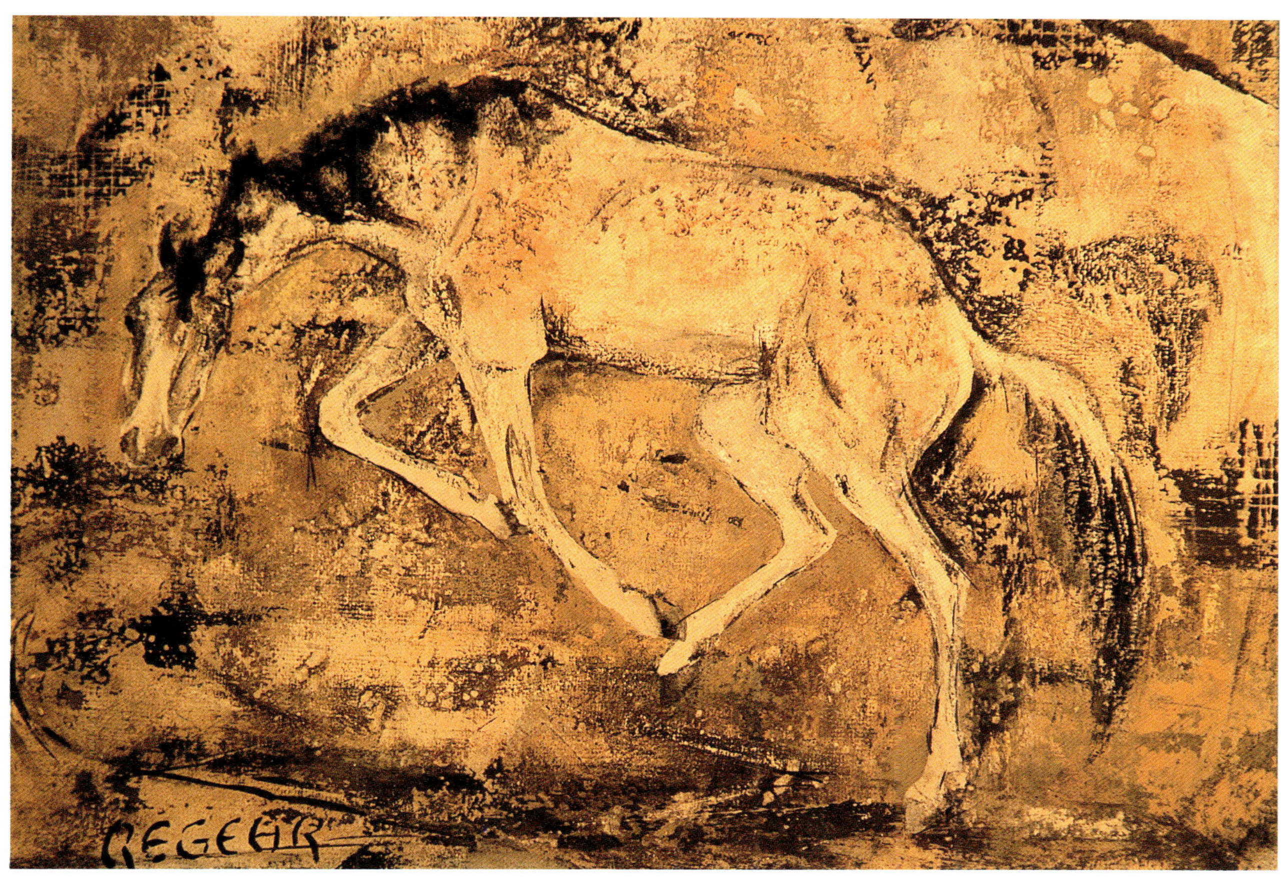

Teaching me to read at a very young age was my mother's greatest gift. I inherited her love of the classics, of which she retains a vast knowledge. Although we lived far out in the country, she insisted that her four children make regular visits to the city library. We had no television and I fell in love with literature. It soon found its way into my special work. I would disappear into the woods for hours, acting out entire novels and reciting poetry and plays. During the course of a week, I would be Robin Hood, Hiawatha, Romeo, Grendel, Odysseus, Fagan, Moses, and all three of the Musketeers. By the age of twelve, I had a sense that my life would also include acting and writing.

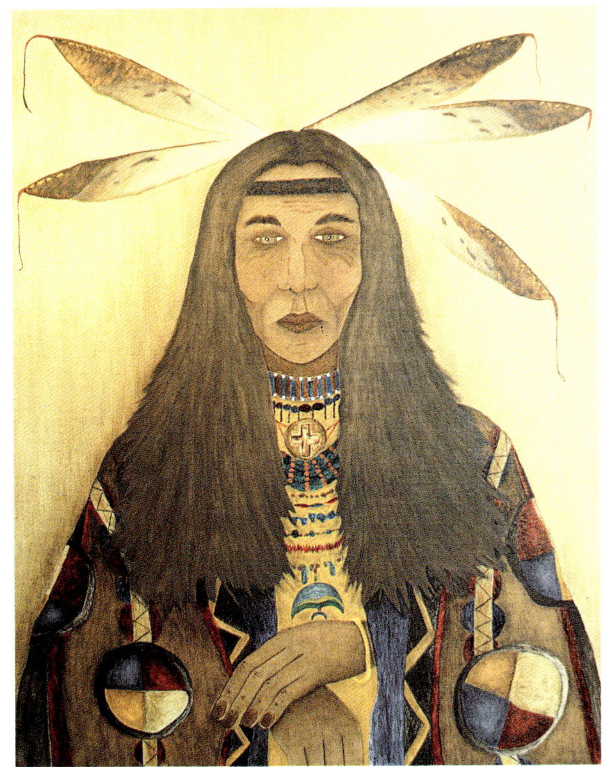

Indian OIL 30" x 24"

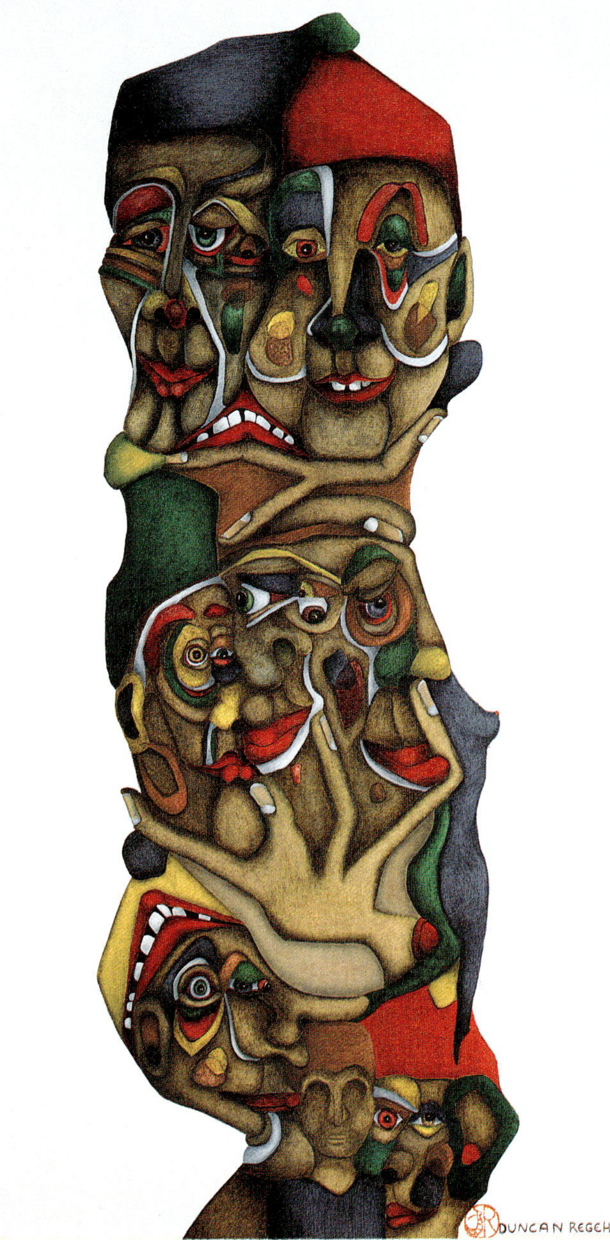

Jugglers
OIL 30" x 15" 1977

Over the years I have learned through a natural process of experience how to focus energy and different states of mind for my mediums of expression. All require emotional investigation. To act, I must become an extrovert. Writing and painting are more introverted art forms. To juggle them all, to switch back and forth amongst them, or join them together by related themes, has always been wonderfully complicated. During my teens and early twenties, focus and concentration often eluded me.

In 1969, Dr. Ralph Allen, who later produced *Sugar Babies* on Broadway, formed a theatre company called Victoria Fair. I auditioned and was hired as the youngest member of the company.

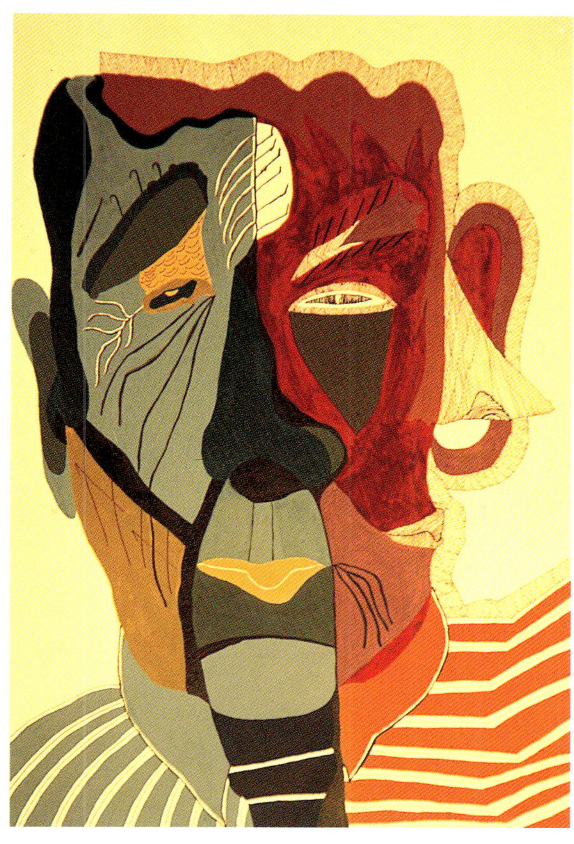

Dr. Ralph Allen
INK AND WATERCOLOR 16" x 12" 1972

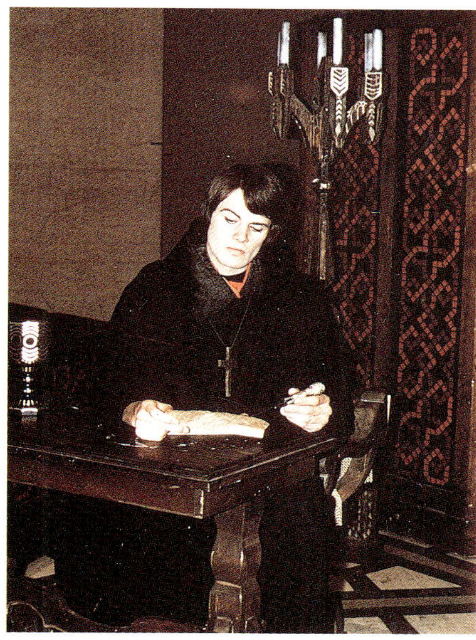

A production of *Justice Not Revenge,*
directed by Dr. Ralph Allen,
Victoria Fair Theatre Company, 1971

Ralph, a brash, good-humored, extremely well-educated man, terrified me. He threw me in at the deep end of Shakespeare and the classics by generously giving me strong roles in his productions. Some of them, I feel, were far beyond my age and ability at the time.

After my audition, I remember standing before his desk while he leaned back in his chair and passionately expounded to the ceiling that I must treat every part, no matter how small, as the starring role of the show.

During this lecture, Max, his equally passionate Schnauzer, vigorously embraced my lower leg. I broke out in a sweat. The vice-like grip of canine amour is unshakeable, and there wasn't a bucket of cold water in sight.

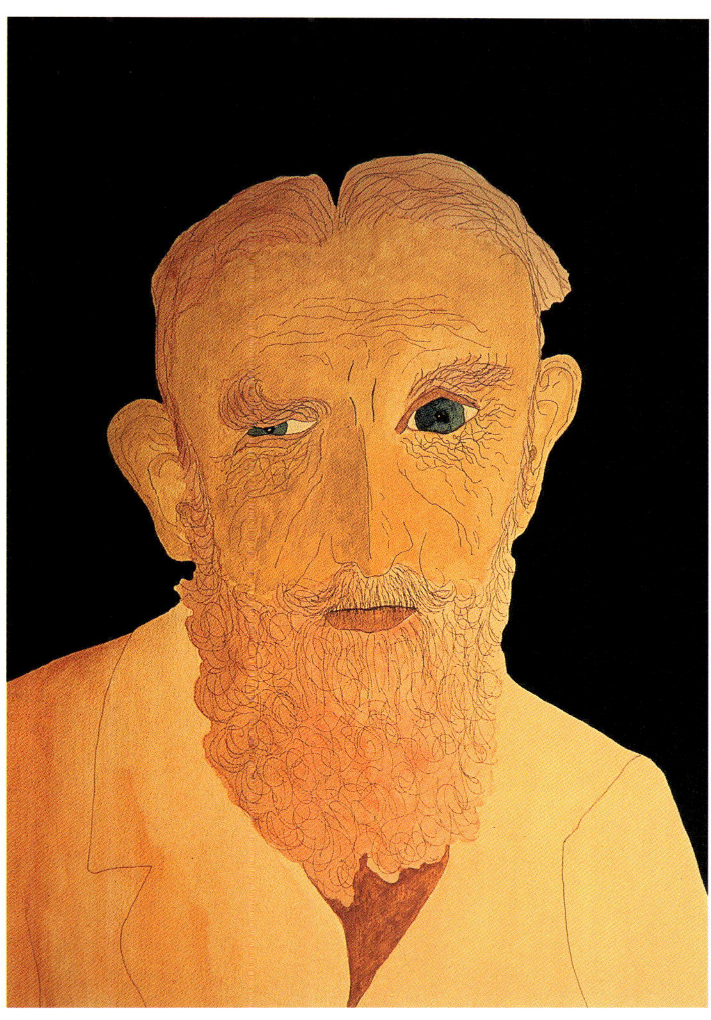

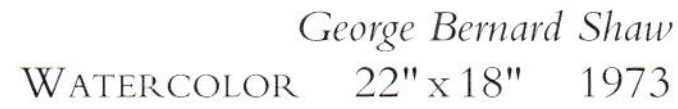

George Bernard Shaw
WATERCOLOR 22" x 18" 1973

Lady Bracknell
WATERCOLOR
24" x 18"   1972-1973

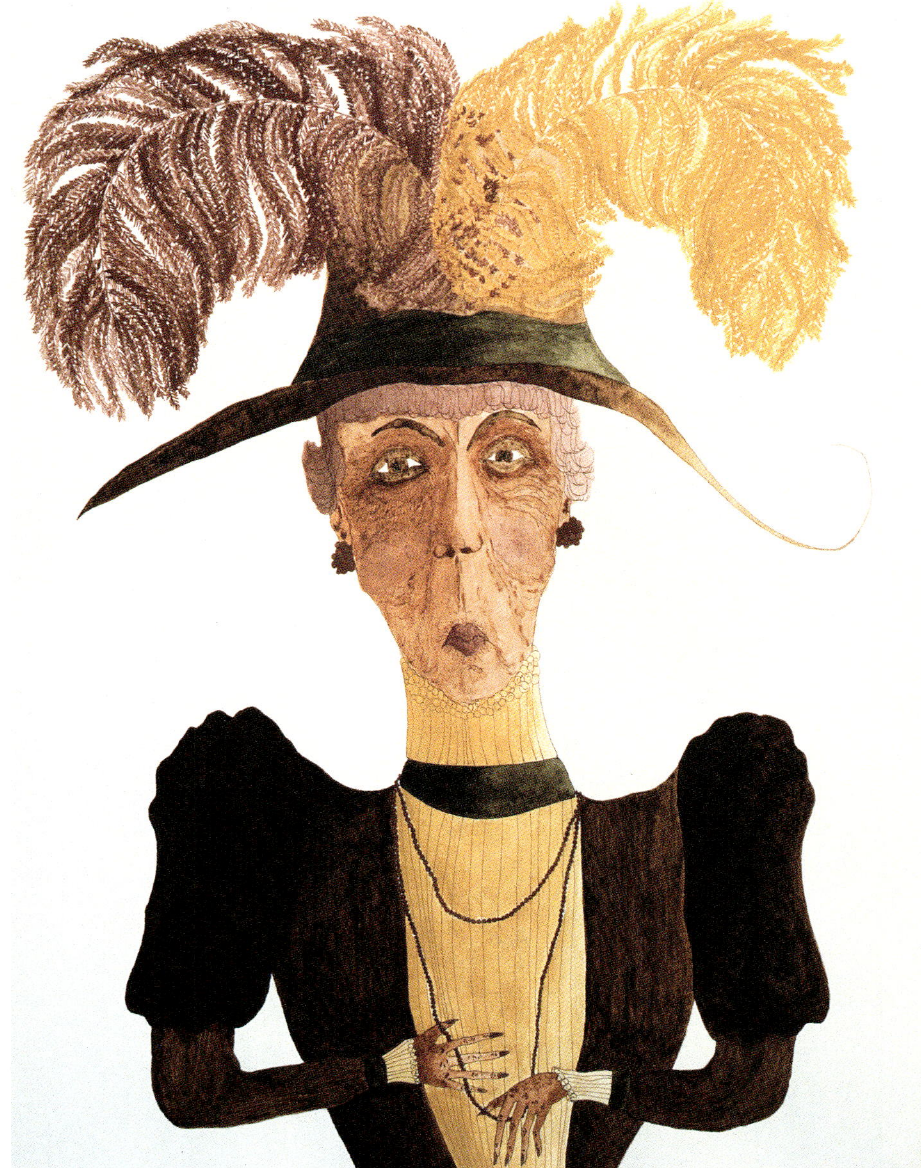

Ralph continued on the importance of concentration.

"It's all there in the material, Regehr, focus on that. Work with the audience, but don't let them distract you."

My concentration was already split between trying to impress Ralph with my mature attitude and the hopeless effort of dislodging the lovesick Max, who was steadily rocking himself into a frenzy. My whole body strained.

After what seemed like an endless sermon of praise to the sacrifices one had to make for a life in the theatre, Ralph brought his speech to a climactic finish. At the same moment, Max went rigid with ecstasy, coughed once, and slid to the floor in a wheezing heap.

Ralph swiveled around to face me, leveling his forefinger like a Colt 45.

"And let nothing," he fired, "I repeat, *nothing,* deter you from the path of your career!"

"Yes sir," I rasped. My throat was dry. "Thank you, sir."

I quickly headed for the door, dragging my ravished leg behind me.

"Oh, by the way, Regehr . . ."

"Sir?"

He knelt down to stroke Max. "You got the job, ya' know, so don't be so damn nervous. I want you to concentrate, but I also want you to relax. Like good ol' Max here," he laughed, "I hope I make myself clear."

Upon hearing his name, Max sat up and began eyeballing my other leg with a penetrating look of lust.

"Very clear, sir." I stumbled out of the room, muttering under my breath, "More than you'll ever know."

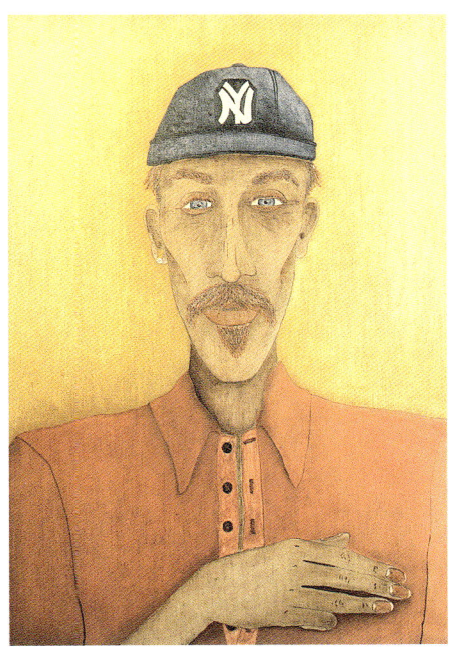

James Brown OIL 24" x 18"

After Holbein OIL 15" x 11" 1993

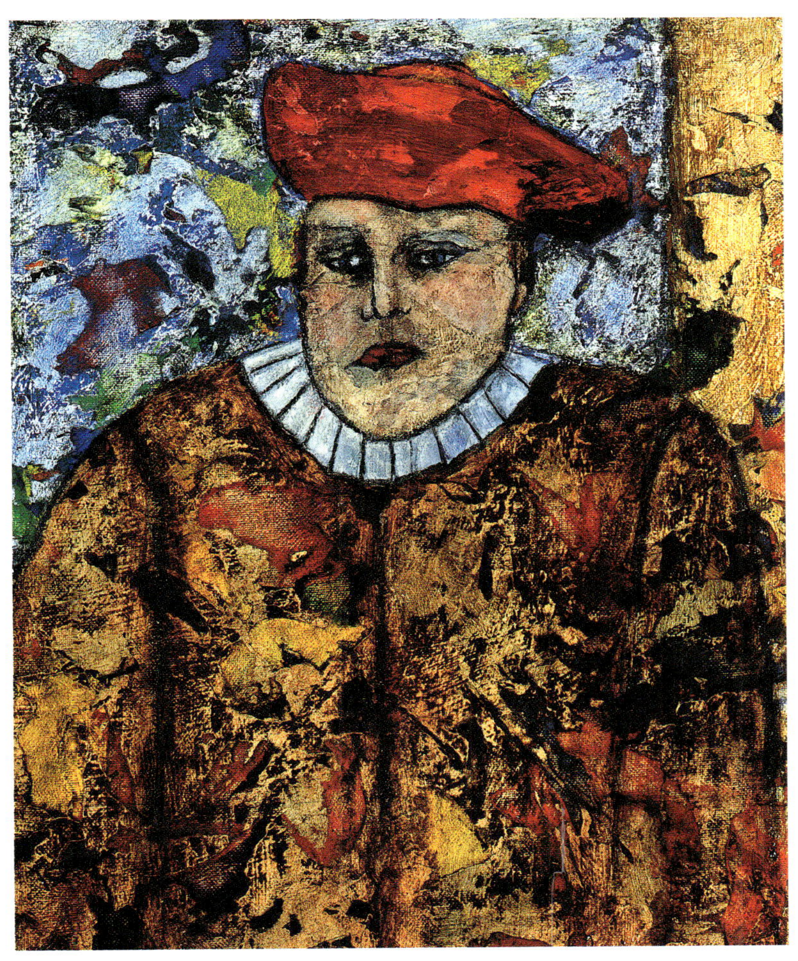

Painting people has always been my strongest interest. Most of my characters are imaginary, but literature, film, music, and theatre have always made an impact. Acting, in particular, has helped to guide my process for developing personalities on canvas.

Nearly all of my early portraits are devoid of background. I wanted nothing to steal focus or upstage my subjects. Eventually, I allowed background to enhance the central image, but even today many of my paintings are not graced with detailed settings.

Discipline was not an issue in the face of a natural drive (which has never left me) to produce work, but with so many activities to attend to, I often wondered if I could do justice to them all. Sometime during the early 1970s, I grasped the concept that creativity was not on a schedule, it *was* the schedule, and that all my expression came from a single core. I could "speak" in as many different languages as I chose; the "voice" would always be mine.

I began to recognize the importance of life outside of work and to appreciate experiences which at one time I had dismissed as mere distractions. My relationships with women and my adventures through travel account for some of my richest experiences. They have proved to be limitless sources of inspiration; as vital to work as working itself.

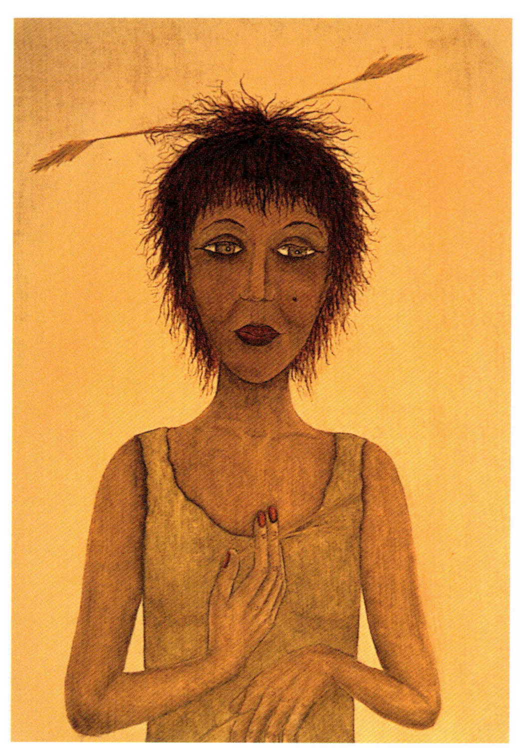

Girl in the Park Oil 20" x 16" 1973

I have no idea where the term "falling in love" came from; it may have something to do with swooning. My personal method has been to plunge headlong (and with any luck, buck naked), into the fathomless and dangerous waters of romance.

At fourteen, I breached the virgin shoreline in the arms of an older woman. I think she was all of eighteen. The event itself was so unremarkable that I cannot even remember her name. With apologies to the lady in question, I must confess that it was also the first time I got drunk. I was so ill from over-imbibing that the morning found me literally hung over the cold steel tracks of the Canadian Pacific Railway, surrounded by puddles of liquid pizza. My recovery took four days. Along with my virginity, I am certain that I lost at least half my brain cells. I had to wait another three years before the real tidal wave hit.

I first plunged into the true love of Carole May, a magical girl I had known since childhood. I had been attracted to her free spirit since the age of eleven; at seventeen I was enchanted. She was a dark, beautiful ocean in whose depths I submerged my adolescent passion. I could have drowned in her forever, but the swells of ambition washed me ashore, and love was driven out to sea. We were together almost three years before we parted. In that time we also lost our child, which created a lasting rift of guilt and a bond of sadness between us.

Blood

Opposite the note pad and your broken glass,
A certificate of sacrifice, left behind
To be filed in darkness,
For the child left behind
Knows no memory of its blood,
But our crumpled severance list,
Now lying in stiffened pools of wax,
It reminds forever.

I rearrange the news clippings
And align your strangled hairbrush
Overgrown with dead split ends,
And set the drained bottle
Beside the ashtray brimming
With your cremations, embossed
With your red kisses, my orchestration
Embalmed with your fallen smoke, I breathe

And once more search the glass we shared
For your fingerprints over mine,
To sense again, any spare element of union
That might speak to me of genesis.
But there is no redemption in these vestiges
No blood to trace amongst these empty shards,
For grief decants only ritual,
And seance only conjures the lost.

—DR

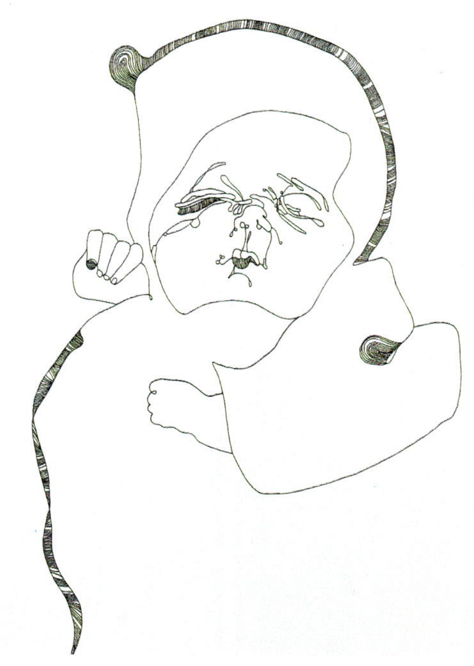

Pocket (Line Drawing Series)
Pen and Ink 14½" x 11½"

As Stu in Sam Shepard's *Chicago*,
Vancouver City Stage,
Fall 1973, post pneumonia

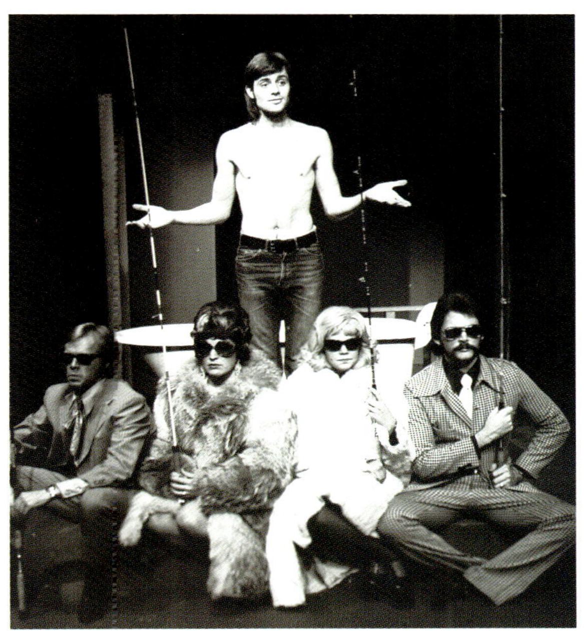

Lack of funds, losing the child, and my career obsessions ultimately sank the relationship. I have often looked back with regret, but also with gratitude for the memory of a passion which over the years has frequently been the stimulating force behind a number of paintings.

My subsequent philandering was both a misguided quest to rediscover the romance of that relationship and a vain attempt to forget the unhappiness of its demise. The following years in Vancouver were wild ones.

By the spring of 1973, after performing and rehearsing as many as four different stage productions at once, recording radio plays in the morning, partying at night, plunging into various female oceans, and painting — often on no sleep at all — my health and my work fell apart. I came down with pneumonia.

It seems an obvious revelation, but during a bout of delirium it occurred to me that if I nurtured my physical self, I could work with greater vitality. I decided that I needed a long life in order to produce all the ideas that glowed beneath the surface of my fevered carcass.

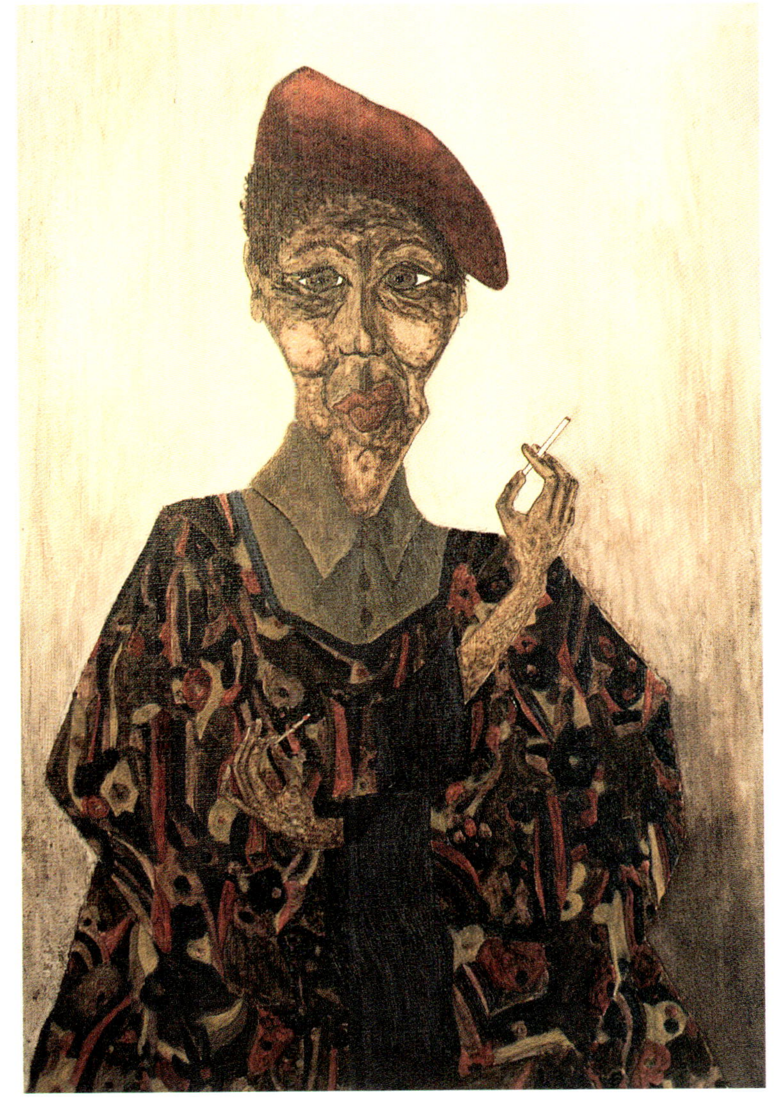

Decadent OIL 24" x 18" 1977

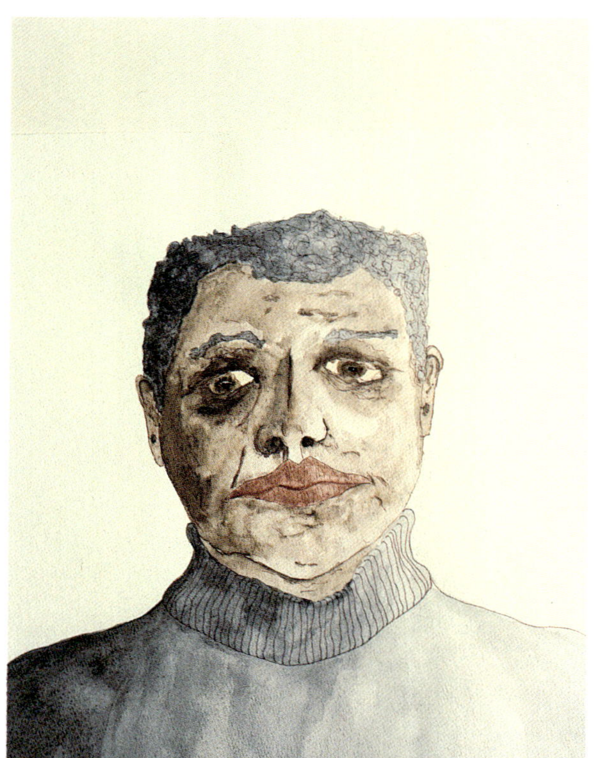

Old Boxer
WATERCOLOR
28" x 17" 1979

I rose up from the cold coals of pneumonia a very determined phoenix. Having already set the precedent for the scope of productivity I relished, I set about amending my life by eliminating the parties and at least fifty percent of the oceanic skinny-dipping. I then introduced a vigorous two hour workout that continues as a compulsory daily regimen and an important cornerstone to the focus and energy behind my work.

I was later to add amateur boxing to my list of physical endeavors. I had always abhorred team sports, preferring the one-on-one (and in this case, the toe-to-toe), as a greater personal challenge. I felt a need to grapple with dangerous forces. After some fifty-odd fights, most of them unofficial, I came to the conclusion that my greatest adversary was me. To engage that force did not require the conscious infliction of violence upon others, but a cross-examination of internal objectives. My devil's advocate, or *doppelganger,* has been my worst enemy, for he strikes from ambush, desecrating purpose, creativity, and ego.

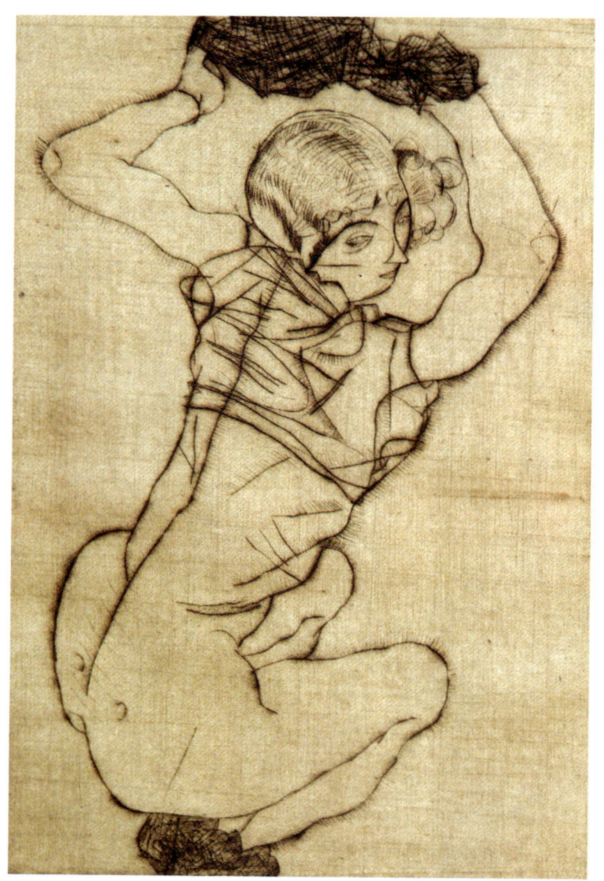

EGON SCHIELE
Squatting Woman
17/100 DRYPOINT 1914

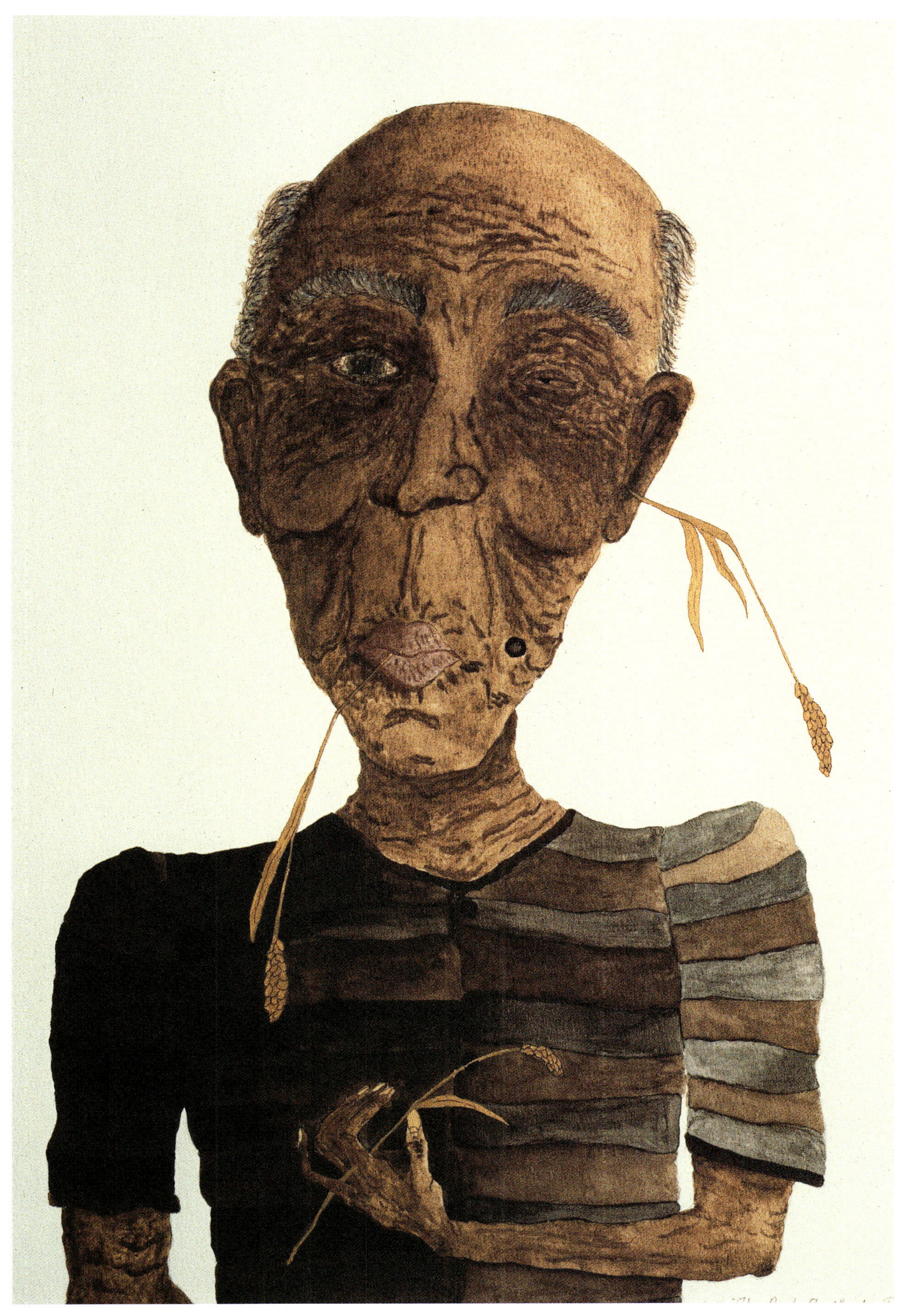

Park Fool WATERCOLOR 17" x 13" 1973

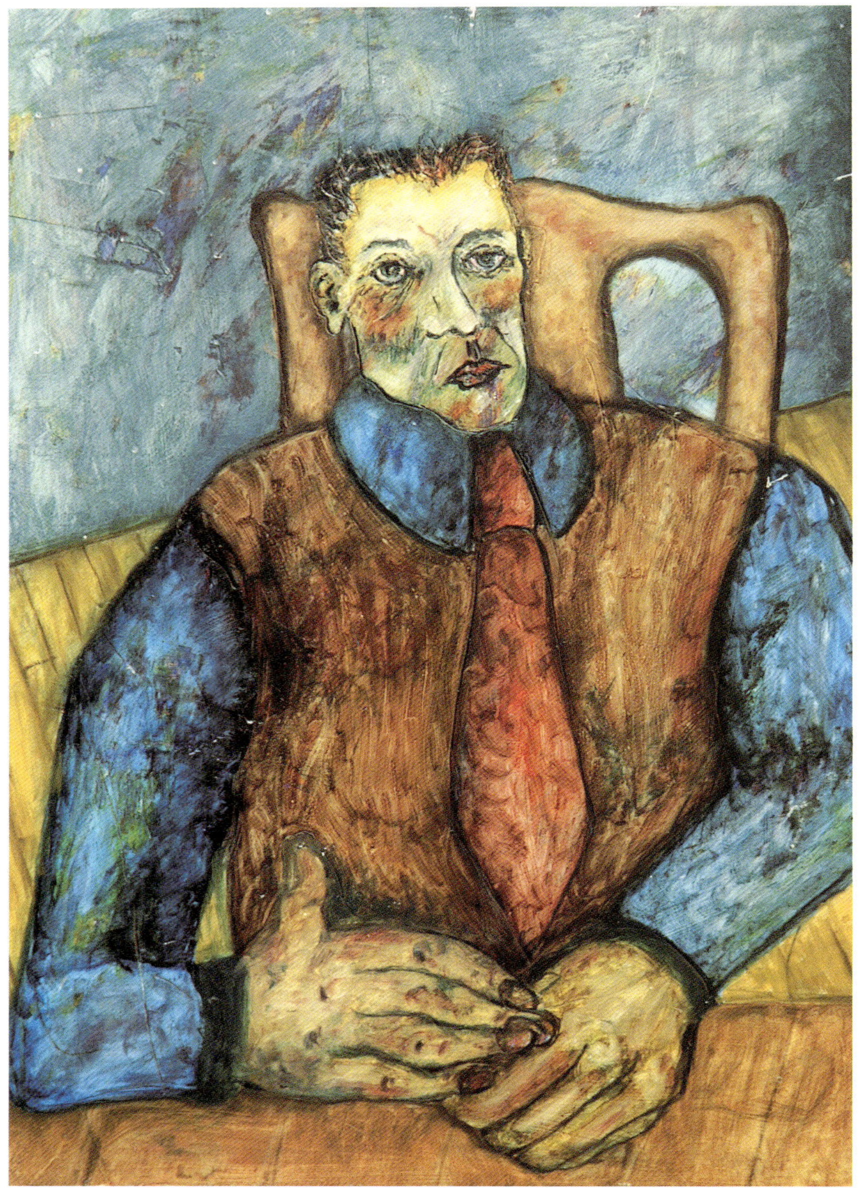

Waiting for Oskar Oil 30" x 24" 1990

Along with my decision to improve myself physically, I resolved to extend my knowledge of art history and to study specific artists, both past and present.

I developed a strong interest in several areas of 19th and 20th century art, most notably Expressionism and Romanticism; with a proclivity for the Pre-Raphaelites and the Secession group of Austrian artists: Gustav Klimt, Egon Schiele, and Oskar Kokoschka. I have also admired the contemporary work of Lucian Freud, Frank Auerbach, and the late Francis Bacon.

Emulating the individual styles of painters has never interested me. There are innumerable forces which incline creativity. I suspect the impact of other artists' work upon my own to be very slight.

My studies have given me to understand that the strongest influences are usually hidden from the artist but I doubt if this is true of myself.

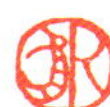

II

TO SEA...
OR NOT TO SEE

Shakespeare

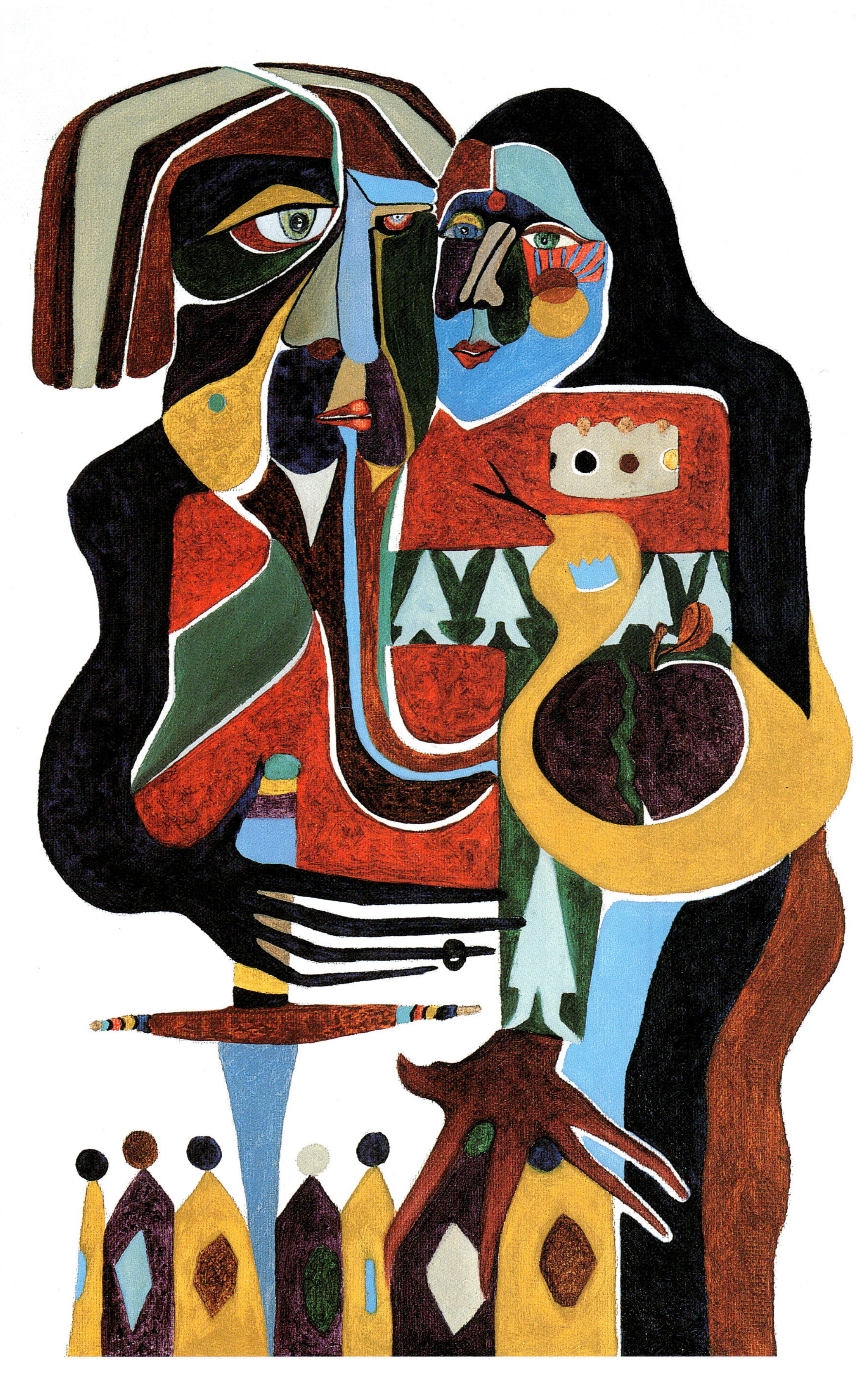

Macbeth Oil 17" x 11"

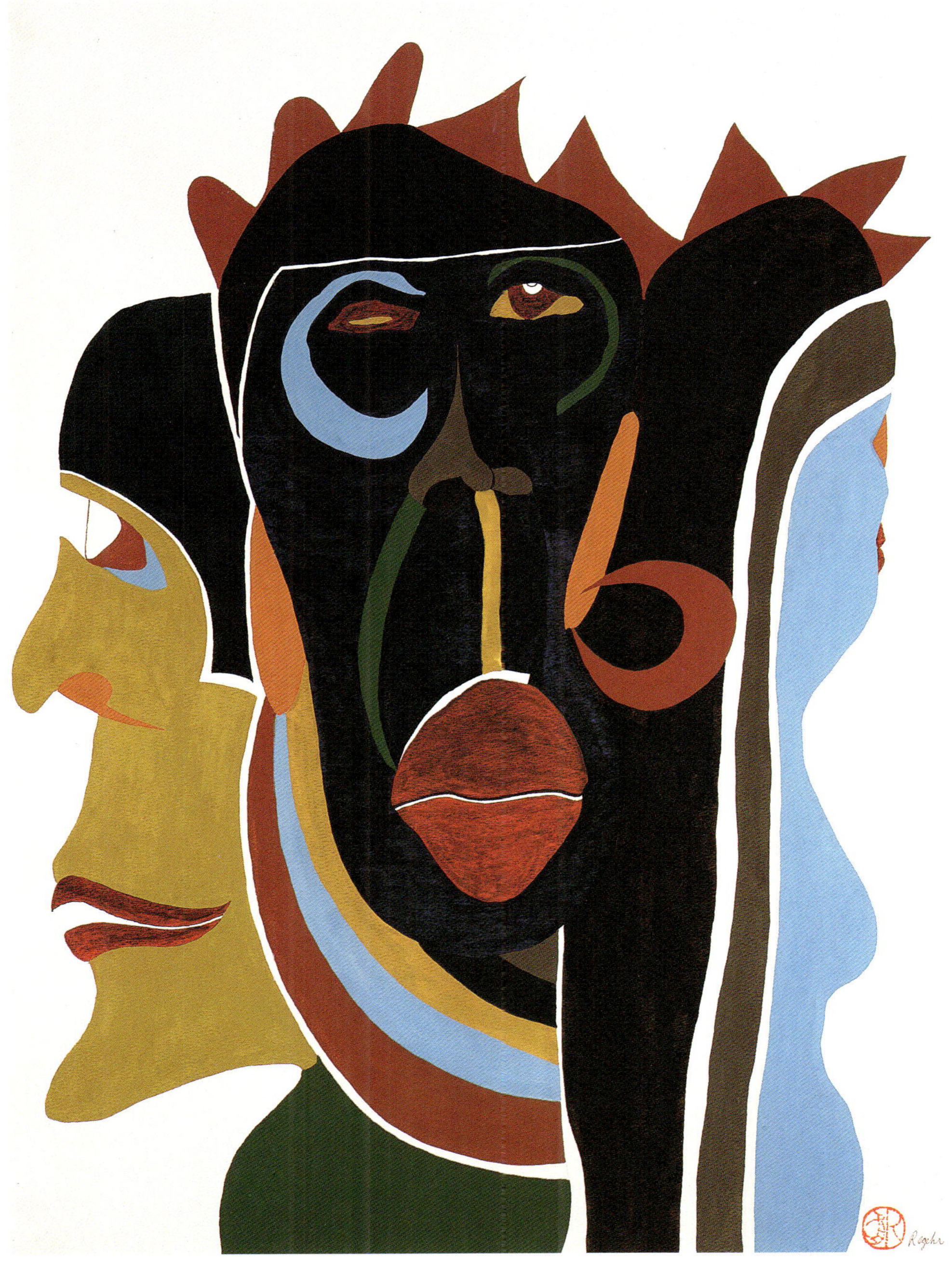

Othello WATERCOLOR 24" x 18" 1974

IN 1974 I MARRIED FRANCINE WURSTER, a vibrantly sensual actress from Chicago. That same year I joined the Stratford Shakespeare Festival in Ontario.

The characters and scenes of Shakespeare's plays are so richly layered they breach reality. Similarly, many of the lead players at the festival were burdened with top-heavy personalities, usually perched upon a delicate fulcrum of psychological insecurity. Along with the plays, they became the resource material for a new series of paintings.

Artistic director Jean Gascon introduced the longstanding members of the company as "The Stratford Royalty." The hierarchy was calculated and it served to intimidate newcomers who might rise too swiftly above their stations.

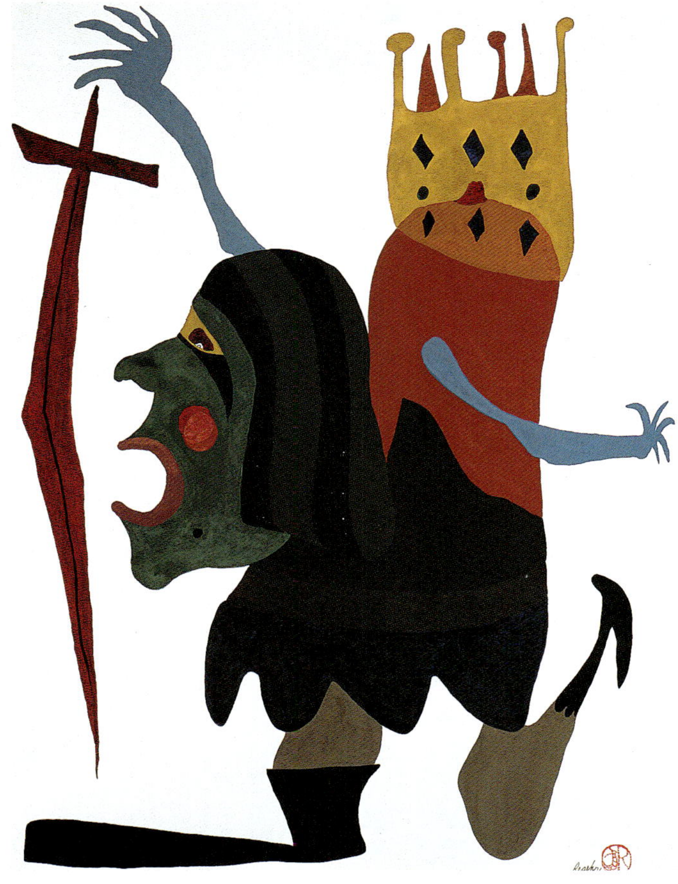

Richard III WATERCOLOR 24" x 18" 1975

The tallish juve
Stratford Shakespeare Festival, 1974

I remember one star of very short stature (a legendary giant in his own mind) who, upon noting that he was to share the stage with a tallish "juve," announced in acid sibilants to the director: "Whenever I make an entrance, I want whatssshisssname, the hulking blue-eyed number in the loincloth, to ssstand well to the back!"

And so I did. I retreated into the world of my art and the honeymoon arms of the vivacious Francine.

We were very happy for a while, but for the most part ours was a bedroom relationship. Francine became understandably frustrated with not working and having to spend so many hours on her own. Everything I was involved in excluded her. I lured her into the world of antique collecting (a vice I have never been able to kick) and the study of art history. Neither helped, as Shakespeare and the creation of my new paintings gradually monopolized my time. We fought and loved like untamed shrews.

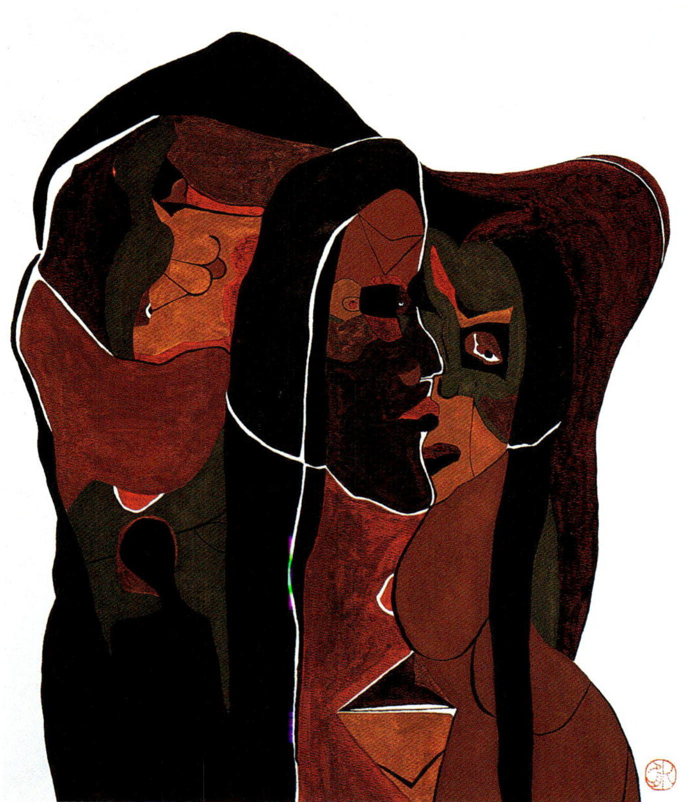

Romeo and Juliet
WATERCOLOR
24" x 18" 1974

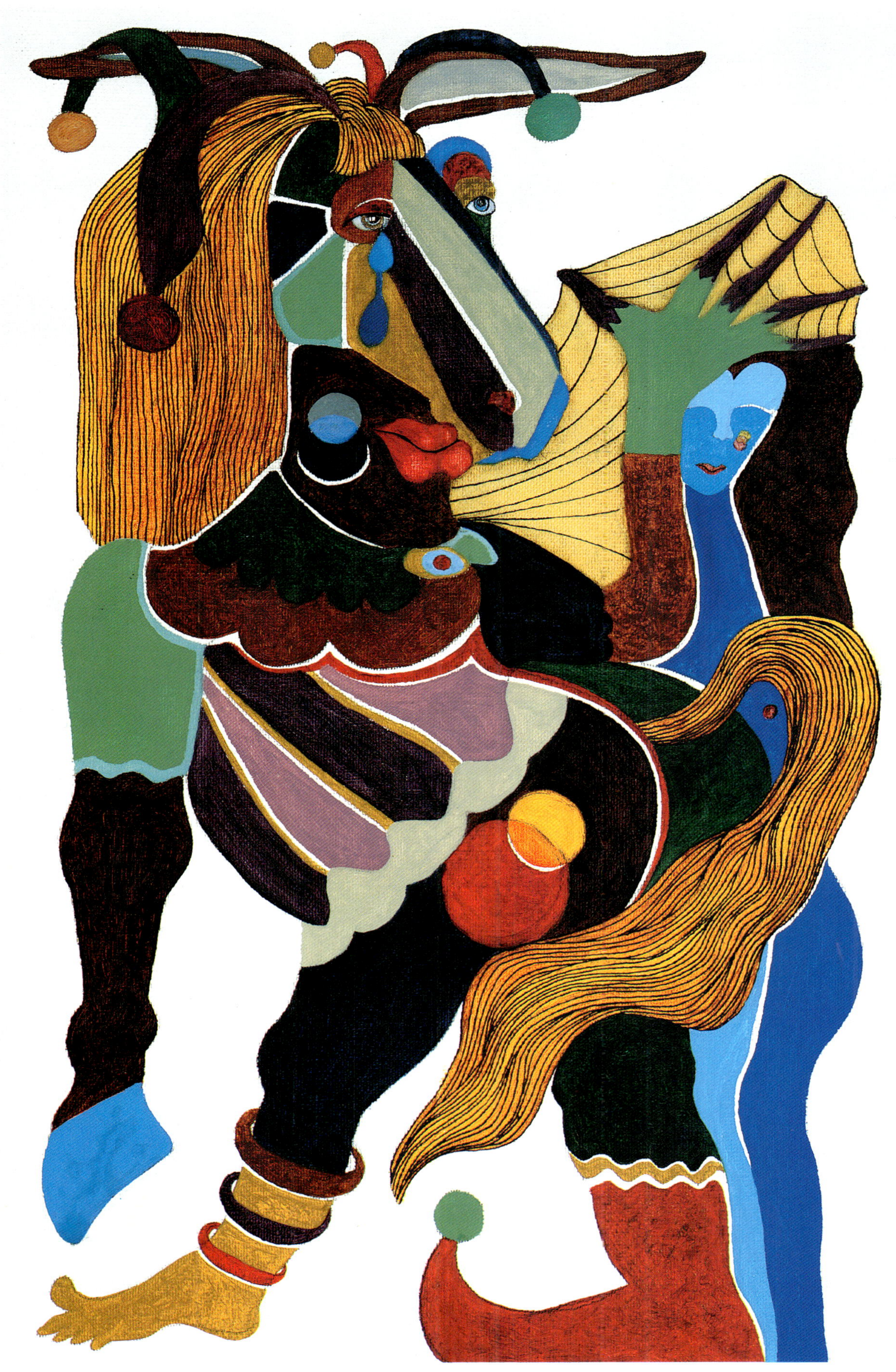

Bottom Oil 17" x 11"

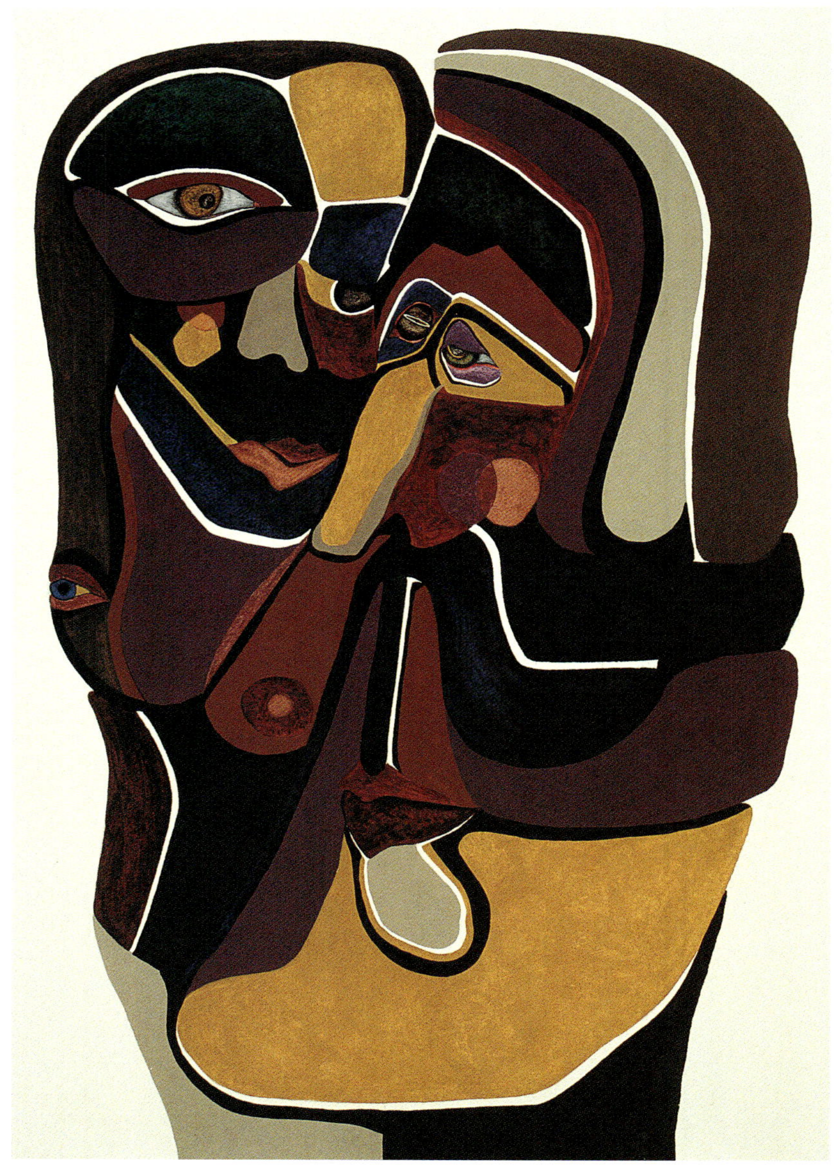

Claudius WATERCOLOR 24" x 18" 1974

In Toronto, long after the festival ended, I was still engrossed in Shakespeare. The plays and players are powerful and complex. By separating and defining shapes and symbols with a clean-line approach, I hoped to condense and simplify them. I blocked them out in deep but brightly contrasting colors. The resulting style was theatrical. Accordingly, the pieces took on the look of marquee posters.

A production of *Hamlet* in the spring of 1975 took me to Montreal, which meant a three month separation from Francine. I met MorWenna, a smashing Welsh actress, with a flaming sea of red hair. I barely held my breath before plunging into those fiery depths. Instantly committing marital suicide, I surfaced for air only at the end of the run. The color of 'Wenna's hair and the pale cream of her skin haunt many of my later canvases.

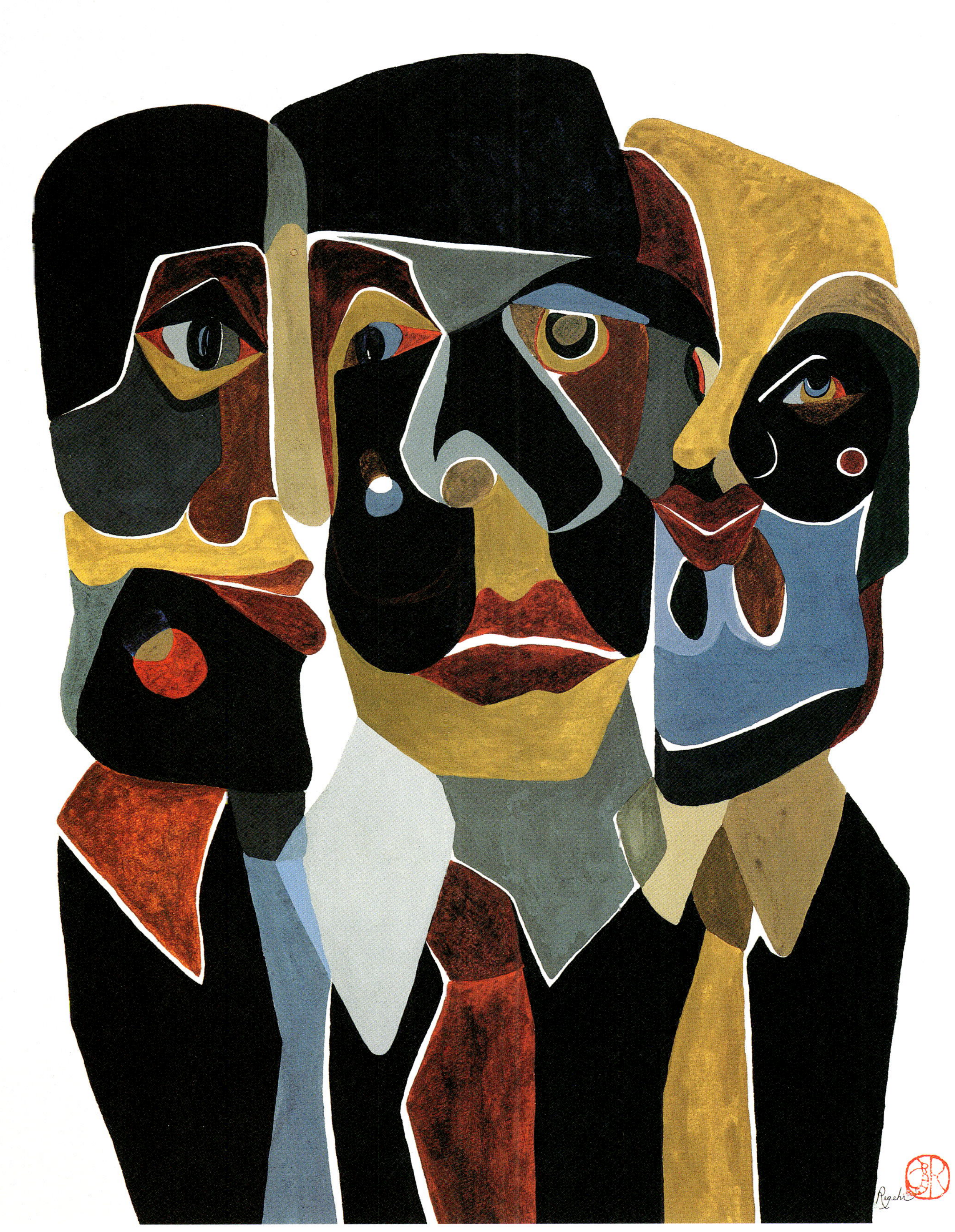

Conspiracy, Merchant of Venice WATERCOLOR 24" x 18" 1975

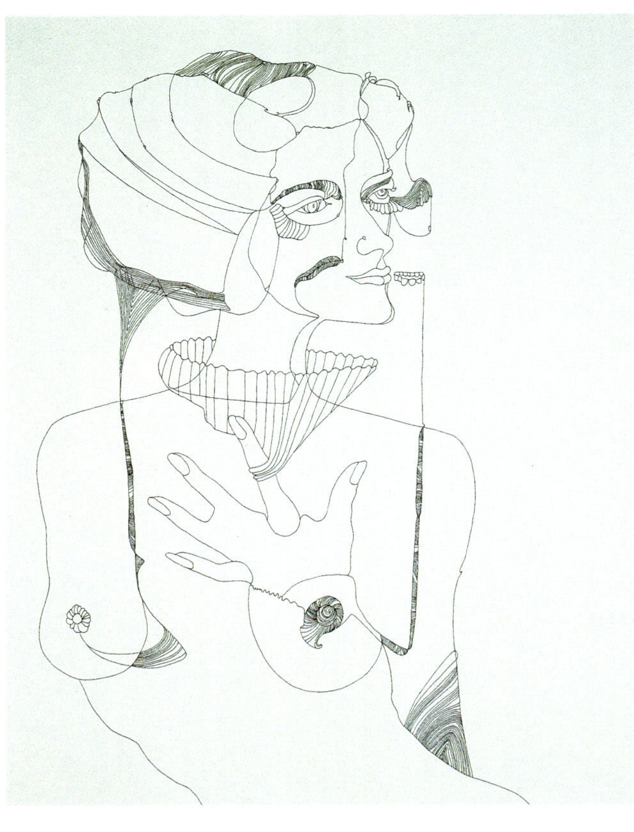

MorWenna
LINE DRAWING
24" x 18"   1989

I returned to Toronto to face my other blazing tempest, Francine. I arrived expecting to be burned at the stake of infidelity, only to discover that Francine had found solace in the arms of a doting stage director.

I could hardly blame her. She was lonely. Even when I was with her, I neglected her for my own selfish endeavors. In truth, we were incompatible. The only place we shared a remotely similar point of view was in the bedroom.

The finale of our relationship was exciting, if painful, but it contributed much to my paintings.

It may only be imaginative hindsight, but it seemed that the more we screamed at each other, the redder my reds became. The ensuing cold silences spread as dark blues and greys. Our hopeless attempts at normal communication left narrow gaps of spared white, while sessions of apology produced earth tones, which quickly changed to scarlet or crimson whenever remorse rekindled ardor.

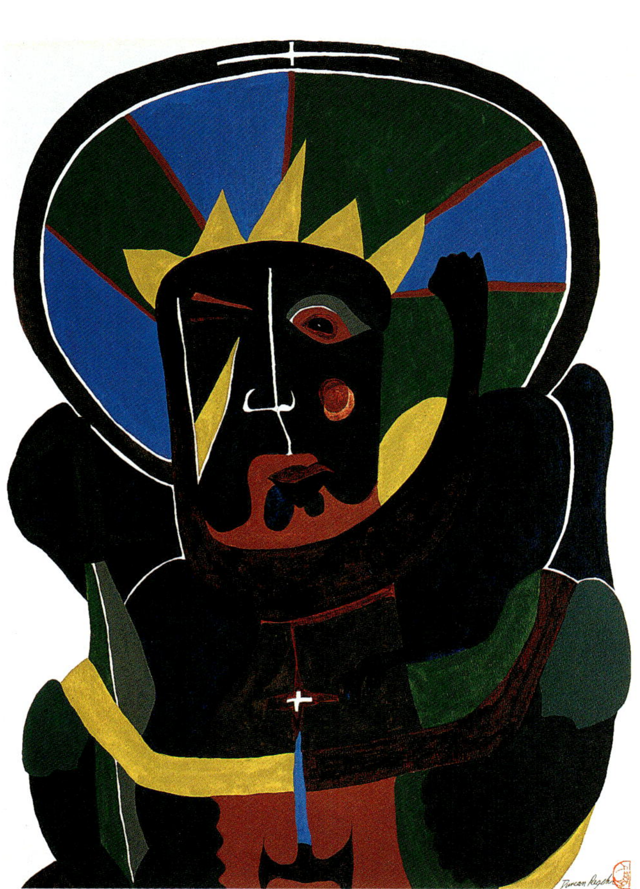

Henry VIII
WATERCOLOR
24" x 18"   1974

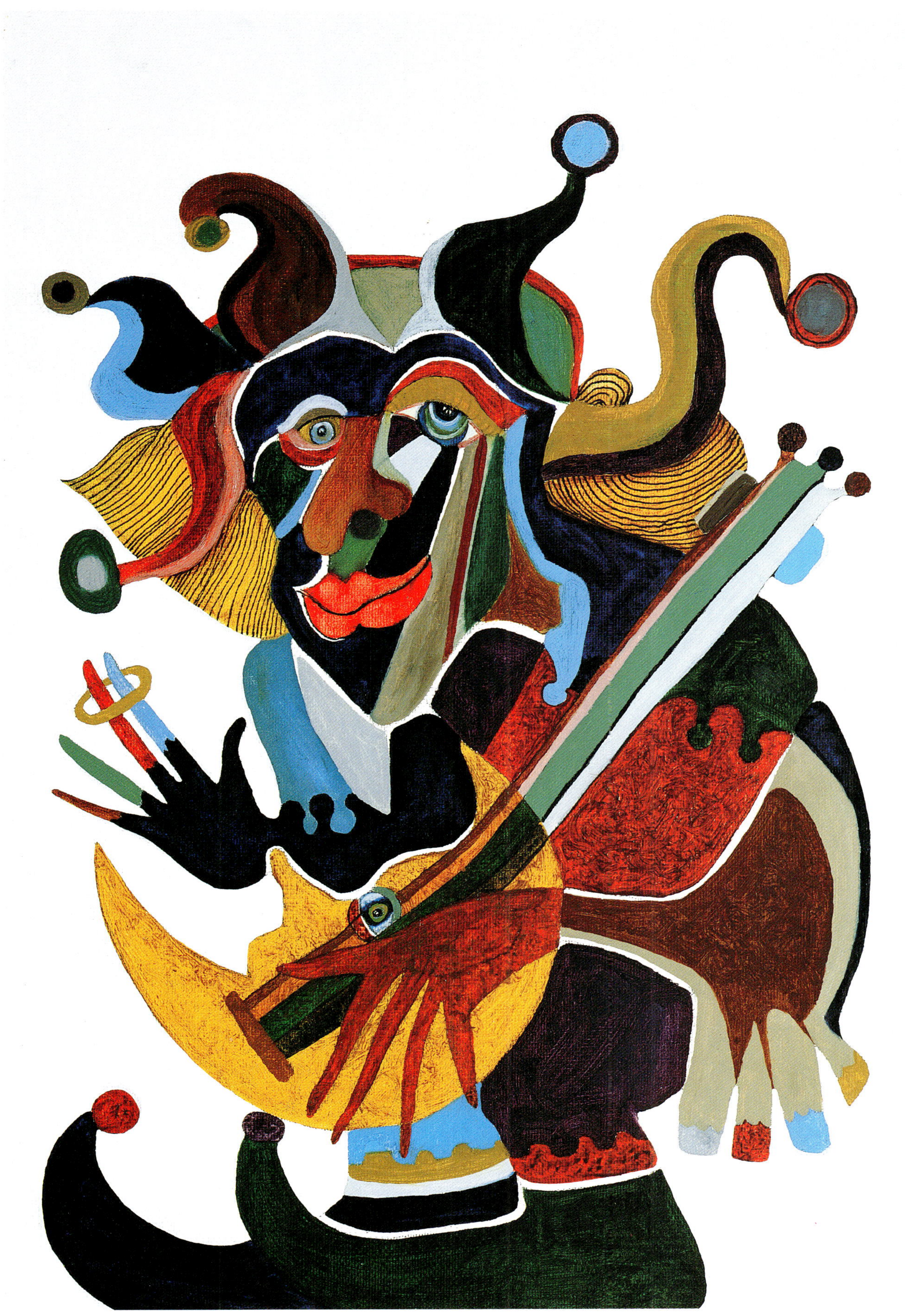

Feste Oil 17" x 11"

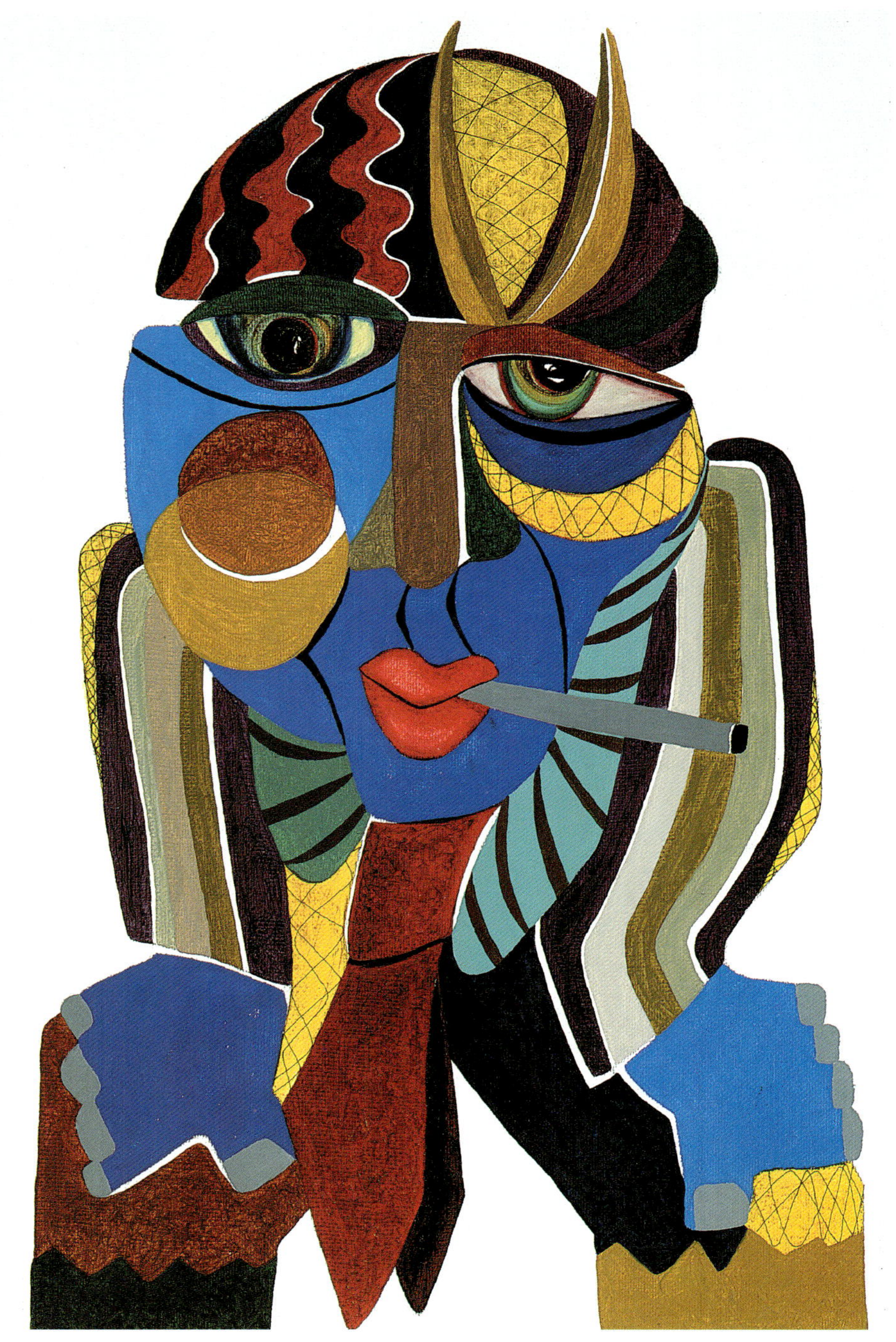

Iago Oil 17" x 11"

As I sat at my easel, Francine would practice singing with a vengeance. She had a voice as powerful as Ethel Merman's but much more melodic. It grew in volume according to the length of time I spent working. Her vocal eruptions had the potential to shatter all manner of things fragile. I hesitate to add our relationship to the list, but I should point out that they failed to break my concentration, as my resolve to continue painting also increased with each decibel mounted. By the time we separated, she was hoarse with laryngitis and my ears rang for months with the apt refrain, "Black is the color of my true love's (heart)."

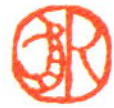

III

THE INFIDEL'S DOG

Religion

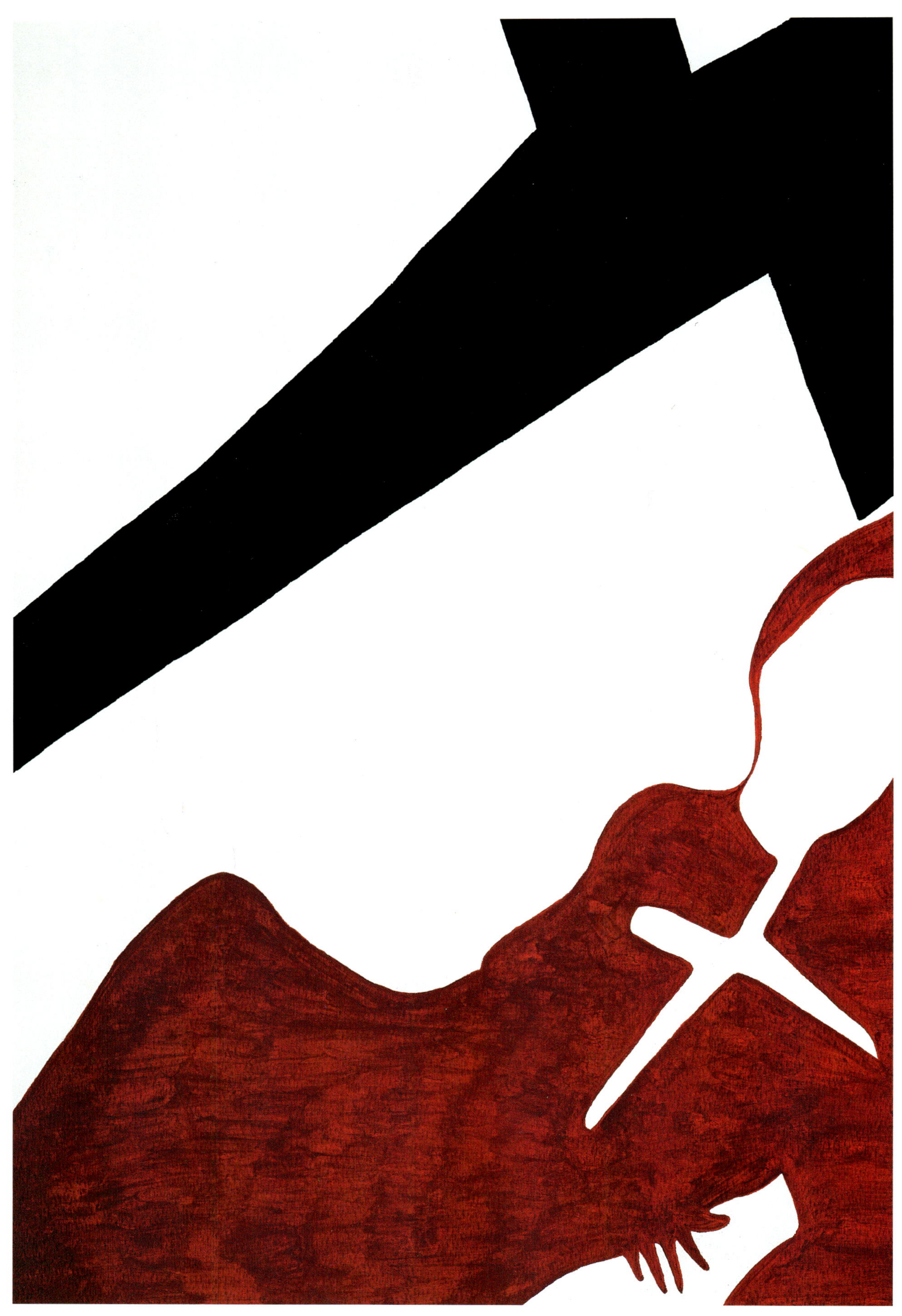

The Dying Cardinal WATERCOLOR 18" x 12" 1975–1976

DURING THE LATTER PART OF 1975 through 1976, I lived in the second floor flat of a large house near the edge of Toronto's High Park.

Dutch painter Henry Poesiat and his wife rented the attic flat. Their lovely daughter Anya occupied the small suite adjacent to mine.

Henry, a Surrealist, taught me a great deal about investigating the untapped regions of my psyche and how the unconscious could manifest through automatism and dreams, which he valued as poetic experiences. He maintained that automatic techniques enabled the mind to bypass normal constraints of logic and produce images of unexpected brilliance.

I felt insignificant showing my work to Henry, but he offered only encouragement. Upon viewing my portraits he said, "Hands can be the window to the soul, hang on to that. They often convey secrets untold by the face, or the rest of the body."

As a lover and a soul mate, Anya helped me to speak freely of things I had remained silent about for too many years. Far into the night, we would discuss subjects her father had initiated earlier in the evening.

Sinner WATERCOLOR 18" x 12"

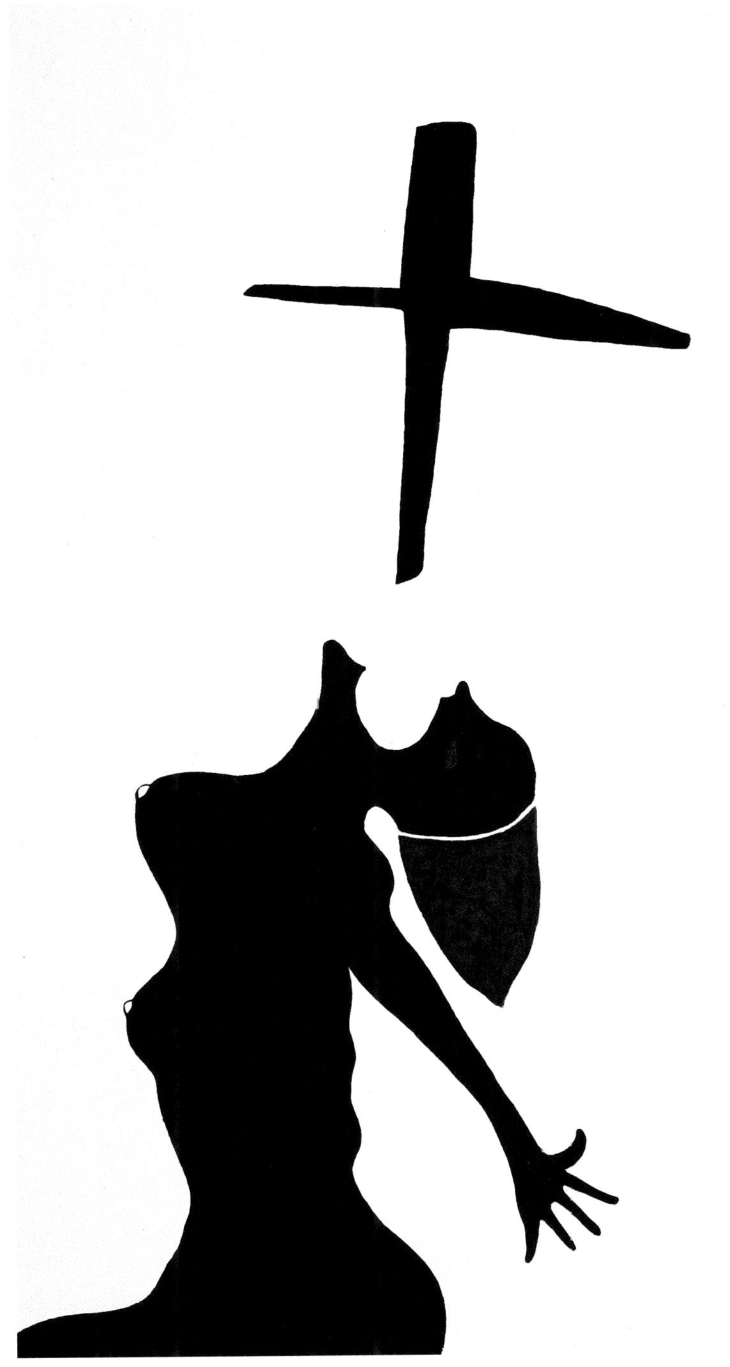

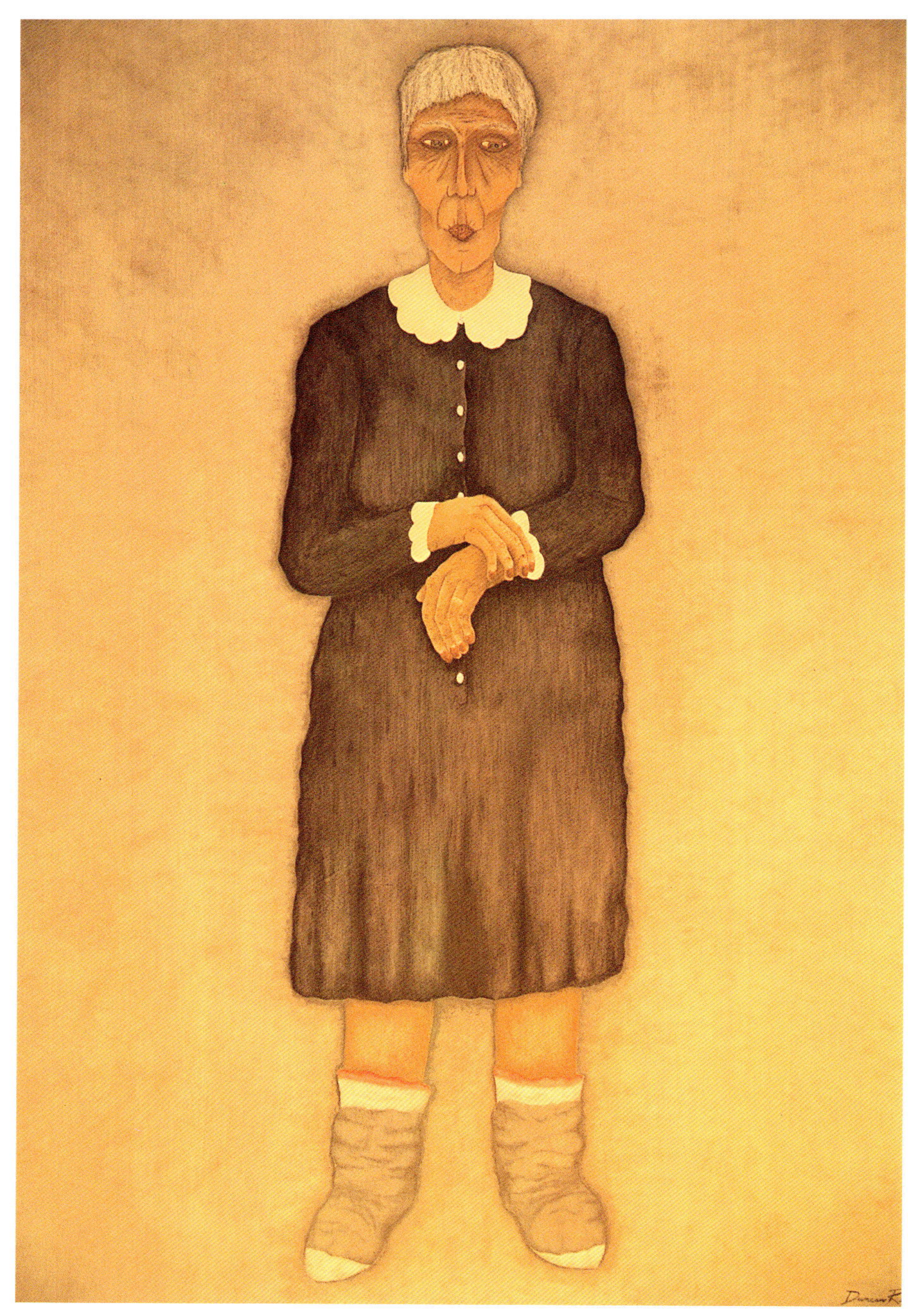

Widow of Faith Oil 48 x 36" 1978

Theology was a subject I had avoided since the day I was cast out of Sunday school — for telling the teacher that I did not believe Jonah had been swallowed by a whale. "A shark maybe, but then he'd be chewed up into little tiny pieces. The Holy Bible's full of dog muck!"

When I told my mother I had been expelled for repeating one of her comments on the Bible (the bit about Jonah was my own), she corrected me, "No dear, I said *dogma,* not dog muck." But I have continued to use the old term ever since, often with regard to my own writings.

The Hook
WATERCOLOR
24" x 18" 1975-1976

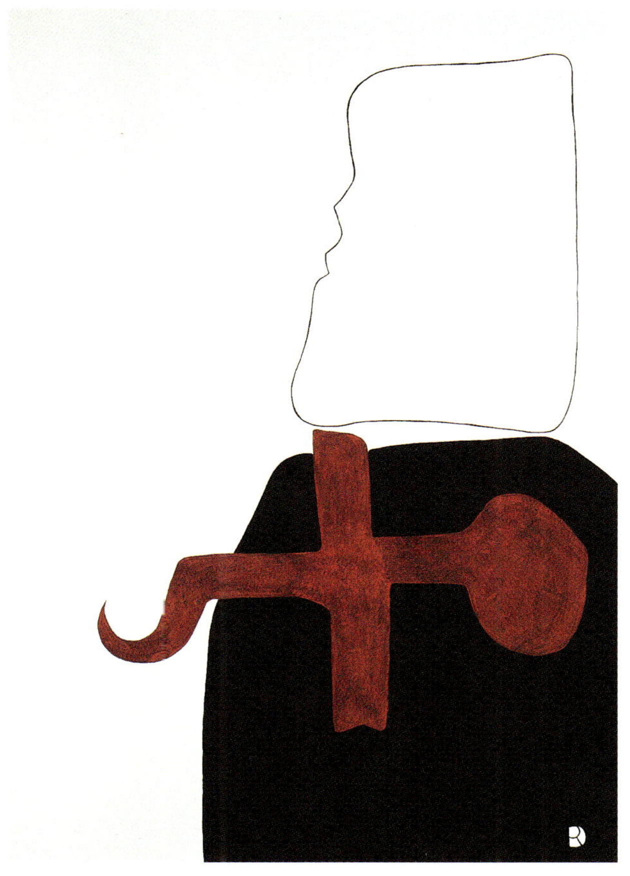

My father was brought up a strict Mennonite. A faith he rejected after it rejected him for joining the Army in World War II. It was no fault of his, but I grew up loathing most organized religions, especially Christianity. The following is an excerpt from my journal, dated Christmas Eve 1976:

My relatives are obsessed with the afterlife. Rarely rising from their knees long enough to experience this life, they will bear the self righteous yoke of Christianity to their graves.

Long ago, it seems to me, the Christian church lost sight of its basic ideals. More than any other religion, it has become divided into sects that avariciously wield guilt as a blackmail tool to wrest money from followers. Surely it is time to start over with a simpler form of unification.

Heaven forbid it should be another clone of Catholicism. That rabid hound is tunneling under the mountain of its own hypocritical dog muck; undermining its wealthy foundation by not condoning birth control, thereby helping to increase global poverty through overpopulation. The fabled new messiah better bring a large shovel to clean out the kennel and bury the bones.

It was not a happy Christmas that year.

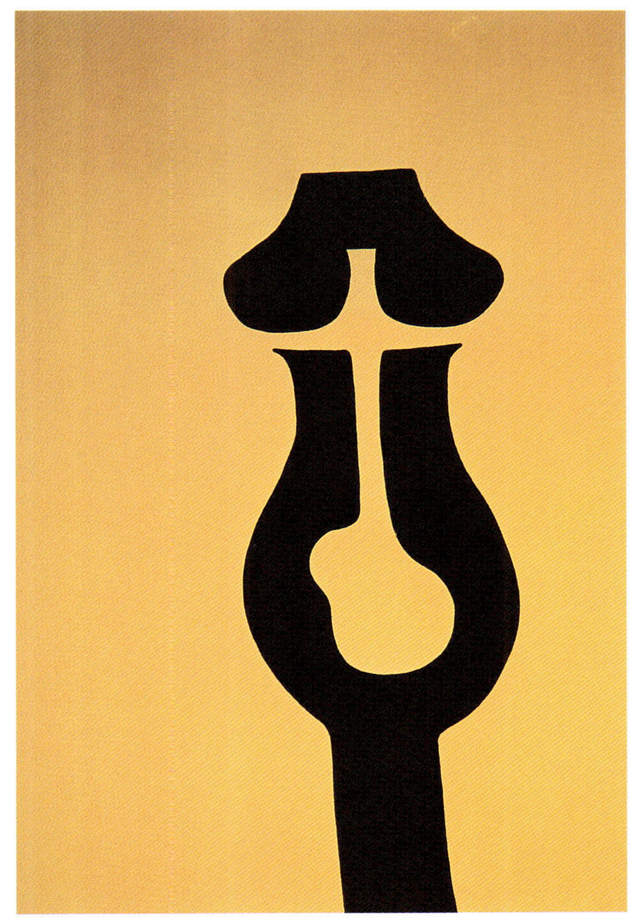

Gestation
WATERCOLOR
24" x 18" 1975-1976

The private world on the edge of High Park Forest allowed me to look deeply within myself. One would expect that environment to be therapeutic, to encourage a quiet, philosophic state of mind. Quite the opposite occurred. My long talks with the gentle Poesiats and my subsequent meditations unearthed demons. I began to have terrible nightmares. Alone in the woods, I felt as though I was being followed. The dark episodes of my past had become predators, lurking in the undergrowth, waiting to pounce.

Sometimes I would see the faces of my friends transform into castigating masks of my religious relatives. In the night, I would awaken with women from my past, lying dead beside me on the sweat soaked sheets. In the worst of my dreams, I would be with Carole May, making love over and over again in a field of hay and flowers while covering a faceless child with her long dark hair. The woods were full of winter skeletons, their branches like witches' fingers, clutching and pointing with imprecation.

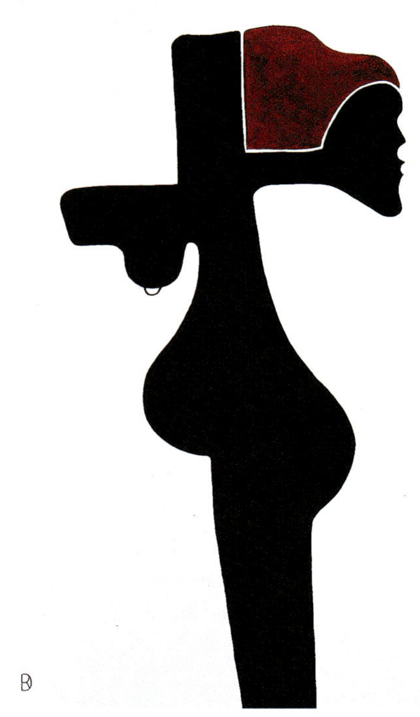

Crucifixion III WATERCOLOR
24" x 18" 1975-1976

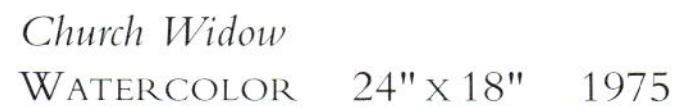

Church Widow
WATERCOLOR 24" x 18" 1975

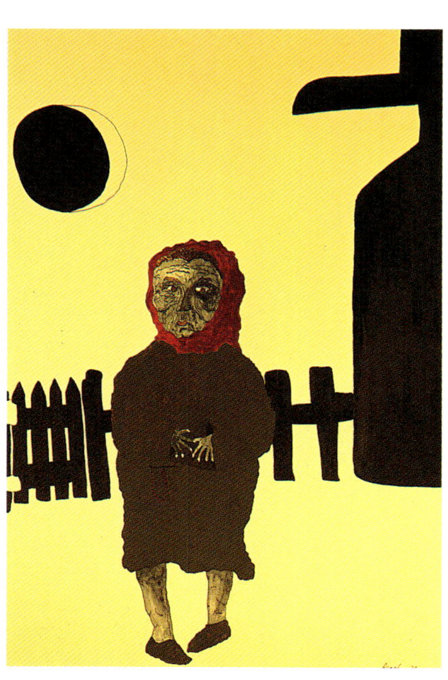

Fleeing Priest WATERCOLOR 16" x 12" 1975-1976

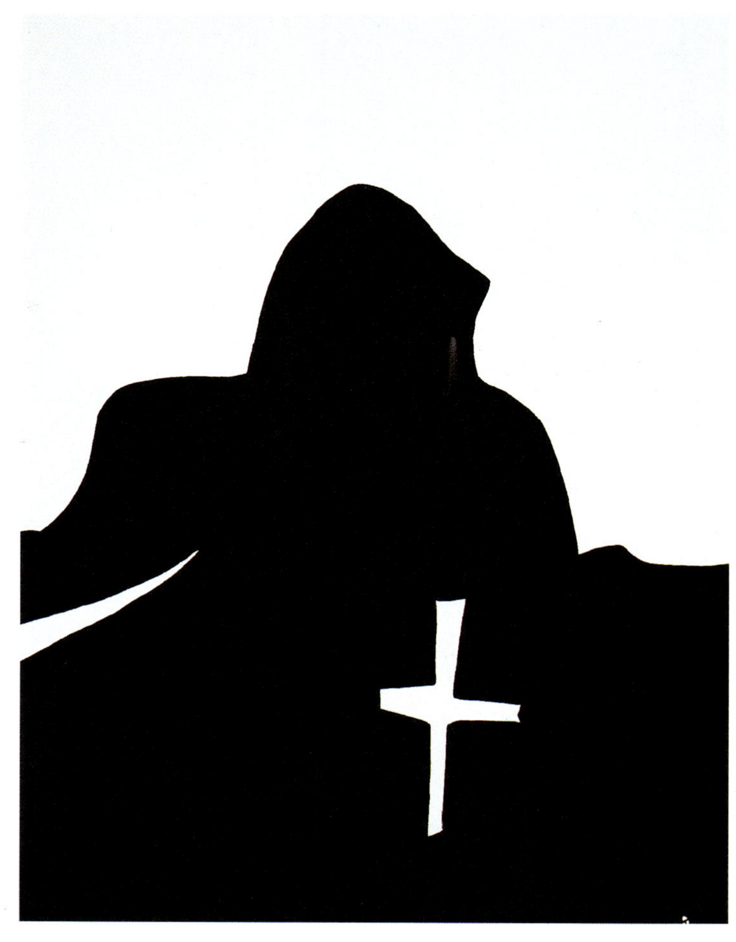

Cur

Peace strolls with you on a forest path,
freshens your spirit by the sea,
(drowns suspicion there)
smothers instinct in the scent of gentle wildflowers.
Anticipation evaporates, resting on a sunny stone.
You are unprepared for the chasing dog.

It is suddenly there,
panting garbage dump smoke
on the far edge of a golden meadow,
or very near the narrow stream too broad to leap,
too close to the fallen log across.

It roots along the other side.
Huge and snuffling, spreads stink
with back legs that shred your footprints out of the earth.
The carrion muzzle growls froth.
The forest air fills up.
Pausing on your scent to self bite old wounds,
it whines for slaughter.
Then crosses over,
ripping up plants, cold trails it scalds with urine.
Chasing and shaking the helpless living,
it cowers from rocks that lie perfectly still.

You run,
eyes held breath closed.
You meet on the road
unleashed from peace, a nervous system prepared.

Instinctively it lunges,
then halts short.
Eyes glaze,
dissatisfaction barks in the smoke.
Disappears . . .

You call out:
Who's dog is this?

you call

Who is this dog (you belong to)?

—DR

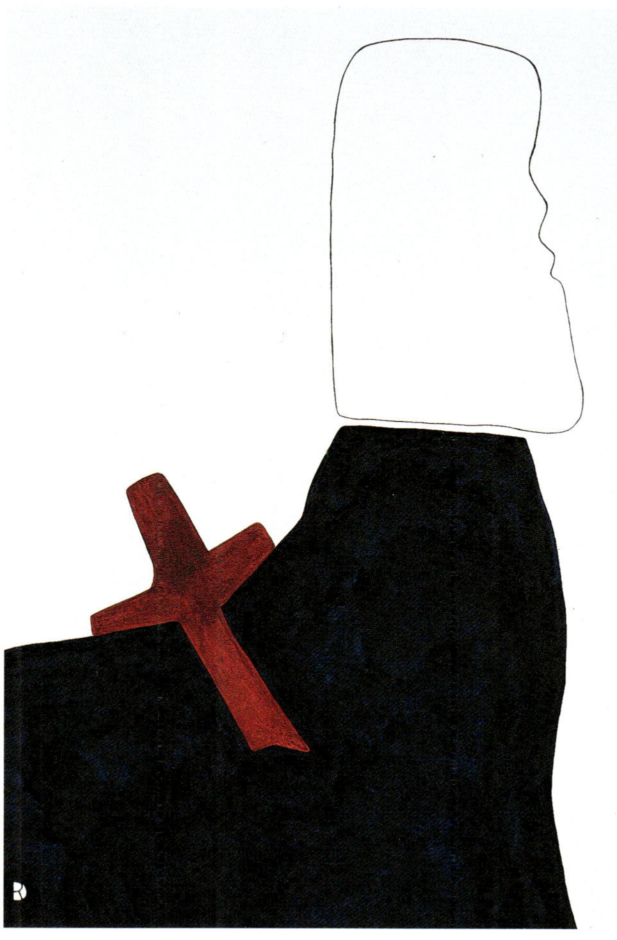

Priest Sphinx WATERCOLOR
24" x 18" 1975-1976

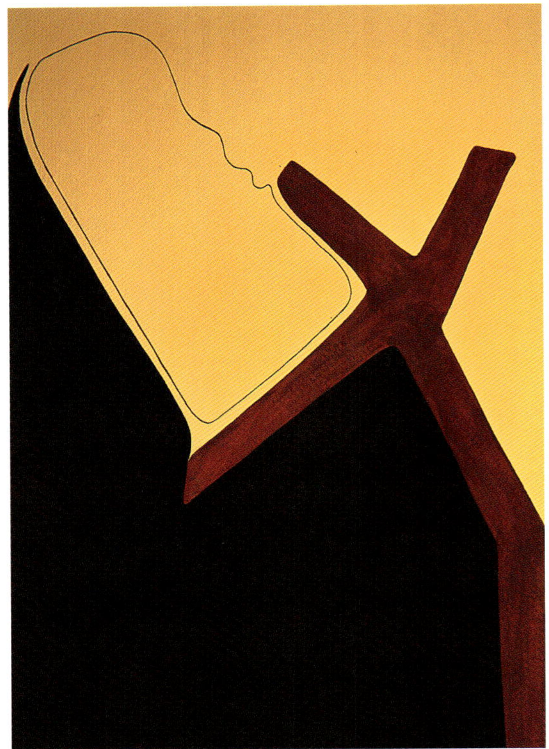

Easter Priest III WATERCOLOR
24" x 18" 1975-1976

Crucifixion I WATERCOLOR
24" x 18" 1975-1976

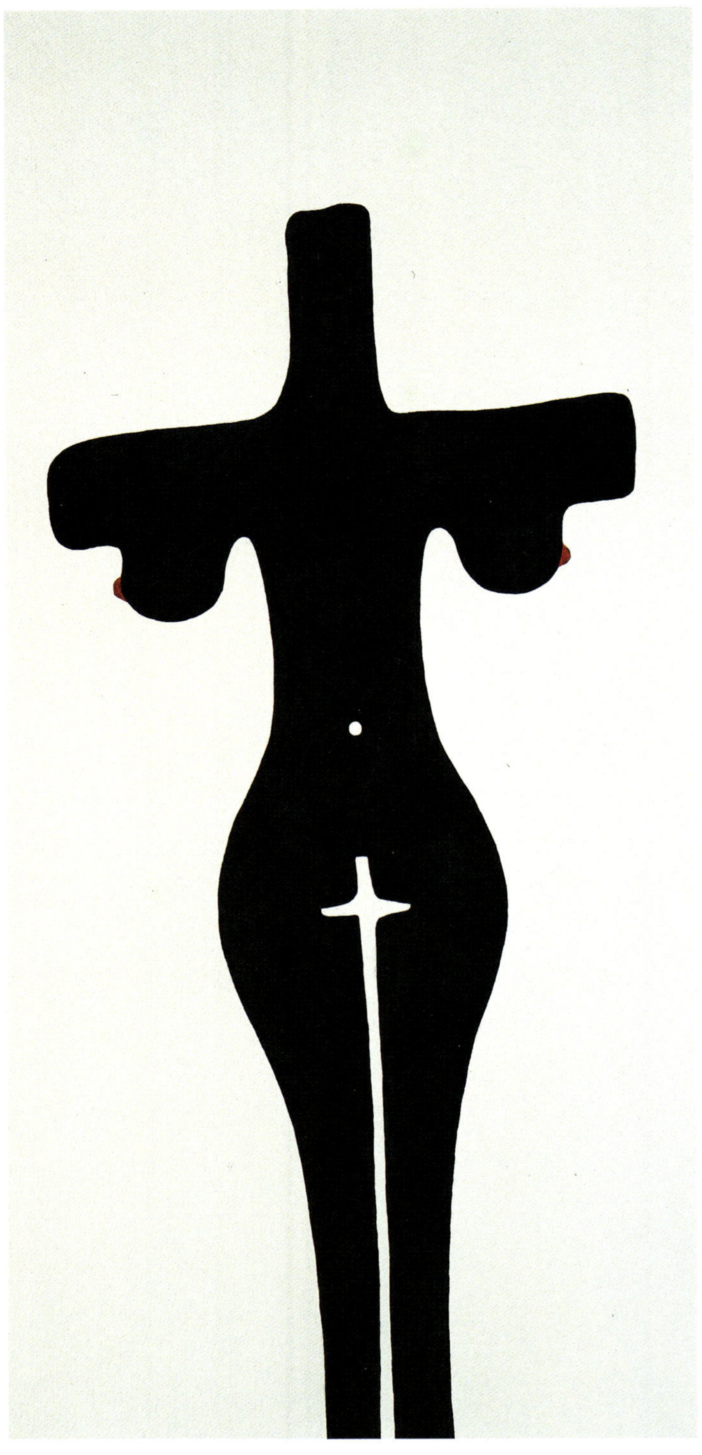

I lacked a criterion through which I could seek spirituality, and while I had an established format for inner morality, I had little faith in it. Any act might be considered sinful, depending on which dog muck one's subconscious consulted. I was guilt-bound by my love affairs and the loss of my child.

At times I may have been unfair and unfaithful, but my worst transgressions were always against myself. Murder is evil. My sins existed as evil because my past indoctrinations labeled and instilled them as such. From day one at Sunday school, I had been taught that we are all evil from the moment of birth. I was drenched in dog muck from head to foot.

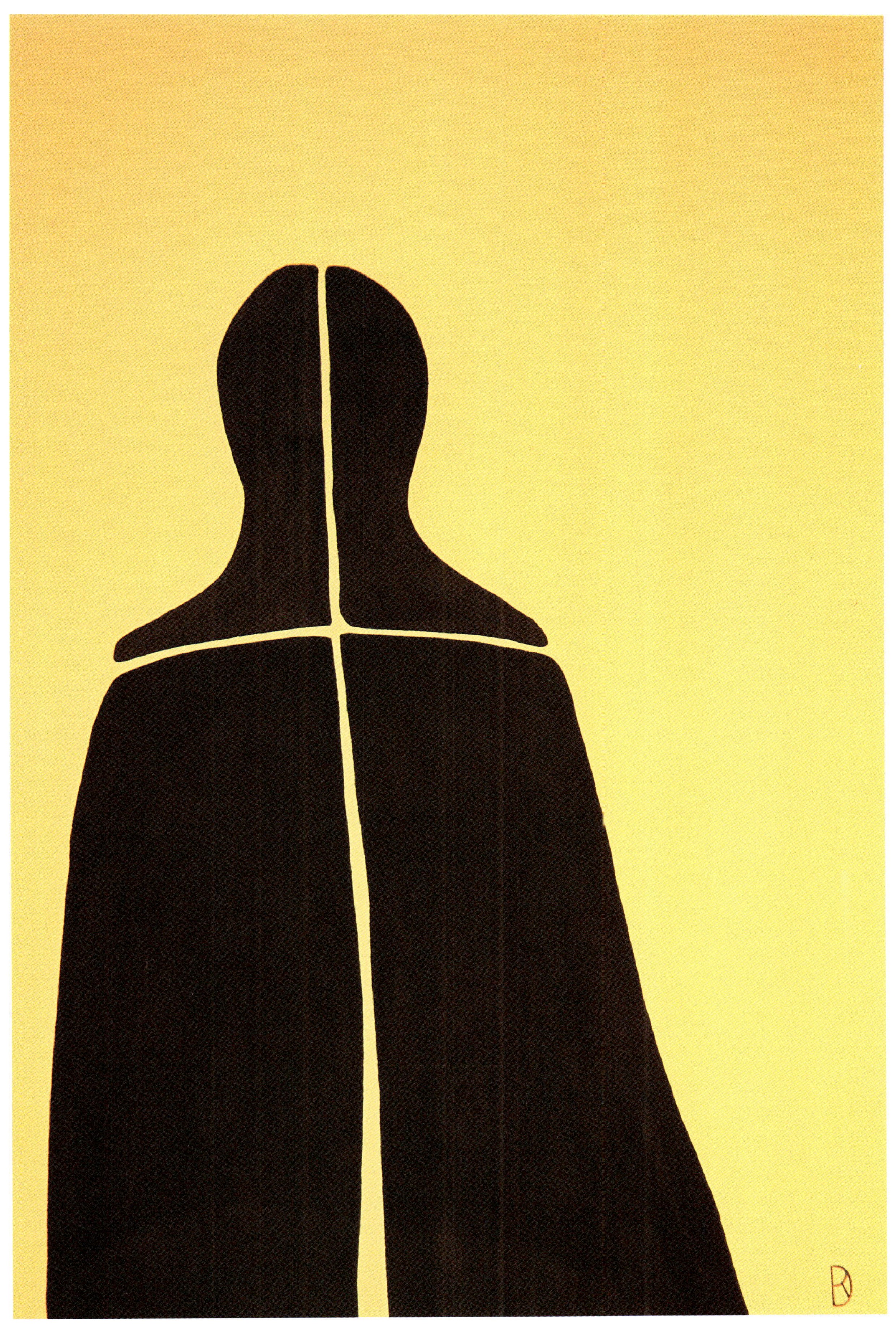

Holy Phantom WATERCOLOR 24" x 18" 1976

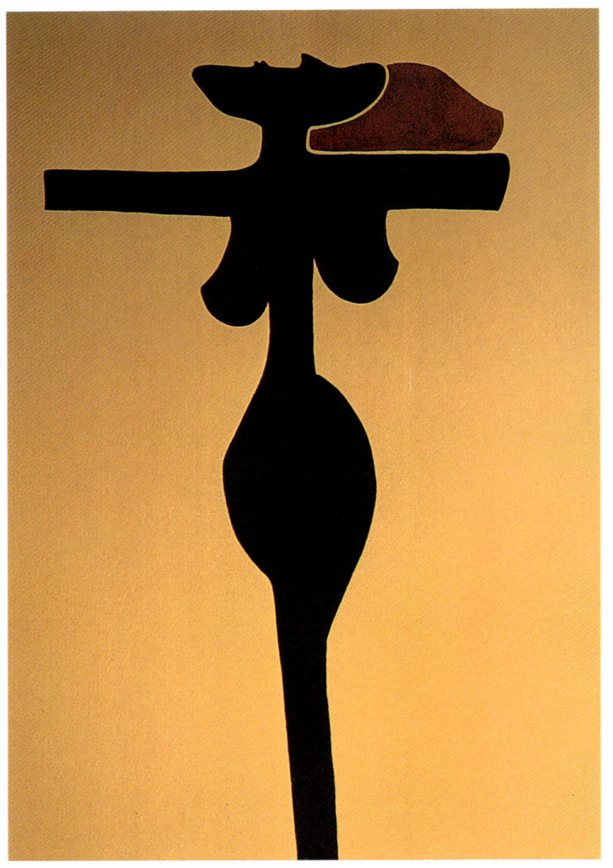

Crucifixion VII WATERCOLOR
24" x 18" 1976

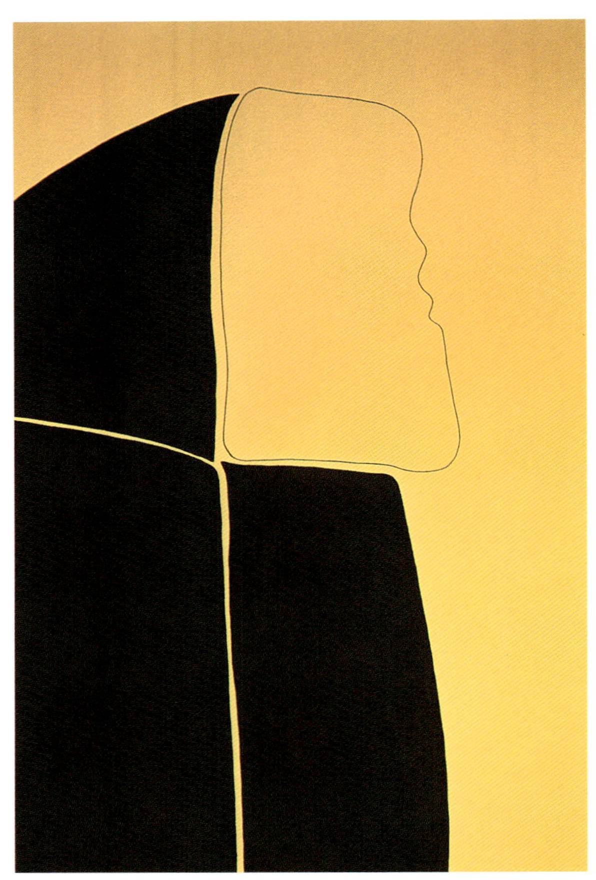

Easter Priest WATERCOLOR
24" x 18" 1975-1976

I washed myself clean in watercolor. I composed flat, symbolic images involving crosses and priestlike figures, often outlining a blind featureless face and sacrificial or misogynic shapes of women. While the paintings appear to be a comment on the malignancy of the Christian faith, they are also the manifestations of my guilt and supposed sins.

The work acted as an exorcism. It helped to bring about a simple awareness that laid my demons to rest. Devoid of dog muck, that awareness would later blossom into a broader, unfettered form of spirituality—understanding myself as being one with all things.

I count religion but a childish toy,
And hold there is no sin but ignorance.
—CHRISTOPHER MARLOWE

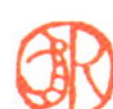

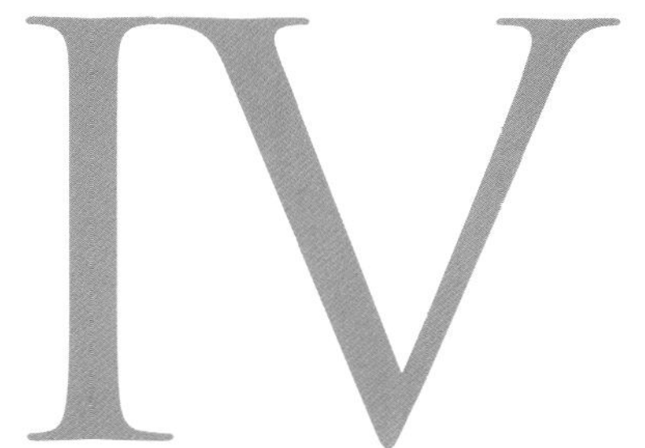

HOLLYWOOD AND THE PRE-RAPHAELITE VOLCANO

Geoscapes

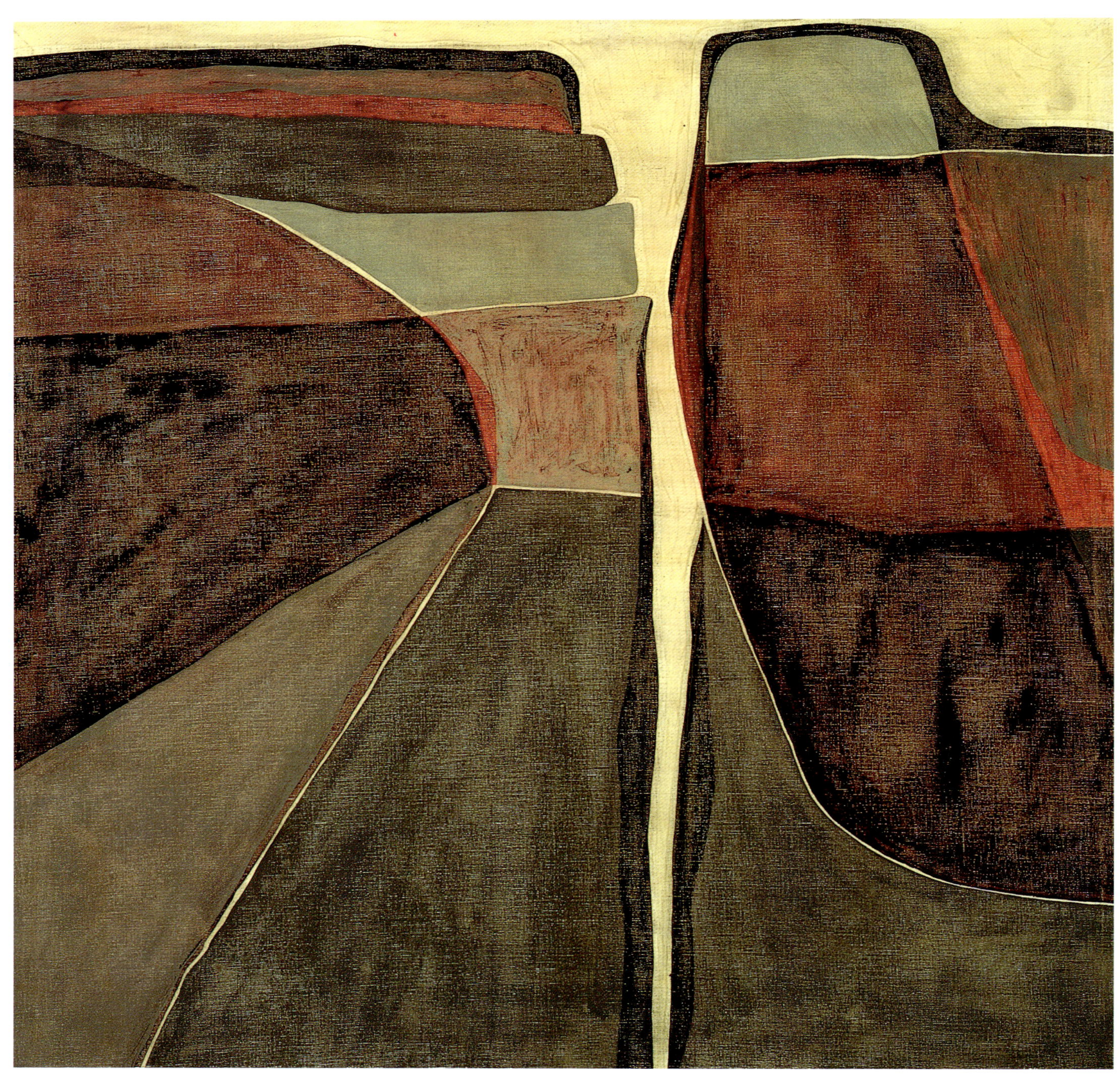

Geo II Oil 48" x 48"

Catherine and I met at the opening of an art gallery in Toronto. I had been living a hermit's life for some time in a shabby little studio flat near Old Cabbage Town. She had left her home in England a few years before and had just thrown in the towel on an acting career to pursue other artistic endeavors — pottery and photography. Falsehearted men were not part of her master plan, so I consider our eventual attachment to have been nothing short of a miracle.

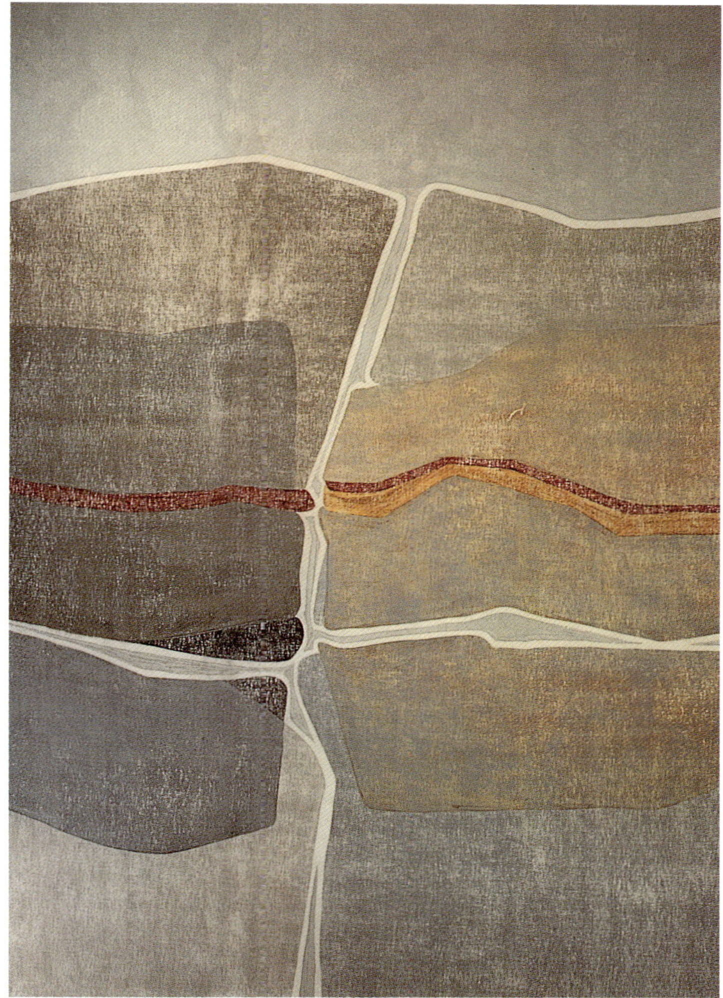

Lode Oil 96" x 72"

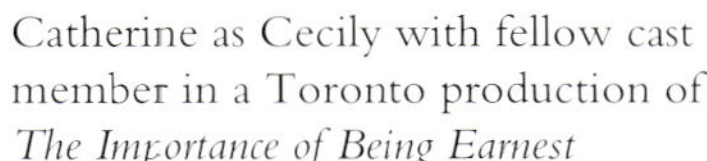

Catherine as Cecily with fellow cast member in a Toronto production of *The Importance of Being Earnest*

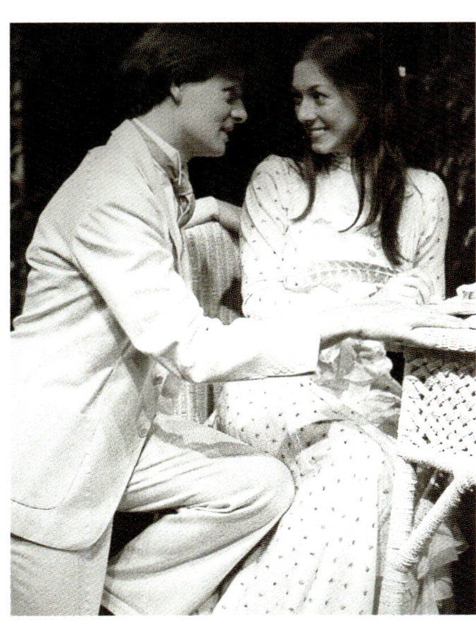

Journal excerpt, April 3rd 1977:

. . . where else would love find me but at an art gallery on April Fool's Day? I haven't written for three days.

Love at first sight? Blind lust without a second thought is par for the course, but this is different. After three days, I am still in shock. It all seems very cliche and absolutely right. She is like a faerie princess, escaped from some Pre-Raphaelite masterpiece.

We literally saw each other across a crowded room and "knew." I know that C. knows that I know that we both know that we have known each other forever. So is this it?

I am without funds again, having emptied the biscuit tin on rent. Thank God, money seems of no importance to C. We are both broke. Last night she gave me her last five dollars to buy a meal for us, steak tartare a la McDonald's. I hope the gallery sells another painting soon, or I will have to skip out on the lease at month's end. At least I will have beautiful company joining me for the midnight flit. Life is wonderful.

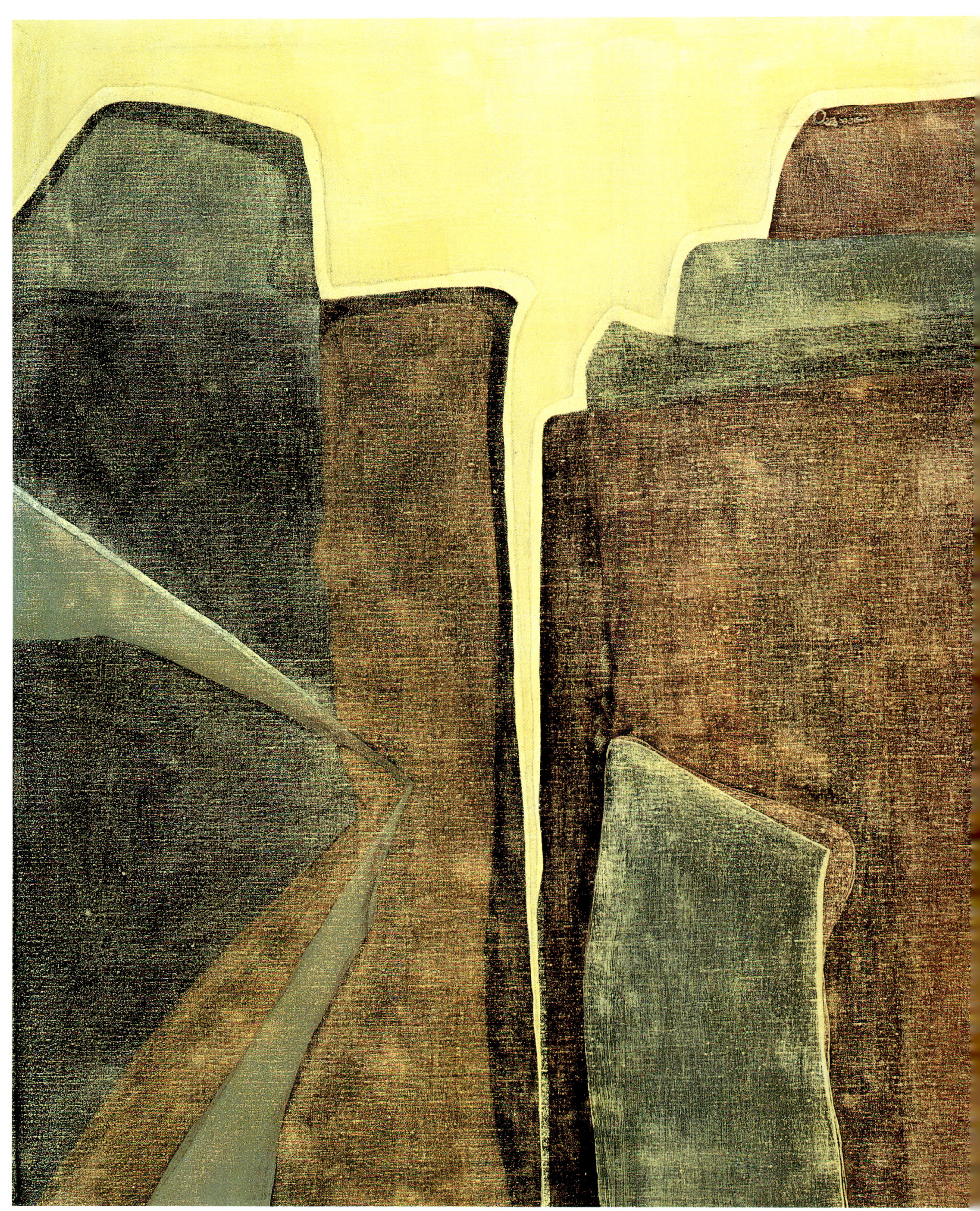

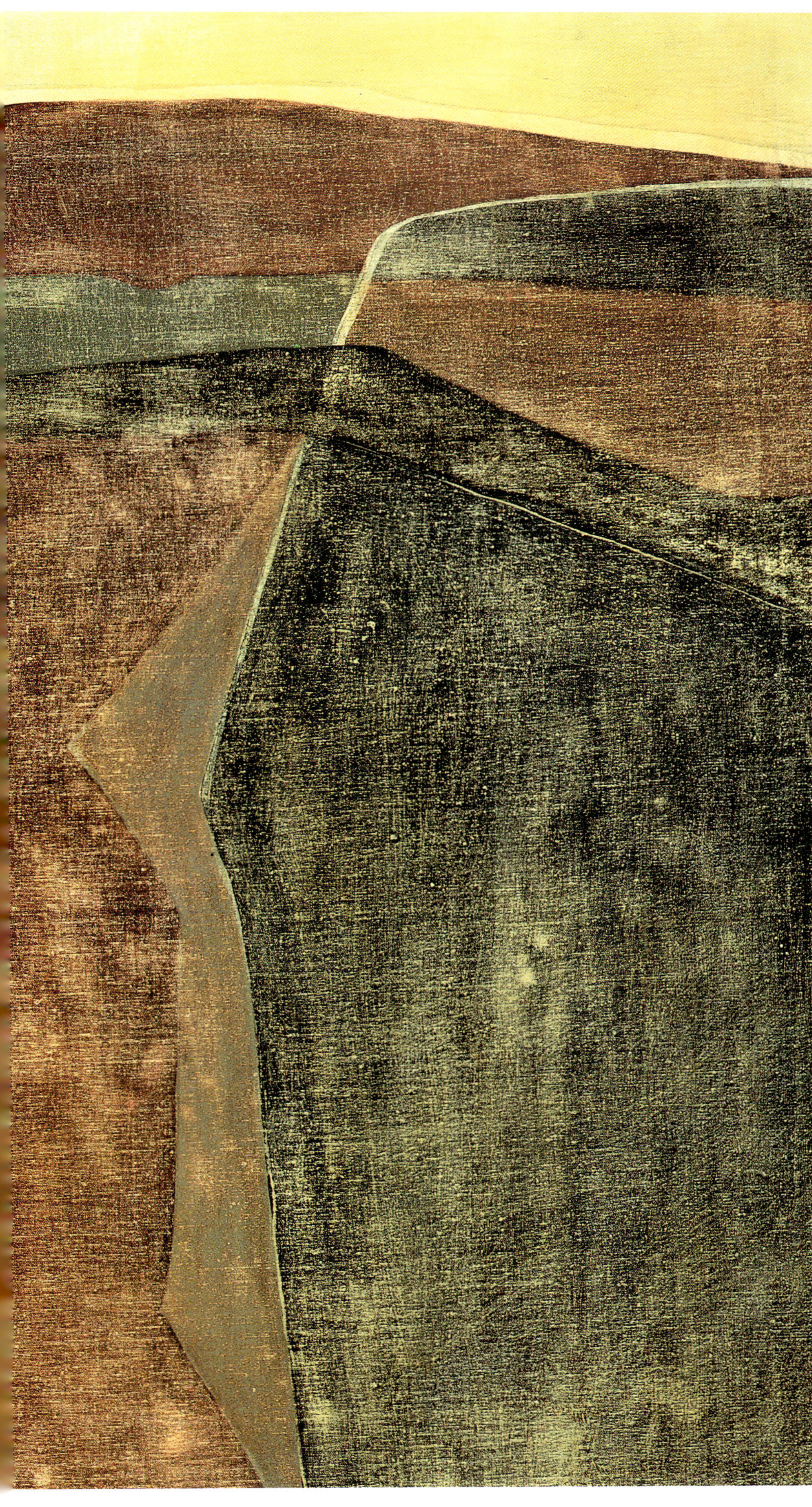

Geo I Oil 40" x 50"

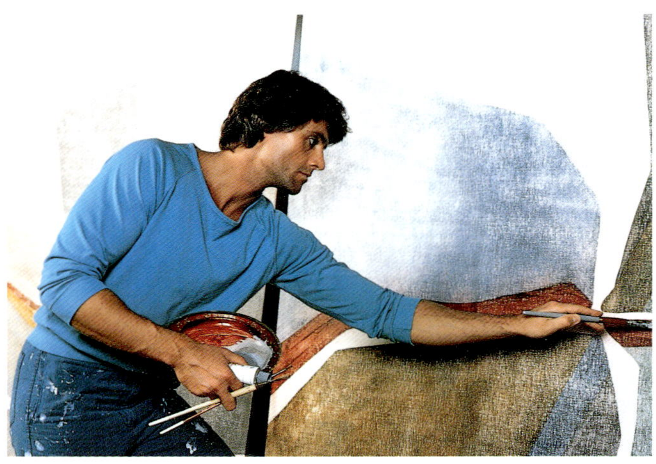

In the studio

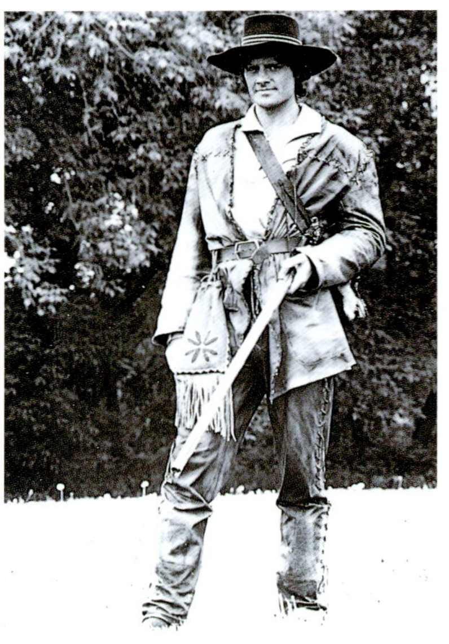

As Kit in the television series *Matt and Jenny*

Disengagement Oil 96" x 72"

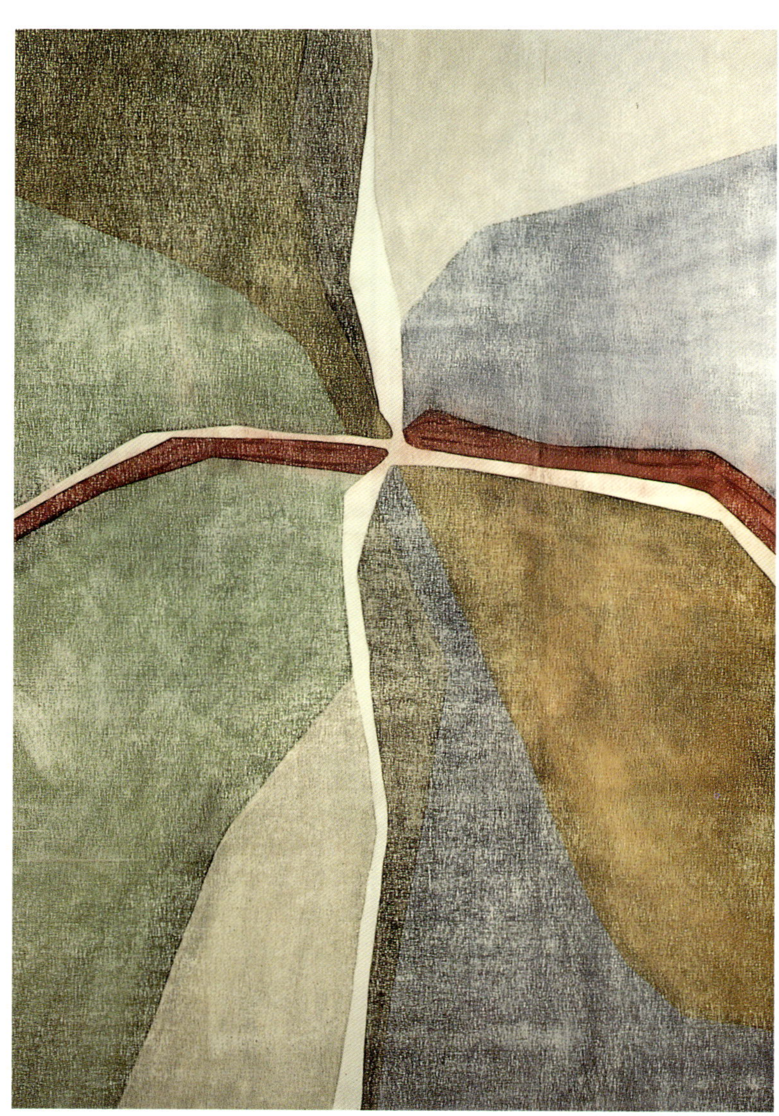

For Catherine and me the world of art was our matchmaker and so it remains — a strong binding factor in our relationship.

She has never directly influenced my work, although many are convinced that she appears quite often, if subliminally, in my paintings. Her love of the arts accompanies a gentle tolerance for that selfish tenacity which forces artists to place work above all else. I marvel at her strength of spirit and remain eternally grateful that she continues to put up with me.

Twenty six episodes of a television series called *Matt and Jenny* finally provided us with enough capital to make a long intended move to Los Angeles. We arrived in the fall of 1980 and rented an apartment in Westwood.

Typically, I attacked everything at once. With Catherine's help, I procured an agent within a week. Within three weeks I had a job offer and a work permit in process. I was painting even before we had unpacked.

My first impressions of Southern California inspired a new series and style of painting, Geoscapes.

I was struck by the parallels I saw between the fragile social/political climate and the equally fragile geographic/geologic environment. The analogy gave me a constant sense of disengagement. Having physically and psychologically moved away from my old home served to reinforce these feelings. My new home abounded with violent scissions, temporary upheavals and long standing rifts.

It was only in my mind that I juxtaposed the class delineations, economic gaps, dichotomy between the sexes, the segregation amongst the races and the divisions in every layer of L.A. society with the earthquakes, volcanic faults, fissures, decomposing strata, and the eroding cliffs between land and sea. On canvas, I made no attempt to paint or connect my social/political observations.

Rift Oil 36" x 48"

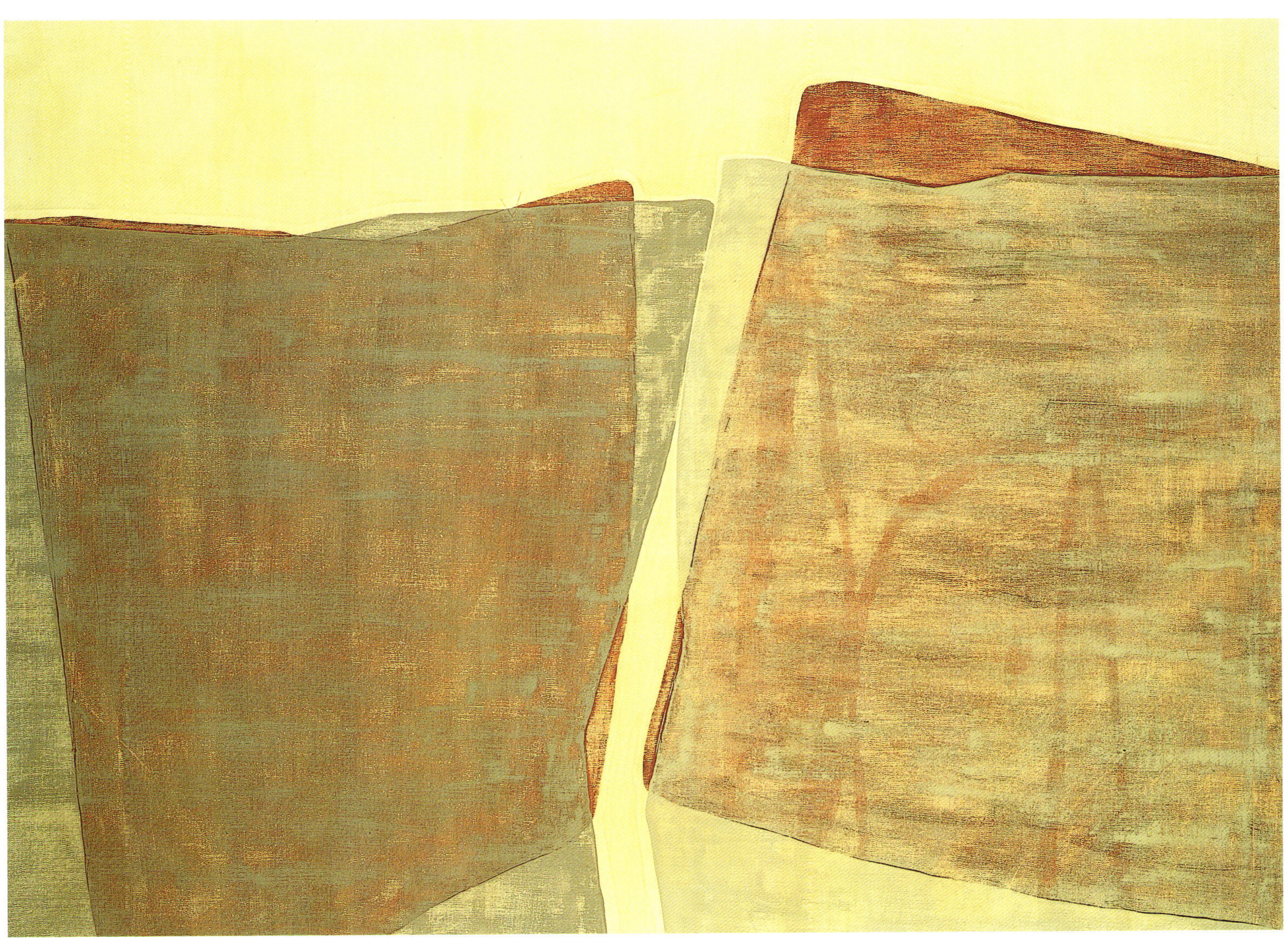

Vesuvius (TRIPTYCH) OIL 48" x 144"

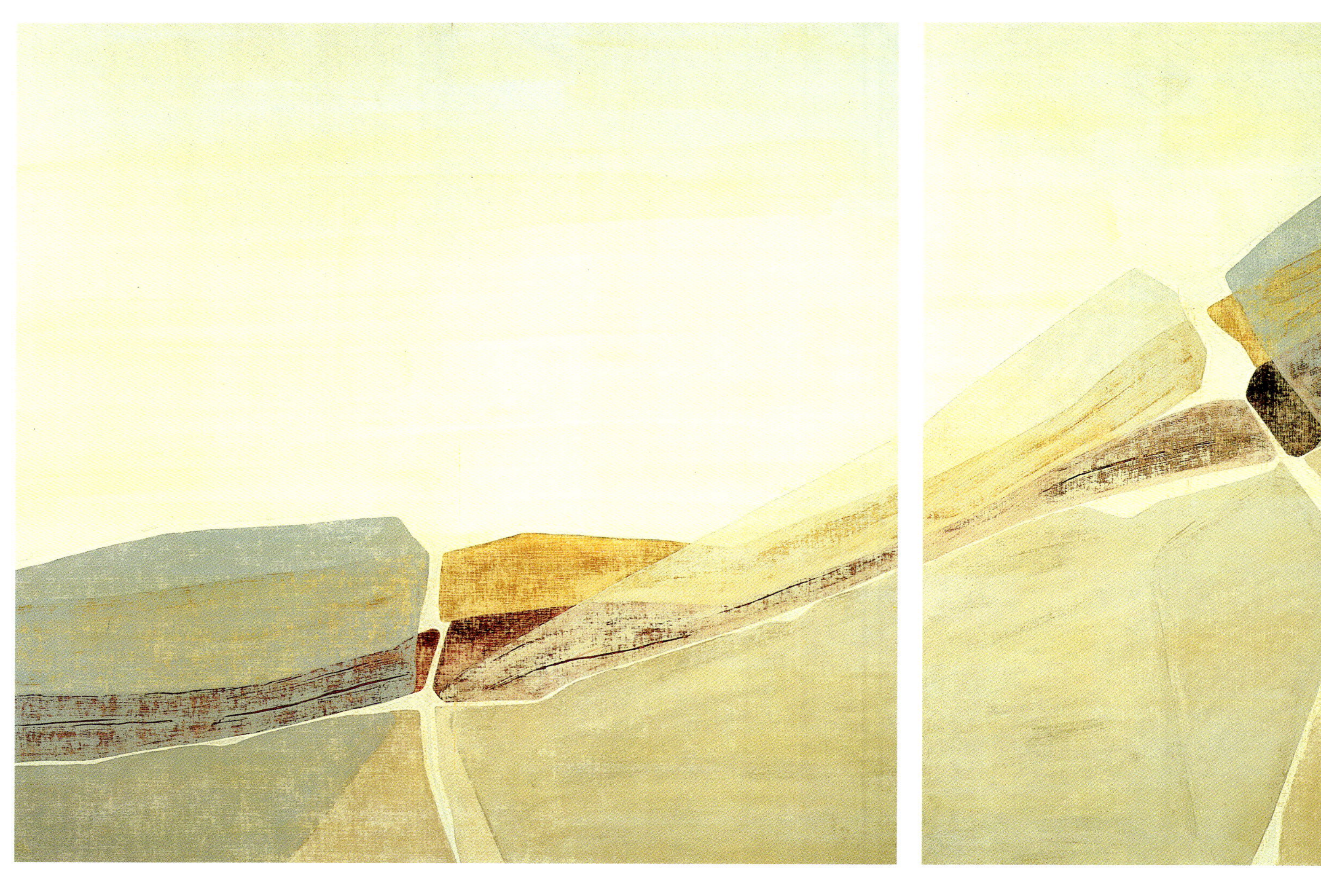

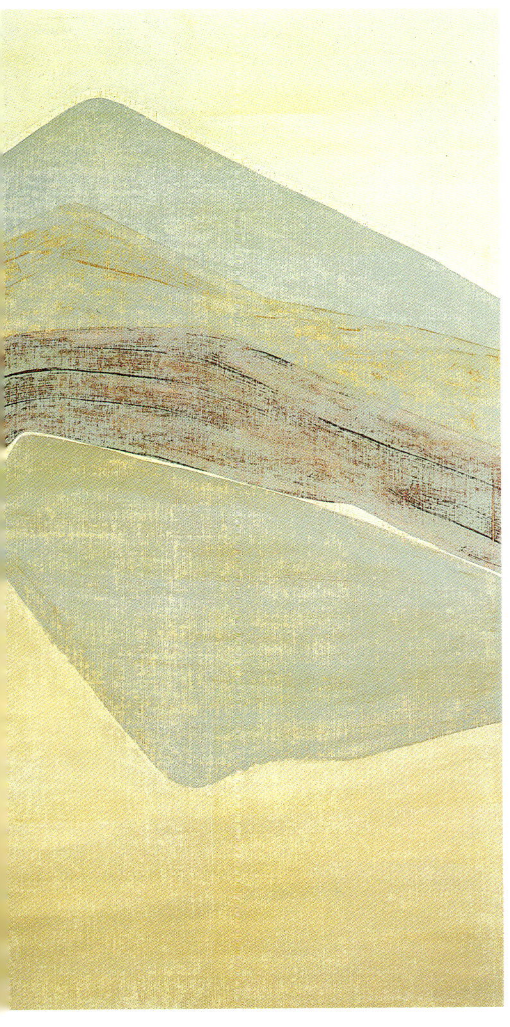

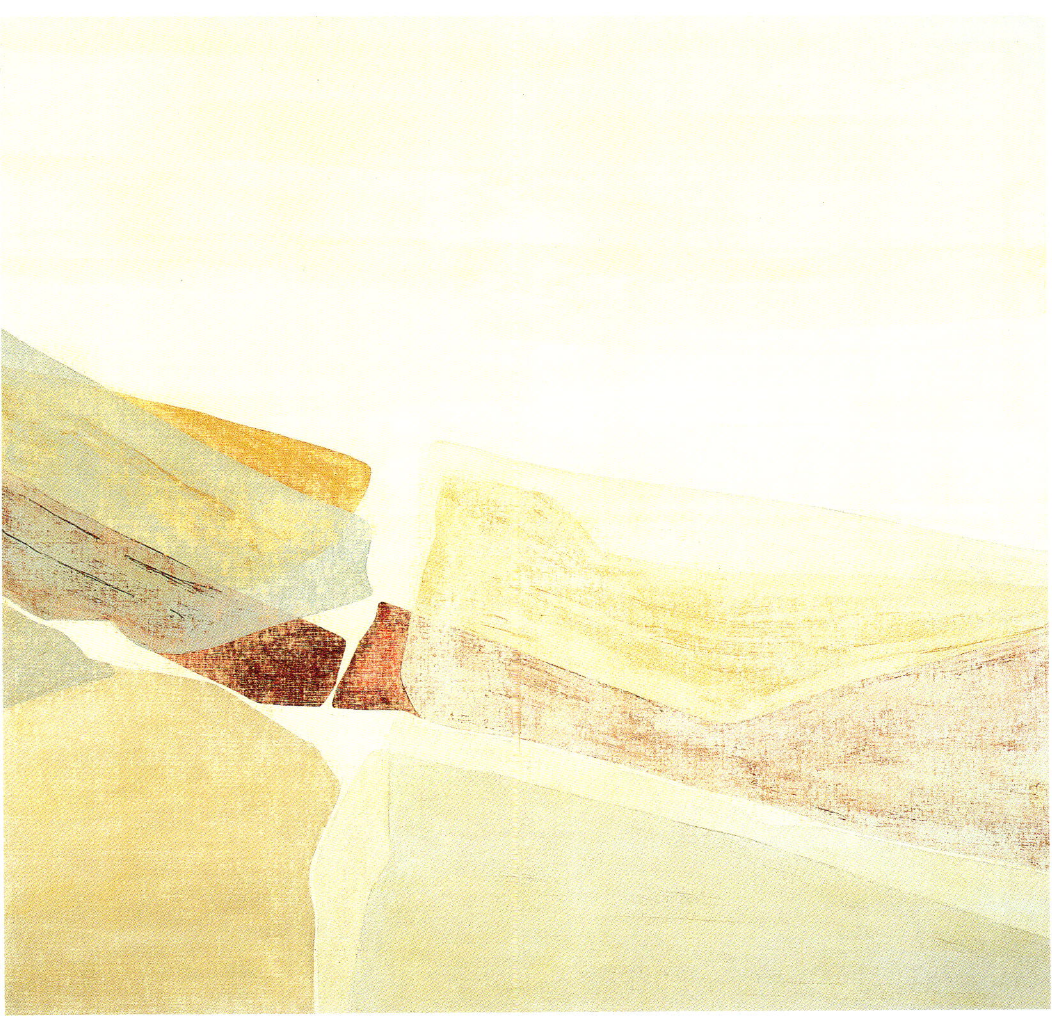

The resulting oils were gratifying to make. Particularly the larger canvases. A triptych entitled *Vesuvius*, which I painted after a trip to Italy for the filming of *The Last Days of Pompeii* (a diversion from California, but nonetheless related by similarities of geological circumstance and societal development), was for me, the linchpin of the series.

Vesuvius was later hung in the living room of our home in Toluca Lake, California. When we put the house up for sale in 1988, a prospective buyer who was about to enter into escrow suddenly insisted, very rudely and vehemently, that under no circumstances would he purchase the property unless *Vesuvius* was included in the package. Catherine erupted like the notorious mountain itself. After burying the unfortunate man under a stream of molten verbiage, she then discharged him (smoldering) into the street and promptly burned his realty papers to a crisp.

If I had ever entertained dreams of a large remuneration from the triptych, they went up in smoke in that instant. I had no idea she felt so strongly about the piece. Perhaps she saw some of her own character in the power of its gentle sloping surface, belying a subterranean volatility.

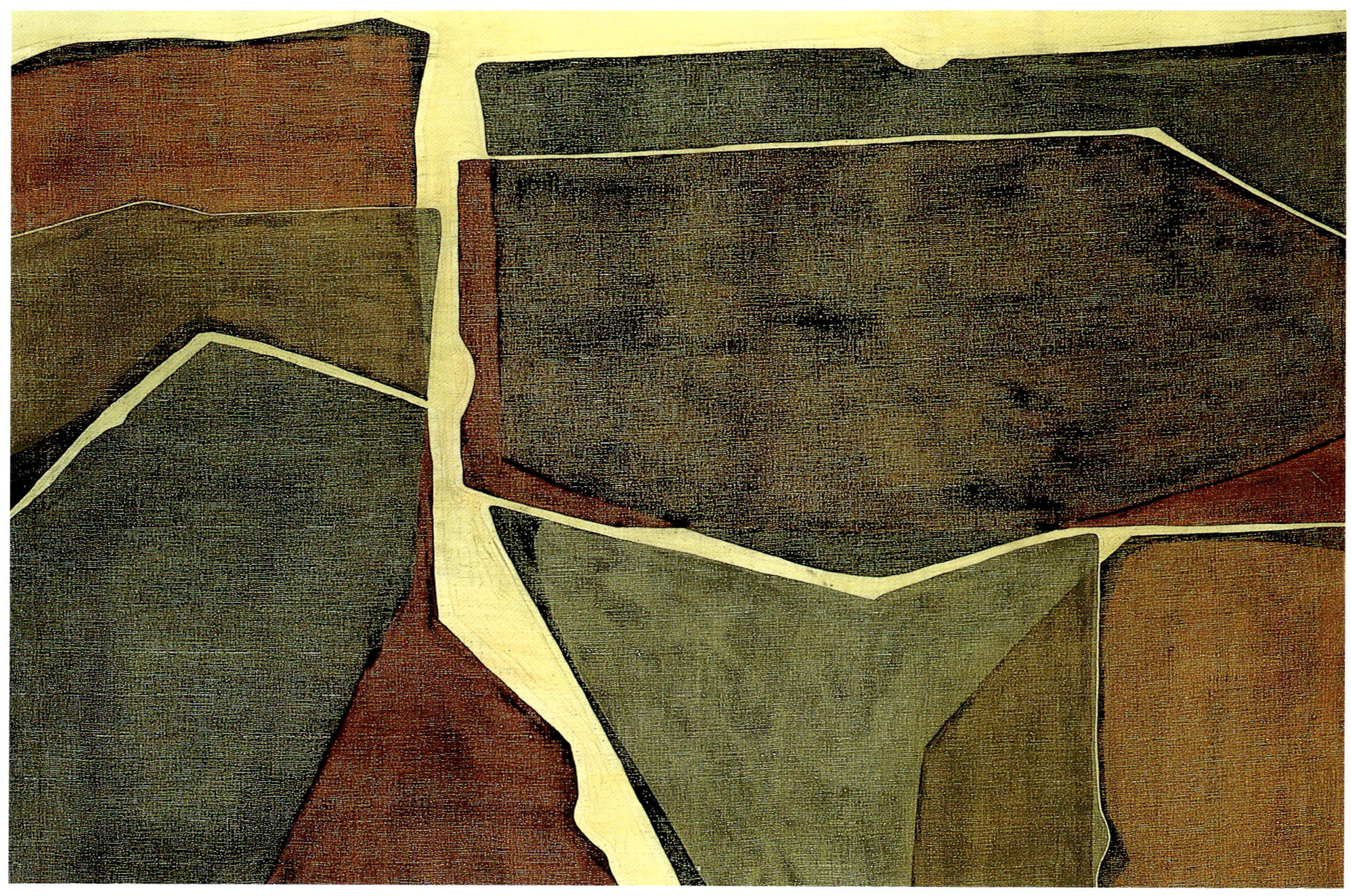

Geo VII Oil 36" x 48"

Dogstones

Dogstones
Stray from the ocean bed.
Mishapes on this shoreline grave,
Crouch before a sanding wind,
Cringe before the tidal sculpt.
Beaten, smoothly crippled
Are mongrels at the heel of land.
Dogstones have no masters.

Godstones
Were Dogstones, cast for empire cities.
Well muzzled as the building blocks of art,
They hibernate within the tower,
Stand guard above history's tomb.
As holy altars etched with praise,
Enshrine a timely script.
Godstones own their masters.

So feral rocks are seeming tame
When the avalanche is hewn and chained.

Godstones leapt from Jericho's walls,
Broke loose from David's leash
Uncaged, the rabid tore Vesuvius' slopes
While granite bit the feeding hand,
That stoned the bleeding prophet
And held the healing witch down
At the bottom of the sea... to rise again as

Dogstones
On this shoreline grave.
I see myself in each of them
And all of them are parts of me.

—DR

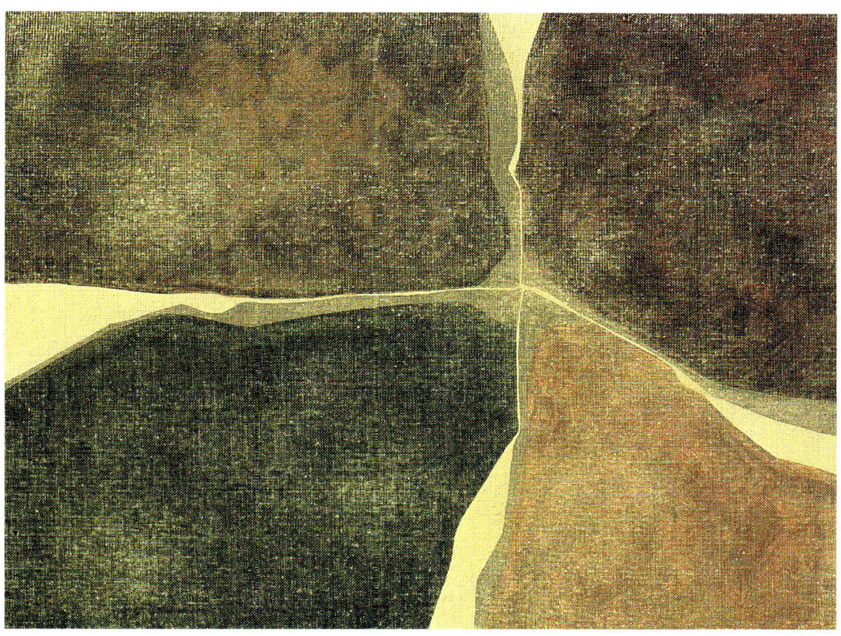

Convergence Oil 40" x 50"

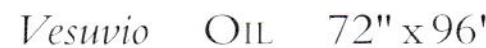

Vesuvio Oil 72" x 96"

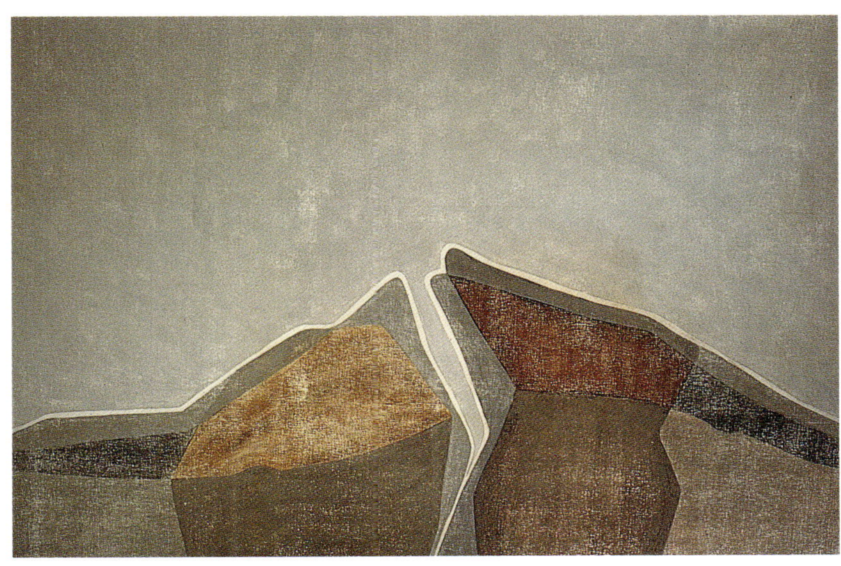

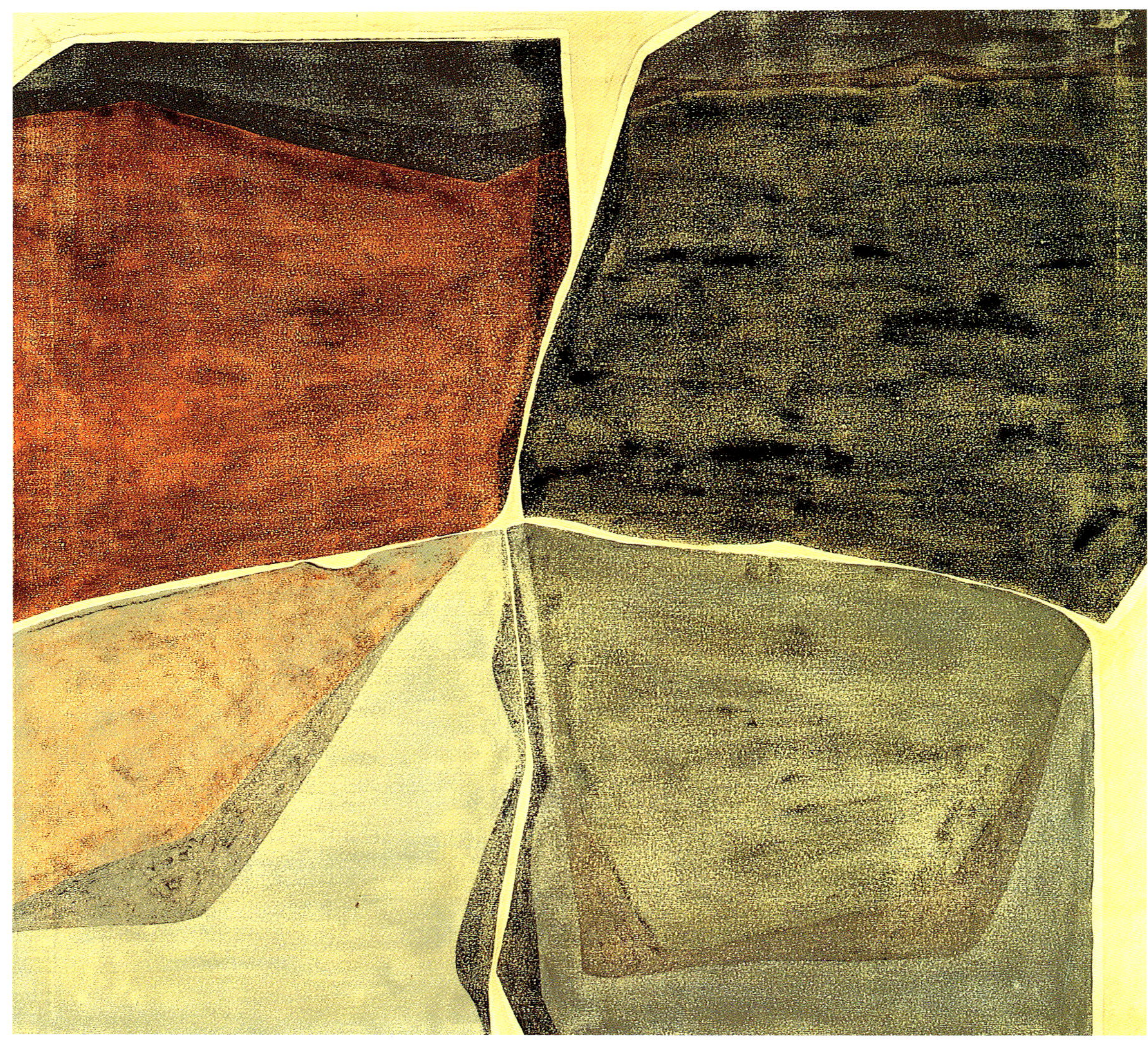

Disengagement 9 Oil 40" x 50"

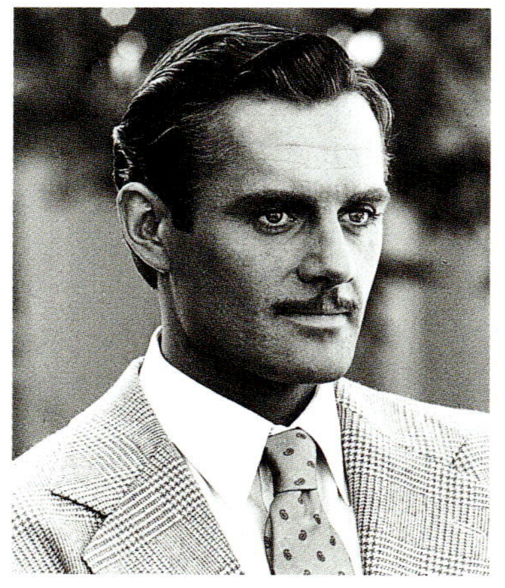

As Errol Flynn in
My Wicked, Wicked Ways

From 1981 to 1985, I sporadically continued with Geoscapes and portraits. Much of my life was taken up with introducing the thespian side of myself to the Hollywood community, which involved endless meetings, dinners, and auditions. I cherished whatever small bites of time I found for the easel and my typewriter. During those years, I was a regular in two television series for Warner Bros.—*Wizards and Warriors* and *V*. I also secured starring roles in a number of TV pilots, movies of the week and mini-series, such as *The Blue and the Grey*, *Goliath Awaits*, and the aforementioned *The Last Days of Pompeii*.

My Wicked, Wicked Ways was a breakthrough in 1985. It helped to establish my presence in the public eye and allowed me to be slightly more selective in my choice of film roles. Without the constant burden of cattle call auditions, I had more time to devote to writing, painting, and film development projects.

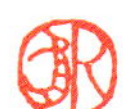

V

GIFTS FROM MERLIN

Henge

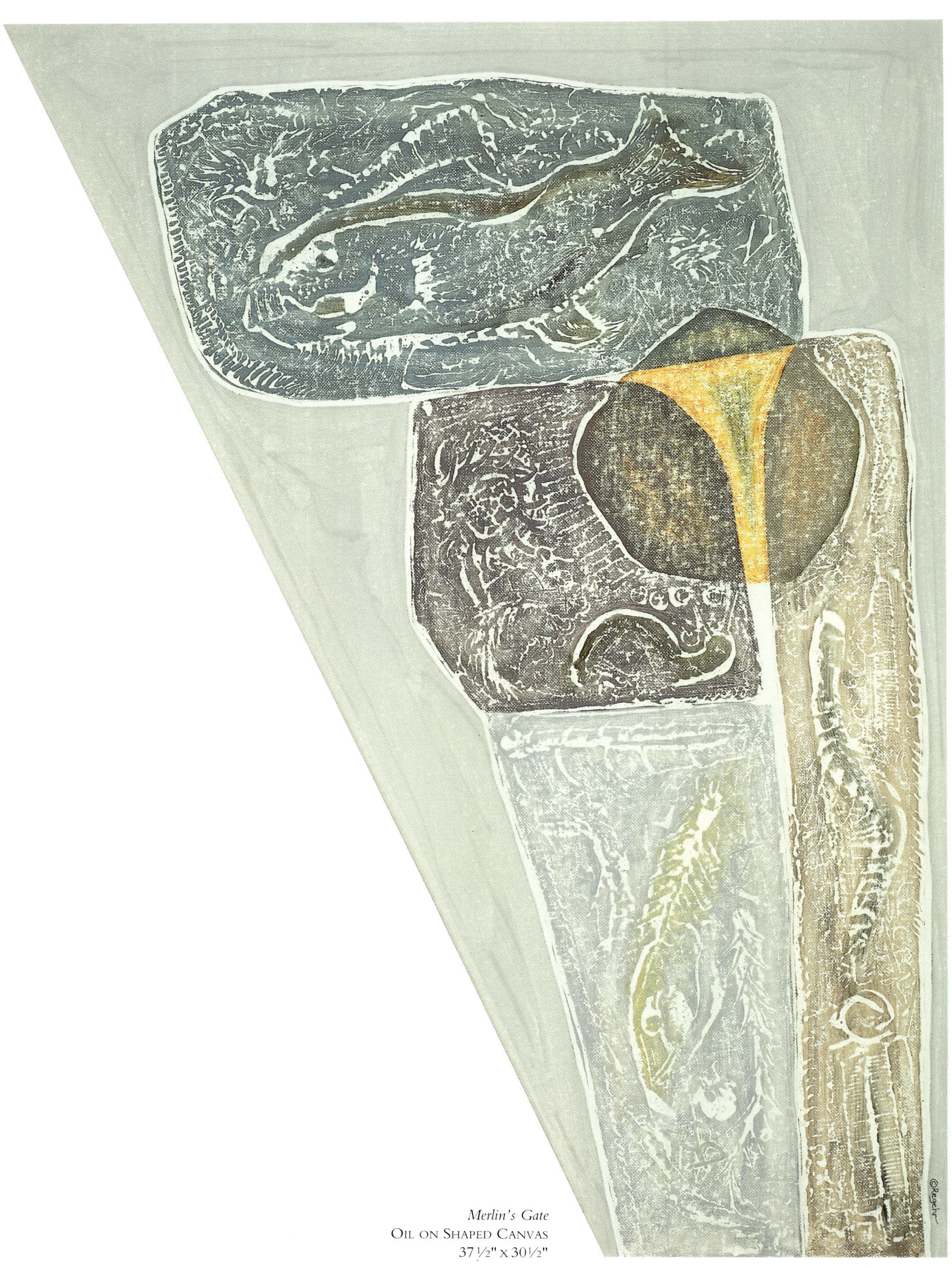

Merlin's Gate
Oil on Shaped Canvas
37½" x 30½"

Engraving of Stonehenge by
William Stukeley, 1792

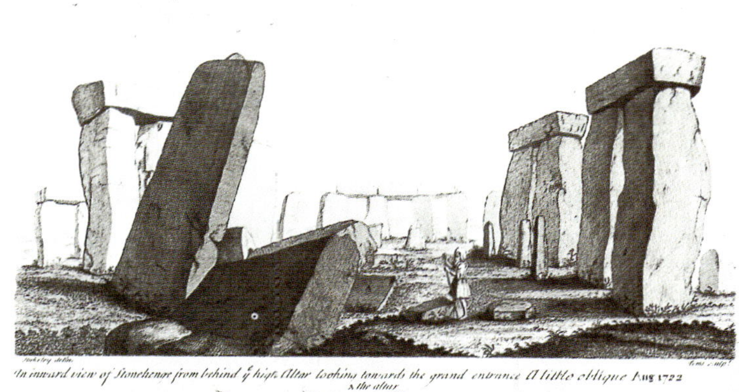

THE HENGE PAINTINGS were a natural evolvement from Geoscapes.

While traveling in Britain in 1978, I visited many ancient stone walls, circles, and monuments. Stonehenge was awe-inspiring as a place of great mythology and spirituality. Although I did not use any part of it as subject matter, it was the catalyst for the Henge series.

The following text includes notes and excerpts taken from my journal. Parts of them were published as an addendum for the premiere Henge exhibit at the Los Angeles Warner Center Art Gallery in November of 1986.

When I first saw Stonehenge on a slate grey day in November 1978, it appeared very small and unimportant, almost lost on the far crest of the horizon. It was only when I arrived at the foot of the stones did their true majesty become breathtakingly apparent.

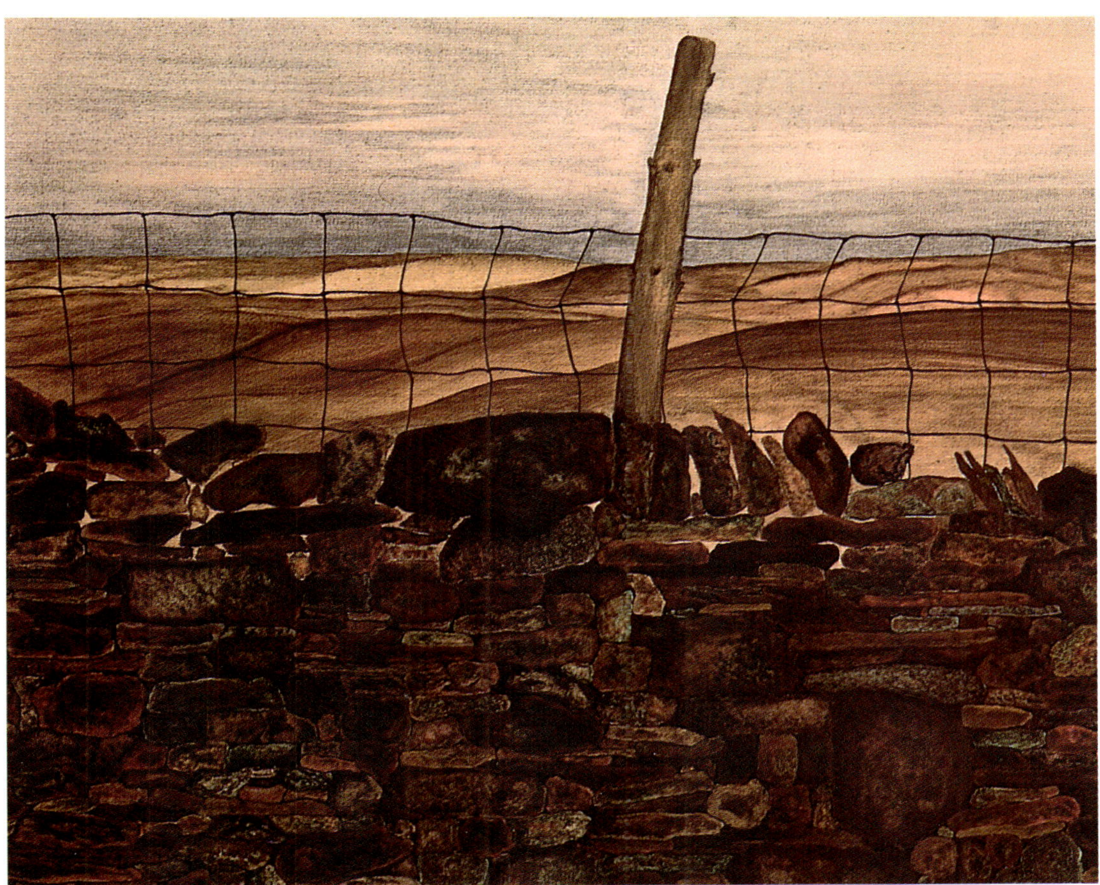

Top Withins Wall
at Haworth, Yorkshire
OIL
16" x 20"

The first thing I noticed was that vandals had freshly spray-painted graffiti on some of them: "Save the ponies," with a large picture of a horse being stabbed by a knife.

The second thing I noticed was that there were no people meandering through the roped-off silent forms; the exception being an old tour guide, who approached me with a certain air of hostility, carrying a rather large cane in his hand. I came to know him as Mr. Edinburgh.

He announced, "Stonehenge is closed. Can't you read the signs? Them damn vandals defiling again!" I apologized for intruding and explained that I often carelessly forgot to notice signs, even when they were right in front of me. He warmed to me when I pointed out that I was not a vandal and not really a tourist, but an artist. If the truth be known, the real distinction separating these creatures has always eluded me, but the title "artist" seemed to bring about a dramatic change in Mr. Edinburgh's attitude, and he promptly offered to take me on a private tour.

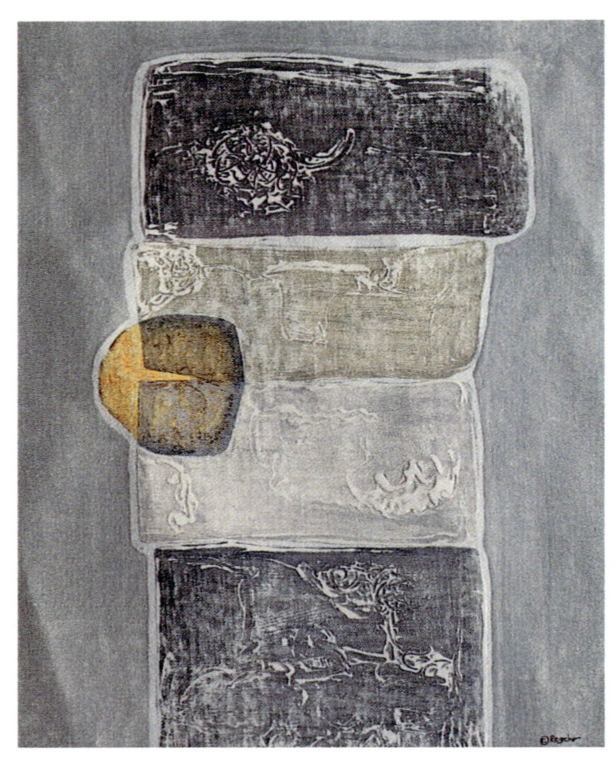

Eclipse I OIL 31½" x 25½"

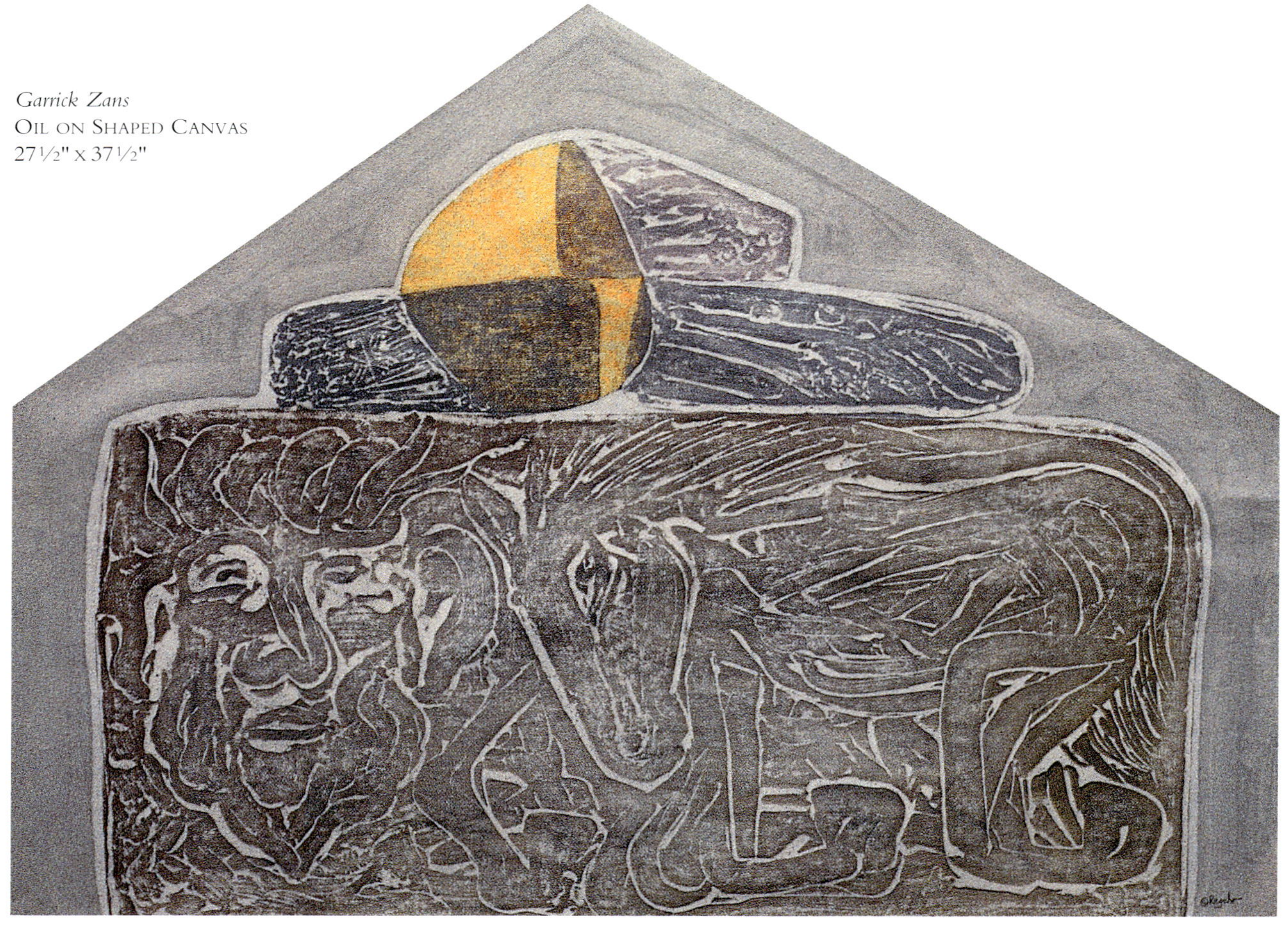

Garrick Zans
OIL ON SHAPED CANVAS
27½" x 37½"

Beakerstone OIL 42" x 32"

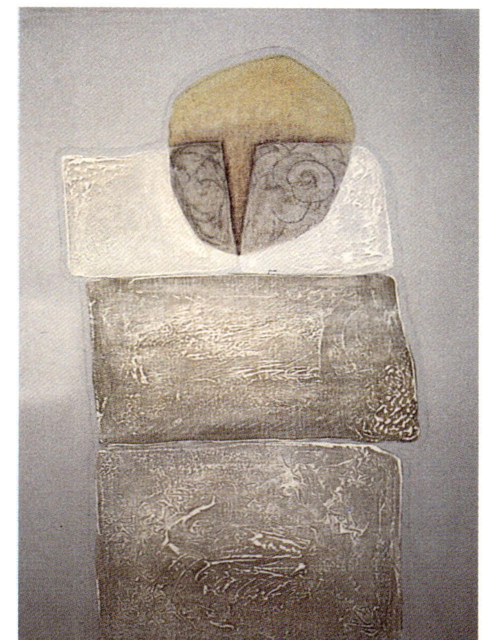

He referred to himself as a mystic and he had taken the job of tour guide because he had a bad heart and believed that the stones had certain healing properties.

> *"For in these stones is a mystery, and a healing virtue against many ailments . . . for they washed the stones and poured the water into baths, whereby those who were sick were cured."*
>
> — GEOFFREY DE MONMOUTH
> C. 1136

Mr. Edinburgh led me past the crude Heelstone, near the entrance of Stonehenge.

I was immediately taken by the gentle power of the place and a multitude of questions crowded my thoughts. The two of us moved like murmuring ghosts through the myriad of Sarsens, Lintels, Trilithons, and Bluestones. I felt as though I were visiting the greatest museum of all time. I was in the midst of the culmination of man, nature and science. All around me were history, archaeology, mythology, theology, and philosophy. There was magic, mysticism, and spiritualism. Astronomy, astrology, mathematics, geology, and geometry. There was everything! Knowledge, time, and space.

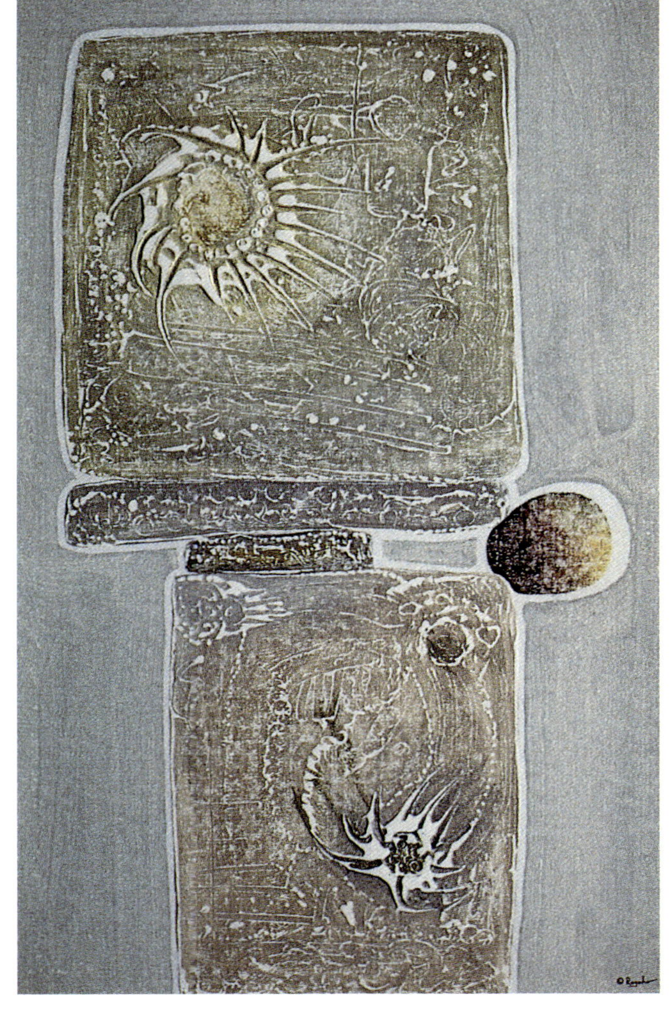

Chronicle OIL 33" x 24"

Morva (Place near the sea)
OIL 39" x 51"

Waiting Sarsens OIL 29½" x 23½"

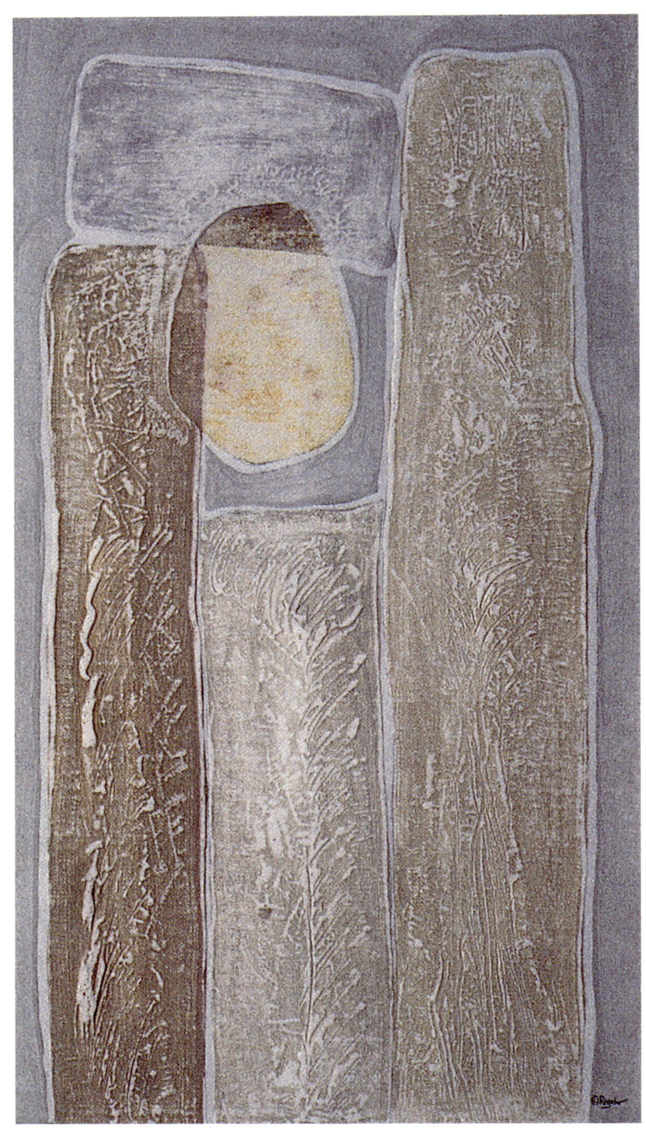

Mr. Edinburgh seemed delighted by my awe and with a very knowing smile, insisted on showing me his three secrets of Stonehenge.

He led me through the Sarsen Circle. I noted that I had adopted his way of creeping along, as though we were walking in a library or church. His constant low-voiced explanations gradually reduced to rustling, sporadic whispers.

We reached the outside ditch of Stonehenge, where he stooped to pick up a flat stone, about the size of a child's palm. He turned it over; there, embedded in the surface of the rock, were the fossilized remains of what appeared to be a seahorse.

I was charmed by its delicate beauty, but I also suspected that someone had probably dropped it there. Then I realized that it was not out of place at all. That small piece of nature was absolutely in keeping with everything else. It belonged there by virtue of its marriage through time to all the elements around it; and if a tourist or a scientist, a Faerie King or a wave from the sea had left it there, it was meant to be.

> *"It is generally averred hereabouts that pieces of these Stones putt into their Wells doe drive away the Toades, with which their Wells are much infected."*
>
> —JOHN AUBREY, 1626-1697

Mr. Edinburgh carefully returned his tiny secret to its rightful place, and took me quietly back through the stones. He began pointing out various bits of ancient graffiti that had been carved or etched into the surfaces at different times during man's history. Then he stopped and gestured towards his second secret.

At first I could not discern what he was trying to show me, but as I moved closer to the indicated stone, it came into focus.

Bronze Age carvings. Two broad-bladed axes and a hilted dagger. I could not help but relate the primitive scraping to the horse and dagger that the vandals had recently spray-painted. Was there really a difference between the carvings and the modern graffiti I had seen earlier? As I looked around me, there were runes, hieroglyphics, drawings, carvings, and graffiti everywhere. All were forms of documentation. Placed there by scribes, artists, lovers, vandals, and of course, tourists. They had all visited and left their marks as part of mother nature's unfolding story.

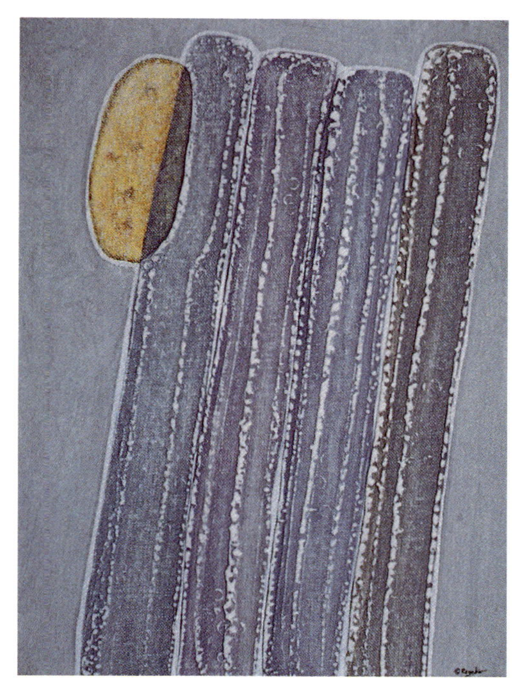

The Pipers OIL 26" x 24"

Logan Luz OIL ON SHAPED CANVAS 32" x 38"

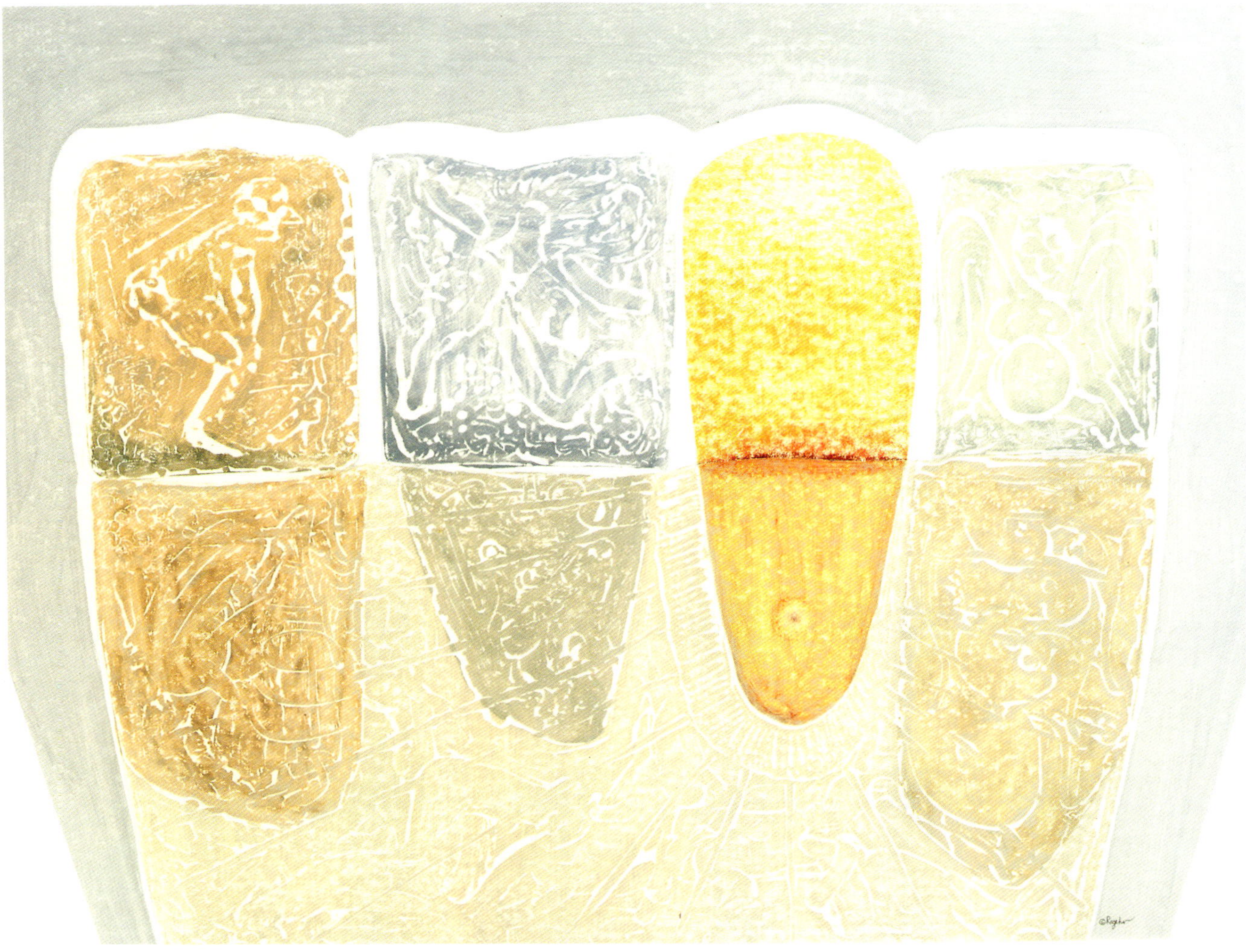

Caerwynnen, The Giant's Fry Pan
Oil 34½" x 29½"

Noon-Day Height Oil 42" x 31½"

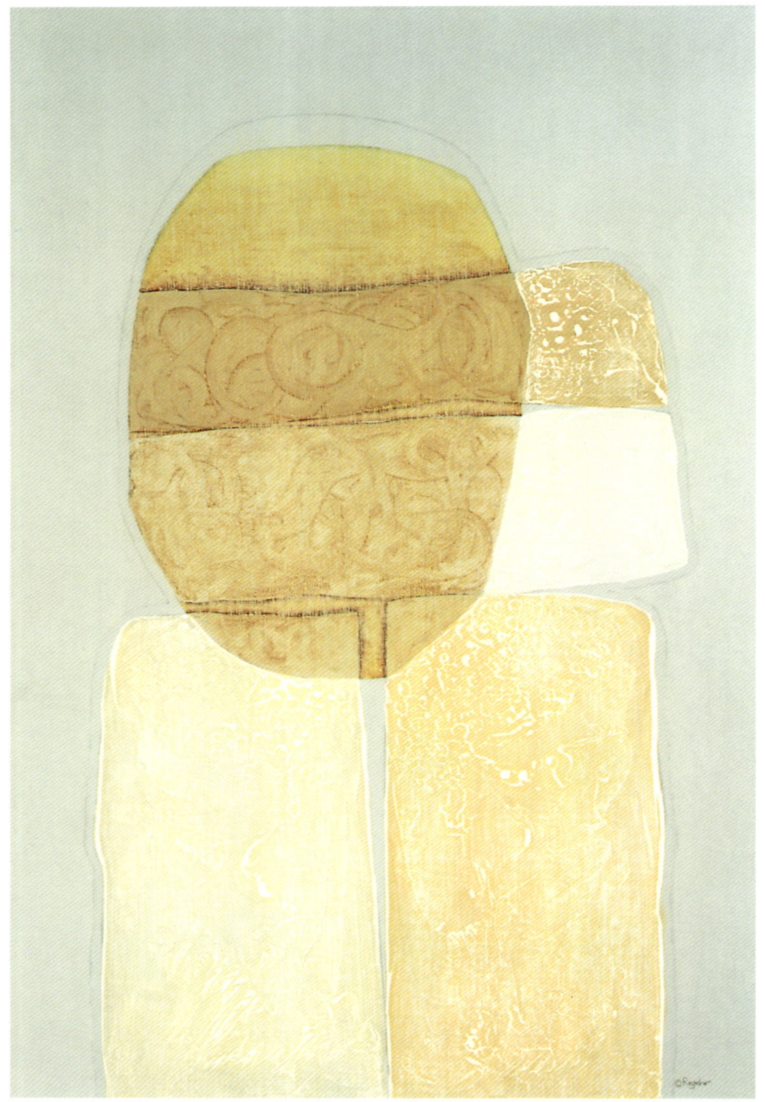

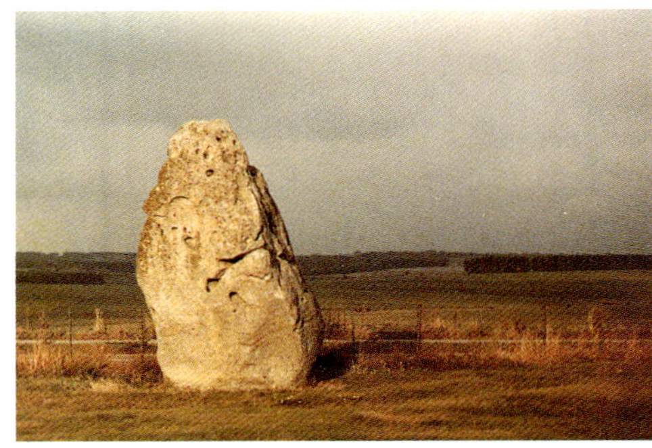

The Heelstone, Stonehenge, 1978

As we moved on, an impression of familiarity brushed past me. Not really déjà vu, although I do not rule out the possibility that I may have been there before, it was near to a sensation of harmony with everything. I began to feel very comfortable and more like a participant than an observer.

Mr. Edinburgh directed me towards the road and brought us to a halt near the Slaughter Stone.

He explained (sotto voce, just in case there were invisible eavesdroppers about), that his final secret could only be seen "on such a day as this." The sky was grey blue with clouds, and only a hint of oscillating glow was evident from the sun.

Slowly raising his arm to shoulder height, and wielding his cane like the wand of Merlin, Mr. Edinburgh, the mystic of Stonehenge, dramatically whirled around to point directly at the Heelstone.

I had not paid much attention to this stone when we had entered, because it seemed very unimportant. A solitary, thirty five ton, crude, Sarsen boulder with a blunt point. One of the few "undressed" stones of Stonehenge. If I had thought it was an unassuming rock earlier, I certainly did not think so in that moment, for it was bathed in the most beautiful colored light.

The stone seemed to grow in stature as its aura pulsated with the shimmering flush of the sun. It was as if the light emanated from within the stone. I felt welcomed by it, as though I were part of it. A sensation of completeness and understanding swept over me.

I asked Mr. Edinburgh how this magical phenomenon, which was clear for all to look at and which appeared (at least to me) to embody the whole concept of life, Stonehenge, and the universe could possibly be a secret.

His reply suggested that with all magical marvels, the "enlightenment" is always in existence, and that although this could only be observed on particular days, one had first to want to perceive it.

"People never look for magic, so they never see it, let alone believe in it."

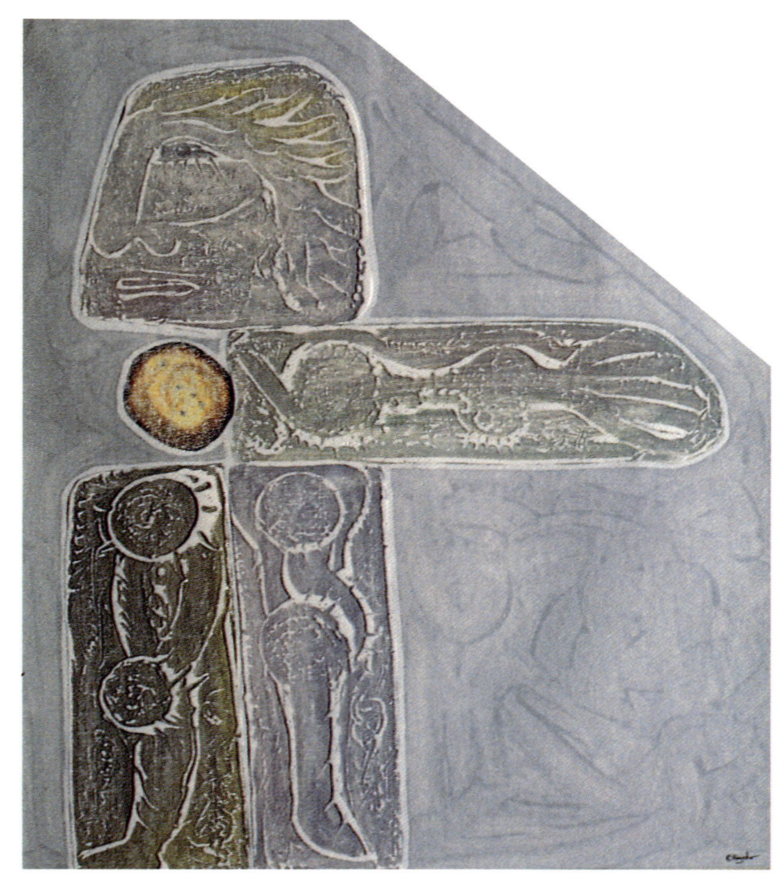

The Blind Fiddler
OIL ON SHAPED CANVAS
32½" x 29½"

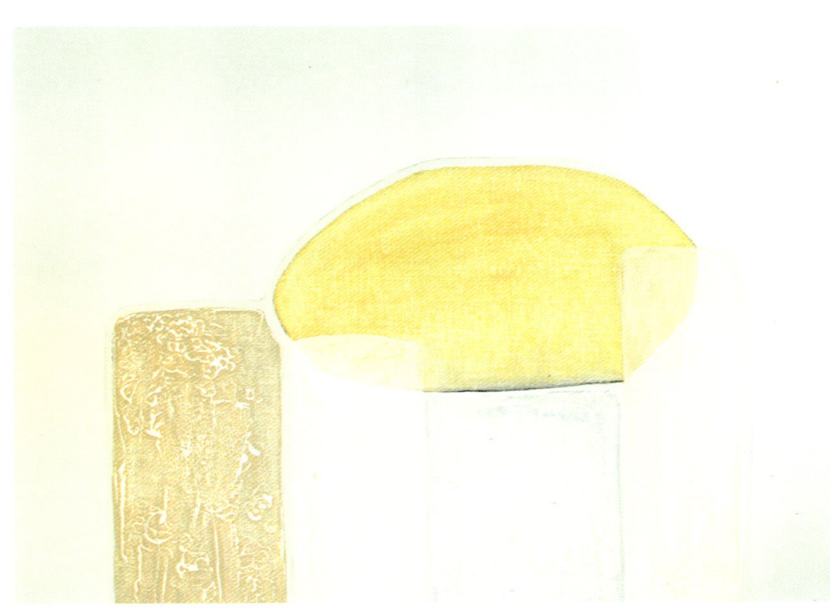

"Then ignorance with fabulous discourse,
Robbing fair Art and Cunning of their right,
Tells how those stones were by the devil's force,
From Afrik brought to Ireland in a night,
And thence to Britannie, by magick course,
From giants' hand redeemed by Merlin's sleight."
—SAMUEL DANYEL, 1624

Afrik OIL 31" x 41"

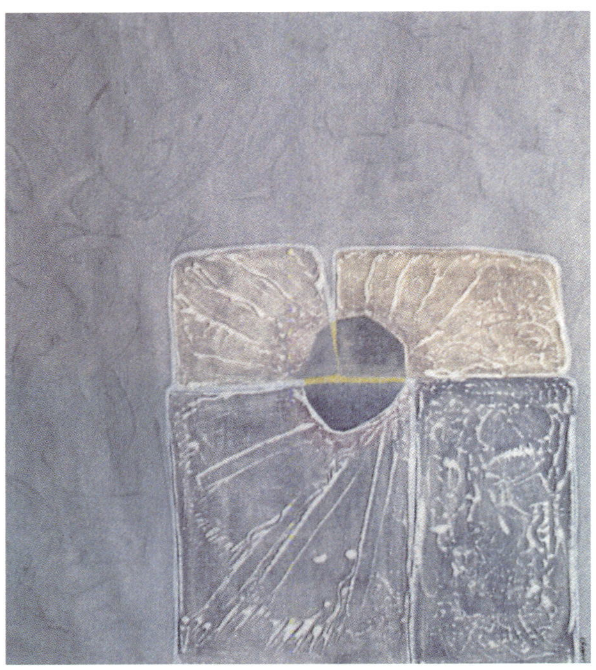

Eclipse II Oil 31½" x 29"

We shook hands and I thanked Mr. Edinburgh for my private tour and for the wisdom he had bestowed upon me. His parting words to me were, "Don't forget to read the signs, lad."

As I drove away, the sun finally broke through the clouds, and its light seemed to envelope the whole of Stonehenge in a farewell glow. I was reminded, once again, that everything is a part of everything else, and I made myself a promise — always to look for the magic.

It was not until the mid-eighties that my experience at Stonehenge manifested itself in the form of paintings.

In almost all parts of the world, there are mysterious groupings or outcroppings of stone. Frequently we are uncertain as to whether man placed them or if they occurred by some other power of nature. Often the peculiar balance of one stone upon another seems too impossible to have been wrought by anyone but a magician.

Unnatural Balance, The Rise Oil 33½" x 37"

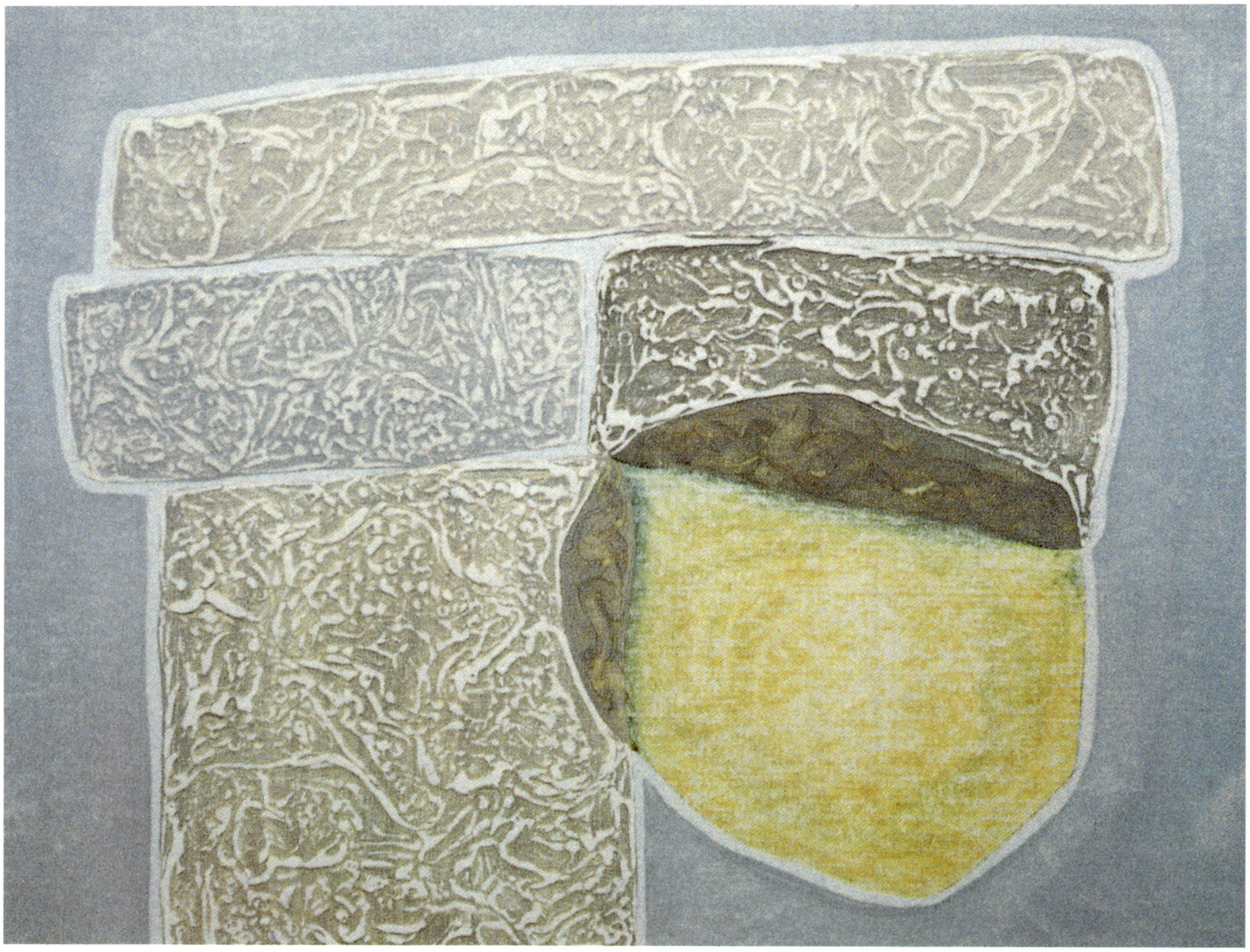

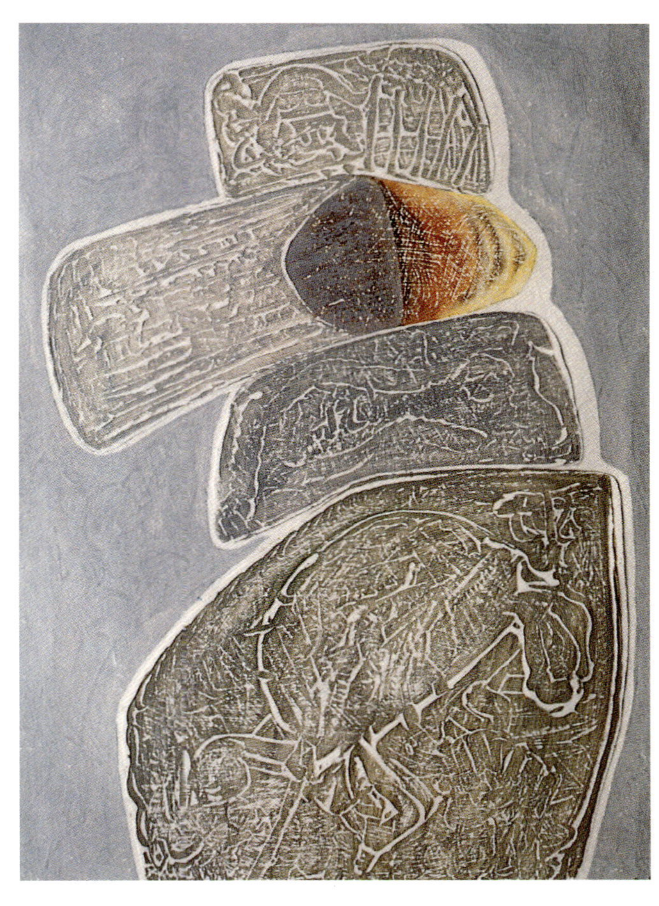

Mulfra
Oil 34" x 26"

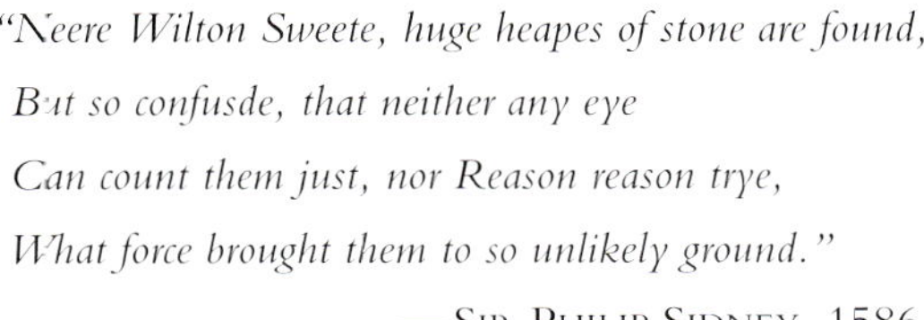

"Neere Wilton Sweete, huge heapes of stone are found,
But so confusde, that neither any eye
Can count them just, nor Reason reason trye,
What force brought them to so unlikely ground."

—Sir Philip Sidney, 1586

As a small boy, I found faces and monsters in the textured cement walls of my basement niche. Today, I see elusive formations in everything—clouds, stones, trees, earth, wood, and the stars. We have a tendency to overlook such visions as being unimportant to all but the simplest of minds, but throughout history, the shamans of our cultures have given names to or conjured magical stories to explain these abstractions.

Developing the Henge paintings brought forth some of my own interpretations. I created balanced shapes, encompassing a mixture of enigmatic images, formulated in such a way as to challenge the viewer to distinguish their source.

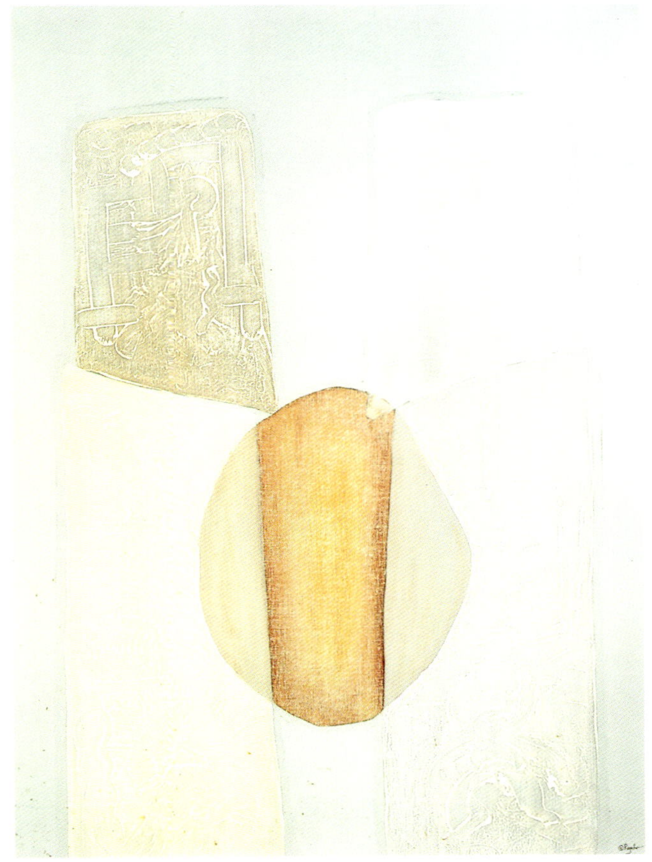

Adversary
Oil 41" x 31"

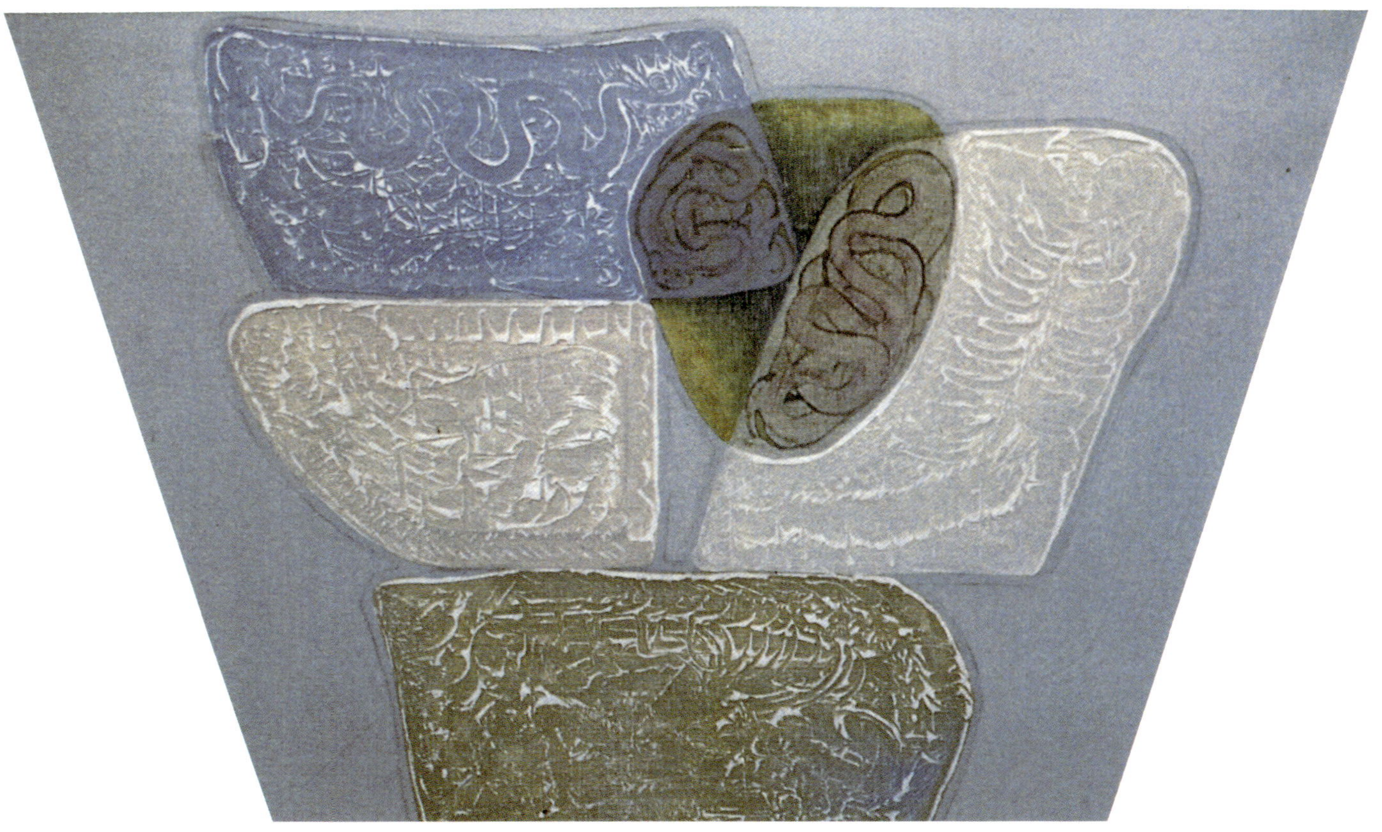

Chun Oil on Shaped Canvas 26½" x 37"

I hoped to convey similitude between science and spirituality. And with any luck, to invoke the understanding that man and nature are of the same indivisible force — Creation; and that each small creation within the greater contributes by way of metamorphosis — a process that includes the de-creation of one thing to become another. The word "henge" means hinge or contingency. Taken to its full extent, it implies the harmonious concept that everything is locked interdependently to a universal cycle.

Rather a lot to ask from simple shapes of paint and canvas, which might only aspire to hang on the wall as the "color scheme link" between someone's drapes and carpet. But that in itself serves to demonstrate that henge exists at all levels of infinity.

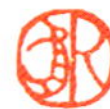

VI

THE AUGUR'S HAND

Smokin' Gun

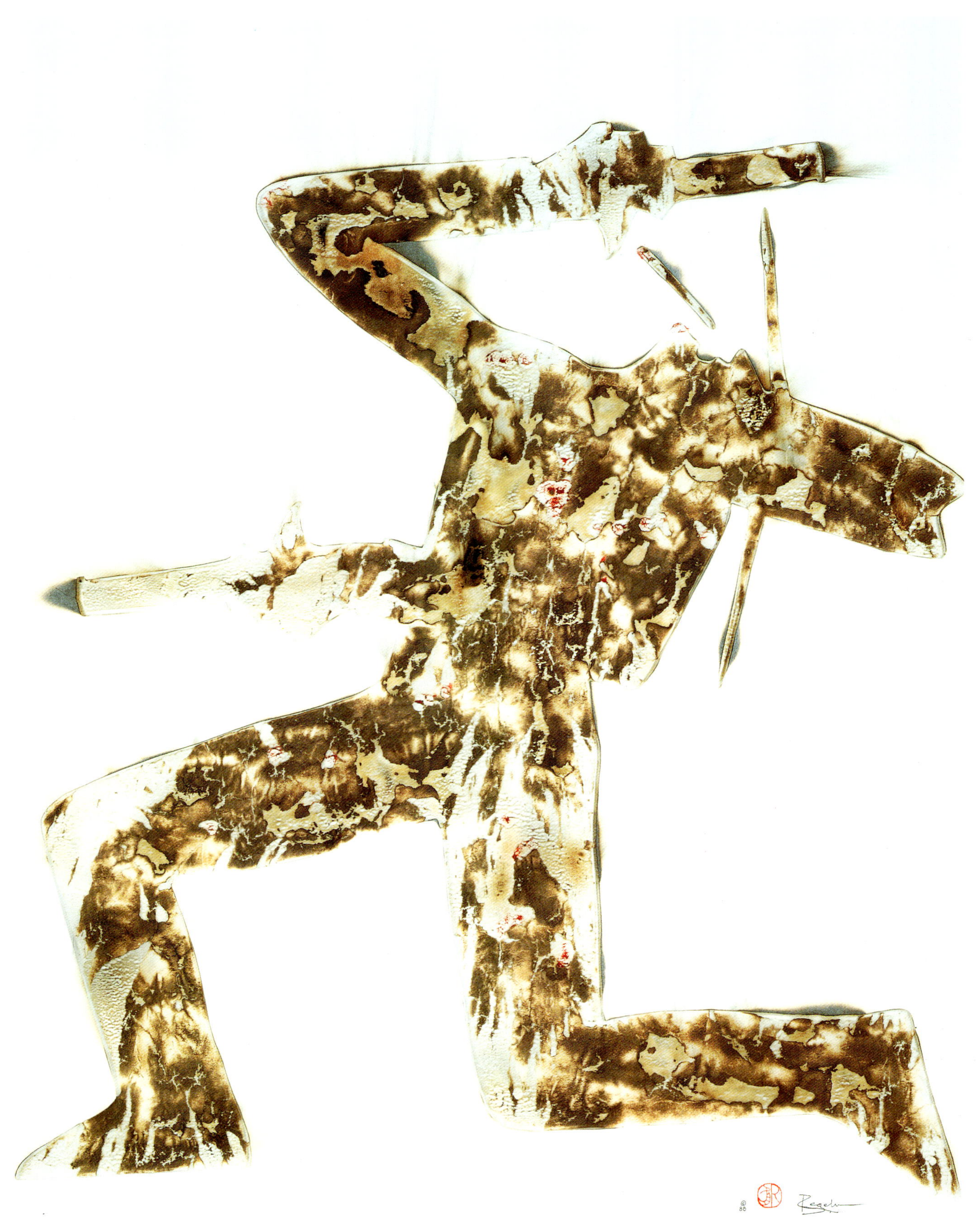

Smokin' Gun No. 56 Acrylic, Charcoal, Styrofoam, Paper 48" x 36" 1988

L.A. Without Mercy

L.A. the un-city,
Vicious bimbo of the West.

L.A. show and tell,
So here, and gone so fast, no past
To remind us of what is forgotten.

L.A. so much.

L.A. like a joke,
That I cannot bear to love.

L.A. incomplete.

L.A. the sex-maniac.
L.A. the genderless,
The intangible cloud . . .

Could never touch my heart.

—DR

Eternal Dusk OIL AND COLORED PENCIL 48" x 36" 1988

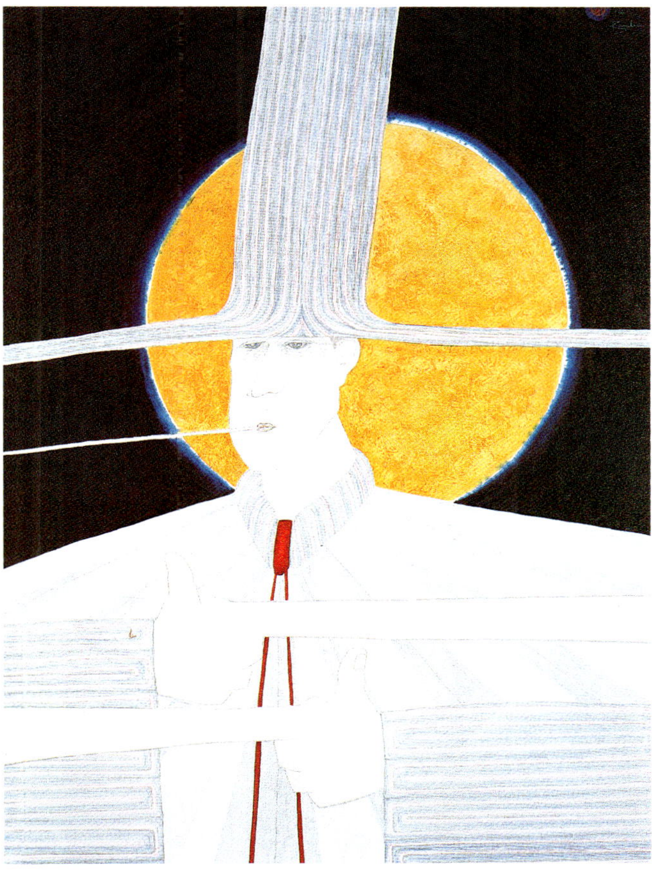

LOS ANGELES has all the diseases for which there are seemingly no cures, yet it is a cultural paragon to the West. I lived there from 1980 to1991.

The first two years in Westwood (when it was still a village) were exciting, but I could never shake the feeling that I had arrived to make a "beginning" near the end. The dawns looked disturbingly like dusks. The sunsets disturbed me more. Like an infected rash across the epilogue of day, wrapped in smoky gauze. That infection spread. The longer I lived there the more frustrated I became.

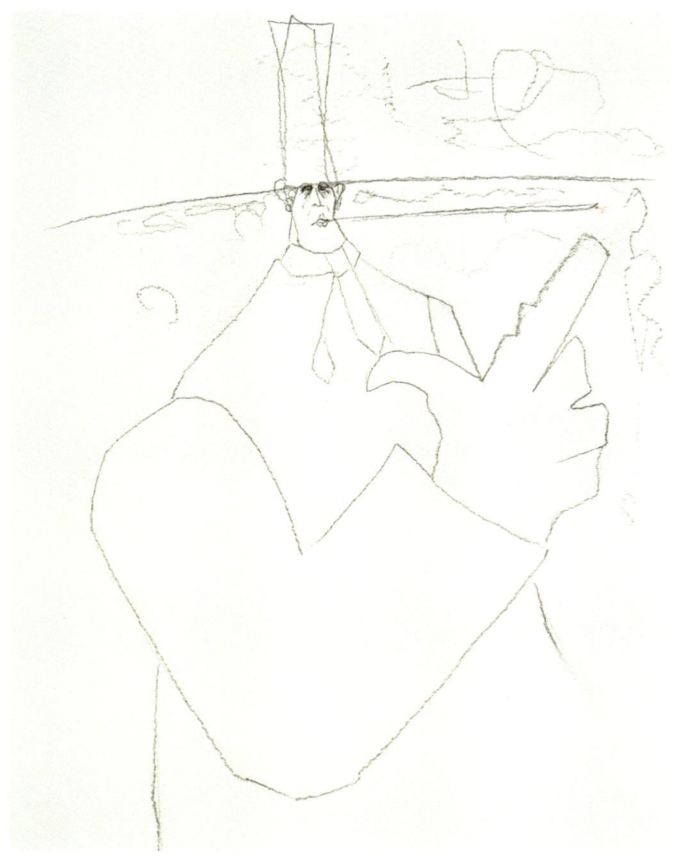

Pencil Drawing 12" x 9" 1988

"Smokin' Gun" was created in 1988. It evolved by way of a purging process with no conscious thought of it ever becoming a thematic series. Day after day, without analyzing why, I drew cowboys on everything from cafe napkins to the misty shaving mirror. My sketchbooks overflowed with satire. Guns for hands and cigarettes like lit fuses dangled from self-righteous mouths. Fierce, fanatically insane, cunning, stupid, ruthless men. Small heads, big bodies, and blunt features. They stalked the borders of my dreams.

Obsessive sketching is not unusual for me, nevertheless I dismissed the caricatures as doodles. My friends, used to seeing me constantly draw a variety of subject matter, finally pointed out just how singular-natured my scribbling had become.

I then realized that I was actually working overtime. So much so, that the work itself had quelled the light of awareness. The drawings were spent frustration. My subconscious was manifesting an image that could encompass all the ills surrounding me.

I was developing a figure of destruction, not a prophet, but an omen that by self example, could bode the future. A metaphor for the western world, whose every negative action returned devastation upon its source: The Man with the Smokin' Gun.

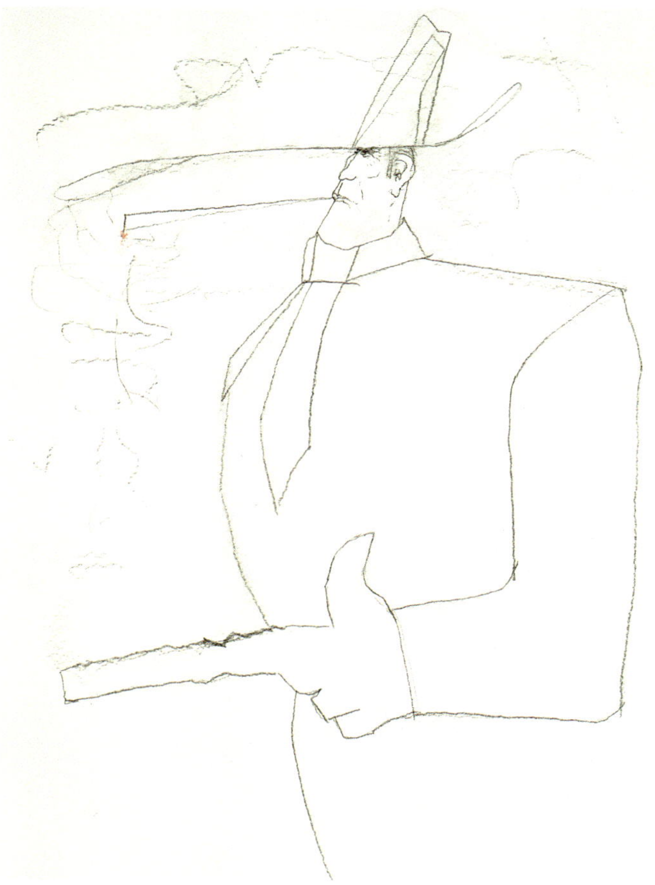

Pencil Drawing 12" x 9" 1988

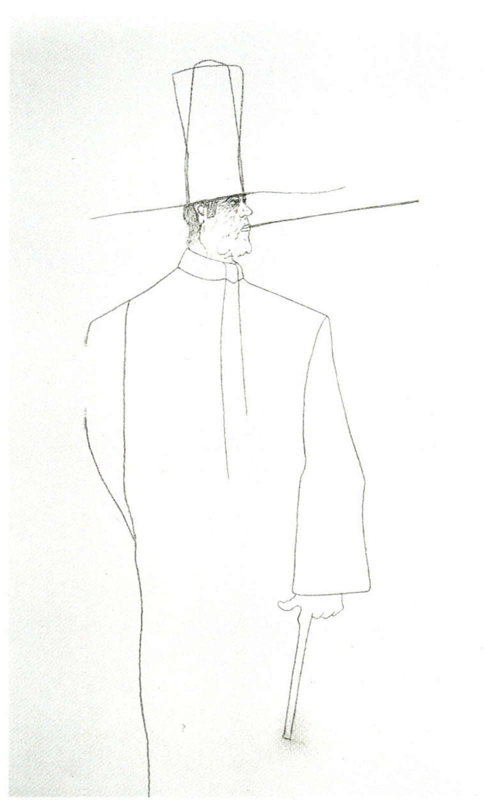

After celebrating this revelation with a group of well-oiled friends, I recessed to my studio and wrote, by stream of (wavering) consciousness, *The Man with the Smokin' Gun (to be read running on the spot)*. Some of the worst verse I have ever laid down, but its rawness seems to work if it is read at an ever-increasing tempo.

I returned to the party and induced my long-suffering companions to further libation and a performance. We staggered through it several times. Our crescendos blasted the heavens and frightened the neighbors. The police came. They were less than sympathetic.

Pencil Drawing 18" x 12" 1988

Hear No Evil, See No Evil, Speak No Evil Acrylic and Cardboard 29" x 39" 1988

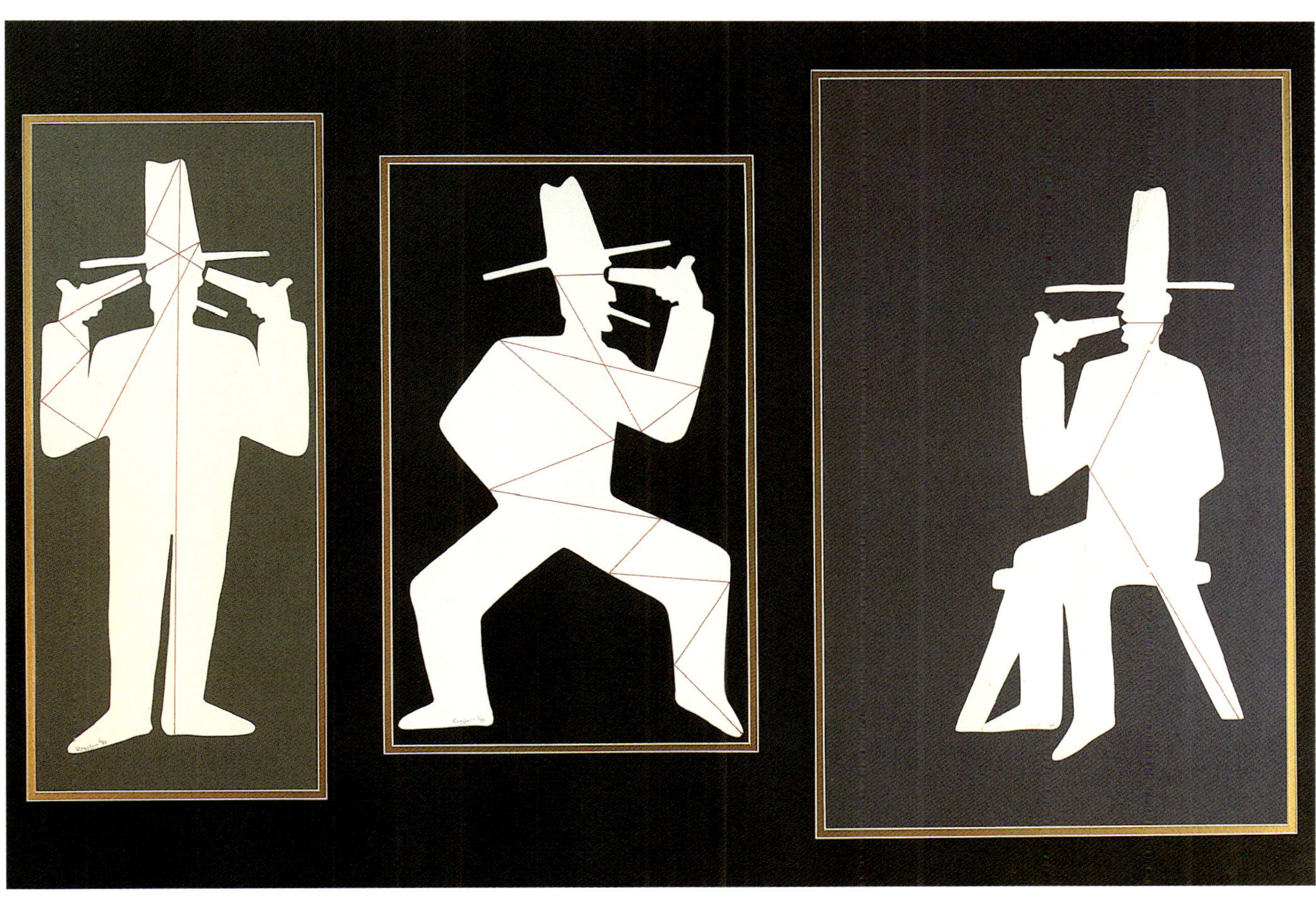

Smokin' Gun No. 59 ACRYLIC, CHARCOAL, STYROFOAM, PAPER 48" x 36" 1988

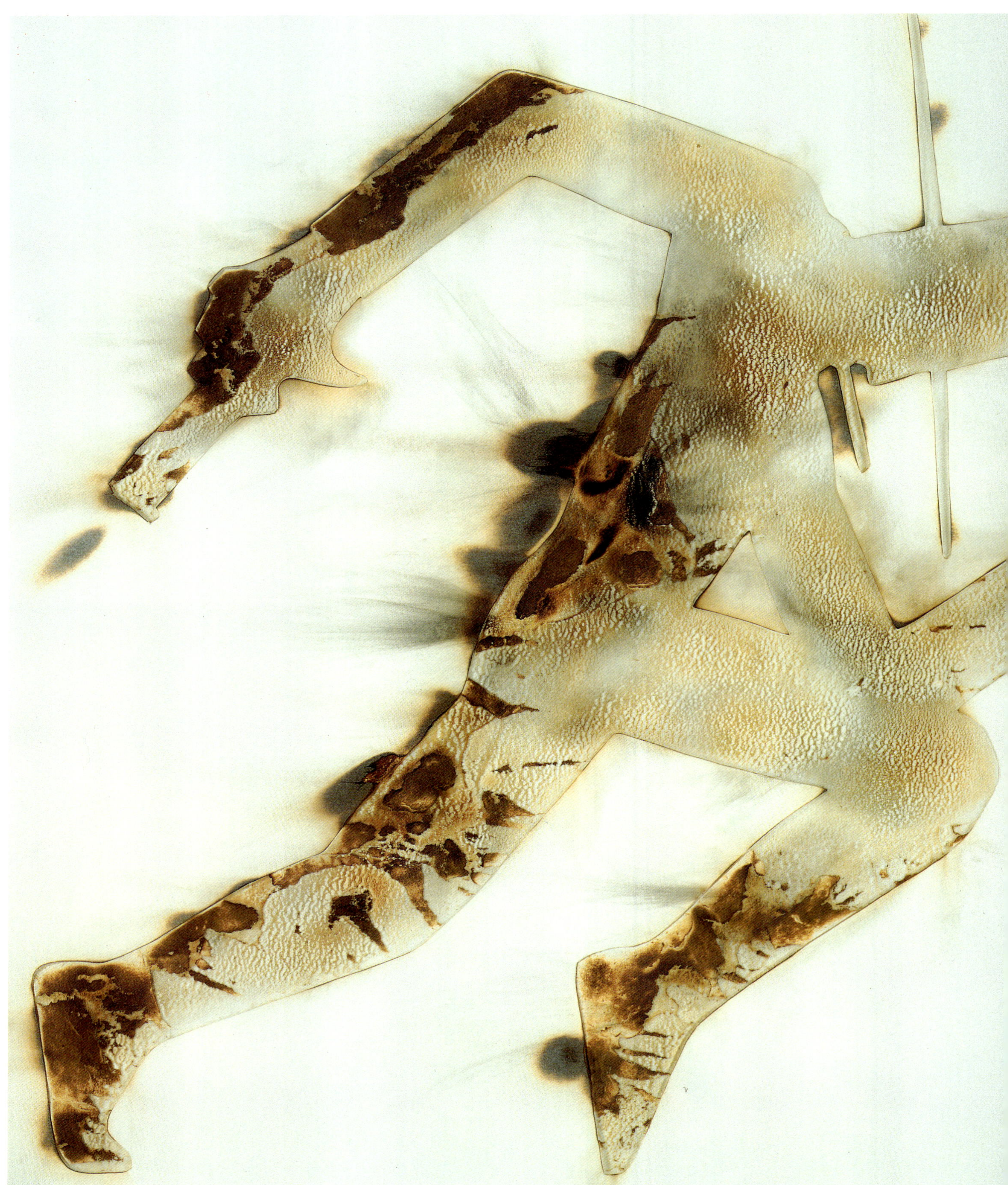

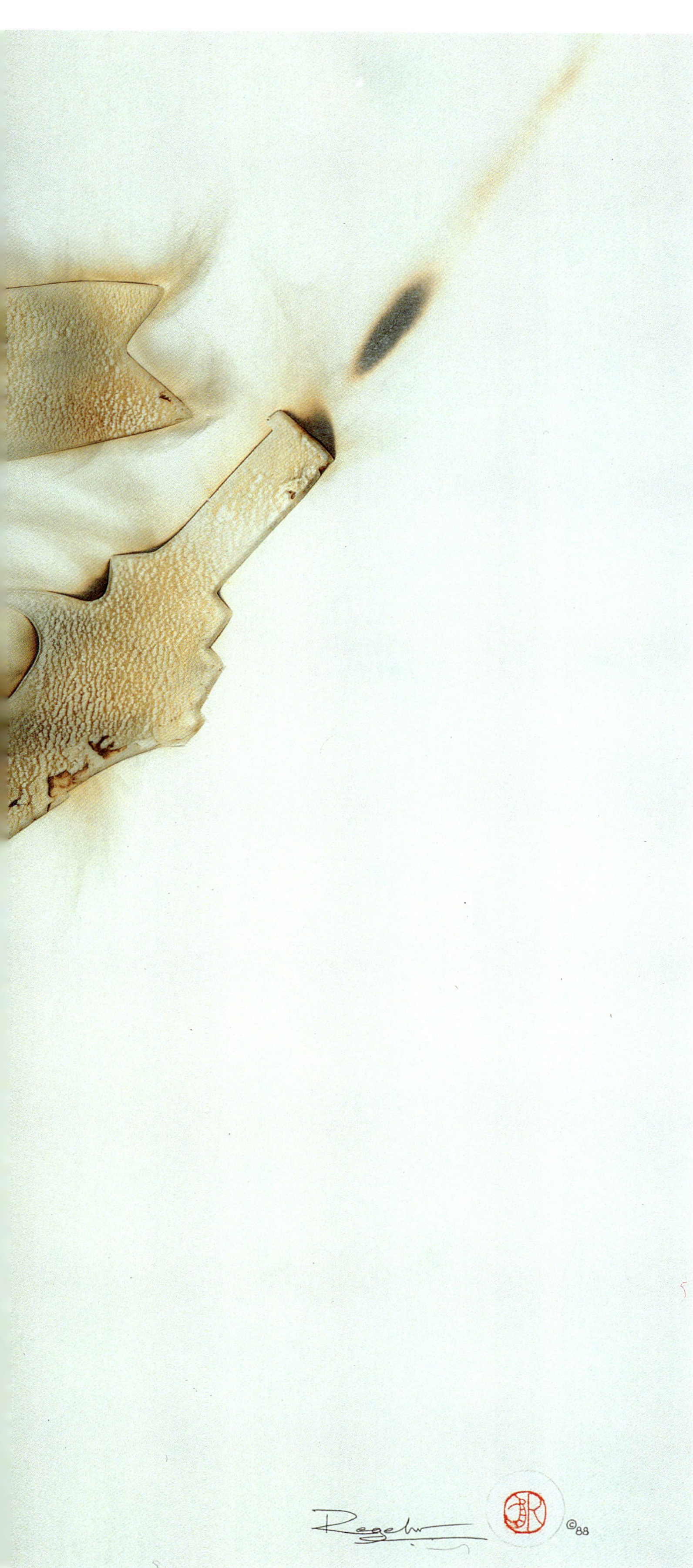

The Man with the Smokin' Gun

(To be read running on the spot)

Voice 1:	I can't see em anymore
	Lock over my shoulder will ya?
Voice 2:	Nothin. All I see is smoke
Voice 3:	Course he's smokin darlin
	And you can bet he's comin
	Rollin like crimson thunderheads
	From the land of the dead
Voices 1&2:	Come on breathe!
All Voices:	Keep runnin keep runnin
	The man with the smokin gun is comin
Voice 1:	With golden eyes that never need to blink
	And a mind that doesn't think
	Of anything but fire!
Voice 3:	No cryin
Voice 2:	No cryin
Voice 1:	Keep runnin he's comin
Voice 3:	Cause where there's smoke
	There's only his desire!

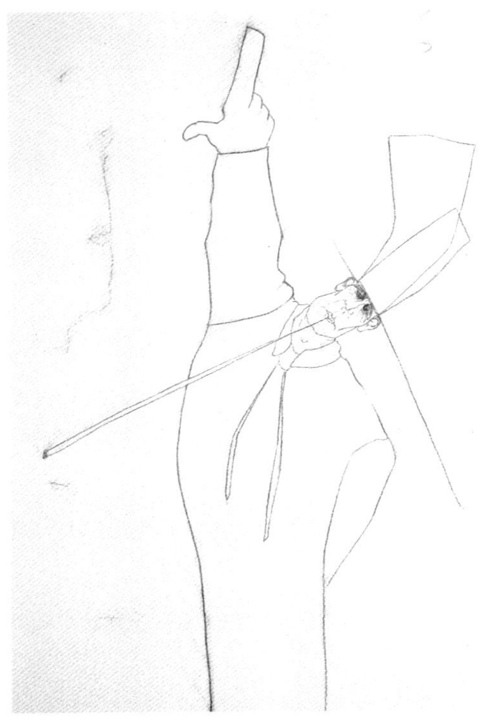

Pencil Drawing 18" x 12" 1988

Pencil Drawing 18" x 12" 1988

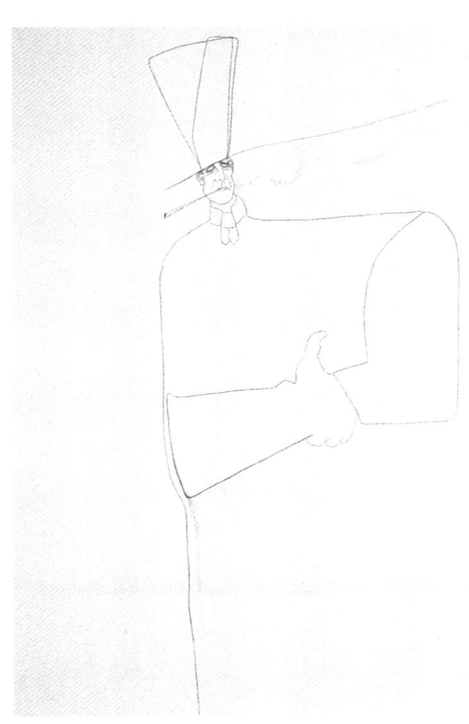

Voice 2:	I'm sorry
Voice 1:	So sorry
Voice 3:	Christ!
	I didn't know he had a gun
	Let alone hunt with one
Voice 1:	Come on run!
Voice 2:	He rode into town so benevolent
Voice 3:	He strode down the street so confident
Voice 1:	So magnanimous to all
Voice 3:	So easy over the wall
Voice 2:	Up to the bar
Voice 1:	Up to the game of cards and
Voices 2&3:	Keep runnin!
Voice 1:	How far?!
Voices 2&3:	He's comin!
Voice 1:	He said he was lookin to hunt for bear
Voice 3:	And I said where?
Voice 2:	You can't find bear in L.A.
Voice 1:	And he shot everyone outta sight
	From high noon through yesterday

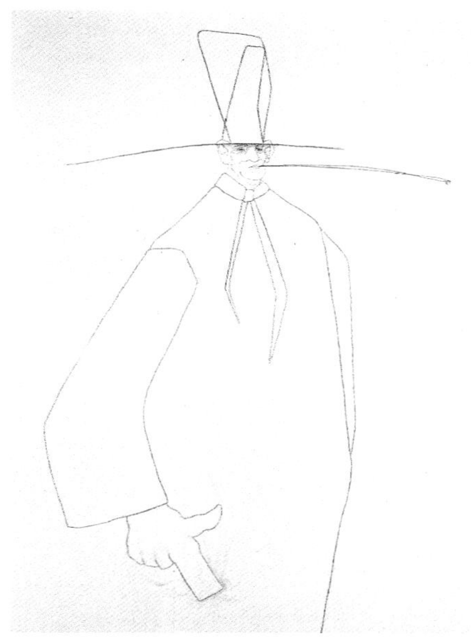

Pencil Drawing 18" x 12" 1988

Voice 2:	Jesus!
Voices 1&3:	Keep runnin!
Voice 2:	I can't see anymore!
Voice 3:	I can't breathe anymore!
Voice 1:	Keep runnin he's comin!
Voice 3:	He burned the house of cards to the ground
	So there's nothin left to be found
Voice 1:	He blew down the western town
	So there's no one else around
Voice 2:	He set the flamin forest on fire
Voice 3:	He torched the church to a funeral pyre
Voice 1:	And through the haze of the blaze
	Of the rampage
Voice 2:	He doesn't faze
	He continues to rage and raze
	For the rest of our days!

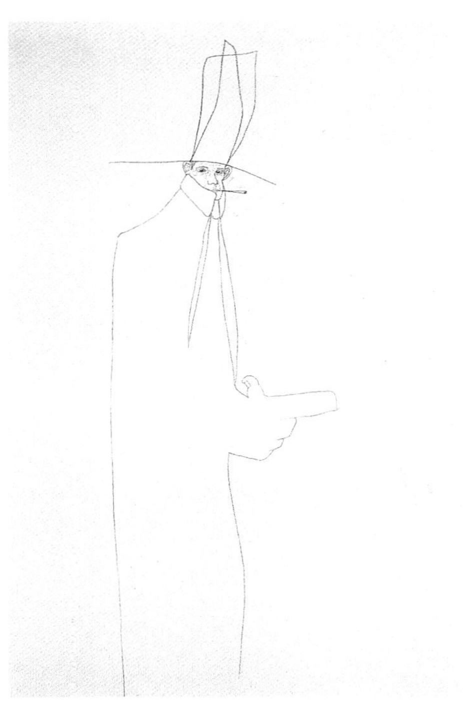

Pencil Drawing 18" x 12" 1988

Pencil Drawing 12" x 18" 1988

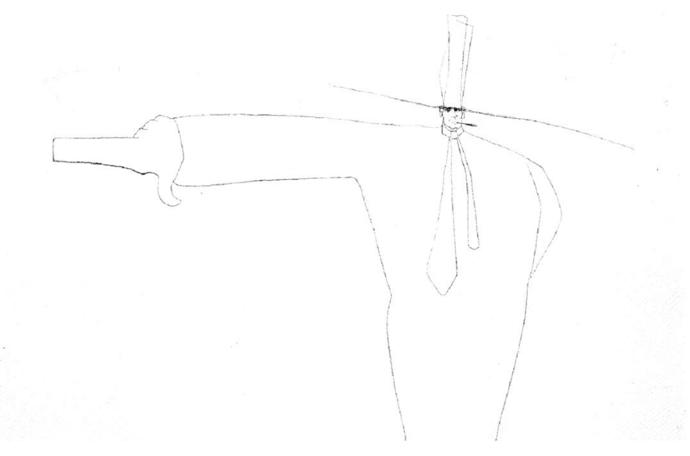

All voices:	So keep runnin!
	Keep runnin!
Voice 2:	I'm outta breath
	And it's a slow death that's comin
Voice 1:	I can't keep this pace
	I wanna drop outta this race
Voice 2:	How long is he gonna chase?!
Voice 3:	Til the sun turns red from the smoke of the dead
	And even his children can't find a hidin place!!
All Voices:	So keep runnin
Voice 1:	He's comin he's comin!
Voice 3:	Keep runnin keep runnin!
Voice 2:	I'm chokin I'm chokin!
All Voices:	And my heart is broken
	Cause the man with the smokin' gun
	has SPOKEN!!!

—DR

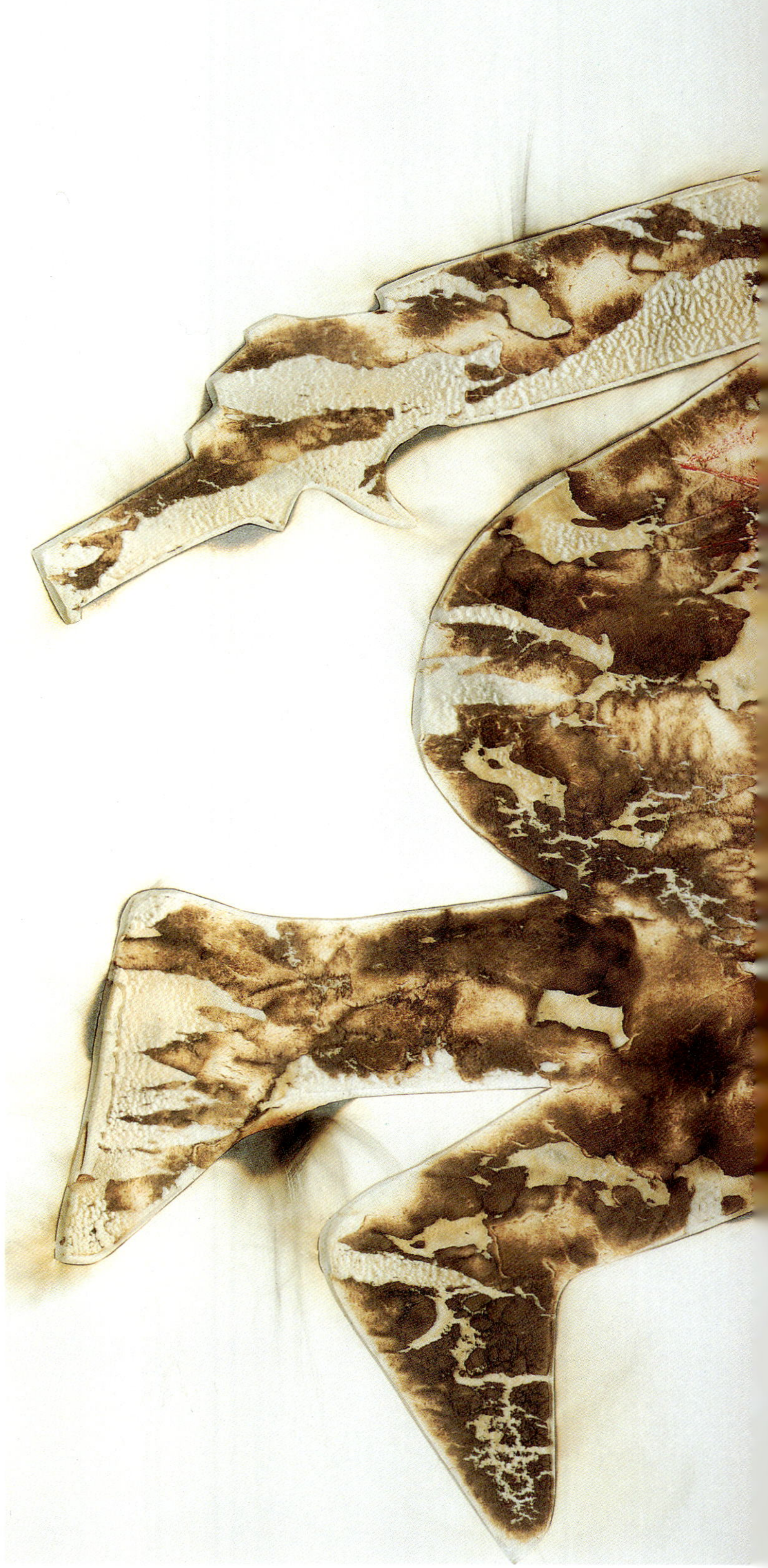

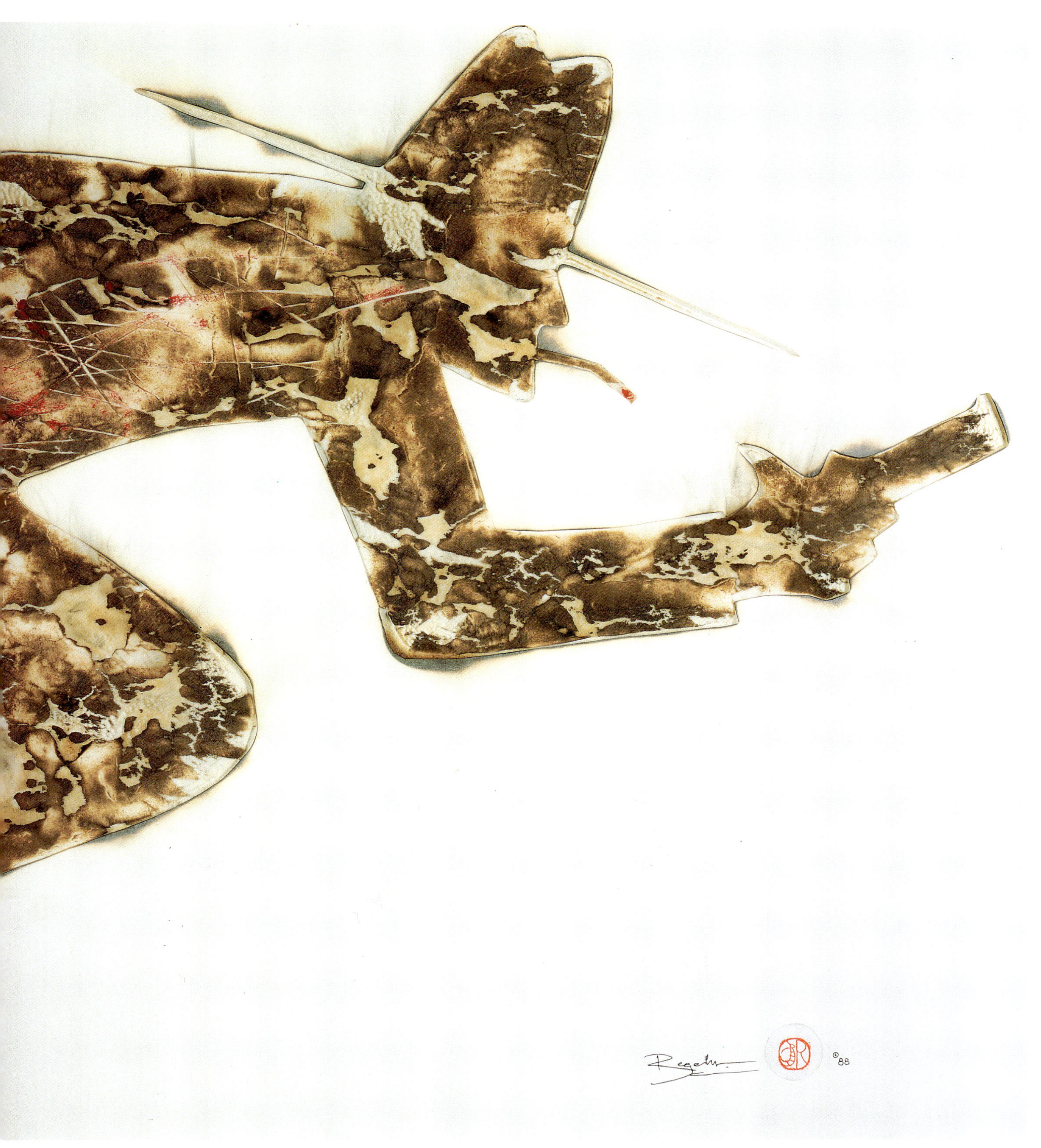

Smokin' Gun No. 60 Acrylic, Charcoal, Styrofoam, Paper 48" x 36" 1988

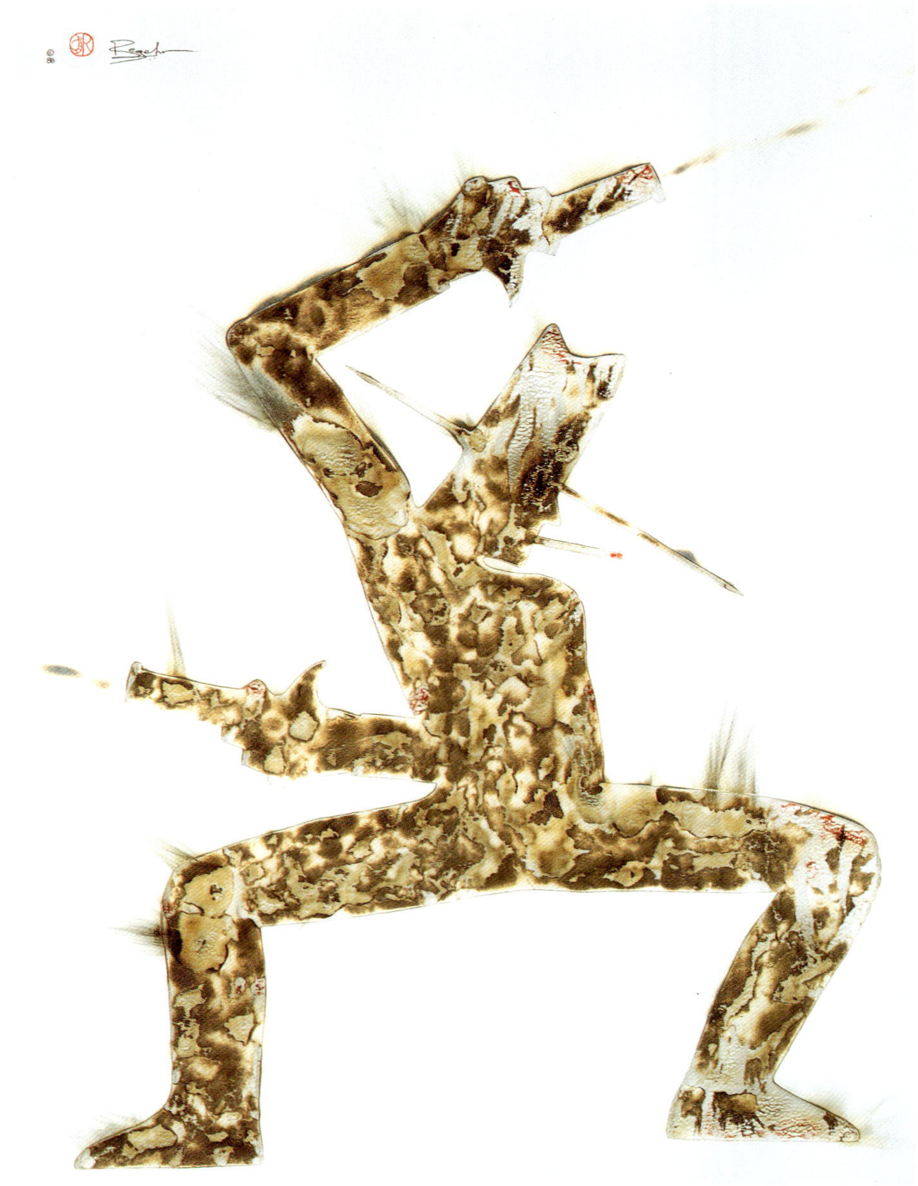

Smokin' Gun No. 58 Acrylic, Charcoal, Styrofoam, Paper 48" x 36" 1988

I threw myself into the series, using many different styles and techniques. Exploring every avenue that might improve the base image. Oils, acrylics, charcoal paper, canvas, stone, and wood. I used all manner of materials, ending with styrofoam panels.

Styrofoam melts and carbonizes beautifully when extreme heat is applied. With the help of a blowtorch, I created shapes which, for me, hold the strongest images, and perhaps the heart of "Smokin' Gun."

I would stand in the studio garden before the white boards, stripped to the waist, the sun beating down on my neck. Completely ensconced in the role of gunslinger, I would fire up the torch and blast away from the hip—ruining many good pieces by not being able to stop in time. Somewhere deep inside there lurks a pyromaniac.

I tried to retain three symbols in each piece:

The Gun: An instrument of betrayal. Whether symbolic or real (for there are many kinds of guns), when discharged with malice or lack of forethought, always backfires.

The Cigarette: Indicates cancer, drug addiction, pollution, the wick on the bomb that is about to explode. Cigarettes convey a driving nervousness or an uncaring casualness. Either way, they kill without mercy.

Smoke: A rich symbol that speaks of things burnt or in the process of burning; or it can be the harbinger of approaching flame.

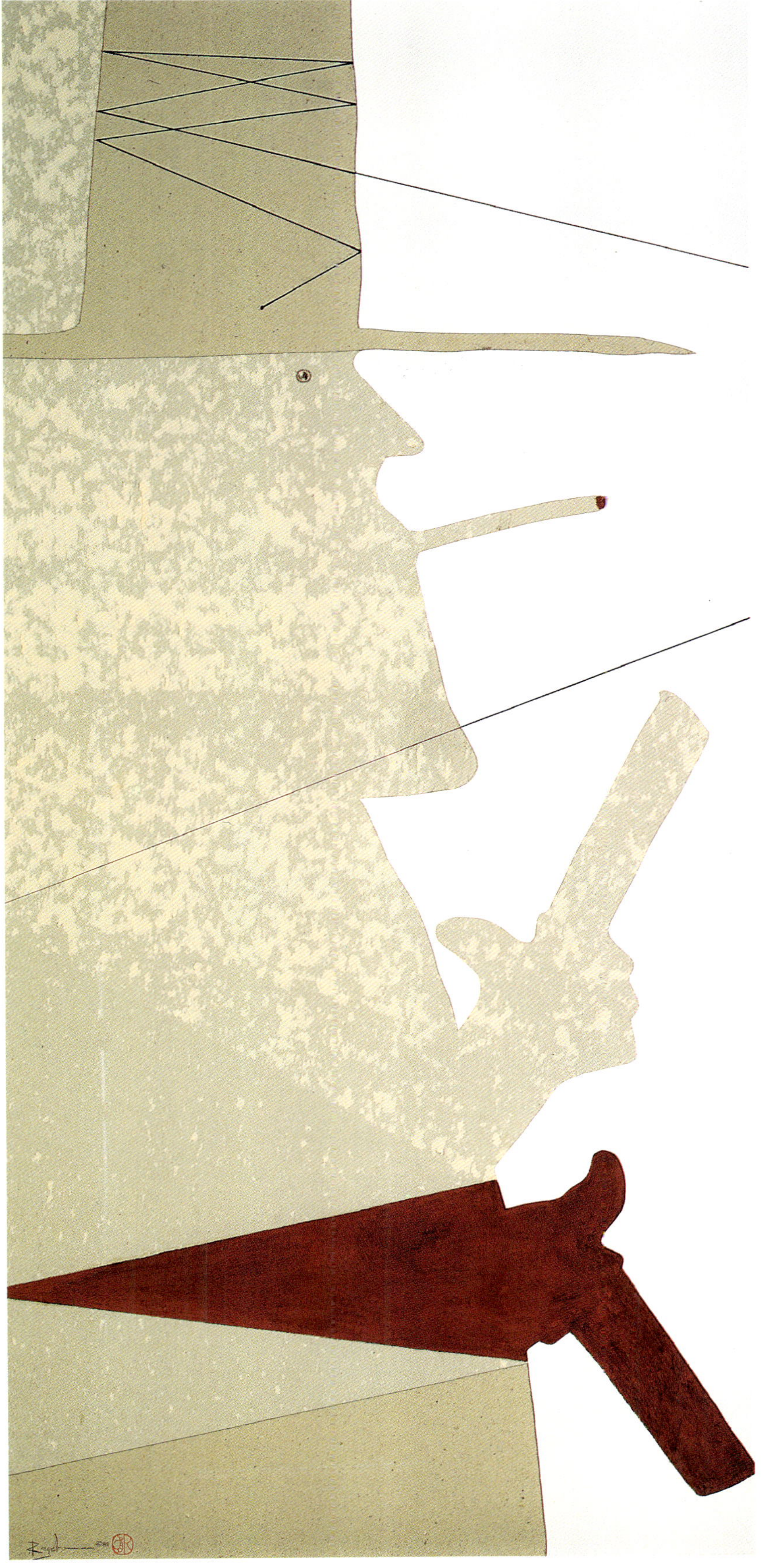

Ricochet OIL, ACRYLIC, CARDBOARD 60" x 26" 1988

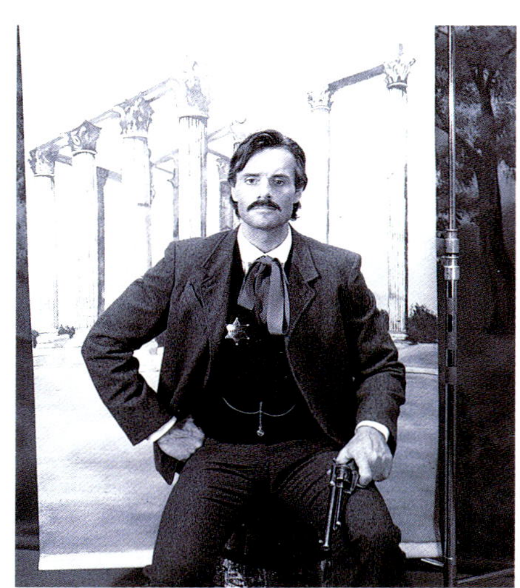

As Pat Garrett in *Gore Vidal's Billy The Kid*

In many ways Smokin' Gun was a pilgrimage to a mythic entity. Halfway along my blazing journey, I was offered the role of Pat Garrett in *Gore Vidal's Billy the Kid*, for Turner Network Television.

Serendipitous luck, and fuel for the fire! Pat Garrett was a sociopath obsessed with hunting down another sociopath—William Bonney. Each man dedicated to the quest of perpetuating his own way of life as the only way to exist. Mythic heroes both, they helped to sire the American Way. Their legend is deeply imbedded in the genes of western philosophy.

My life was completely immersed in the land of the Smokin' Gun. All my creative mediums focused simultaneously on the same theme. This released a great energy which fed and drove itself to produce an enormous body of work.

The Smokin' Gun exhibit opened at the Los Angeles Wiltern Center in December of 1988. When I stood in the gallery and observed the work as a whole, it scared the hell out of me. It had evolved from fear and suppressed anger. While there is humor in some of the pieces, the series offers no answers or hope, only warning and despair. It was the truth, it was the future, and it was as unrelenting as "the man" himself. I felt like a doomsayer.

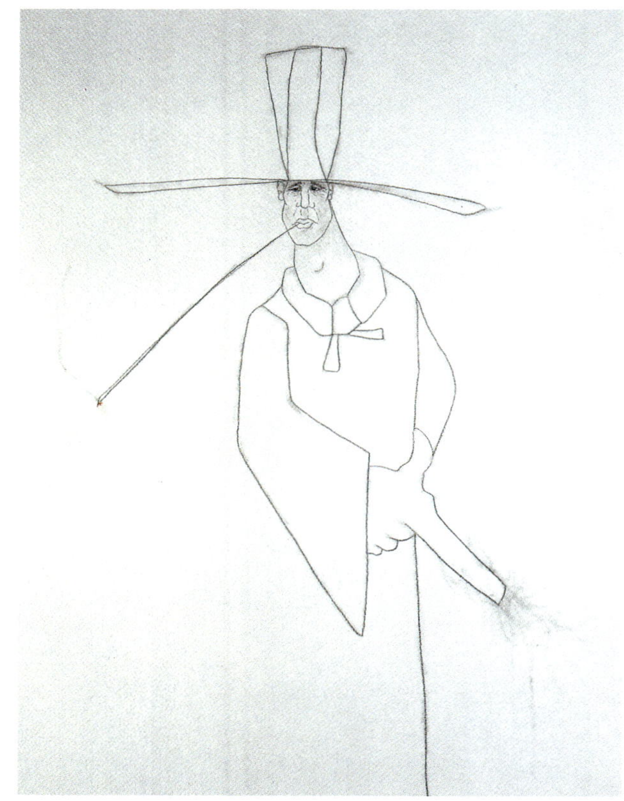

PENCIL DRAWING 18" x 12" 1988

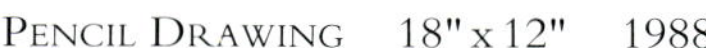
PENCIL DRAWING 18" x 12" 1988

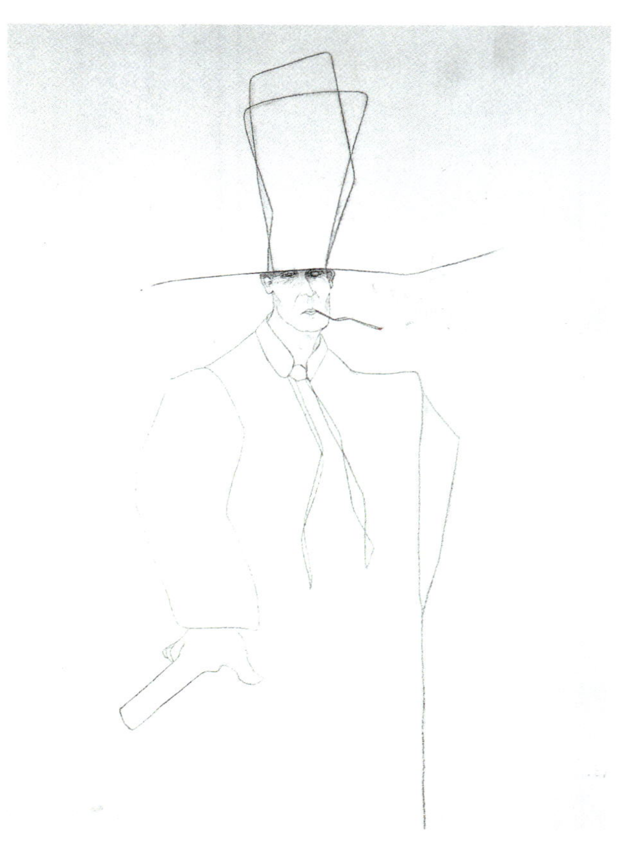

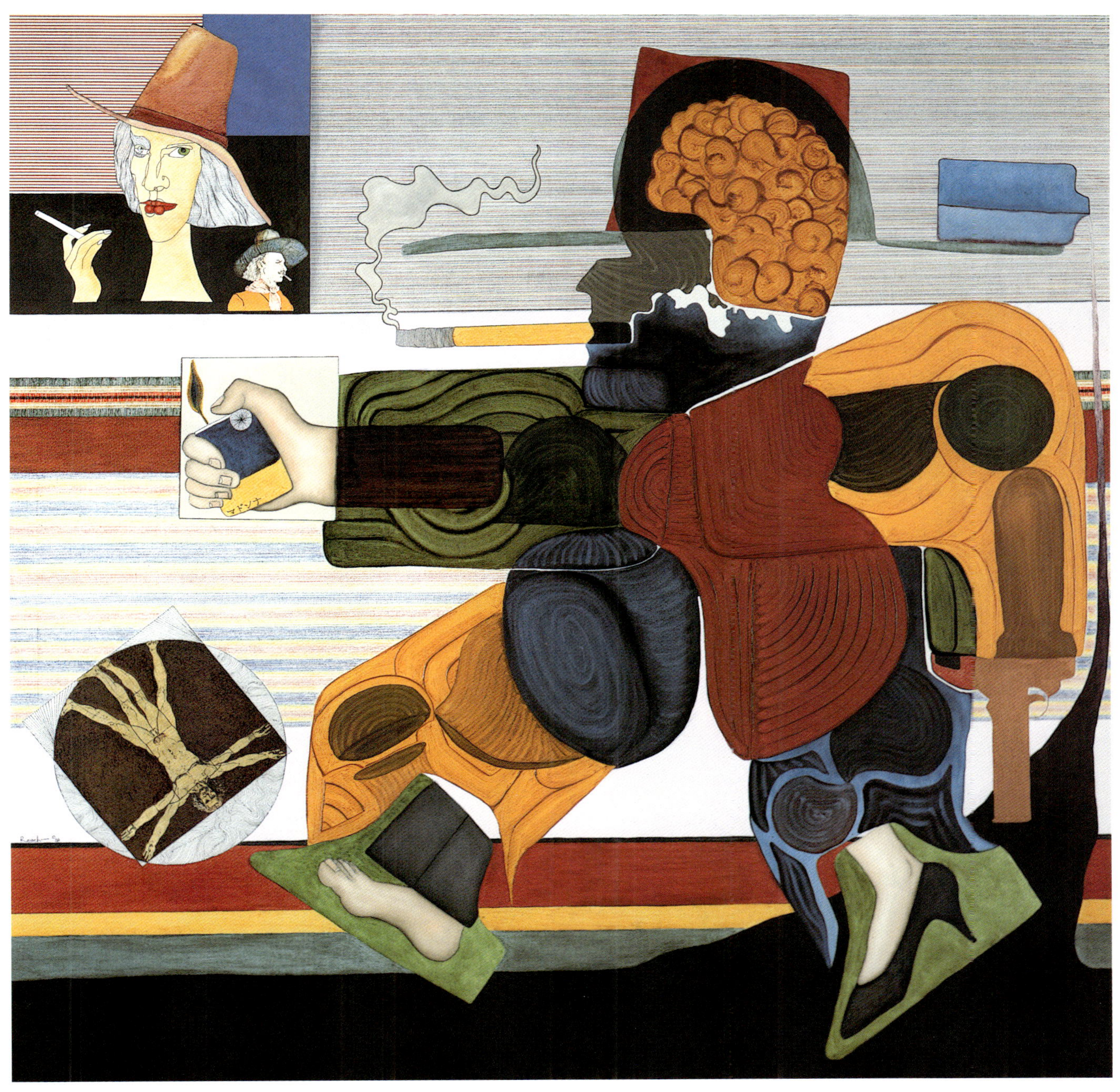

Smokin' Gun No. 18 Oil, Acrylic, Ink 48" x 48" 1988

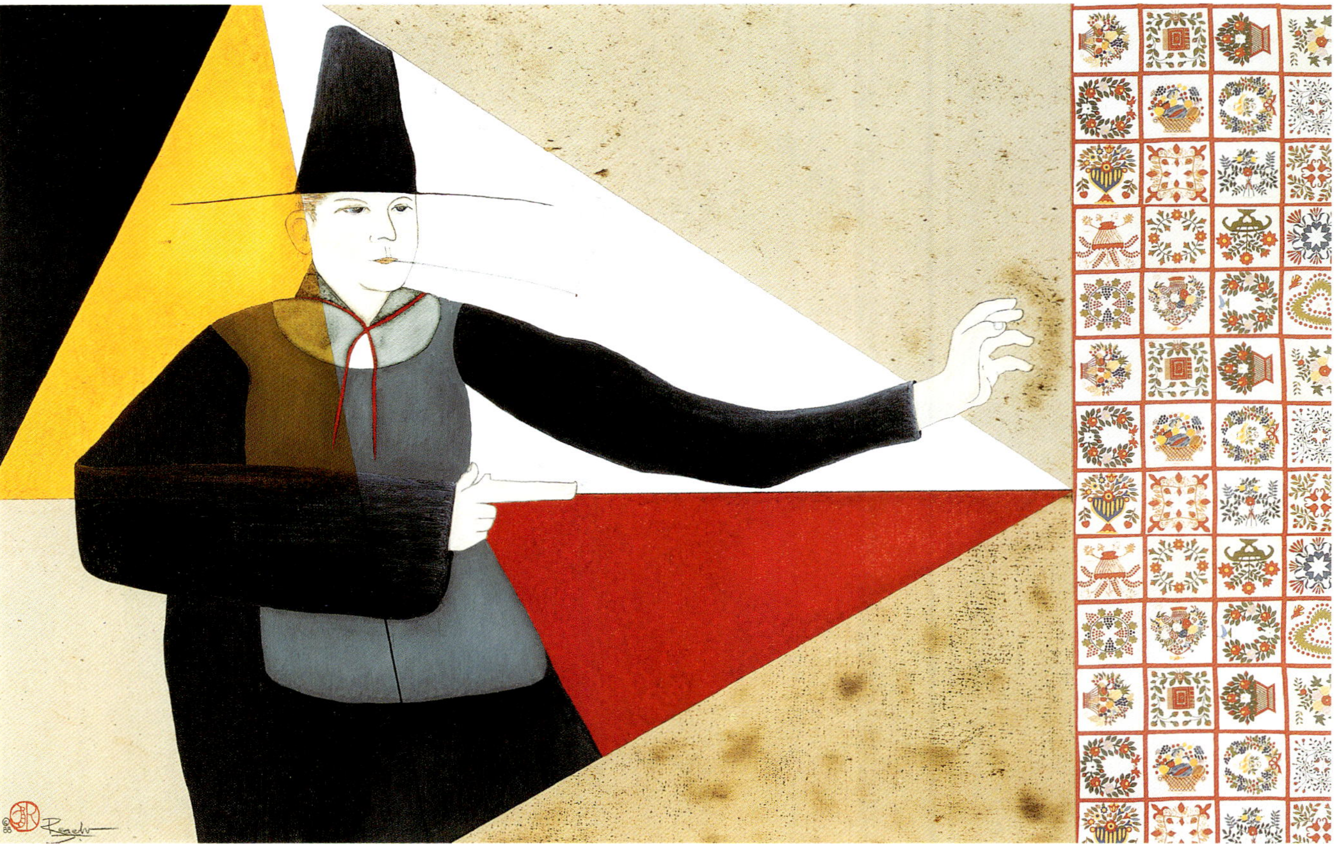

Pilgrim OIL, ACRYLIC, CHARCOAL, PAPER 29" x 39" 1988

I resolved to approach my future work with a broader awareness. To include social and/or political elements as integral parts of a theme instead of swamping my entire vision with them. Allowing the process of total immersion occasional moments of respite would encourage greater clarity.

This was the greatest bestowment of Smokin' Gun, for it gave me growth and a new path to follow. A path that would also eventually lead me away from L.A. We have our truce, our visiting hours, and I retain custody of my soul, but the crystal sphere is never clear of smoke, and the truth still smolders within.

In absence my vision grows
For I dwell in the elsewhere view
And look beyond from there.
I have grown,
And I have grown far enough away
To care easily and deeply in the distance,
For the city where angels die.

—DR

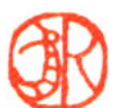

VII

A SINGLE THREAD FOR CLARITY

Line Drawings

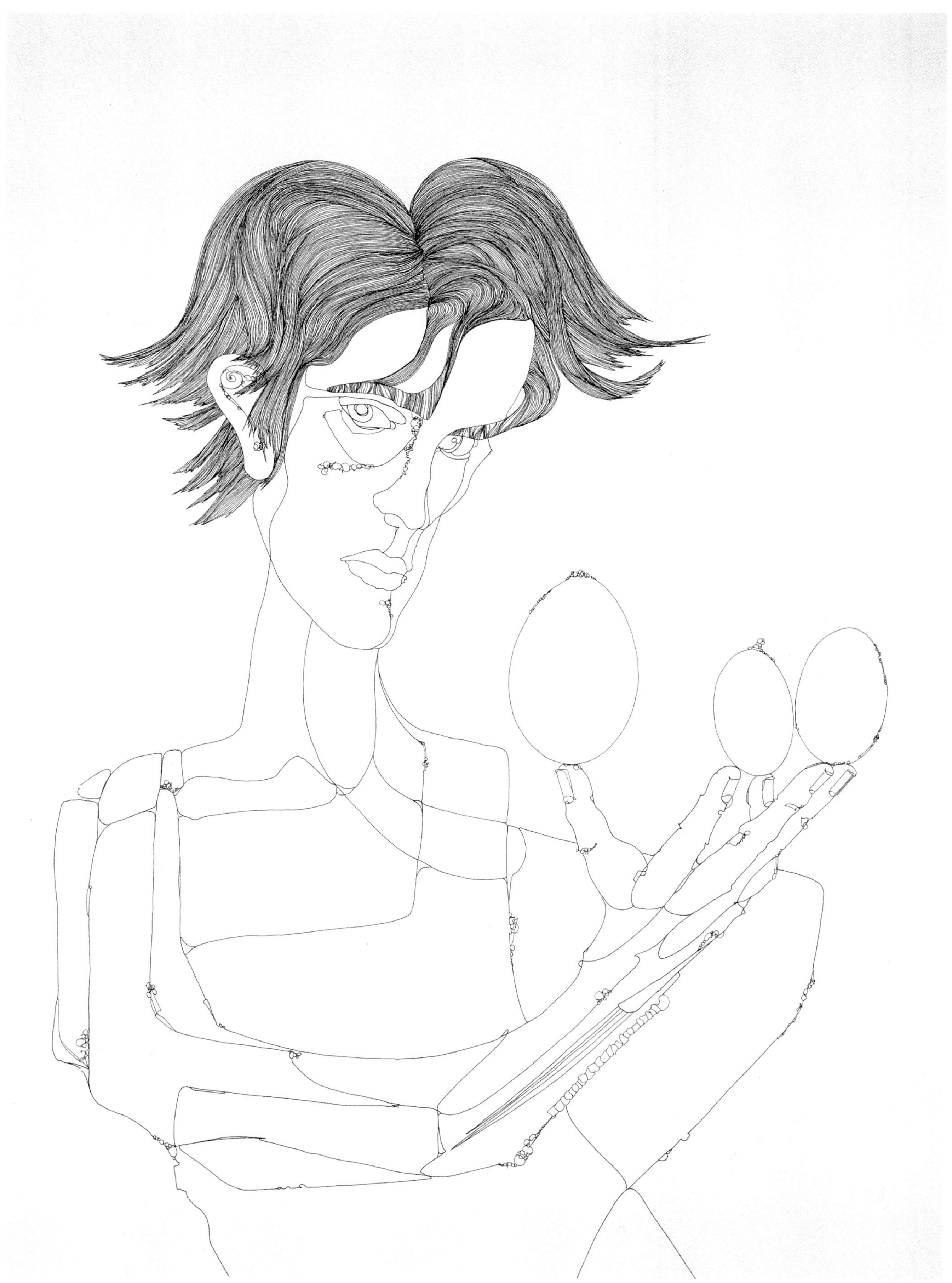

Carbon Faerie Pen and Ink 24" x 18" 1989

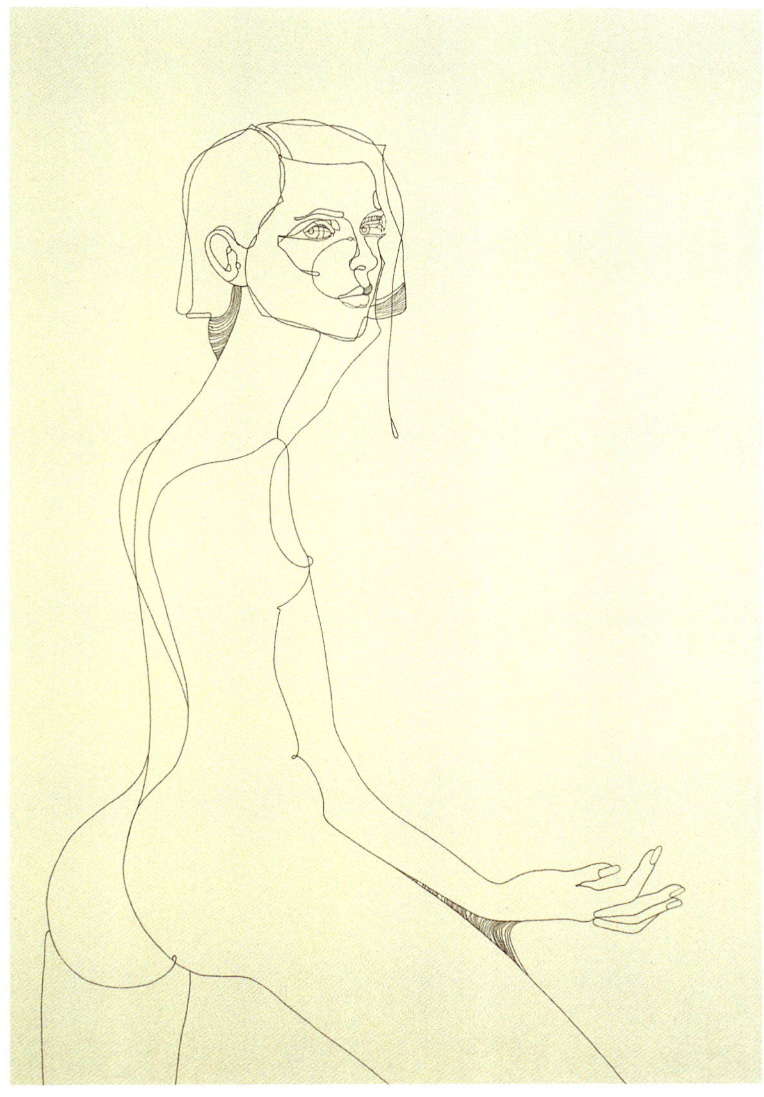

Angel Pen and Ink 24" x 18"

Angel and the Deep
(*An uncolored definition*)

Black,
the sacrificial Deep,
where fallen colors relinquish
identity for coalescent sleep.

White,
the reflecting Angel,
bids each color, separate
through wings of light and purity.

Angel hovers,
Deep beckons.
Penultimate contrast strikes the air.

No greater definition to clarity upheld
than on the threshold
before wings dip the surface
and gentle grey is borne.

—DR

Clarity and Gentility. After the cease-fire of Smokin' Gun, I sought both. I found them sleeping in pen and ink.

I awakened them to act as the guiding reins for line drawings. The harness for black and white.

The medium has been important to my drawing skills since childhood, both as an exercise and as the preliminary sketches for larger works.

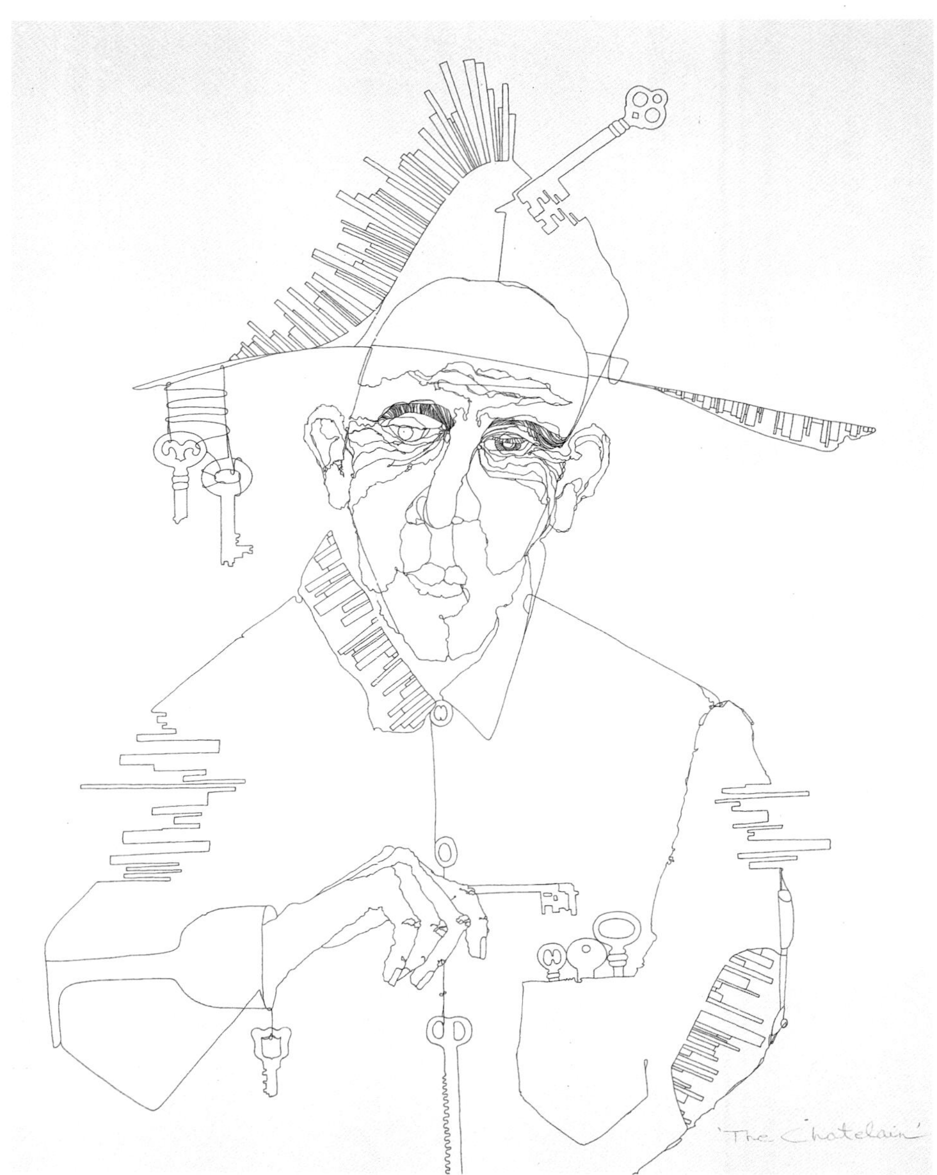

The Chatelain Pen and Ink 24" x 18" 1989

I returned to Henry Poesiat's "automatism." I let the imagery come forth unbridled. In contrast to that easy flow, one hand or the other strictly controlled the pen, singularly, from start to finish of the drawing. Deeply scoring the paper, almost never lifting the pen from the surface and rarely pausing—for a blot would soon form—I incorporated any mistake as part of the final image. Erasing the ink was impossible.

The slip-ups became cover-ups, often giving birth to incredible tangents that grew more complex as I went along, especially when mistakes occurred within mistakes. Because they were all quickly absorbed into the progress of the line—and allowed to find a place in the scheme—they were no longer errors but important additions to the drawing. Some of my greatest flaws became treasured symbols.

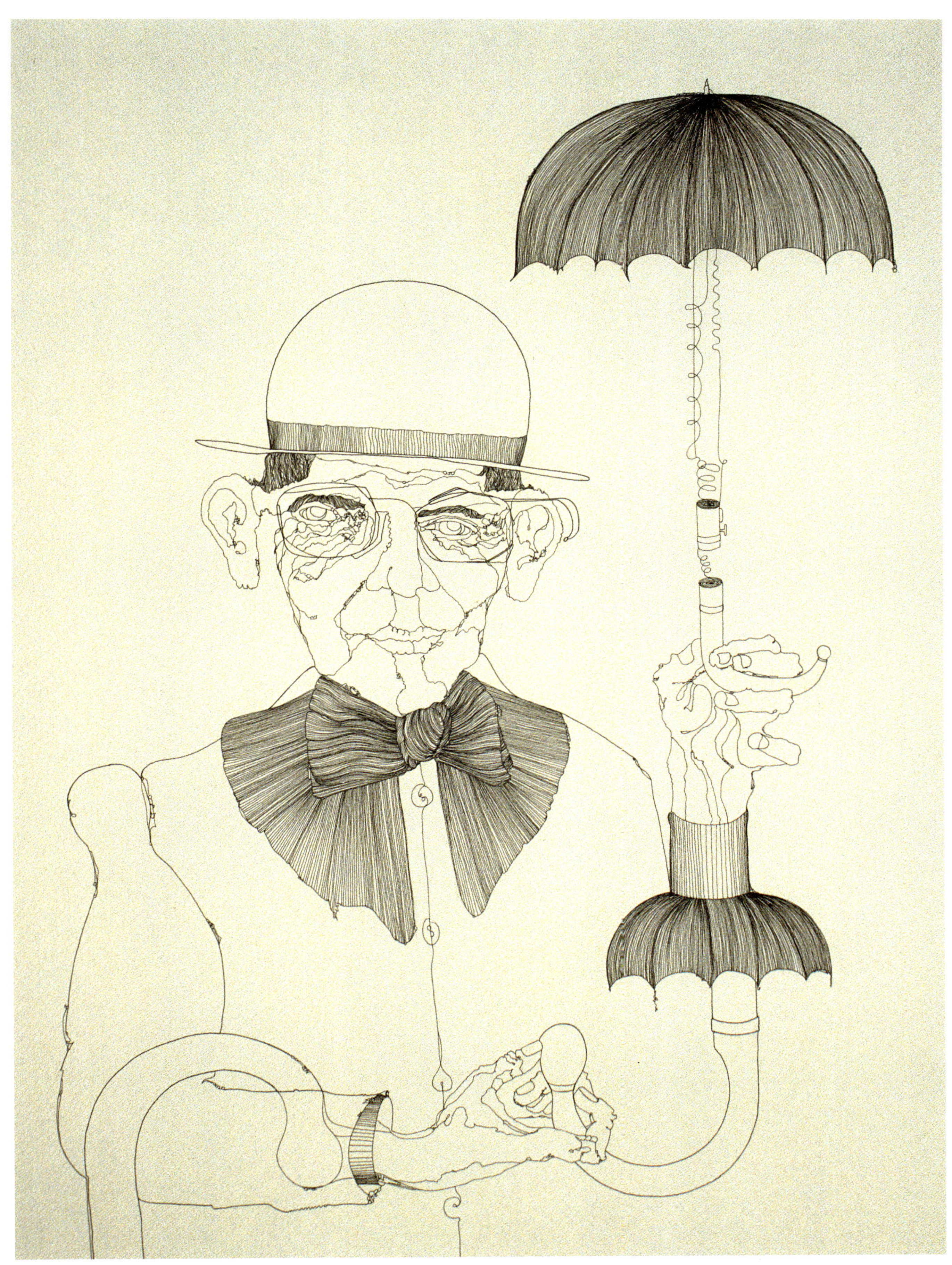

The Rain Maker PEN AND INK 24" x 18" 1989

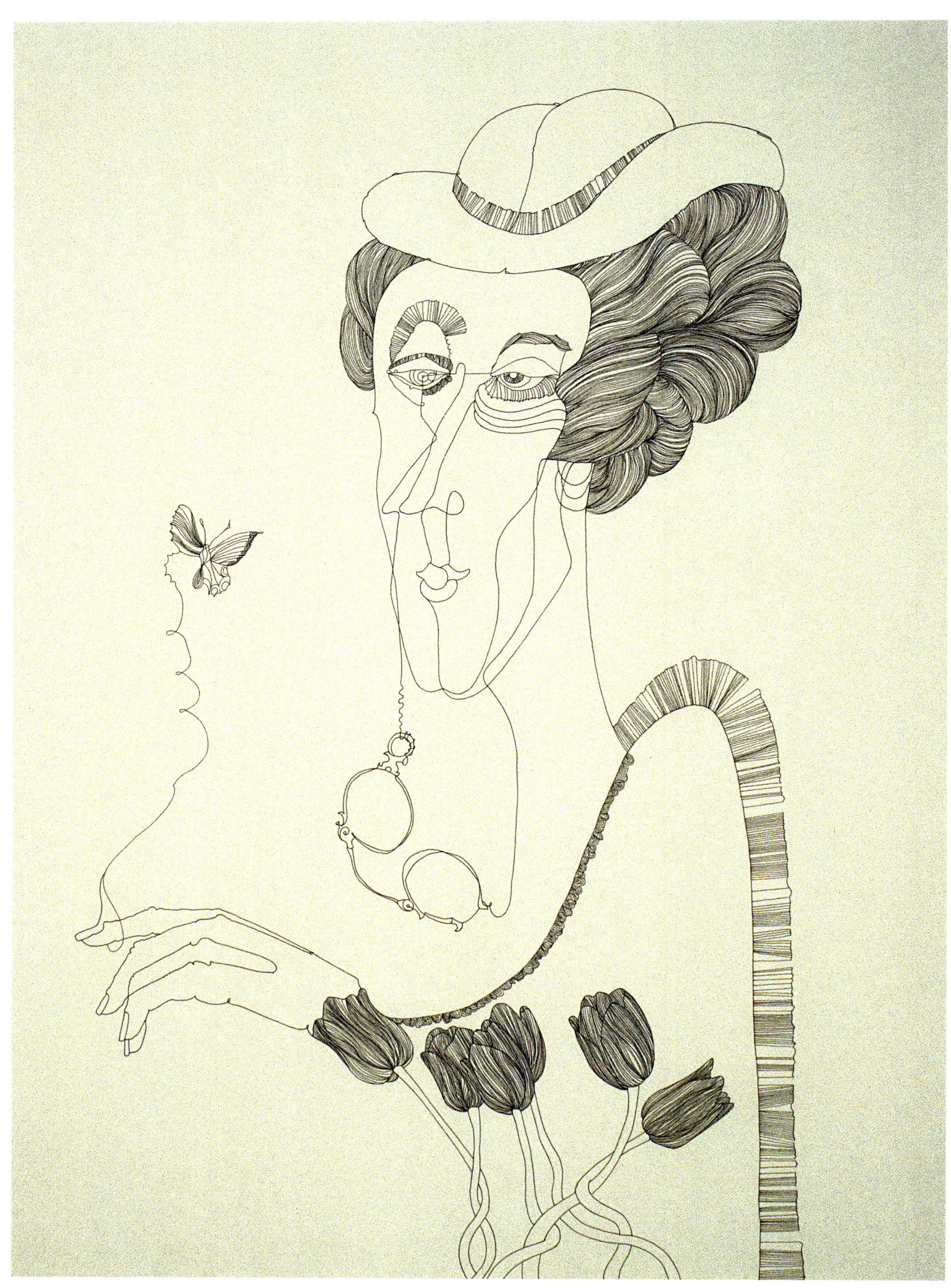

Miss Plummer Pen and Ink 18" x 24" 1989

This spontaneous system of rectification resembles a technique that eighteenth century potters applied to Chelsea porcelain. The craftsmen would paint flowers, fruit, or insects in such a way as to modify pinholes and bubbles formed in the glazes by the firing process. They used the shapes of the imperfections to guide their choice of subject matter. An elongated bubble would become the abdomen of a butterfly; a round one the eye of a bird. Their careful selections were made primarily from the world of nature. My system was based on immediacy and included a broader, wildly eclectic range of choices.

In the end, there were no faults to my errors. The final drawings were either complete successes or total failures. In cases of the latter, I would start over with aspirations of repeating myself, but would inevitably stray, quite happily, to create something entirely different.

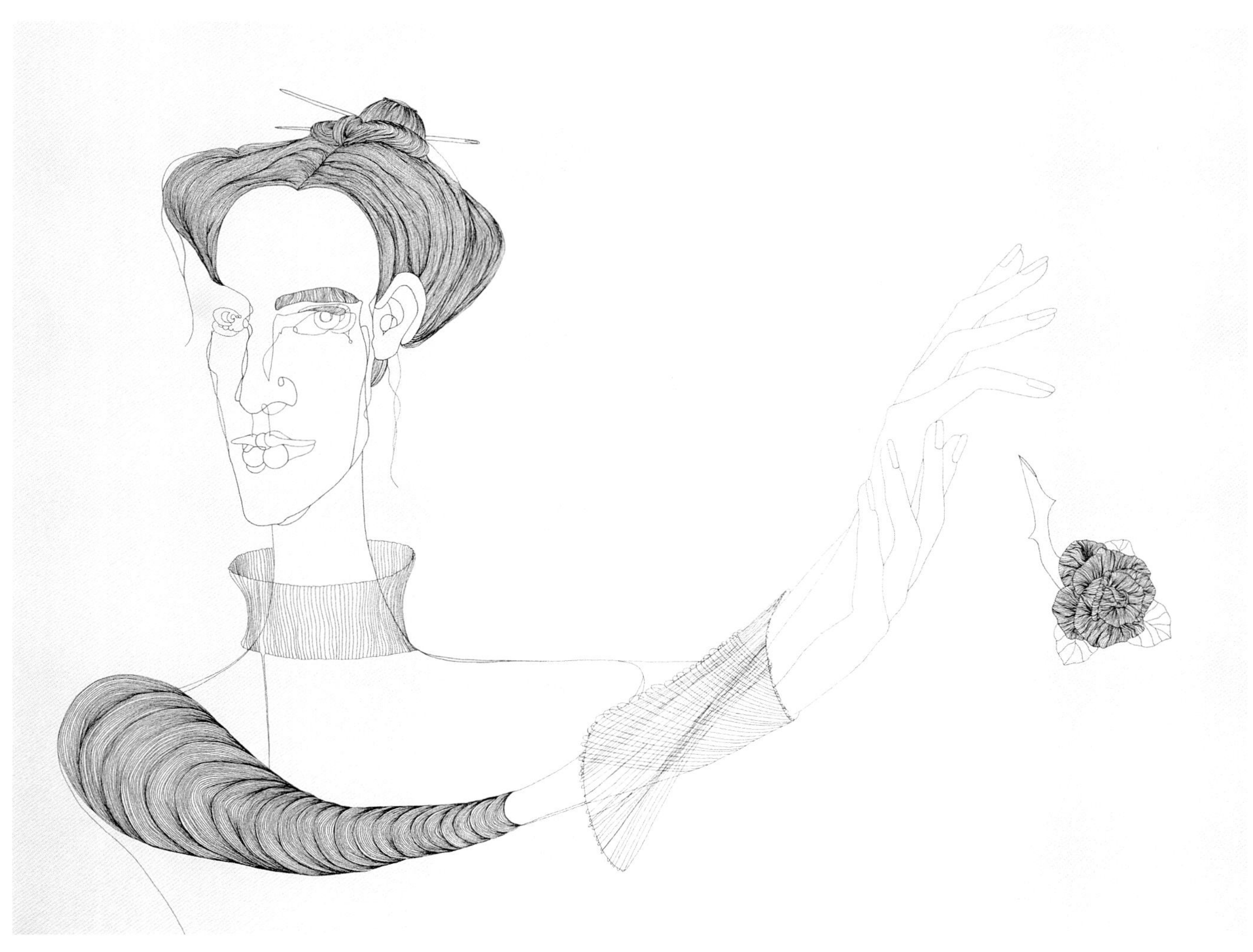

The Seamstress PEN AND INK 18" x 24" 1989

I was figure skating on paper, employing hard precision to accommodate freedom of expression. The resulting illustrations took the form of symbolic portraits. By subconscious osmosis, the work would often align itself with the abstract ramblings of my journal writings and poetry, incorporating faces known and unknown; tapping into my dreams and bringing forth forgotten memories. All the ideas contorted onto the paper, transformed by the separate will of my imagination.

The theme of each piece unfolded as the drawing progressed. At times becoming apparent only with the ending movements of the pen. I would emerge from a session of drawing as if from a trance. There is no sense of time in that state. It is as if the mind exists on some other plane, with no relation to the constant changes of the physical world that are the gauge determining our chronological understanding of time.

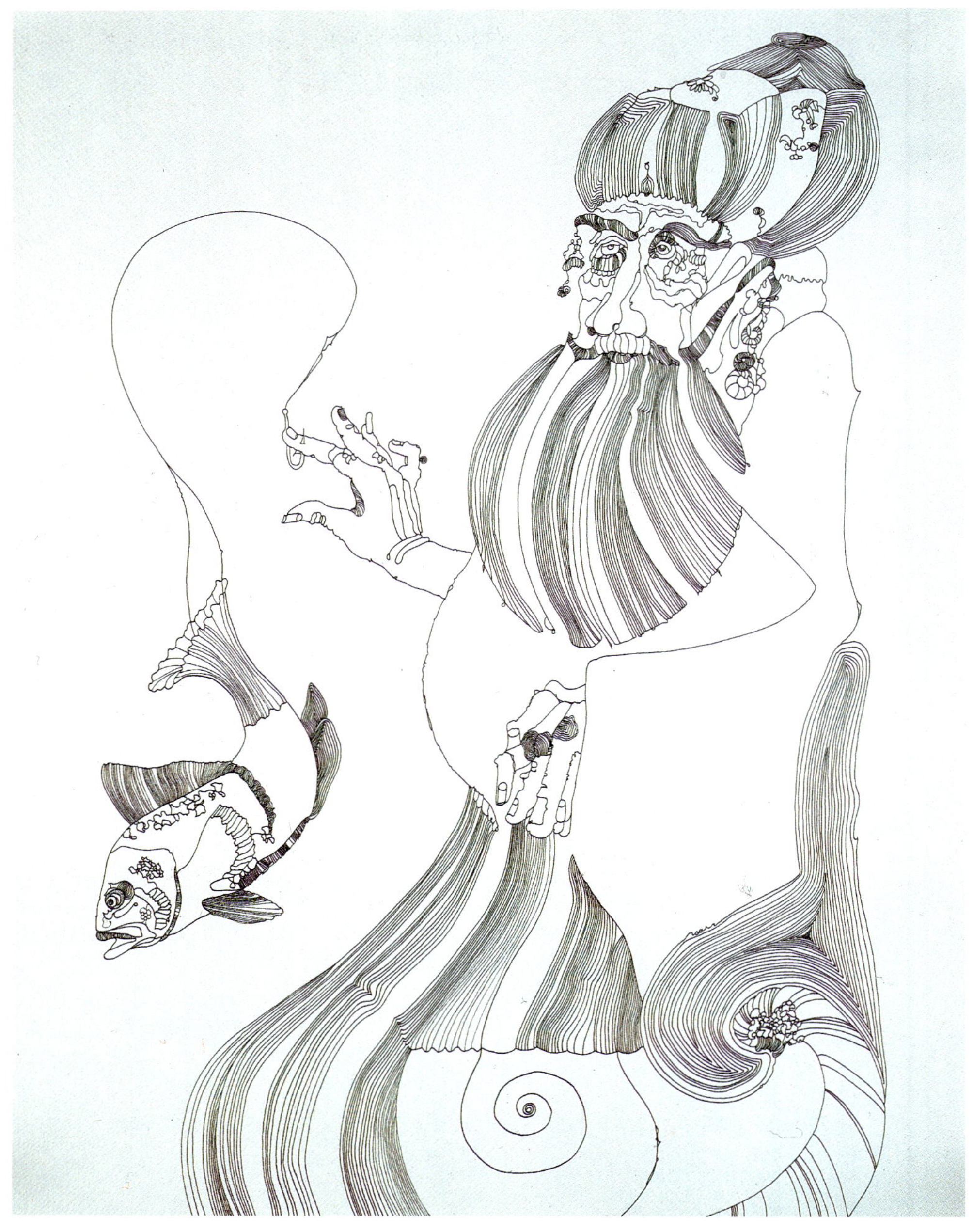

Of Proteus and Wordsworth
Pen and Ink
24"x 18"   1989

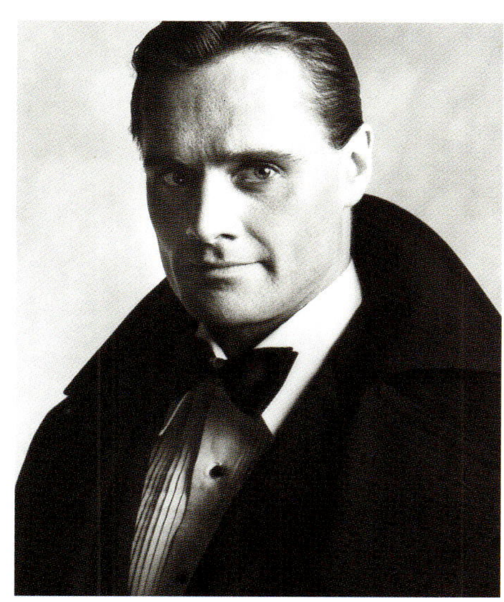

As Dracula
in Tri Star's
Monster Squad

The Fox-El Zorro CHARCOAL 15" x 10" 1990

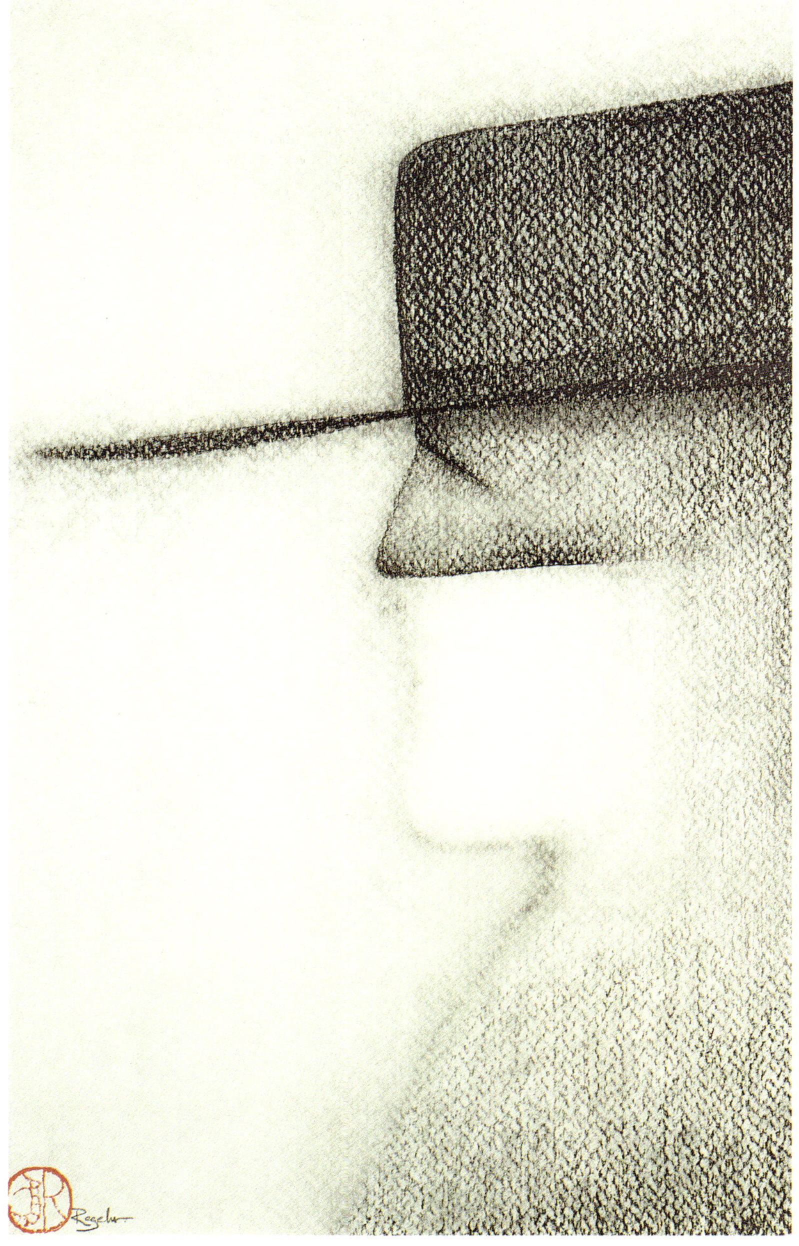

Black has been the "color" of the costumes for many of the characters I have portrayed, including Prince Blackpool in *Wizards and Warriors*, Charles in *V*, *The Banker*, Lydon (in gladiator mode) in The *Last Days of Pompeii*, Dracula in *Monster Squad,* and most recently, *Zorro*. The color seems to follow me like a shadow, and to wear black as an actor is to don the cloak of hidden powers. I enjoy it for brief periods but find myself longing for respite from the stigma of oppression and, dare I say, the evil that it often conveys.

Similarly, with the line drawings, they craved relief. I introduced colored pencil and so contrived a different approach. The suspended-line technique of pen and ink that had engaged automatism so closely was set aside. Replaced by my standard fidgeting (drawings composed by both hands, switching back and forth). I manipulated the pencils to create translucent shades, resembling those of watercolor. In contrast to the deep-limning pressure I applied when using the pen, this required a feather-light touch. The resulting images had an airy, dreamlike quality.

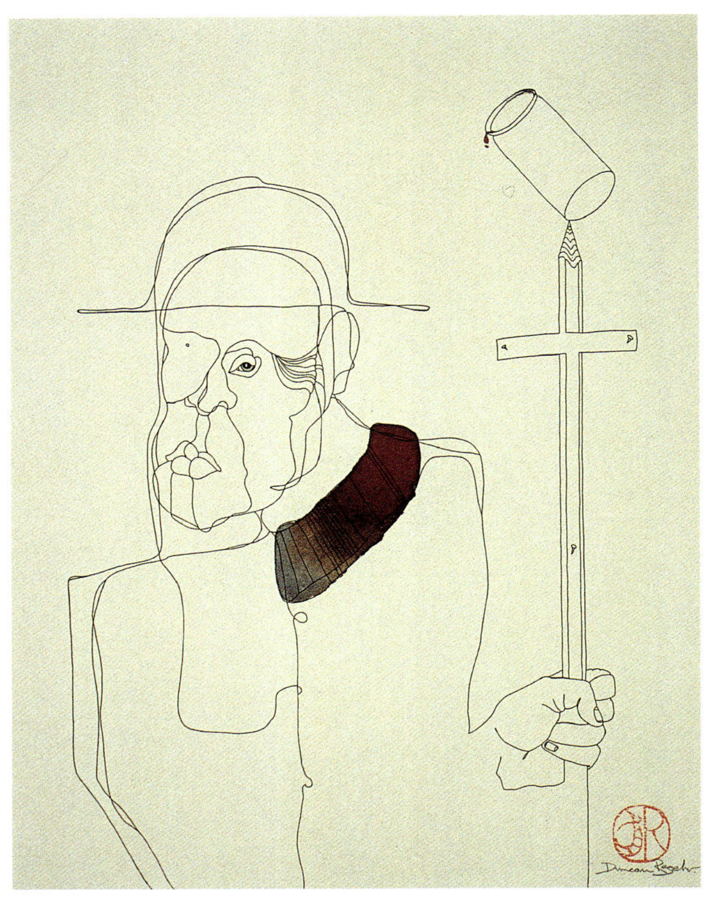

Mennonite
Watercolor, Pen and Ink
14" x 18"   1989

I also recomposed some of my established ink drawings with color, embellishing them into fuller visions with both pencil and/or watercolor.

I have referred to line drawings in the past tense in order to explain their progression and to establish a period of time when I focused on them as a single project. In truth, they are a continuing series, which I place on hiatus from time to time while concentrating on other projects.

Most of my other series work, with the exception of early portraits and landscapes, are thematic in a general way. The separate pieces within those series relate like bees in a hive — their collective existence has a singular purpose — feeding the queen bee. That is not to say that if you had seen all the paintings, you would have seen but one. Instead, each piece gains individuality from its presentation of supportive ideas, which generate the overall concept.

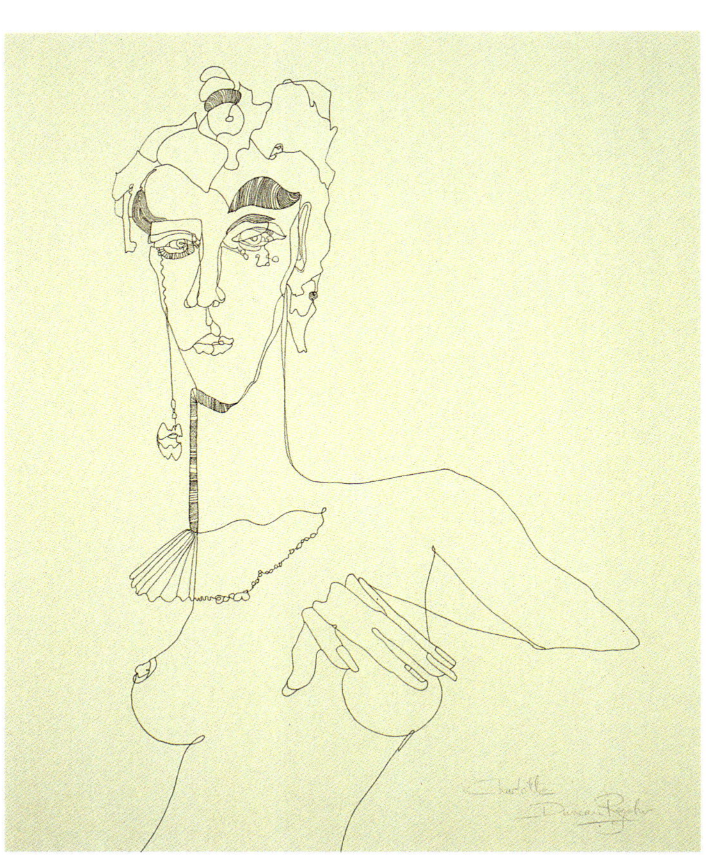

Charlotte
Pen and Ink
24" x 18"   1989

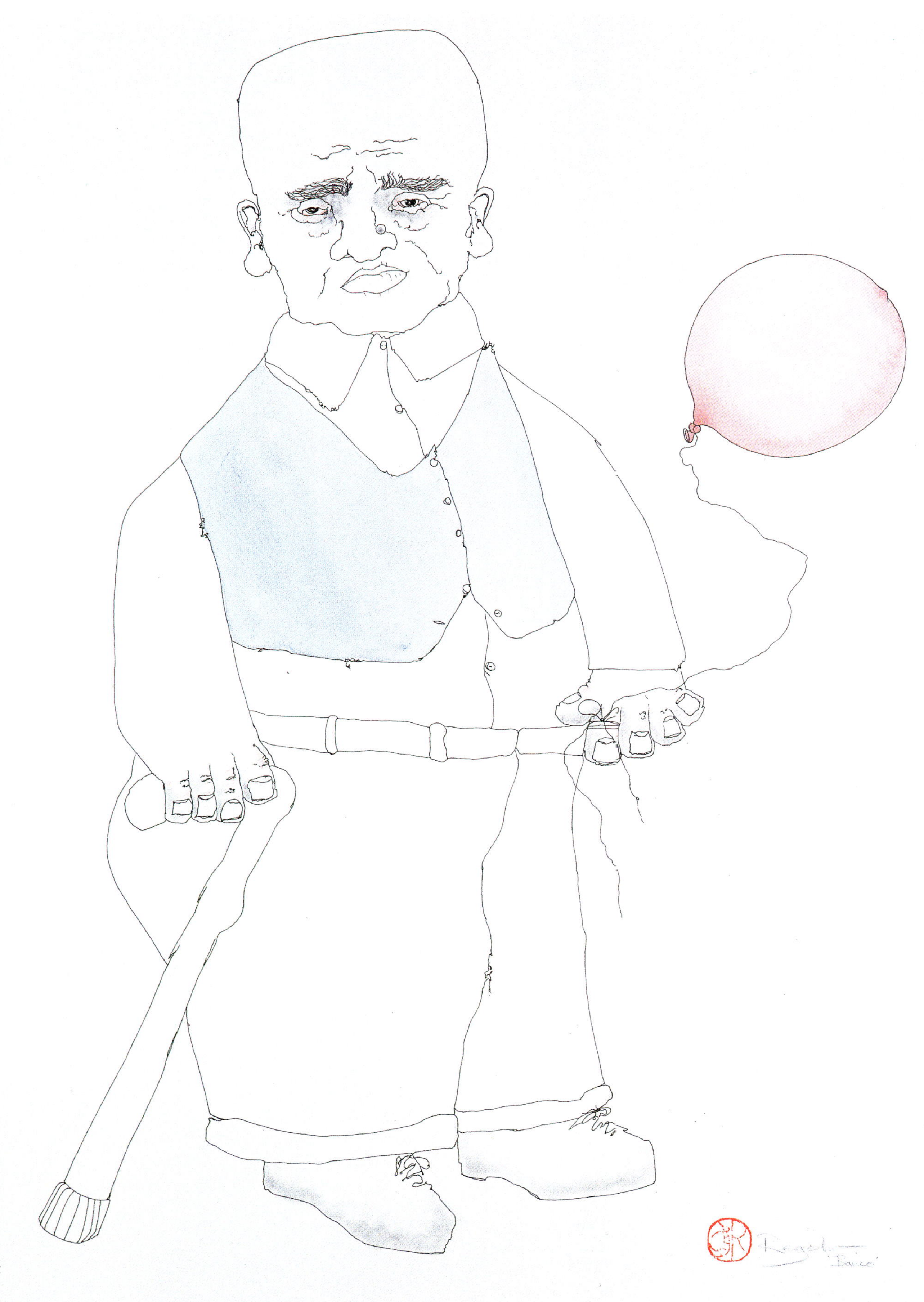

Banco Pen, Ink, Watercolor, and Charcoal 24" x 18" 1989

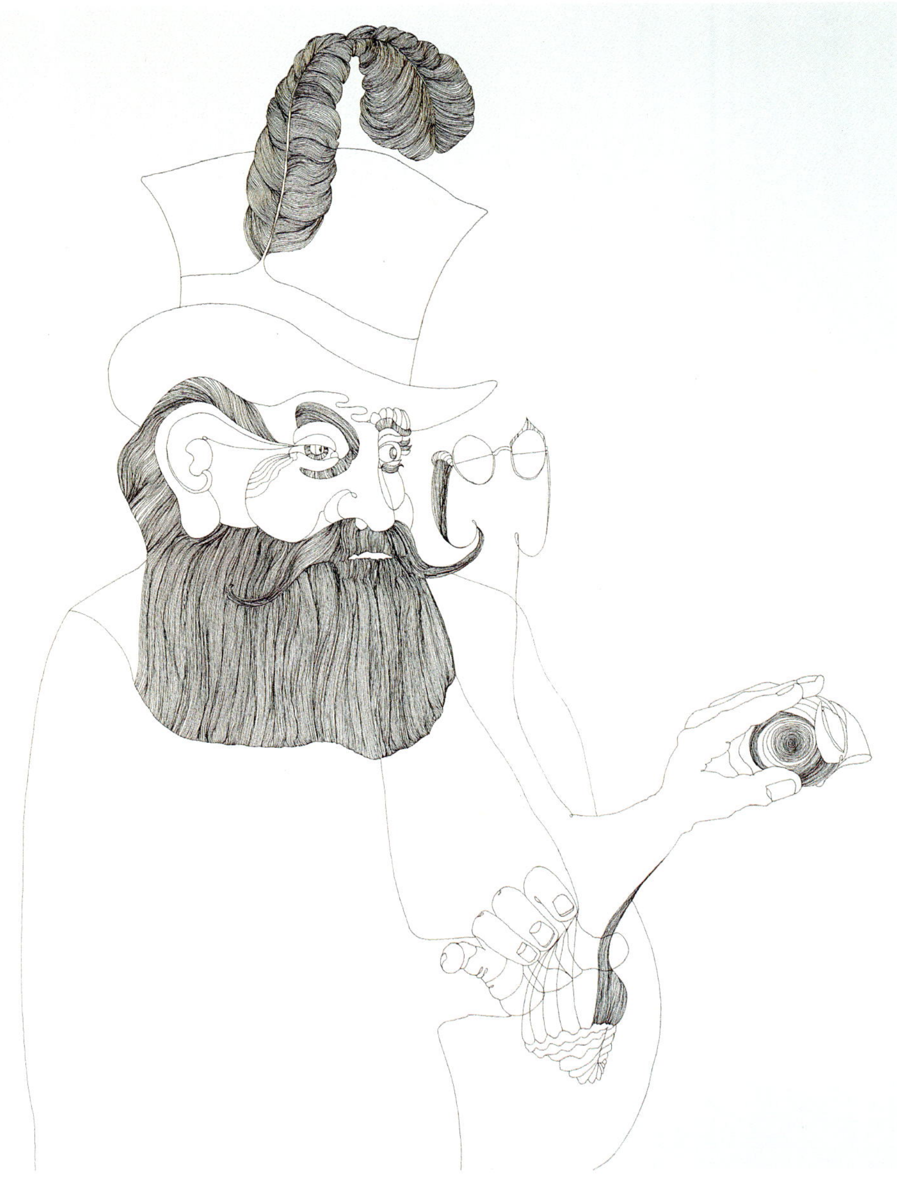

Curator PEN AND INK 24" x 18" 1989

The line drawings possess themes unto themselves. Like the poetic imagery paintings, each work has its own story to tell. The technical style is not the only common factor linking the pieces. There is an all-encompassing grand theme which flows as a constant stream from the wellspring of subconscious expression. Since that is full and fathomless, the complete thematic scope may never be realized.

Angel drinks from the well of the Deep,
Laughs color forth to the Skies,
There Mystery flys and Muses weep,
A rain of riddles to my eyes.

—DR

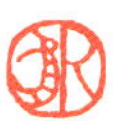

VIII

THE GRAND THEME

Poetic Imagery

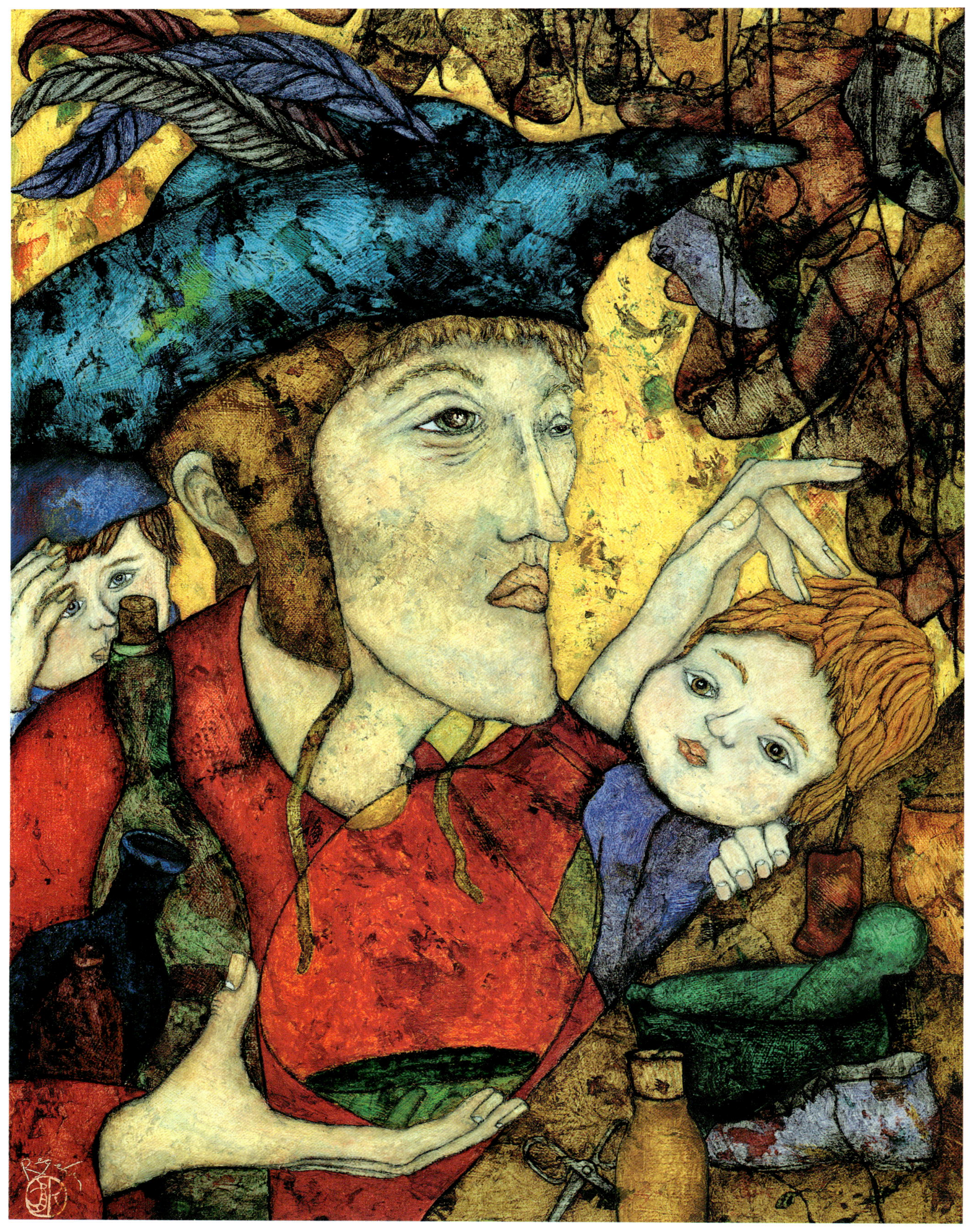

The Apothecary Oil 24" x 18" 1993

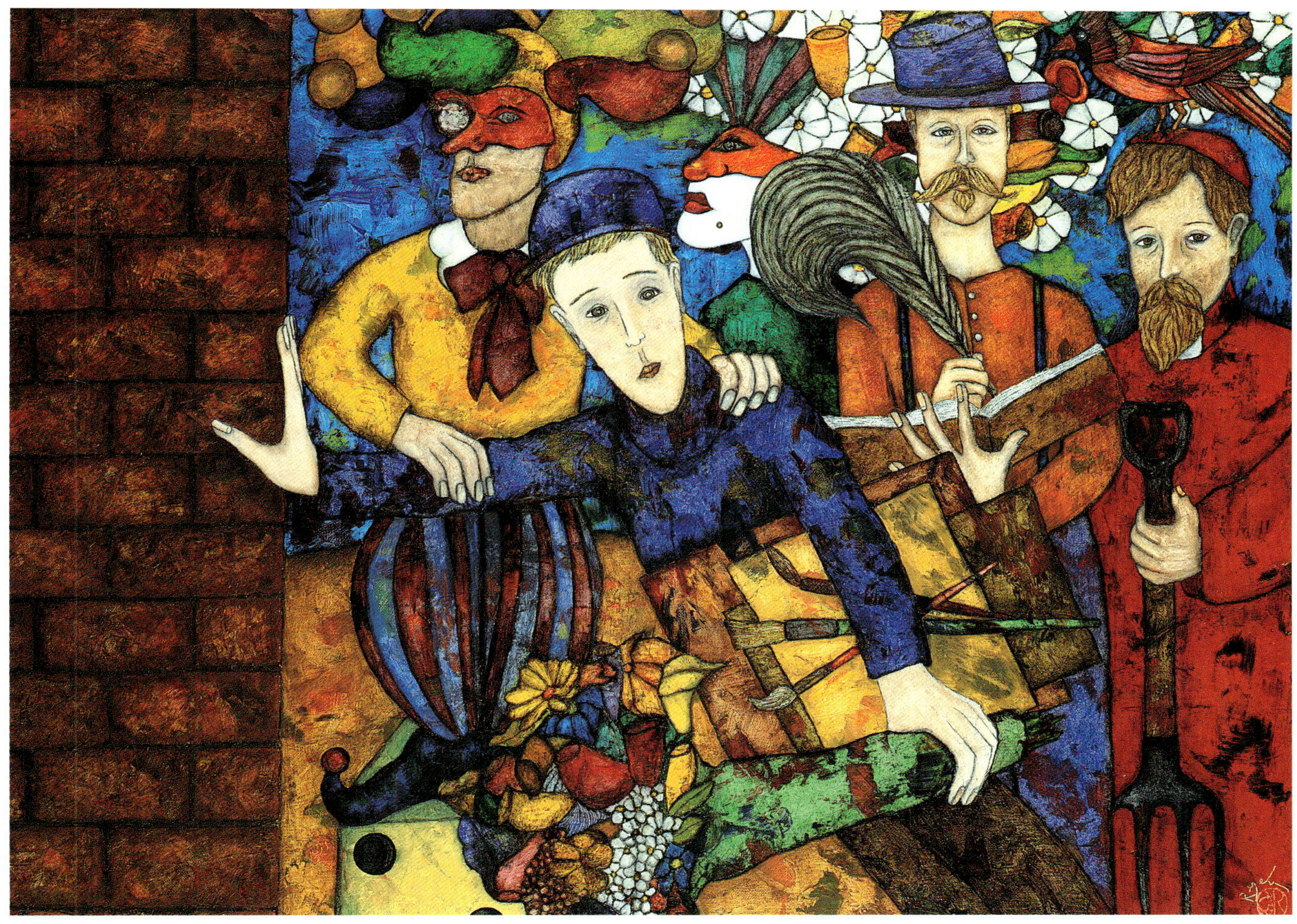

False Dharma OIL 24" x 33" 1993

As Zorro

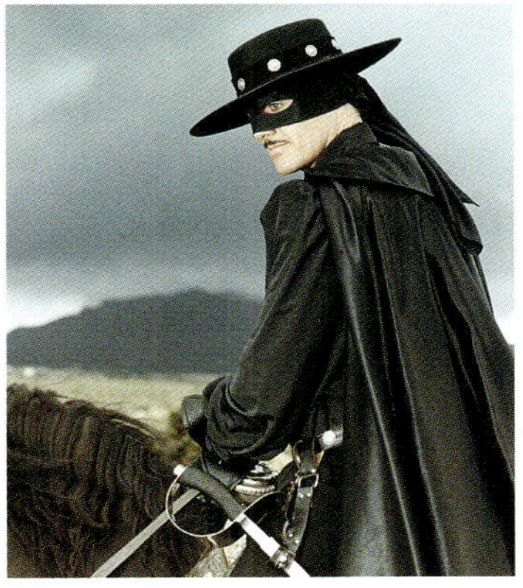

CATHERINE AND I decided in 1989 to move our main residence from California to Washington state before the end of 1991. So began my commuter's relationship with Los Angeles.

It was also a year for much long distance travel. In August I began filming eighty eight television episodes of *Zorro* just outside of Madrid. Over the next three years, I spent many months living in Europe.

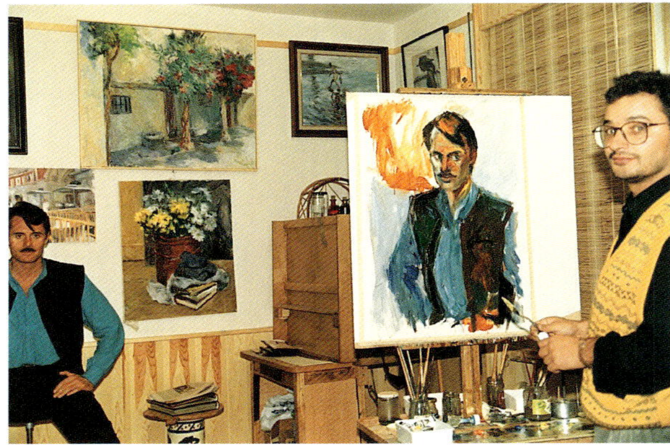

With Jesus Brovia, sitting for a portrait.
Madrid, 1990

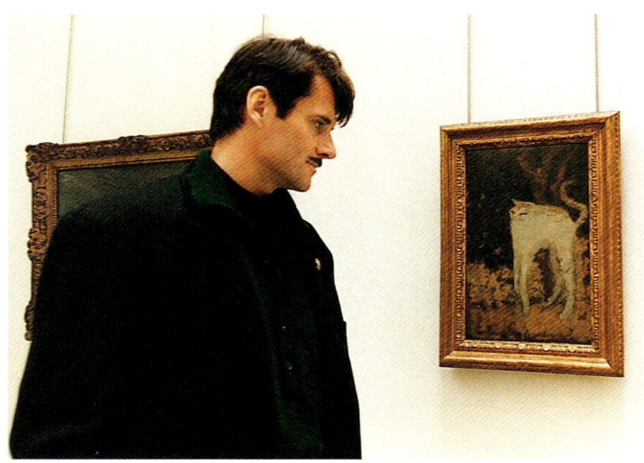

Visiting Musee d'Orsay, Paris, 1989

Zermatt, Switzerland, 1990

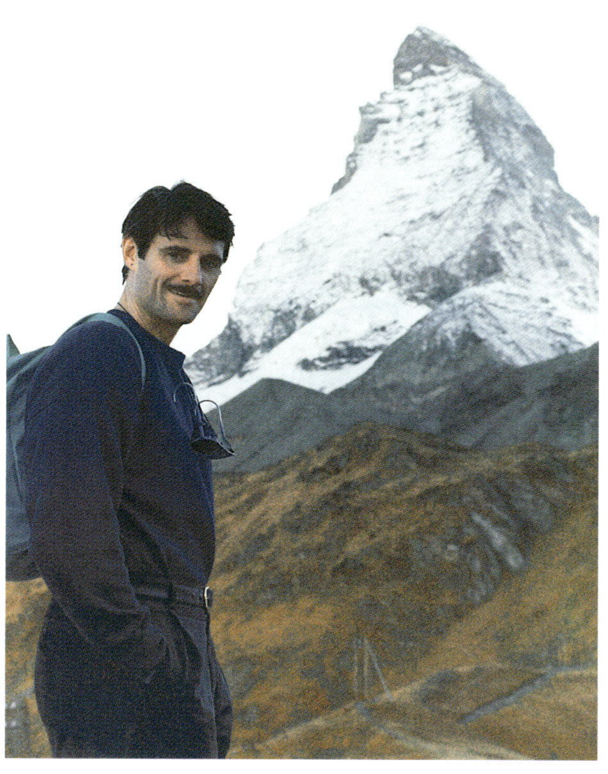

This was a period of enormous growth for me and I have no doubt that it will be reflected in my future art. I sketched and wrote prolifically during hiatus from the show. I traveled throughout Europe visiting art galleries and met many artists in different countries. Our friendships and exchanges of thought continue through letters and the language of our work.

I began mountaineering in Switzerland—an endeavor that goes far beyond being a sport. It presents the ultimate challenge to body and spirit through nature: a frontier that tests one's courage, resourcefulness, cunning, strength, ability, and stamina to the utmost in a situation of inherent risk.

The following is an excerpt from my Journal
August 29th 1990, Zurich, Switzerland:

. . . the mountain can be viewed as the Self. The Climb (which is also the descent) is a pilgrimage—Life, the teacher of the Self. It tests the very essence of being. The concept of Existence is never clearer in the human psyche than when the Elements present Life, to the Self, as pure Survival.

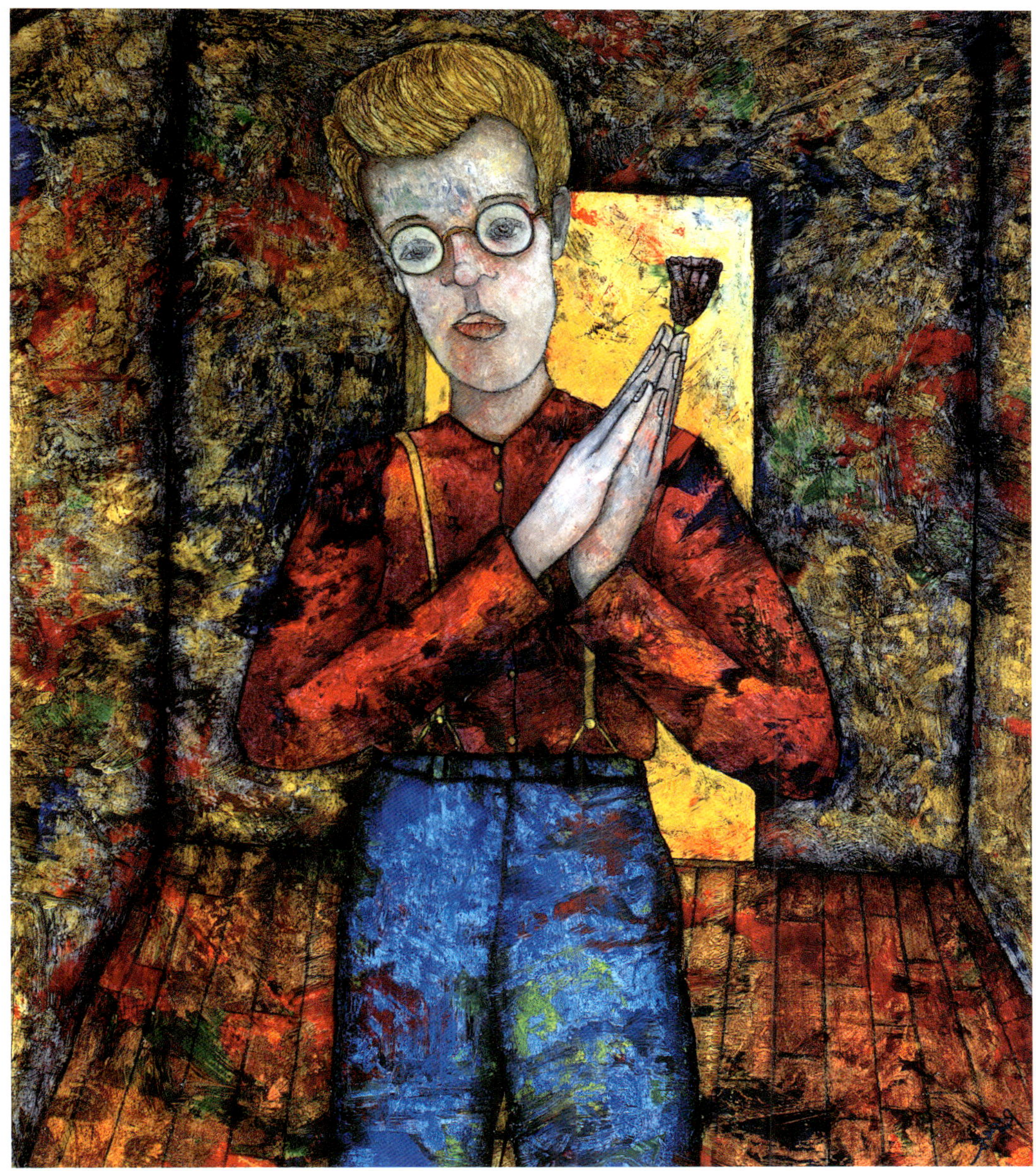

Fraser's Discovery OIL 24" x 20" 1992

The mountain will never be conquered. To deceive oneself into seeking such a thing, will lead only to the emptiness of self-defeat, but the Climb can be achieved, as any ideal in Life can be attained.

To reach the peak requires cooperation with fellow pilgrims (climbers) and a joining with the forces of nature — never fighting or trying to break them, but to learn to survive by living through them.

On the journey upward I strive to respect every encounter, as I will face all of them again later on.

At the top, I celebrate achievement, I look outward in appreciation. In the distance I see another peak, taller than the one on which I am standing. The goal of my Self has just moved to another plateau of Existence. In order to attain it, I must first descend, I must look inward, reliving all that I have learned.

The journey back will be more difficult than the ascent. The moment of achievement is set aside before continuing, so as to fully reflect upon my Climb and my survival thus far — to remember my past.

During my descent I will be re-confronted by each encounter of my ascent anew for I will be challenged by them in reverse, facing my past from the opposite point of view. This is the hardest test of all, but once accomplished, a passage of Life will be complete and I will know my Self well enough to seek a higher Existence.

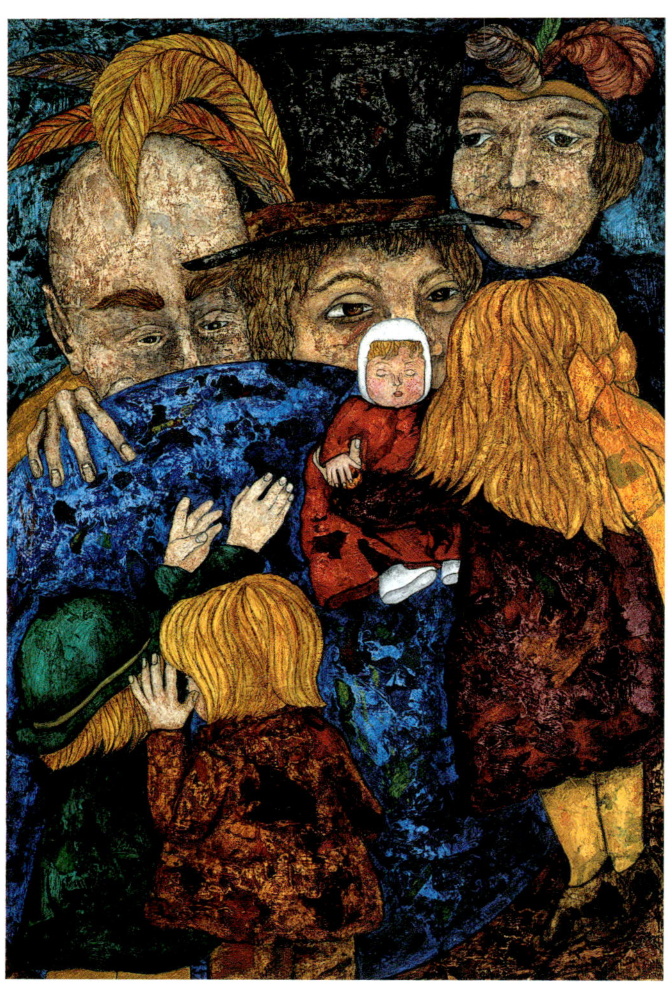

The Keepers OIL 36" x 24" 1993

This book heralds the beginning of my journey into a new style of painting, Poetic Imagery. Imagery of the inner self, joining the past and the present as part of the future.

The working process that creates a poetic image painting is similar to the automatism I use to develop line drawings, in that although the technical application and practical materials differ (i.e., oil paint vs. ink), the state of mind which allows the work to flow from the psyche is the same.

Most paintings of Poetic Imagery simply *arrive*. There is no active search for subject matter. The images happen rather than manifest by direct intent. The more I let go of control, the more readily images present themselves.

At some point during the execution of a piece I usually recognize a definite theme emerging. It is then that supportive elements may find their way on to the canvas. While they do not always occur, these subsequent ideas are conscious enhancements. As lesser components of the synthesis, they allow the greater spontaneous essence of the work to remain intact.

Within all of us there is a level of our unconscious which contains personal memories, ideas, desires, and experiences, which correspond to our individual egos and personae.

In another deeper level of the psyche there is a transpersonal realm which Carl Jung called "the collective unconscious," a realm of transcendental mythology where the collective motifs of the entire human race are housed. Gods, demons, villains and heros portrayed throughout the world's mythologies exist in the depths of all of us. Together these levels of the psyche provide the fountainhead for Poetic Imagery.

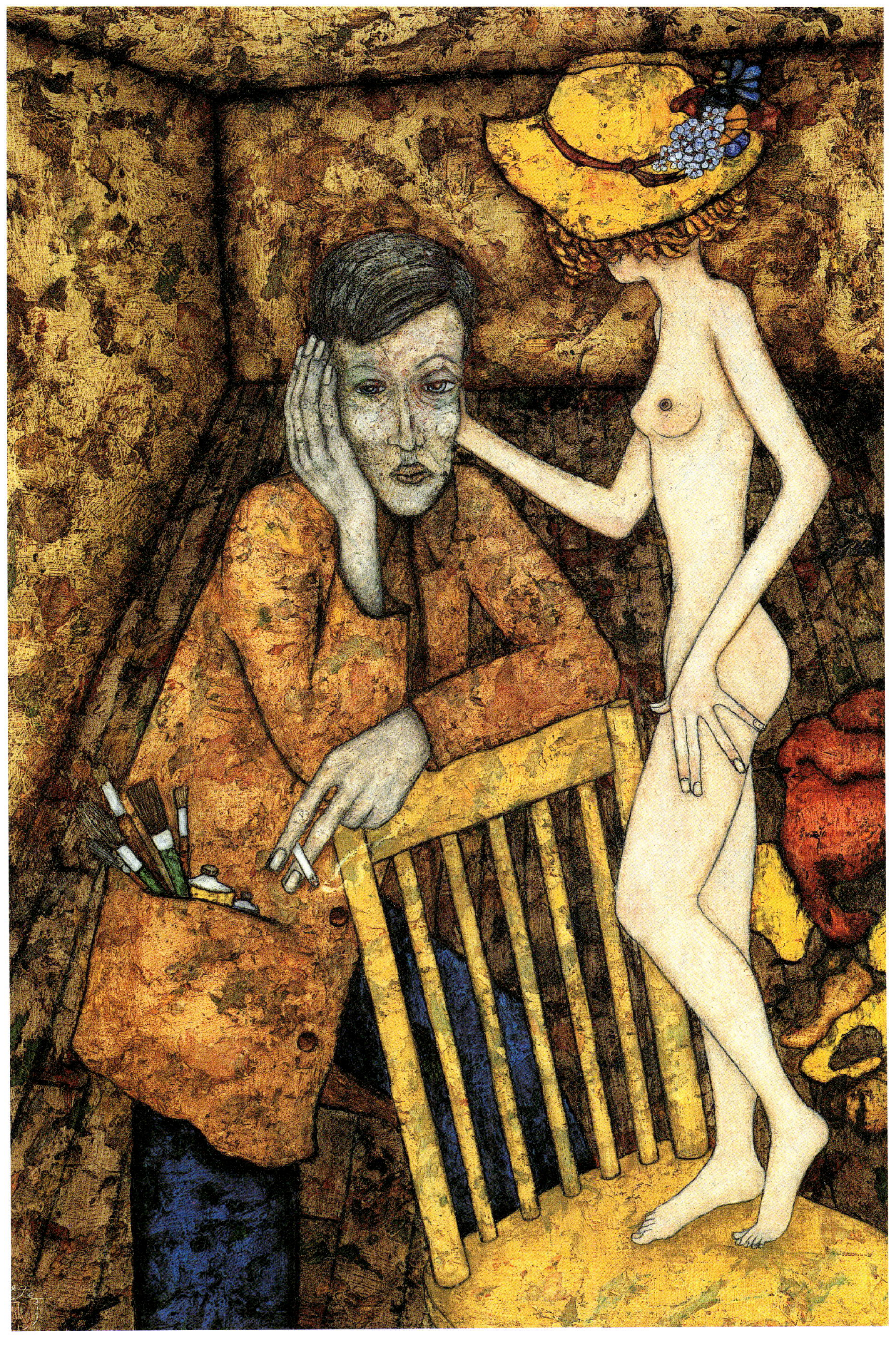

Contre-Coeur Oil 36" x 24" 1993

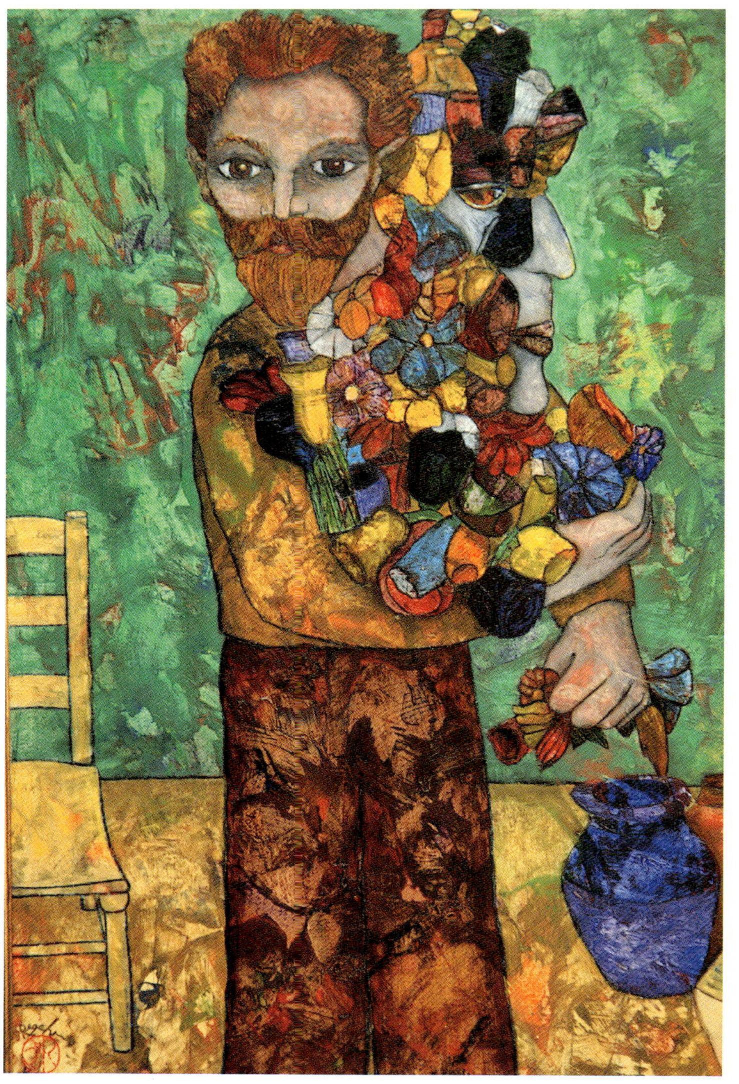

The Gift OIL 23" x 17" 1992

The Stone Prince a.k.a. *Dark Warrior* (see page 179), is a good example of work which has drawn contributions from both levels and combined them into one painting. Bearing in mind that my interpretations of my work are subjective, the main subject could be viewed as a questing hero or a fairy tale prince from the realm of transpersonal myth. But the same symbolic elements which convey that also reveal truths that are directly connected to my ego and persona, and establish the piece as a self-portrait.

As examples of paintings where the levels have separately influenced imagery, *The Blind Cockatrice* (see page 151), serves to demonstrate work of purely mythic origins, while *Contre-Coeur* (see page 95), is a creation from the ego/persona.

Artists from Heronymous Bosch to Picasso have been creating unconscious imagery, mythic or otherwise, as transmitted through their individual enlightened states since the beginning of time. So the foundation of Poetic Imagery is not a novel discovery—its exploration is *new* for me alone. But images conjured from the core of one's inner self bear the very essence of "me-ness" and it is that which gives Poetic Imagery an identity and a definite *look*.

It could be described as a type of Expressionism because it disregards conventional ideas of realism and proportion. It permits emotion to help form shape and color. What is commonly viewed as distortion often conveys important expositions of truth.

The powerful connection to the subconscious suggests that it is related to Surrealism, which has traditionally claimed *to liberate the riches of the unconscious through the primacy of dream*. The notion that a dream can be transposed directly from the unconscious (sleeping) mind to the canvas, bypassing the conscious awareness of the artist, does not work in practice—some degree of control is simply unavoidable.

Poetic Imagery does not exclude remembered dreams from the sleeping state as a resource. They are as much a part of the repertoire as any other occurence, but during its initial stages and in its purest form, the methodology requires suspension of *controlled* artistic vision.

In order to freely tap the inner psyche for subject matter, the working state of mind (while partially disengaged from outer stimuli) is still one that is very much awake. The artistic senses focus on the *subliminal* through a gentle, trance-like condition of *ultra*-awareness, whereby existing images, heretofore unrecognized, become clarified.

In cases where conscious subjectivity has *stepped in* to provide supplementary metaphors, symbolism intensifies and the paintings become allegorical; even more so when complemented by verse or prose.

Poetic Imagery is still evolving. It cannot be completely described by comparing it to past and existing movements of art, or merely as an amalgam of their ideas. Although this may help to categorize it, the influence of other styles is dubious, and descriptive rhetoric inevitably falls short of capturing what is unique about it. Ultimately, it is only through continued work and growth that Poetic Imagery will truly define itself.

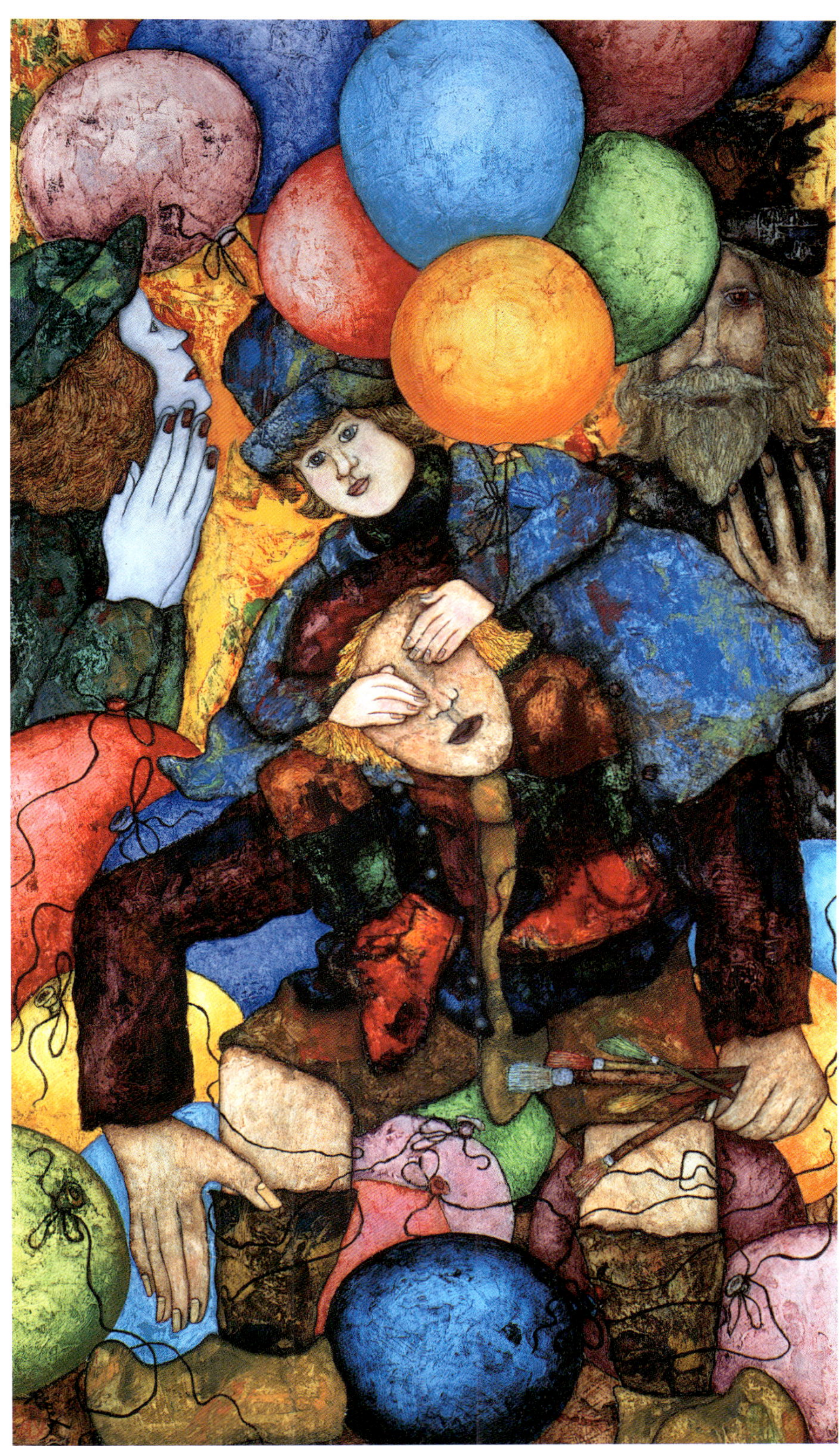

The Quest for the Blue Balloon OIL 36" x 20" 1992

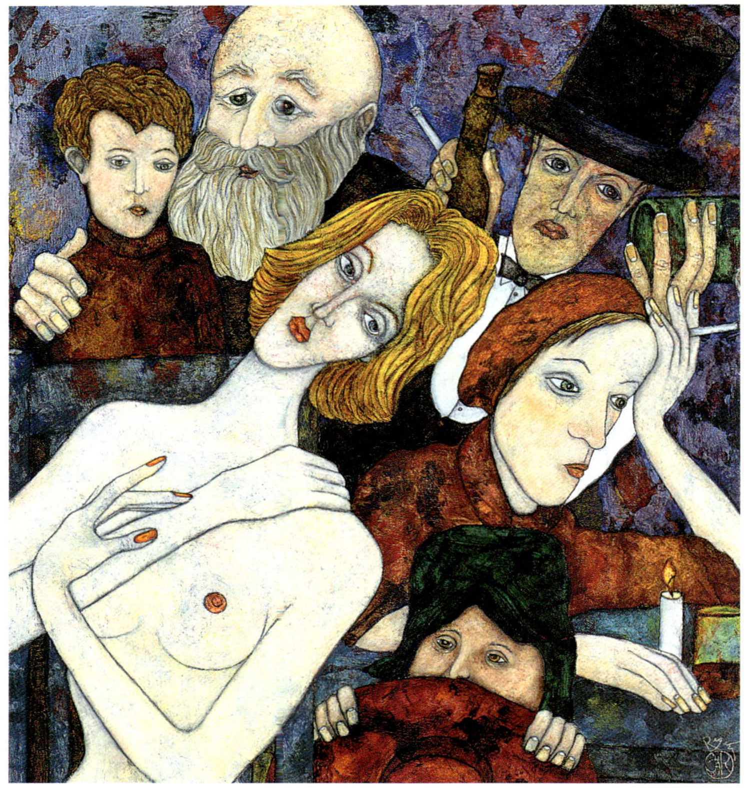

Werther's Legacy OIL 22" x 20" 1993

The Eavesdropper OIL 18½" x 18" 1992

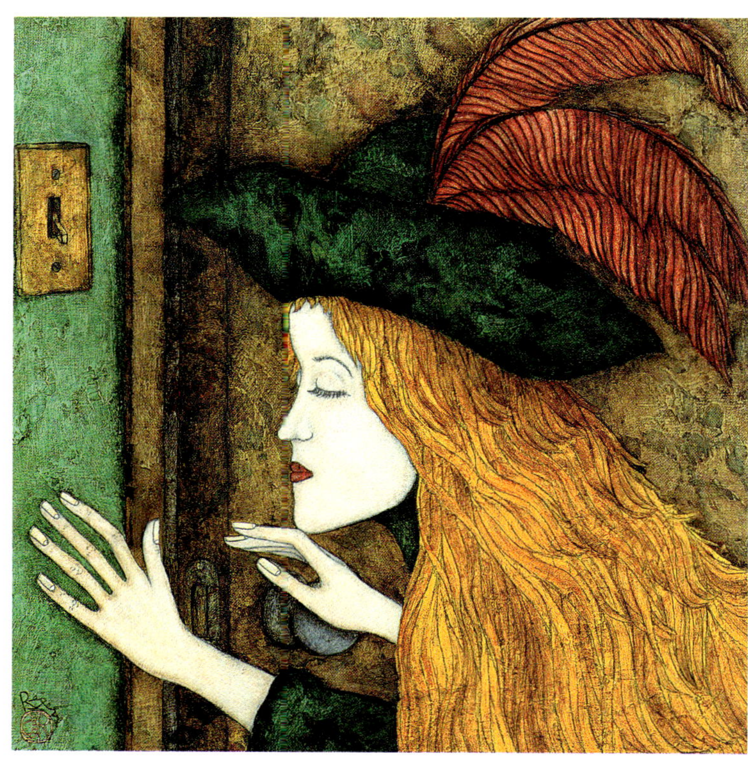

The interpretation of any work is entirely subjective. The diversity and complexity of meanings are endless, so I encourage people to set aside my perceptions of my work in order to explore their own.

I am certain that all artists can relate to the most common inquiry posed by innocent viewers contemplating a piece of challenging work. Inevitably it is one's crowning glory — a creation destined to set the world on fire for its mind-boggling insight and inspired genius.

What does it mean?

A legitimate question, if a humbling one, which can only be fully answered by the work itself. A verbal or literal attempt at illumination is likely to confuse, oversimplify or miss the mark altogether. If the artist could better express feeling or awareness through the language of words, then surely this would have occurred; the creation of the work as a visual piece would not have been necessary.

While it is true that certain themes may be better suited to mediums other than the ones currently hosting them, there are numerous artists who have mixed and matched mediums in order to enhance ideas or to progress their thematic explorations—offering a greater scope of imagery and diversity of insight. William Blake and Michelangelo expressed themselves with passion and clarity of vision in both literature and the visual arts.

This book became a singular work, through combining the written word and visual images.

The Muses speak as nine from one,
That when all is said and done,
The fruitful voice,
Through word and vision,
Bids art from each must come.

—DR

Dress-Up
Oil 27" x 22" 1992

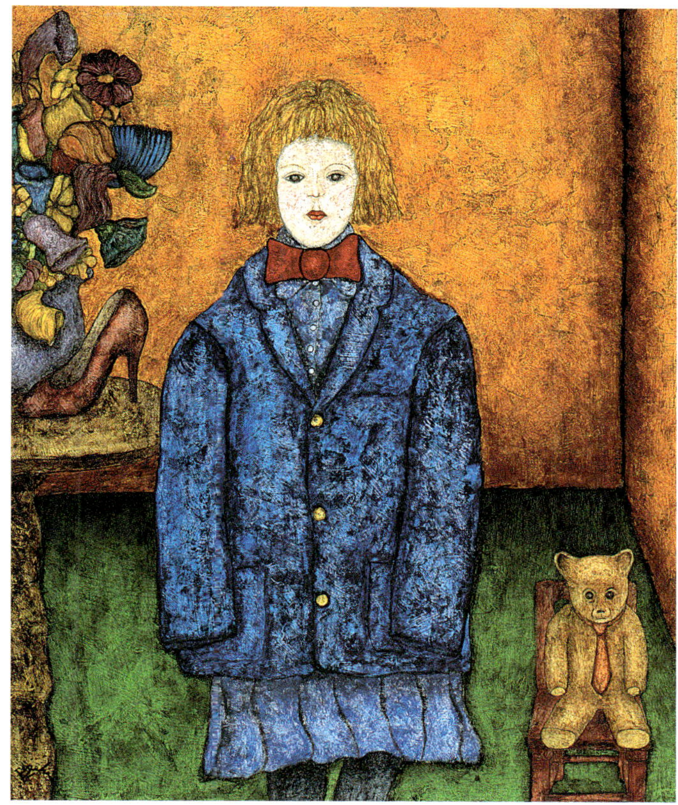

Poetic Imagery had its public debut as a one-man show entitled, "The Poetic Image," which opened at The Goldfield Galleries in Los Angeles on March 18, 1992. The paintings were displayed with accompanying verse, as are many of the plates in this volume.

Like brothers and sisters, the creations that are my poetry, prose and paintings grow up as very different individuals, but they still share similar characteristics of their common womb. Along with many shared or unshared outside influences, they also stimulate and influence one another.

Within the misty domain of Poetic Imagery, there is no law that says each painting must have a corresponding piece of literature. Rather, there are concepts which cross over the mediums, established through creations that are thematically complete within themselves.

I might have produced a poem in 1985 that bears a recognizable link to a painting executed in 1992. During the years between, natural changes and additions (growth) transform the concepts to reveal entirely different literal and visual images. I write and paint numerous works and I find it difficult to keep track of everything, so I keep files and store photographs of all my endeavors. I am often pleasantly surprised to uncover parallels of thought spanning ten years or more. The metaphors have changed and the mediums may be different, but the works can still share the trace of an idea.

Painting is silent poetry,
and poetry is painting that speaks.
—Simonides
6th-5th century, B.C.

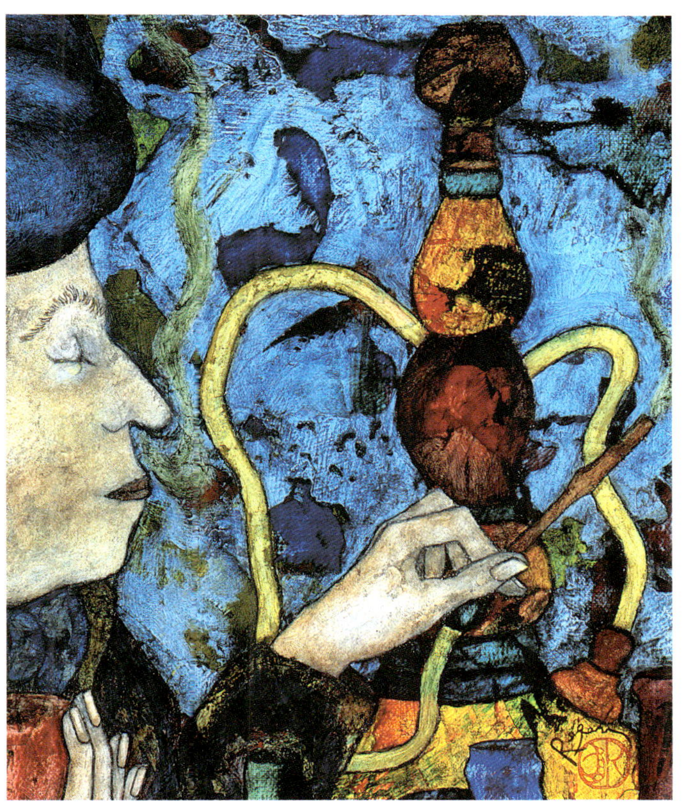

Opium Smoke
Oil 12" x 9" 1992

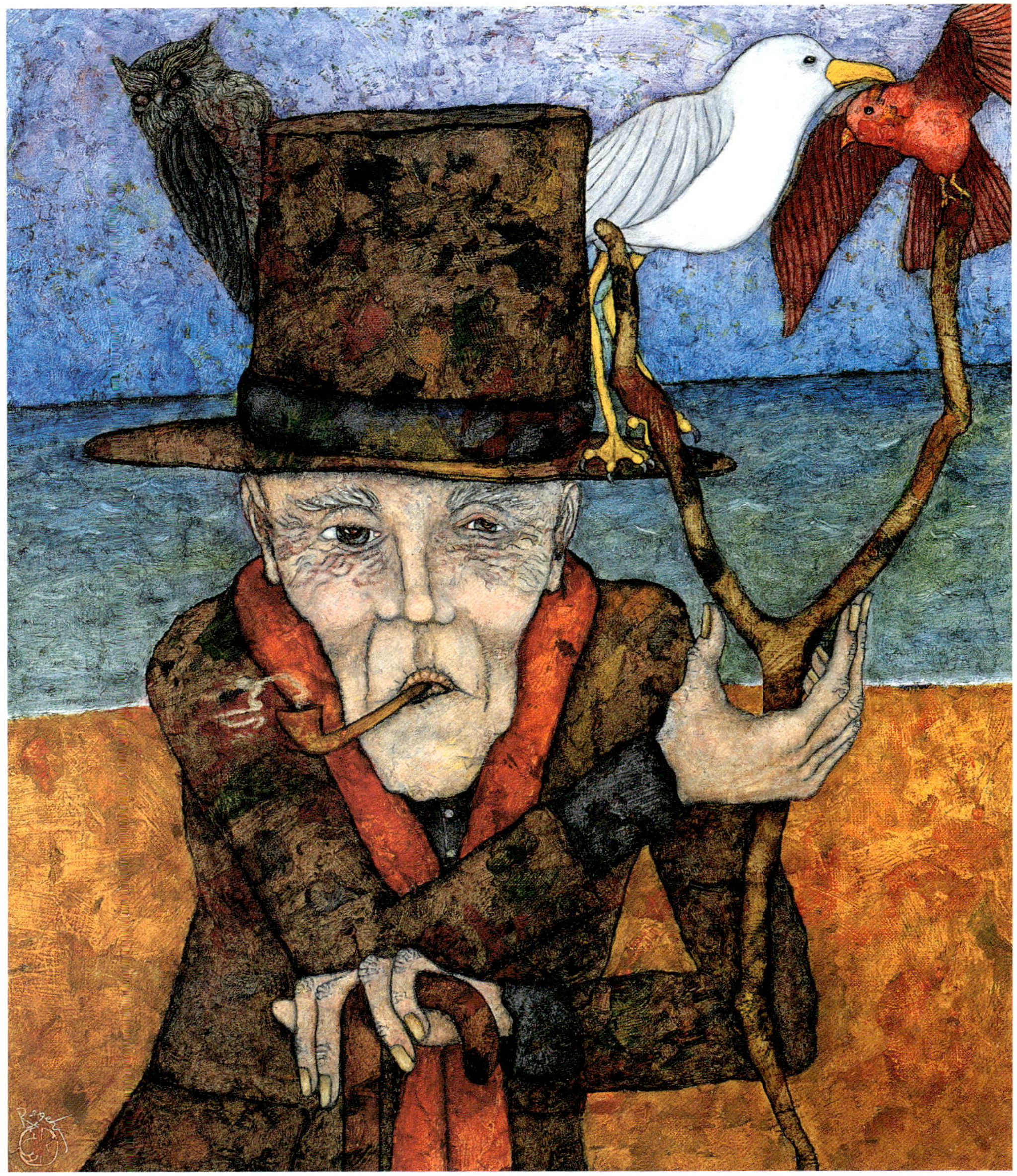

The Dowser OIL 24" x 20" 1992

There is relief and elation with the knowledge that creativity, being its own time clock, imposes no rules, least of all one forcing me to produce only paintings with poems. My paintings do not serve as mere illustrations of my written work, nor do the written pieces exist only to describe my paintings. Each piece stands complete within itself as a separate work, quite independent of any other. The mediums are placed in close proximity to celebrate acknowledgment of their common womb and to suggest that there is an all-encompassing, ever-unfolding grand theme.

I am the sum of my art
Therein lies my life
—DR

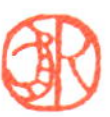

PLATES

THE EMBRACE

Poetic Imagery Series

Oil 30" x 25" 1992

The Spring of Miss Plummer

Child,
I wish to speak to you of flowers.
I watched her collect them every morning,
Small strong hands
Stuffing freshness into pots
Twisting juicy stems to a new will.
Arranging cuts the fingers and stains the nails,
A small price for harmony.
Each bouquet is a signature,
Worshipped in a corner
Faced to the sea
Paraded in crystal
The amphorae embrace
Reflected in casket ebony.
I cocked my head at the row of urns,
Giant mouths made of clay
Halfway through swallowing
Sap and stalk digested out of sight
Compost below the water-line
Microbes in the dregs.
Child,
I am speaking to you of flowers.
This sacrifice is beauty enshrined,
A pause, held living
Yet already dead.

—DR

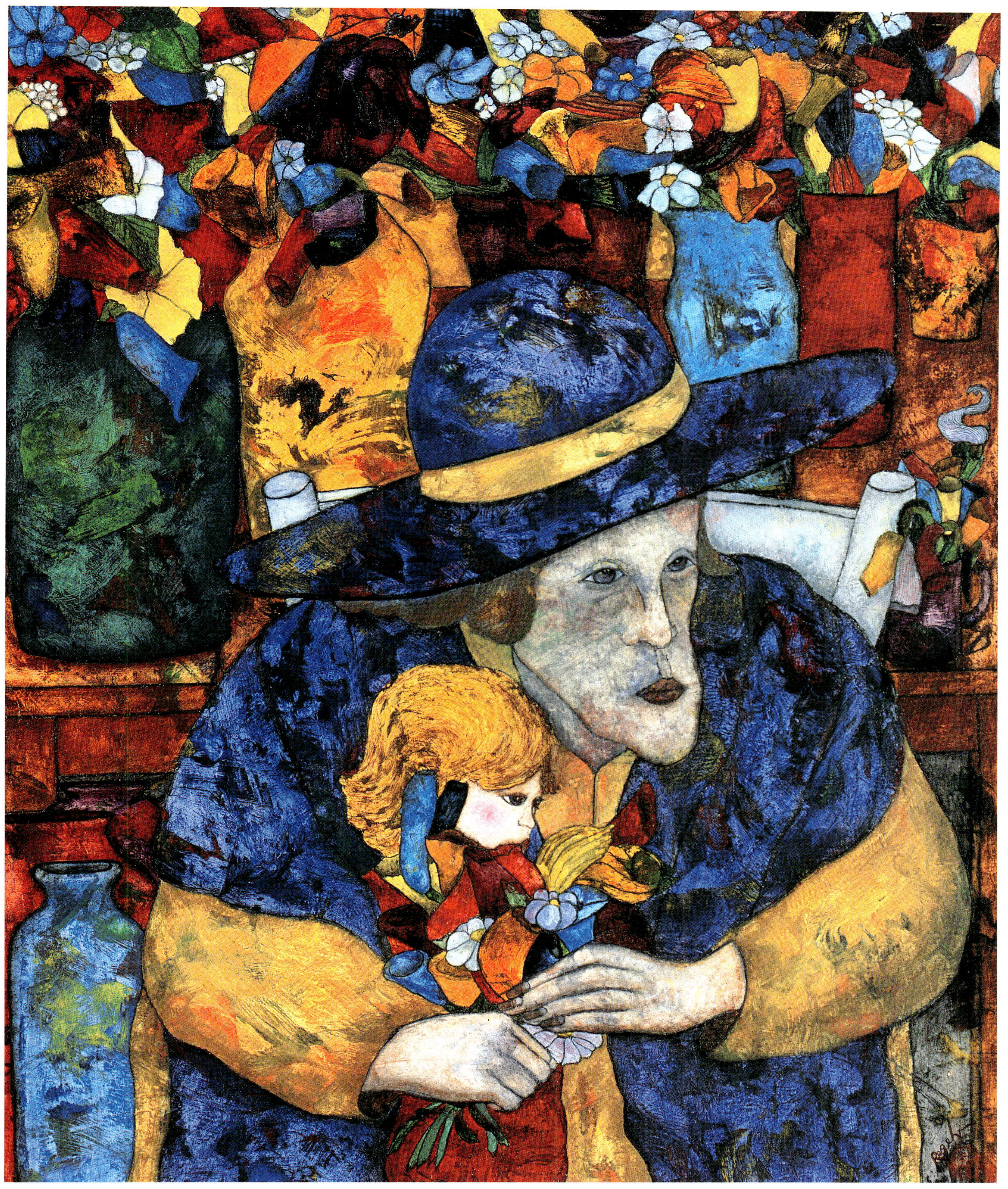

HARMONY

Poetic Imagery Series

Oil 36" x 24" 1991

Killer's Harmony

Her cello plays a moody sky concerto
That should blend hues of grey and lavender,
It is ochre he hears,
The yellowing of newspaper in the sun.

She taps her foot (a colorless percussion),
For him the room swarms with dark purple dots,
The speckled noise of string-pearls drawn tight.

From a balcony,
She should echo forth sapphire into the morning,
It is burnt sienna
Muffled behind filthy windows and curtains he hears,
Stripes of burgundy along the kitchen floor.

Even though the pastoral sighs for gold from a cornfield
Her melody is a hidden stain
Whistling bright red squares from a box in the cellar.

Her hill dance is pitched in bruised green streaks
Instead of tan and umber,
The puckered sound from dried fruit.

All the orange notes are paralyzed within
Chords of deafening white,
Buried behind black hills in the sunset,
He listens . . .

The cello empties
Pale sepia down a long corridor.
Her spectrum flutters,
Indigo and shadows shrink the volume,
He hears the naked color of ghosts,
Music,
Invisible to his human ear.

—DR

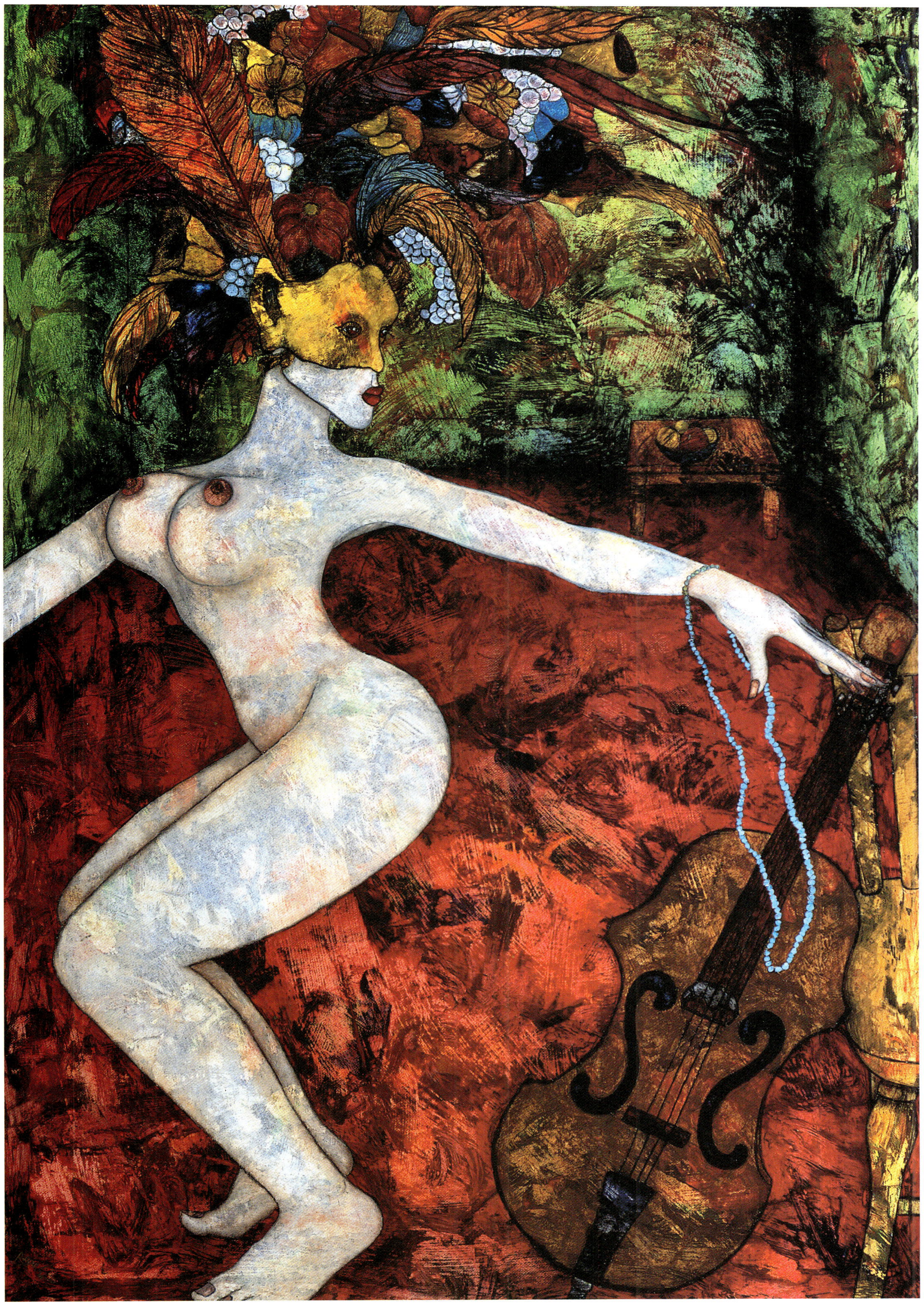

LION FAT

Poetic Imagery Series

Oil 17½" x 21¾" 1992

Lion Fat

A cinder blossoms. Air syphons piquant
The ache is fed.
Near a dark wall
A row of broken backs remain unturned.
On the far side lingers
A naked starving thing.

Empty steeples of glass chime a filtered knell
Where pipermen play bitter flutes for spicecake.
To stained lips the stoker blows his kiss
And dancing eyes become midgeflys sealed in amber.
Behind the veil and the jaded fan
Old deaf Lion breathes fat.
Plumes slink, indigo sleek over hot China green
Black Pleasure creeps along a cool serpent's spine
Into the muse of sleepers.
The purring lung draws water from the Styx . . .

There, ten thousand tired brands
Sank hissing from the wharf.
There, were baptized
A thousand staring heads
Severed, from the voice that gloats.

And here,
Contrition limps on blushing coals
Fawning bed to bed for a nest
On the outer edge of peacock dreams.
Here no joss jars jostle,
The veil fans no robust breeze.
As ashes are becalmed in stain
So ambered eyes, never stray
The fat Lion's gaze.

—DR

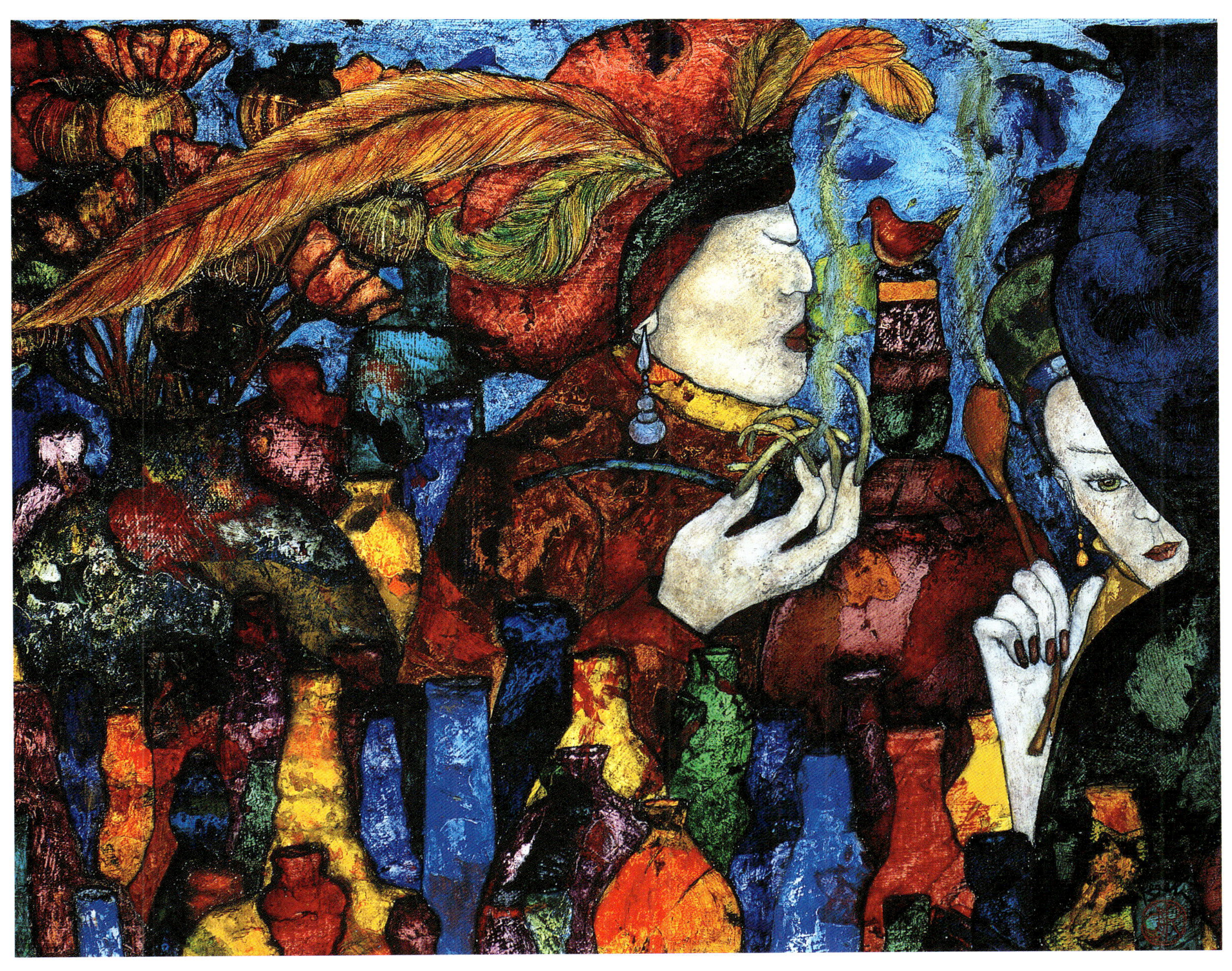

CATHERINE SLEEPING

Oil 17" x 17" 1979

Catherine. The name means purity. Catherine's last name, Campion, is the appellation for a genus of small, red flowers.

True to her namesake, Catherine Campion loves all things pure (and less pure it would seem, as she puts up with me). In addition to being an accomplished writer, she is an avid gardener—her home is always full of fresh flowers and greenery.

Her taste in paintings runs from the early 18th century floral still lifes of Jan van Huysum through the garden landscapes of the Impressionists, to the Pre-Raphaelites, and Fairy paintings of Rackham, Dulac, and the Robinson brothers.

There is an ethereal essence in Catherine. She possesses an aura of tenderness and vitality, which is complemented by her deep intelligence and boundless generosity.

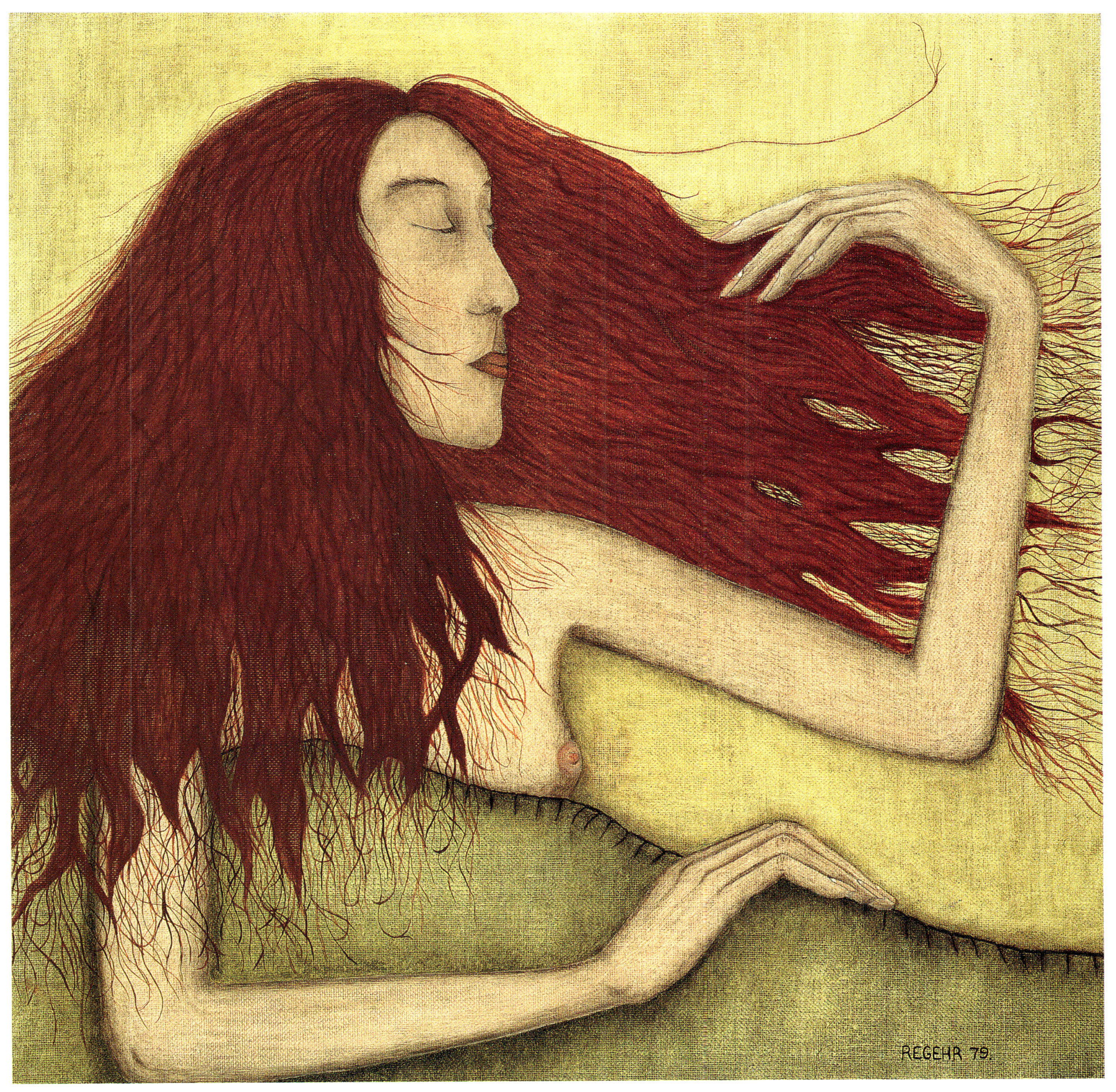
REGEHR 79.

OPUS 68

Oil 36" x 20" 1977

I once lived in a wonderful old apartment building in Toronto that was home to an accumulation of painters, musicians, writers, dancers, and a variety of bizarre characters.

Lawrence, an actor who lived three doors down from me, was fond of conducting music in the privacy of his second floor flat. No sound could be heard through the front window of his living room, which overlooked the entrance to the building, but Lawrence could often be seen from the street, flailing his arms about like a disjointed puppet, his face a contorted mask of intense concentration.

Just as I was entering the building one day, he happened to glance up from his frenzied rapture, and we caught each other's look. He paused, staring at me with his arms locked in mid-gesture. It was like looking briefly into the calm eye of a hurricane, for in the next instant, he exploded into movement with even greater passion than before.

It was only a moment, but the pose he struck stayed with me. The number 17, on the front of his shirt, was paralleled in the configuration of his arms.

As I passed his door on the way to my flat, I could hear the faint strains of a favorite piece of music, Beethoven's Symphony No. 6, Opus 68, Fourth Movement, *Tempest and Storm*.

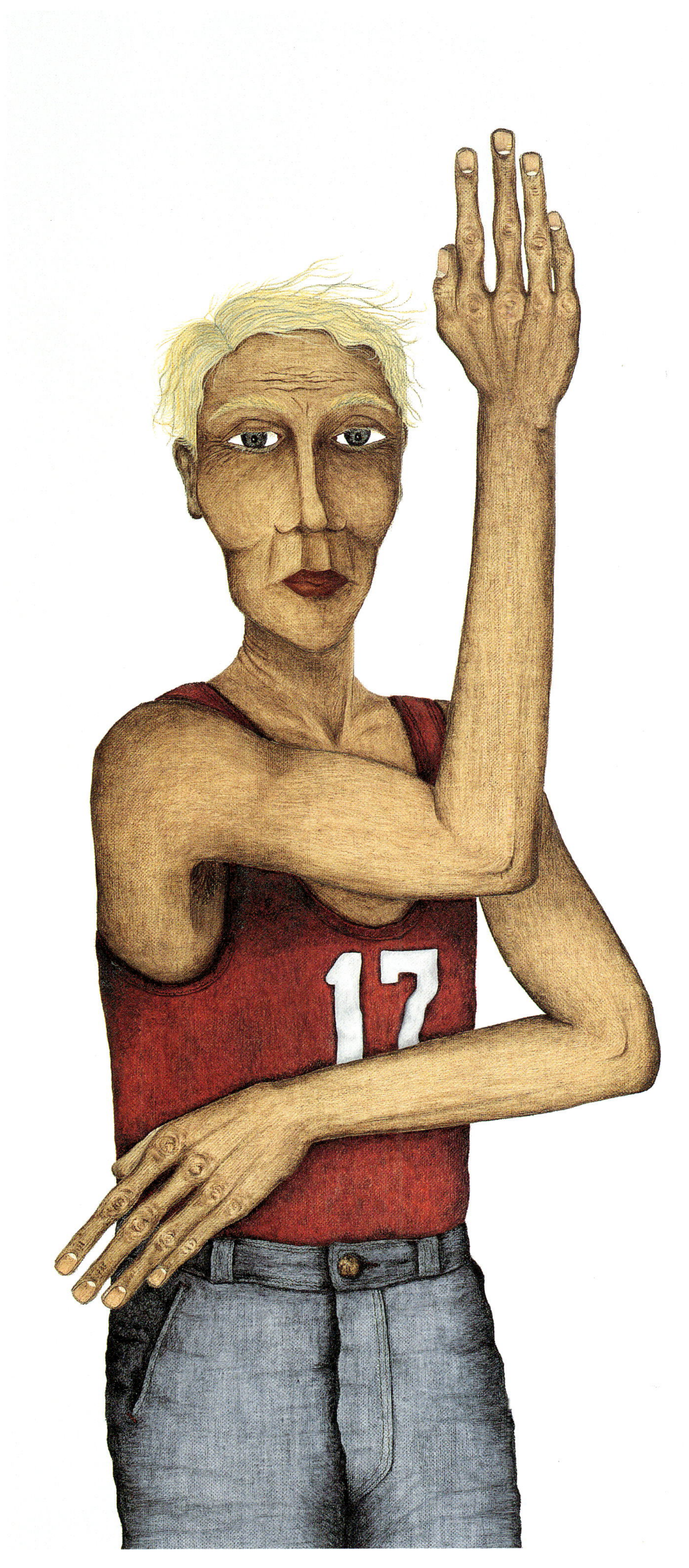
17

NIGHT MARE, NIGHT FIGHT OR GHOST HORSE

Oil 24" x 36" 1973

I enjoy the melodrama of this early canvas. It is perhaps one of the best examples of how my youthful struggles manifested themselves in paint. I particularly like the stormy background and the flashes of silver in the horses' manes.

Like many children, I suffered from nightmares and fought with imaginary demons and ghosts, so there is an intended pun in the title, *Night Mare, Night Fight*. I originally also called the painting *Ghost Horse*.

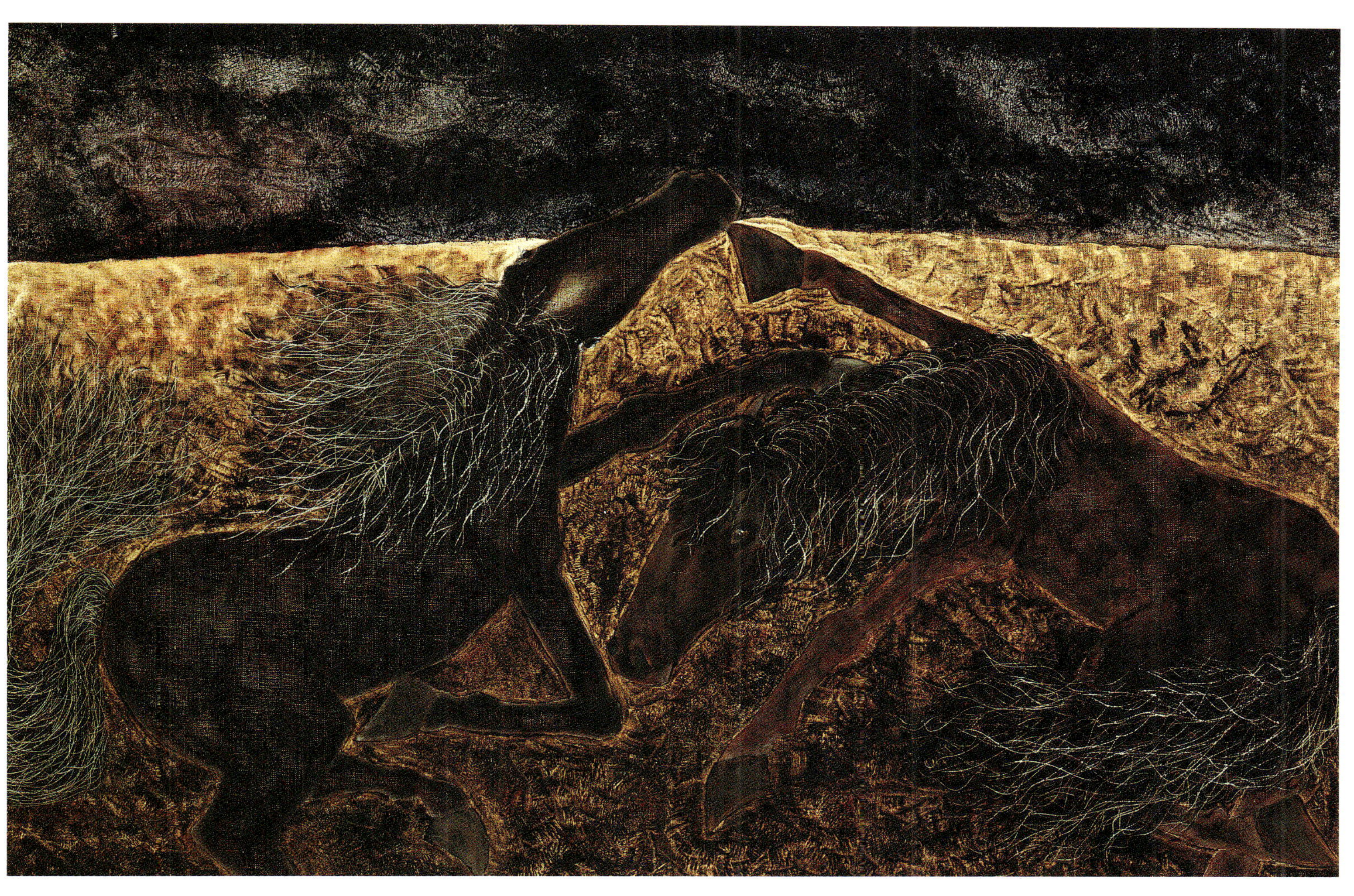

AUTUMN CHILDREN

Poetic Imagery Series

Oil 22" x 18" 1992

Basement Boy

In the autumn, a child
Is stored below the seasons with tubers and broken fruit.
A child of the long fall, ripening
At the bottom of cellar stairs. A subterranean child,
Still, as a row of preserved fruit,
Listening, forehead pounding on a damp concrete wall
As the sound of one hand,
Claps on

Only the ringing in his ears,
Hear the ringing in his ears,
Falling forward through the years,
Just a ringing in his ears.
His love for the ringing in his ears.

His love is asleep in the tears on the wall

Hung from a hook with the headless cat
Alive in the shed in a dead birch withe
Coiled in iron on top of the stove
Stirred in the wood of the kitchen spoon
Stamped in the soul of a shoe
Glowing at the tip of a cigarette butt
Tangled in hair in the brush by the bed
Wrapped in a snake around the hips
Swung in the arc of a skipping rope
Flown away on the sweep of a broom

The autumn child knows the sound of one hand clapping

Close up in the cracks of the floor,
In the closet, that waits
At the bottom of the bumpmedown stairs

To the stare from the corner
With a look in its eye
As blind as a baseball bat

To the ringing in his ears,
Hear the ringing in his ears,
Falling down through the years,
Just a ringing in his ears.
His love for the ringing in his ears.

—DR

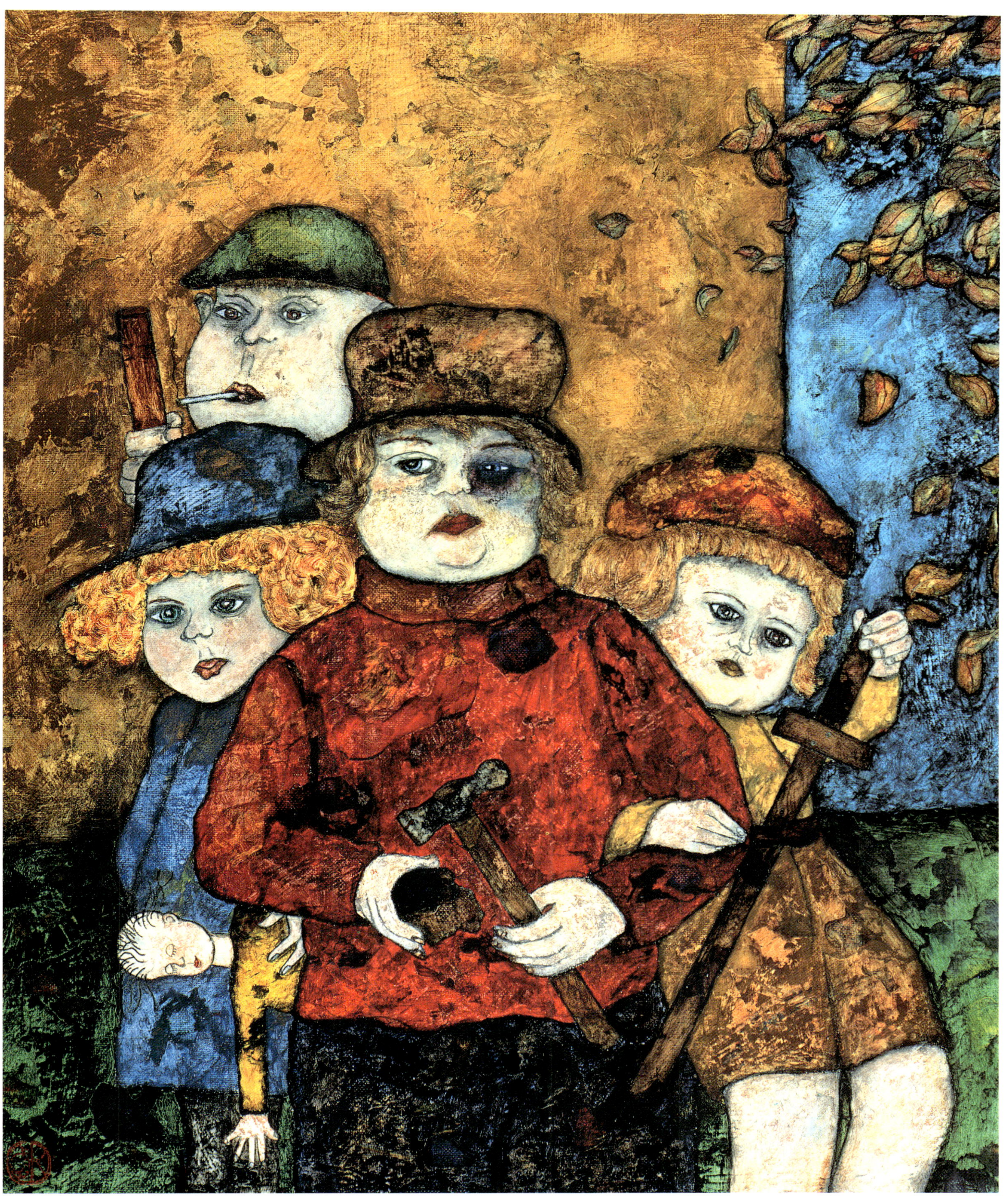

GRANDPA REGEHR—THE CHIEF

Watercolor 18" x 12" 1975-1976

Although I was grateful not to see too much of him during my childhood, Grandfather Regehr nonetheless made a strong contribution towards the attitudes I later developed regarding organized religion. Over the years, he grew in my imagination and memory as a dark, forbidding figure.

A deeply religious Mennonite, he spent most of his hard working life on the farm in Canada, having emigrated from Russia with his family of nine in 1926.

I have long since reconciled my differences with organized religion and the fact that Grandpa Regehr was only one symbol of many to embody my theological ills. But, as small children, my sister Gillian and I were terrified of him. His very presence emanated an aura of fierce, unbending judiciousness. There was no doubt in his mind that as "little heathens" we were destined for the fires of hell. I seem to remember that he almost never smiled.

I thought the clasps on his suspenders, which had the word "police" stamped on them, were special badges. Because he had two, one on each elastic, I was convinced that he had to be the Chief of Police for God and that he would arrest me in the name of the Holy Father if I did anything wrong. I was always very careful to stay out of his way.

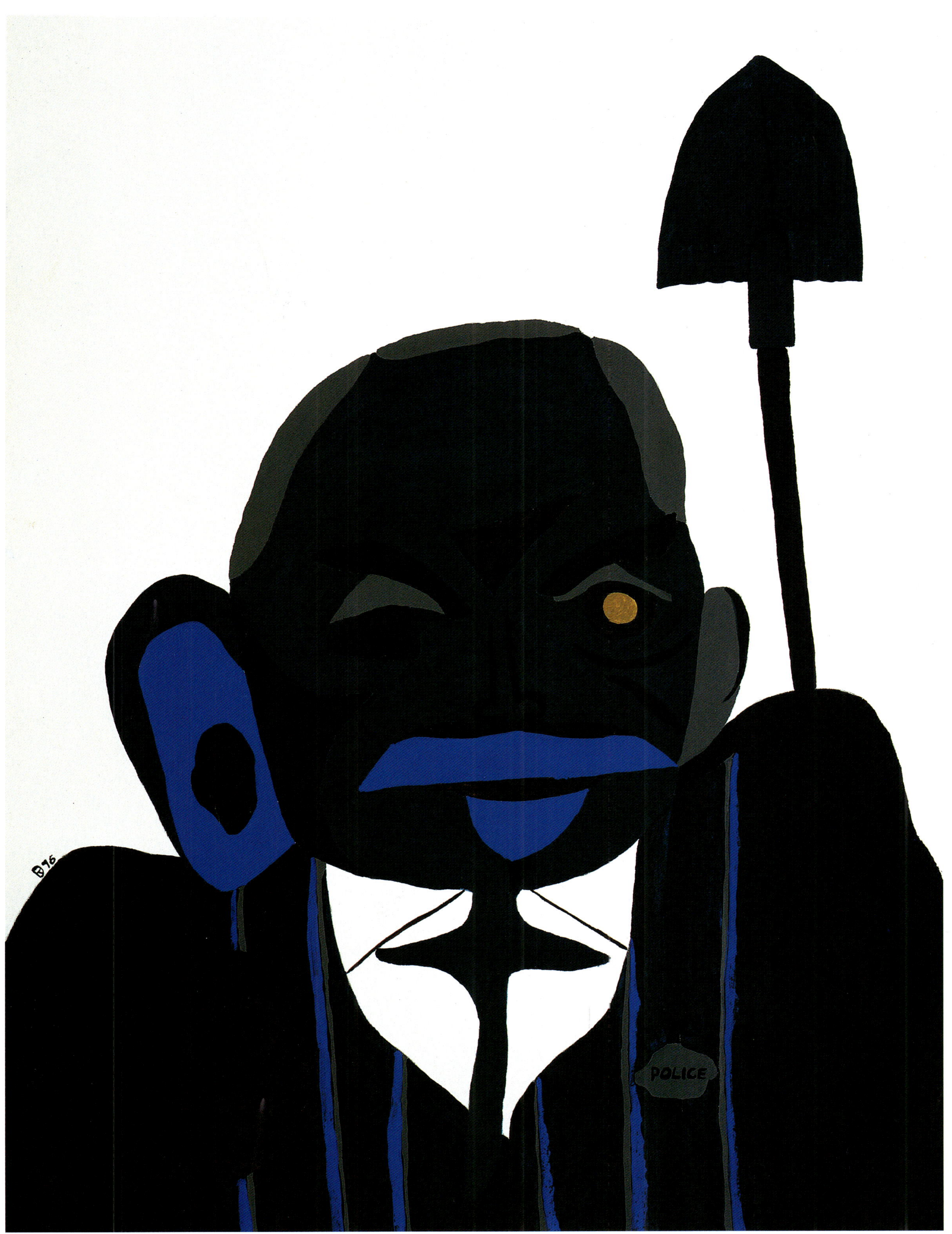
POLICE

MENNONITE

Colored Pencil   24" x 18"   1989

Mennonite thought is characterized by a strong separation between religion and the rest of the world. Severe persecution in the 16th century forced the sect to develop a strategy of withdrawal from society in order to survive. Consequently, most Mennonite (and Amish) groups maintain themselves externally by withdrawal and internally by rigorous discipline.

Mennonites dress in dark clothes of concealment; however, they are well-known for their brilliantly colored quilts. Being famous for their art form rather defeats the philosophy of their lifestyle, and yet the quilts are analogous to the theologic veil that covers their entire world.

The colored materials they use to make the quilts are so rich and vibrant they appear to be on the verge of bursting their seams, but they are locked within strict geometric patterns. Likewise, the lives of the people are contained within the rigid outlines of their faith.

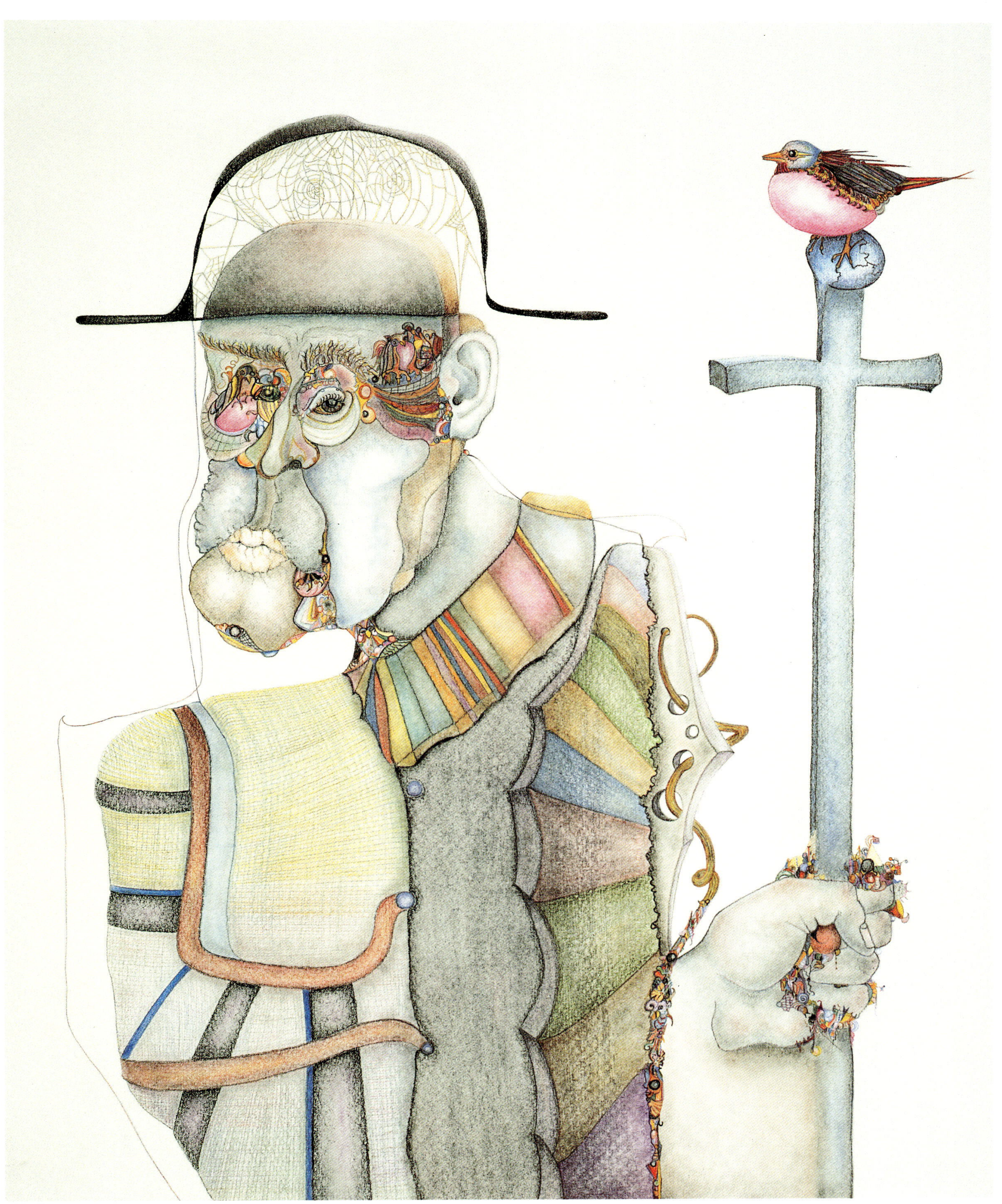

THE MENNONITE

Poetic Imagery Series
Oil 36" x 24" 1992

Mennonite

Dawn.
Under the weight of Jesus' cross
I am numb and very small again.
Like an owl it has swooped down during the night
And pinned my arms to sleep.

I awaken smothered in down and Sunday sunlight.
The cross becomes a shadow cast by quartered window panes above.
I roll over on torn patchwork,
The shadow-cross remains where I once was,
The bed becomes a grave.

I kiss the sleeping Dutch girl,
I kiss her silence, her damp places, her feathered kind places.
I thank her for hiding me inside her.

Last night she wanted to be my mother.
I wanted to be her god.
We trespassed there to escape our wanting prayers
And the Mennonites.

They were scratching at the windows again,
Their singing too loud, their staring too close.
We danced naked before the glass
And fell drunk upon a quilt of fire,
The patterns tore and color burst from prison.

The Dutch girl wakes and asks if I love her. I lie.
On my knees again I make love to her back.
She leaves to sing hymns with her real father's choir.

I rise to walk in the forest.
The Mennonites follow because it is Sunday.
They flit in dark clothing behind beautiful trees.
By congregation they shelter from soaring meadows
And the dangers of wildflowers.

It is Sunday and they watch, too closely.
They whittle the stake. They heat the brand.
They wait to sew the cotton quilt.
It is Sunday, and they wait
To capture color as it sleeps.

—DR

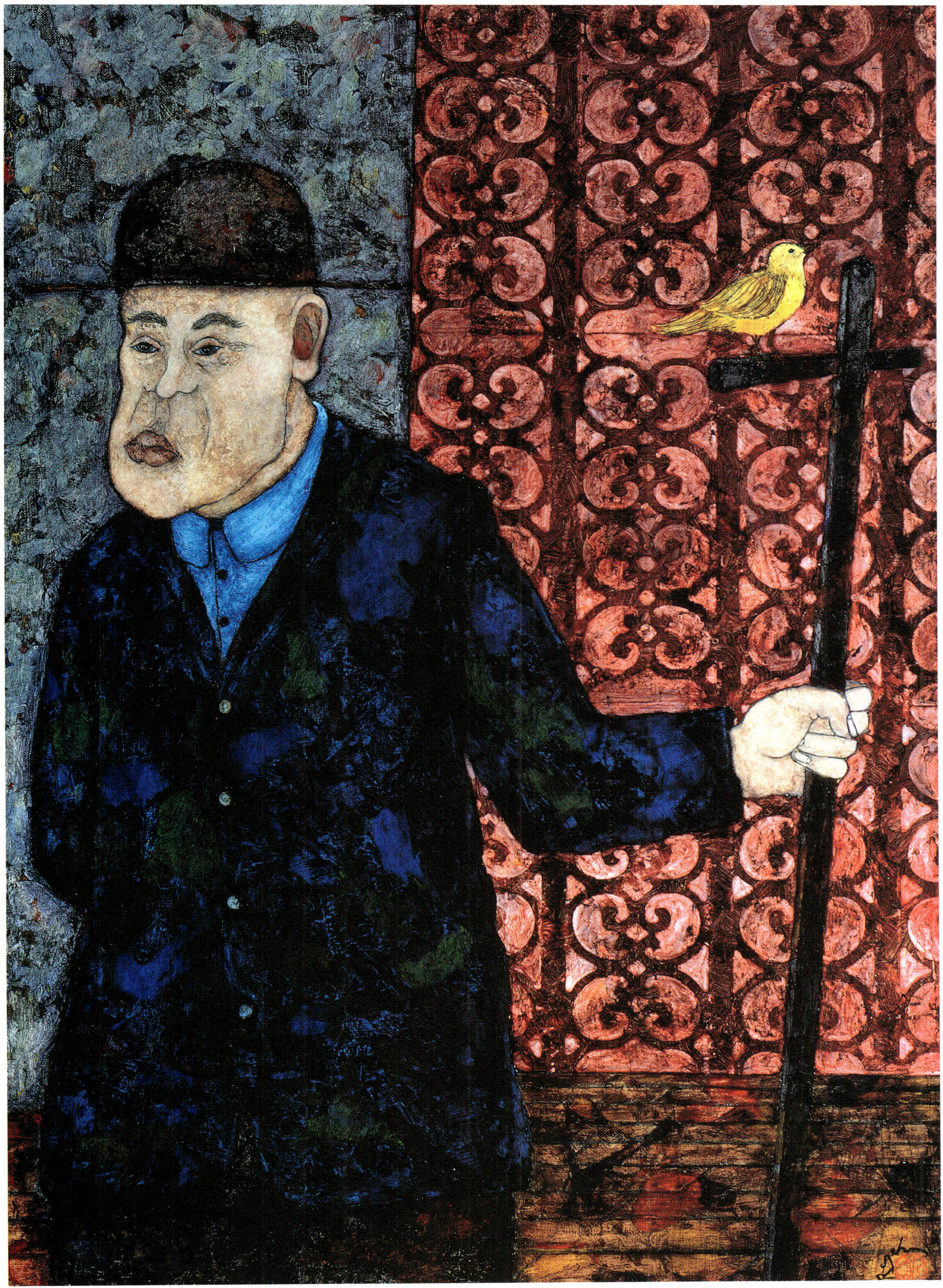

THE FEAR OF BEAUTY

Poetic Imagery Series
Oil 40" x 30" 1991

Nevus

As a boy he lured insects and hummingbirds

It wept from a leak in his skull
Red dapple and royal purple
Descended under the flesh
As patient as creeping lava

He never played
Except Mahler for the flowers,
Precisely and alone

Above the brow it paused, brimming
Spirals spread in careful patterns
Choosing to breach at the temples
Erasing half his face

Behind the mask he hid himself
Behind the shadows of his mother's garden
He concealed both

The veil shed a tear like a small dark slug
It eased and drifted
Sloe trails of filament followed across his throat
Quietly vanishing under his collar

Later he learned Masquerade

Unseen, it swelled with fever
Rapids danced and split his hide
Power cascaded

He raped the scarecrow several times
Left sticky footprints along the picket fence

It poured from his hands over his boots flaming
Down the garden path,
Mother's glories and rows of strawberries
Swept out of the gate and into the forest,
Where the weeds grow natural
As nothing strange with the wild of things.

—DR

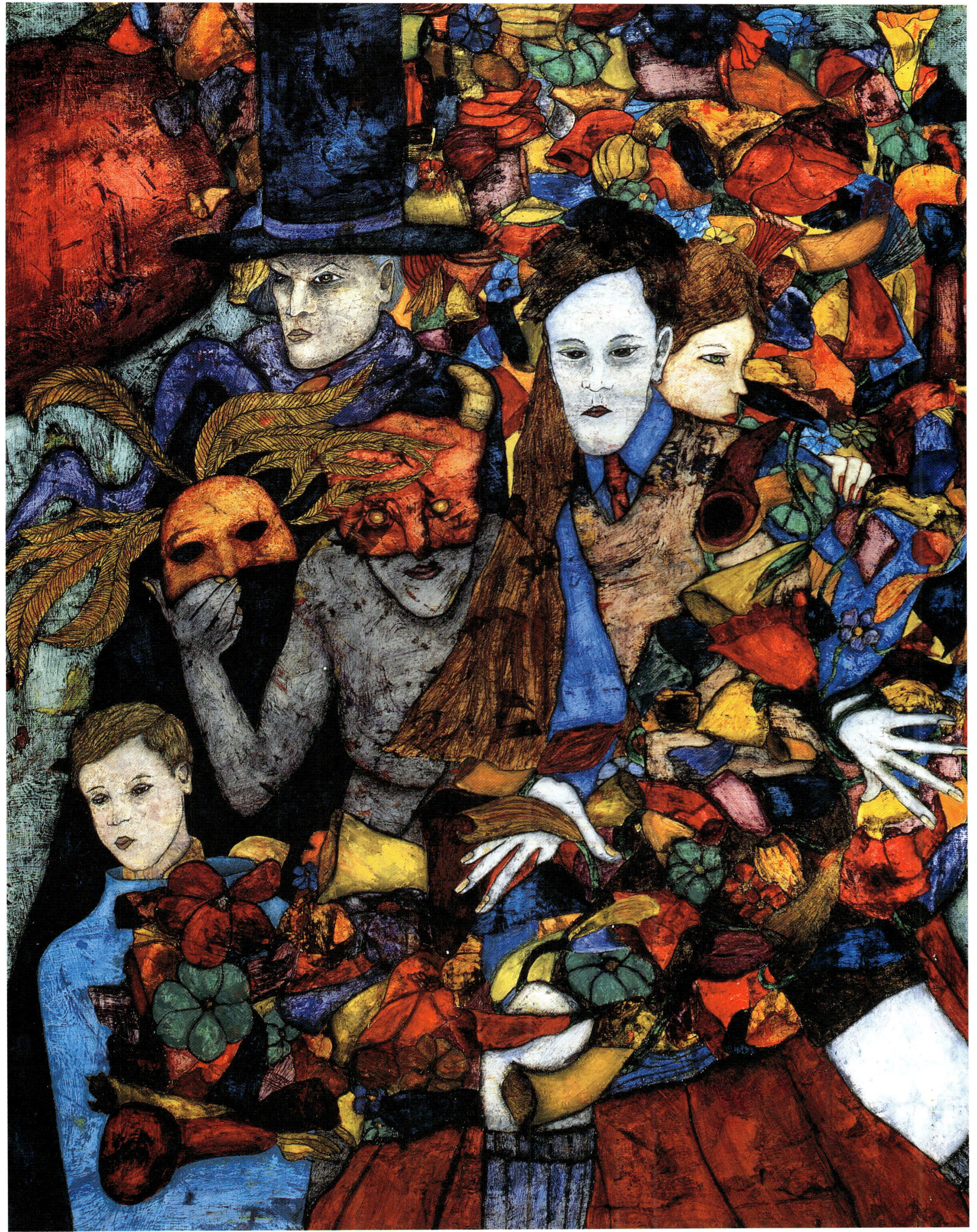

HER WINDOW

Poetic Imagery Series

Oil 26¼" x 20¼" 1991

Her Window

In a cool window
Your strangled lovers hang
From brightly colored threads.

From where I wait
Paralysis has set my eyes
To you,
Swinging on a scented white porch,
Fanning an apologetic breeze
For what cannot be helped . . .
The drug, your rape,
My lover's death by spite.

You lean into the window
As though it is a hearth,
But you are the heat,
I can see your breath condense
Upon my view, your world,
My reflection.
The dry dancing men sway and rattle,
Harmony from strings
So quick and bright and small,
The smallness is overwhelming.

The mobile fades.
Your pattern is less felt . . .
I cannot breach the purpose.
Without anchor or window,
I float from the knowledge
That you will gather me,
To weave again.

—DR

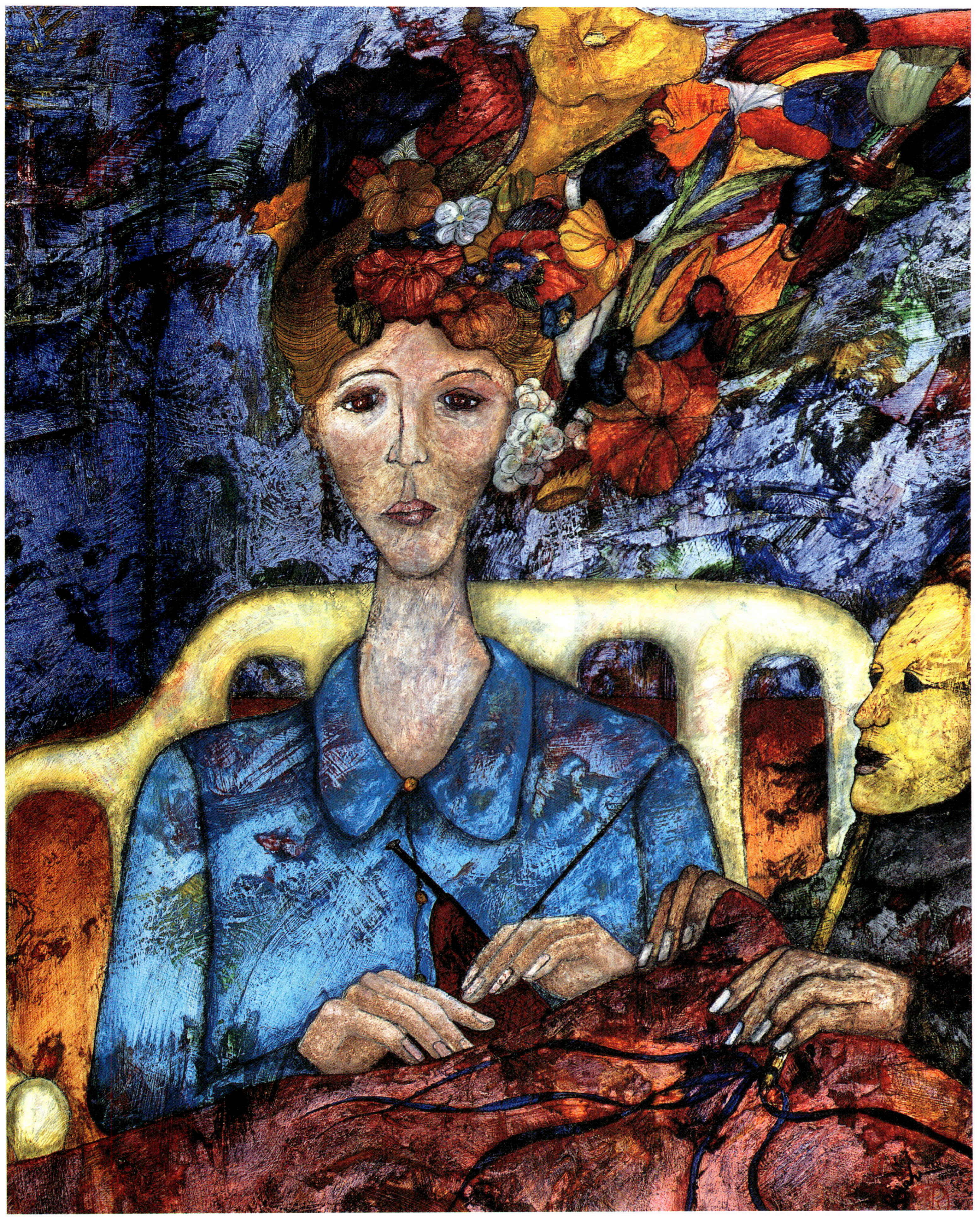

RUSE

Poetic Imagery Series
Oil 24"x18" 1993

Bestowment

Without a secret now,
you lie broken in a broken sleep,
and broken deeper in, your gift
that spills across this pale sheet,
your blessed broken gift, once only yours
now mine . . . a drying mess of red.
This carnage of romance, I would escape.

Quickly now,
chill feet into heartless boots
and I will ease away,
but as lifeless leather saps living flesh
I feel my heat still drawn in you,
I cannot uncuddle naked trust
and walk on limbs, cold-blooded.

Give me Salome's guillotine kiss
as sunderance equal to your own,
and send me stumbling senseless
of my touch, my thoughts, my self
removed from riven innocence . . .
your gift, your blessed broken gift
so red against your white.

The sacred bait of poetry
disguised a hollow voice with ruse,
and lured your deepest secret
to the shallows of base desire,
but your trust, too bountiful,
overwhelms this snare, as void . . .
it is impossible to steal a given gift.

Your gentle trap is merciless,
a guileless vice with velvet jaws
that gives, and gives, and gives
no quarter for false verity,
but holds your truth as mine . . .
I am forever caught, within
the deepest part of you.

—DR

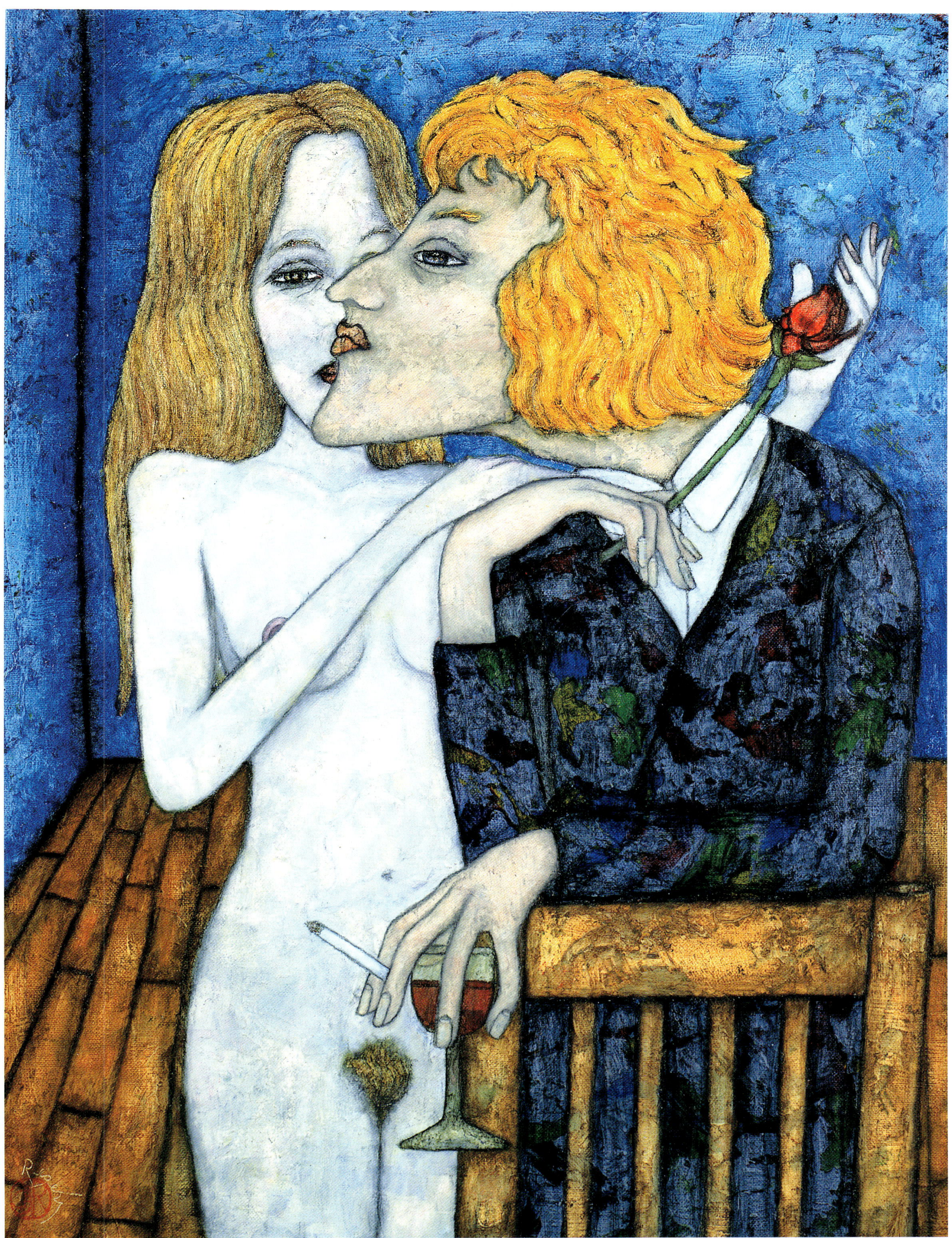

THE CRITIC

Poetic Imagery Series
Oil 16" x 14" 1992

No Blooms from Dogbane

You were chewing oleander again,
We could smell it in the streets
Steaming up from the sewer,
The breath of your parlor song.

And there you are in the corner again,
Leaning like a pigeon
On the edge of a broken stool
Waiting for the kick.

Your words, hung by the neck,
Crack my face in your mirror,
Curse at my life with your destiny,
Can only weep upon a page.

I cannot be strangled
By your suicide lines
Or slashed with the dullness of blackboard nails
That screech across my verse.

I have watched you lovingly
Shove those fingers down your throat,
And laugh with a shaddenfreude's hope,
That I would slip in the puke of your despair.

But the classroom I have left,
Is your barrelhouse,
Where the rafters, carved with unfinished scrawl,
Wait for your swaying shadow to make the news.

In back, rows of squatting dancers,
Read deeper meaning
Into your handwriting on a toilet wall,
But never drink your song

Of oleander,
Your sewer song, spiralling downward,
Flushed far from dancer's minds,
Unsung beneath the streets.

—DR

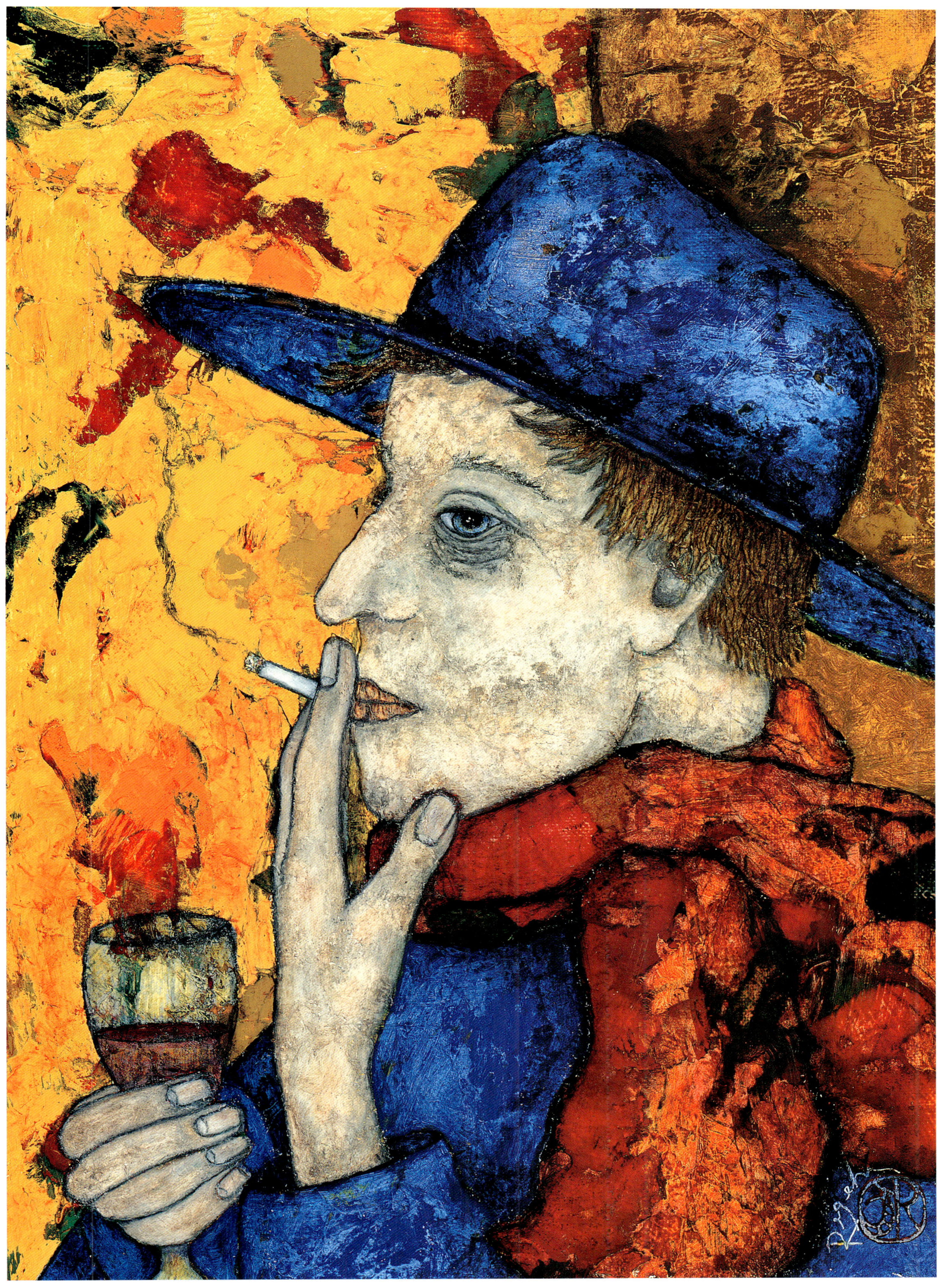

THE WAG BOY

Poetic Imagery Series

Oil 24" x 20" 1991

Actors are the only honest hypocrites.
—William Hazlitt, 1778-1830

The Real Robin Hood

Opening night I was drunk with you.

I wore a moustache under a slanted fedora,
I played your death mask with a slanted smile,
I sang the eulogy in a theatre of myth,
I faked you for an encore when the lights shone brighter,
I slipped the friction of your killing fame.

The morning after,
I stand distorted in the steam,
Almost naked before a naked shaving light.
I inspect for traces,
Wiping greasepaint clots from the corners of my eyes.

I release a blade upon my neck
To scrape over wincing contours,
Re-sculpting,
Dreamshaping the cartoon.

The wag boy (the real Robin Hood)
Peeks around the sweating "mirror mirror."
Twinkling, he places a finger beside his nose
And leaps (the hero)
Through the storm and mists,
Into the place behind my eyes!
To govern,
To rehearse,
To weather the day sitting
On the throne of other's fancies.

—DR

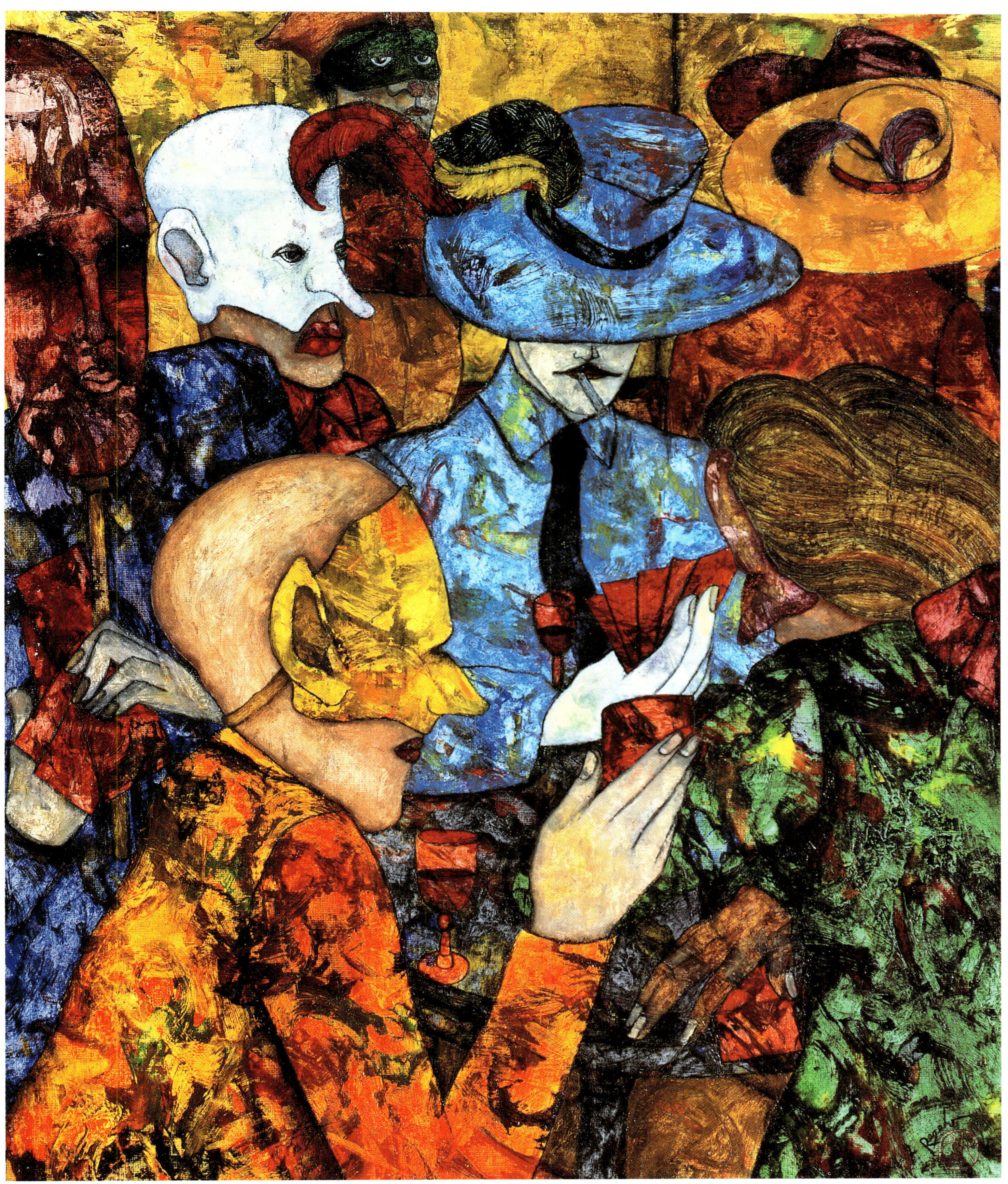

DOPPELGANGER

Poetic Imagery Series

Oil 19" x 8" 1992

A *doppelganger* is a wraith or apparition of a living person, as distinguished from a ghost.

In *The Double* by Dostoyevsky, a poor clerk, Golyadkin, driven to madness by poverty and unrequited love, beholds his own wraith, who succeeds in everything at which Golyadkin has failed. Finally the wraith succeeds in disposing of his original.

The figure in the upper right of the painting holds up two fingers. In contradiction, the resolute gentleman in the foreground holds up *only one*.

One self, or two?

The concept of the existence of a spirit double is an ancient and widespread belief. To meet one's wraith is a sign that one's death is imminent. I have no fear of meeting "me," but then my own *doppelganger* may be no more than a moral counterpart, or simply the darker side of my nature. Doubtless I shall know the truth one day, but not soon.

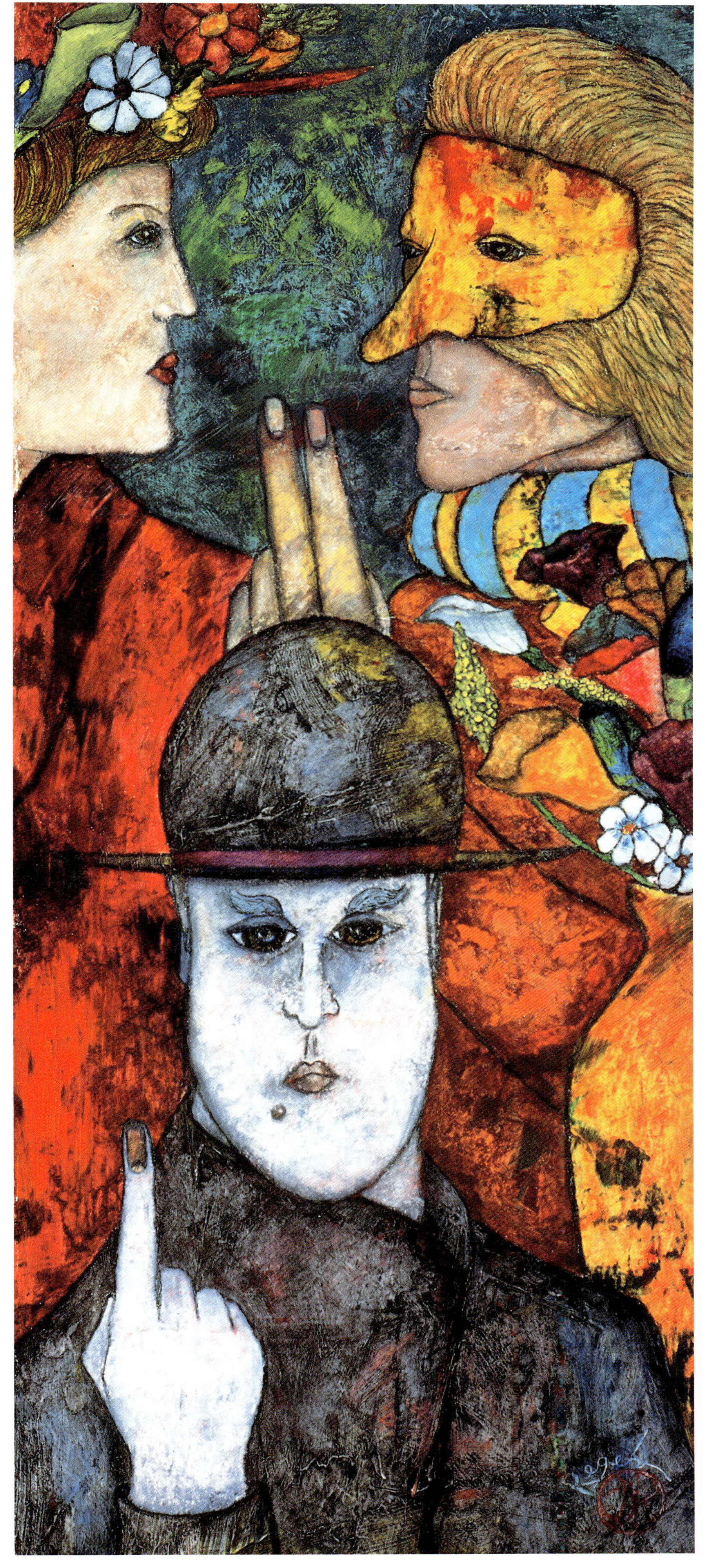

DOPPELGANGER

Colored Pencil 24" x 18" 1989

Doppelganger

We have never been alone,
The room is always swarming with cocktail faces.

I sense a flicker near the window
And I know that you have arrived.
I turn my head in that direction . . .
Nothing.
But now the crowd has a rift from floor to ceiling,
It jags up through the hostess,
Her face is an off-set mask.

The air twitches again,
I snap my head around in time to see . . .
Familiar walls (mismatched now)
And strangers laughing to the off-beat.

I search inside the atmosphere for a blur,
An outline,
Any vagueness in the lonely spaces between invited guests.

Then your silent breath
Singes my neck with nine-tails,
Burning is here,
I reach behind me . . .
Gone.
Your arm slides over my back like a hair-shirt
And I leap for the nearest reflection . . .

It is a woman's crystal eyes.
She thinks I am in love with her
But she only hears my stare talking.
It is you, I cannot capture.

I always play the stoic for you.
Grinning too hard on days of masquerade,
Waving like a fool with an empty glass.

I hide in front of,
You caper behind.
You leave and arrive with my confidence and shame.
You peek and fade, self-righteous
Amongst the living crowd of Do's and Don't's.

Step away
Step around
See me
See you
Know you
Talk to me

alone.

—DR

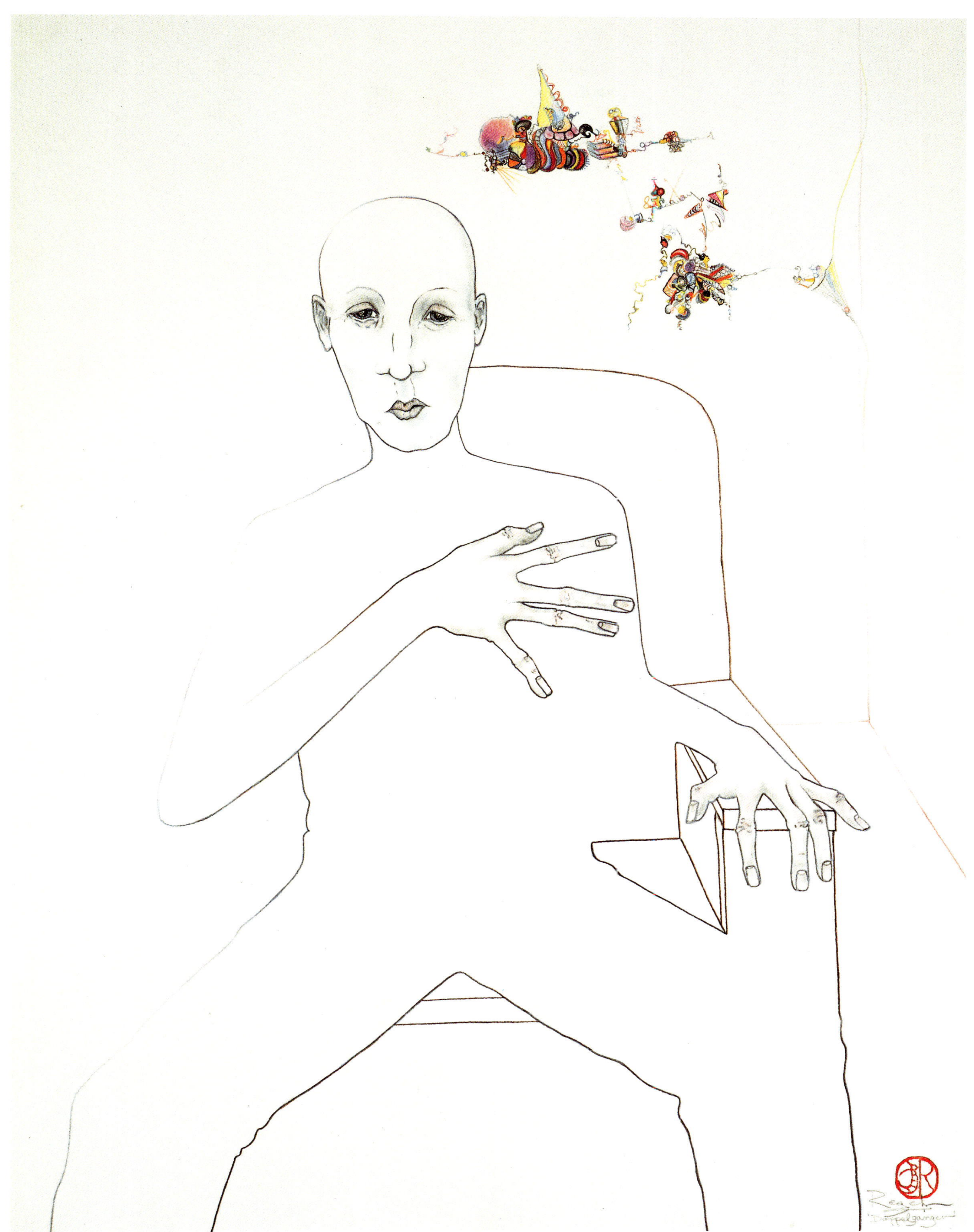
'Doppelganger'

THE NAKED ELF

Poetic Imagery Series
Oil 36" x 24" 1992

Happily Ever After

In my woodcutter's cottage, the door
That leads to fable is locked without a key.
Once upon a time the door fell ajar,
My calloused palm was there to gentle it open.

The princess elf slept upon a floor of polished wood,
Her limbs like fallen saplings lay outspread.
Within her naked form
And in the boards beneath her, flowed remembrance
That we had spliced from a common bole.

The floor cracks widened,
Revealing vaginal patterns in the grains of wood.
And in the deepest corner of her royal flesh
My face appeared, androgynous,
Speaking with her ligneous lips
A language utterly unknown to me.

I am the woodsman, the conditioned foreigner,
Grown away from the orchard,
Grown male, grown petrified
As an axe of stone.
Acknowledged to hew and sew
Outside the fable door.

—DR

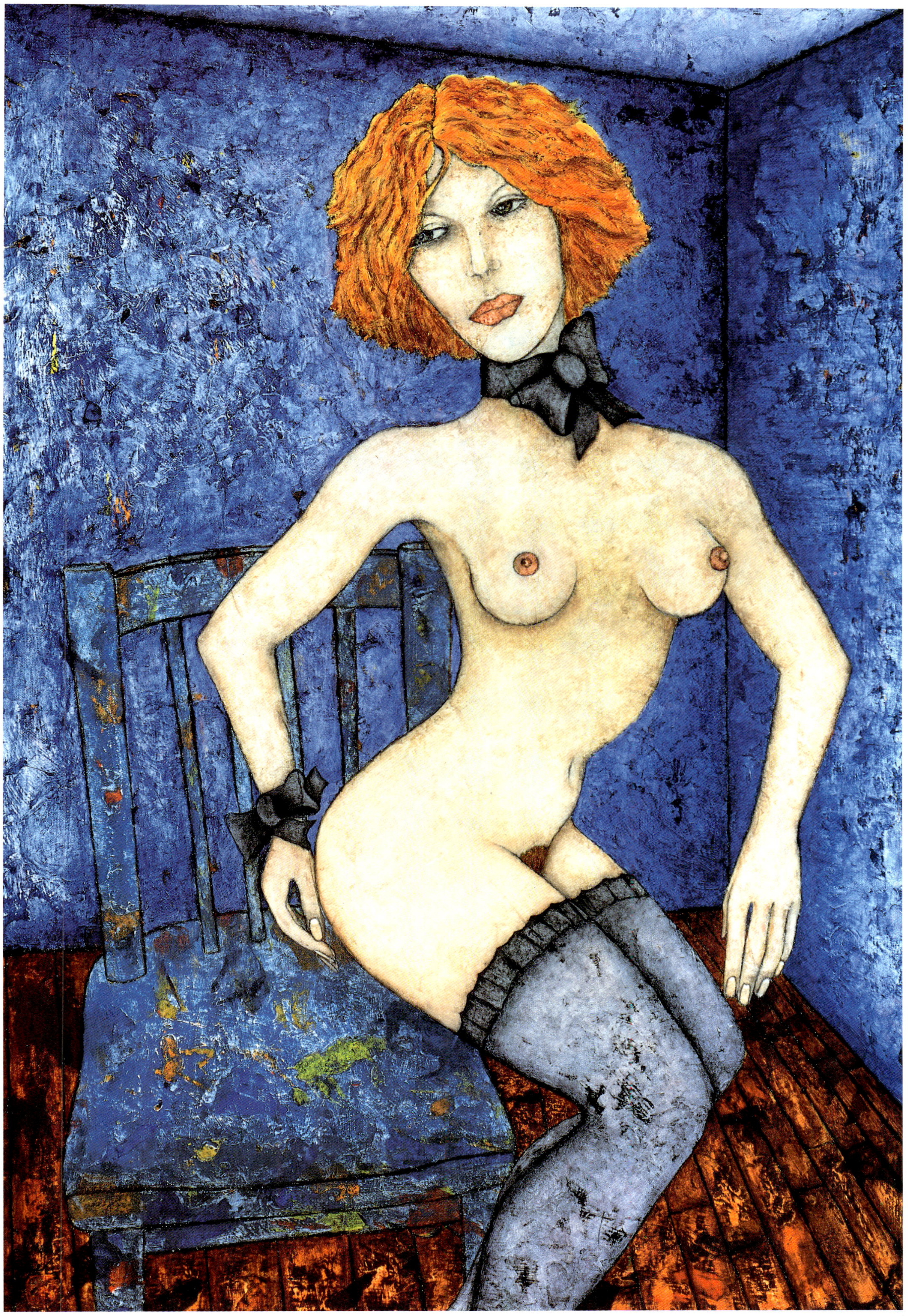

THE SCARLET HAT

Poetic Imagery Series

Oil 36" x 24" 1991

Under the Big Scarlet Hat

Even her voice was red.
It emptied her face when she spoke
She threw it
Down to her high heels like rain
Over her shoulder with rivers of hair
It spattered the walls left behind her
It spread down her breasts like crimson milk
It gathered in pools on her lap
It bled from her fingertips

I have stared at her voice
Within a flame at the mouth
I have seen it dance on high heels
I saw her voice at the picture window
I watched it drain from the scarlet hat
And reflect itself in the mirror
I see her voice overflowing in the hall
Where the echo is a darker red.

—DR

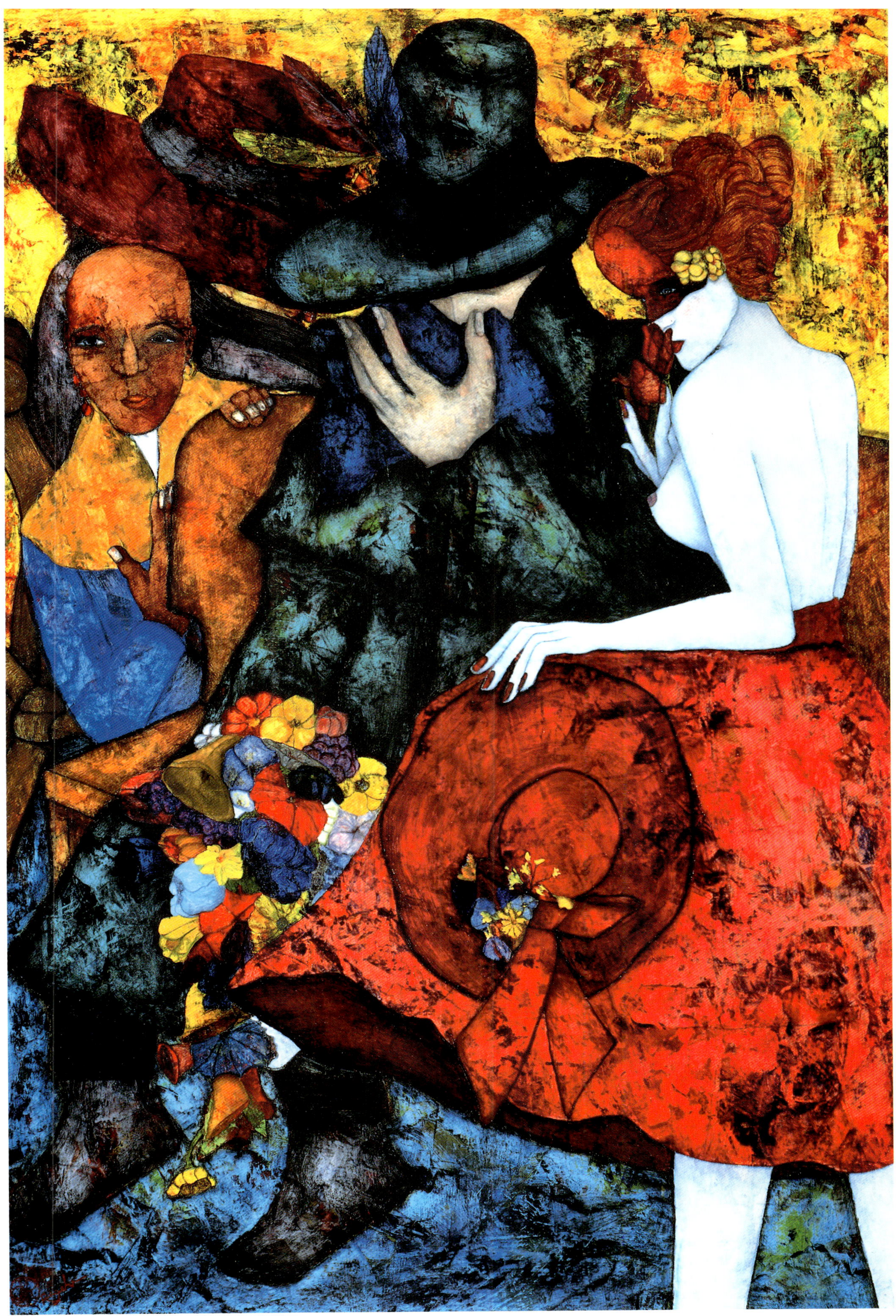

BELLWETHER VIRGIN

Poetic Imagery Series

Oil 24" x 20" 1993

For part of the spring and summer of 1983, I was in Italy filming *The Last Days of Pompeii.*

We stayed in the city of Pompeii for three weeks, using the ancient colosseum there as a backdrop for the crowd scenes and gladiator fights.

Catherine and I became good friends with a lovely little girl who was playing one of the flower maidens in the cheering section.

Every morning without fail, she would meet me at the hotel entrance and walk with me to the film set. She firmly believed that I would lose my way if she were not there to guide me.

Taking me by the hand, she would dutifully lead me through the winding ruins to the make-up trailer, chattering all the way about flowers, her family, and her dance classes. She had a voice like a songbird. I cherished her innocence.

She took it upon herself to strengthen my grasp of the Italian language. A nigh impossible task, but she was persistent and her lessons were a delightful exercise.

My correct grammar was always rewarded with a kiss on each cheek, but I was severely scolded for my numerous mistakes. She would place one hand on her small hip and sigh in mock despair, while ringing the small silver bell she wore around her neck. The number of times she rang the bell graded the measure of my errors. Twice for little mistakes and five or more times in vigorous succession for major transgressions. I would then have to follow her through singsong repetitions of the correct responses.

She was adorable and destined to grow up to become a great beauty. Heartbroken men would follow her like sheep to the ends of the earth, for she was indeed a bellwether.

Nearly ten years later, after completing an oil of a young female nude, I found occasion to use the word "bellwether" as part of the descriptive title for the work.

The girl in the painting is obviously not our young friend, but a virgin who is on the cusp of womanhood and entirely capable of leading men, hocks a'trembling, down the garden path of lust.

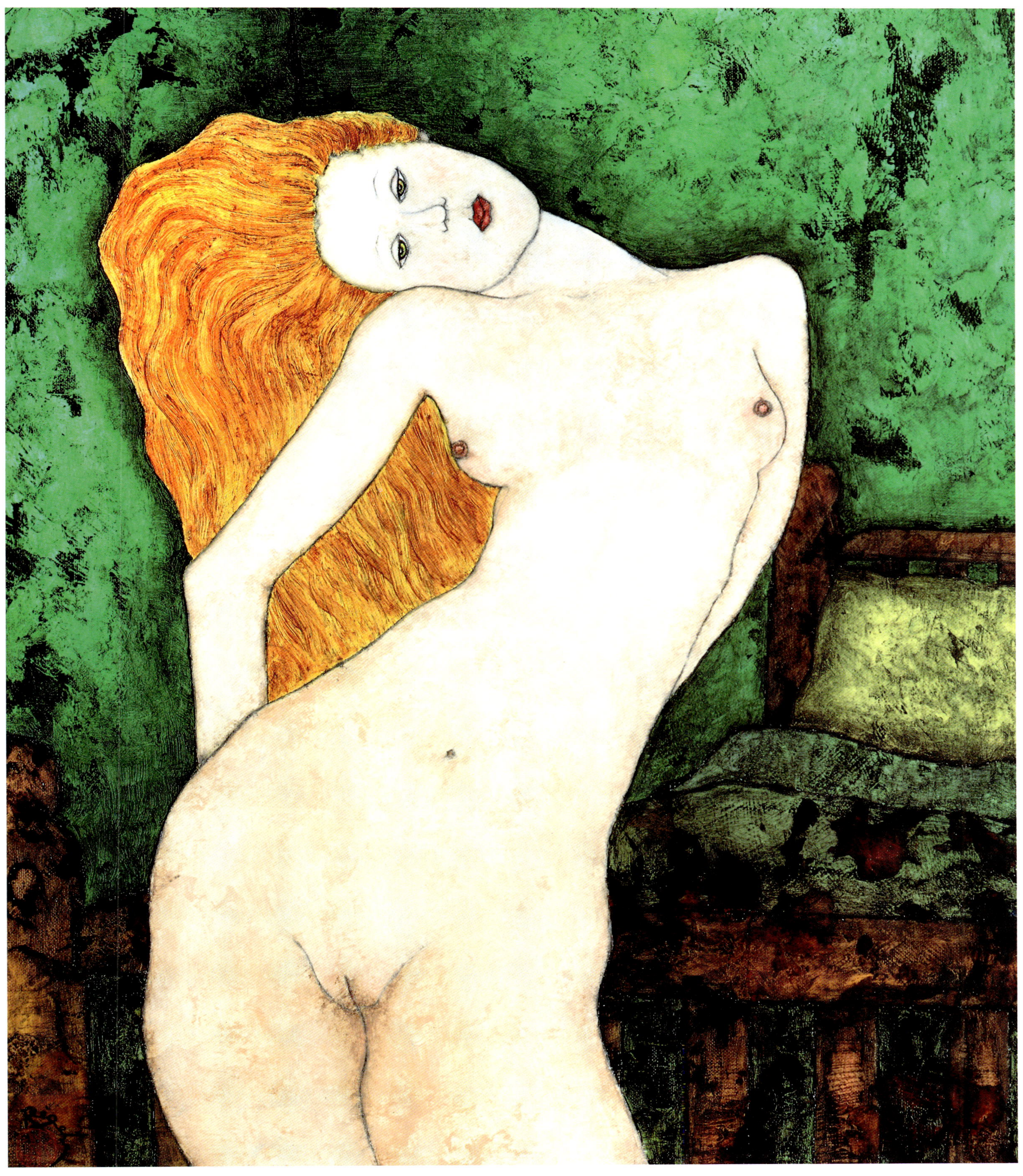

CARTOON LIBERTY

Poetic Imagery Series
Oil 30"x22" 1993

Grey Area

But for the quicksand at her feet
And the heedless slough of spoiled milk
That spilled across her dry-bed creek,
The plain is seedless in her eyes

A vast grey area for a journey unshared,
Where the ashen toll-bridge
That no caring sire could safely tread,
Sheds dead cinders upon her head

She longs for a desperado and the love she fears
To quench the grit between her thighs
But only the vague man, beyond the grey land rides
Pours arid tears, no quarter for the lie

Rail against the past, rail against the dawn
Her standard pale is a flaccid tryst.
As a phallic brace of fencing,
Once strung erect, now rusting lists

By the times gone blind, this is noman's land,
A righteous ground unsaved,
For bound with barbs and wire tines
Is the site for the big woman's grave

—DR

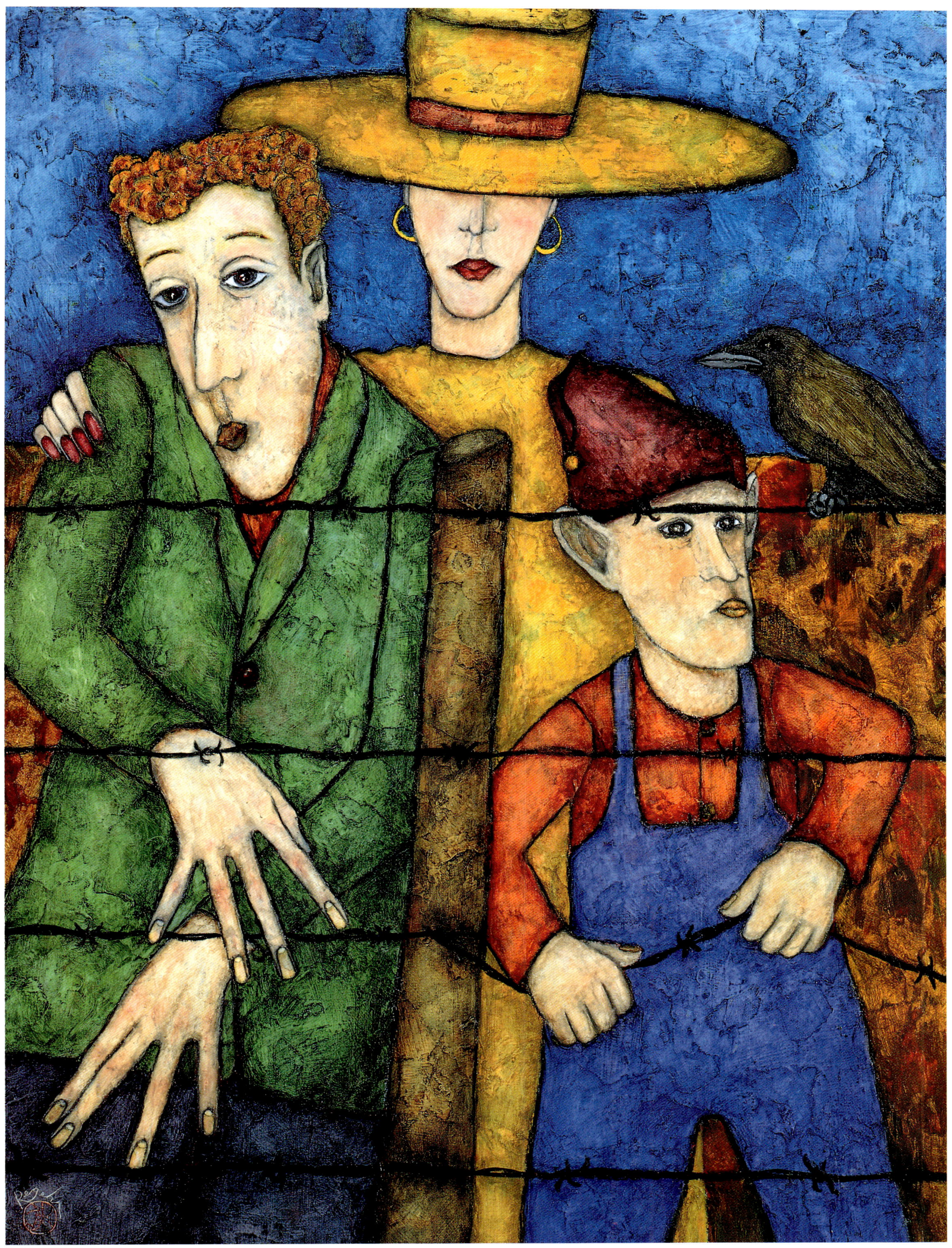

LAMMERGEIER'S LAMENT

Poetic Imagery Series

Oil 32"x21" 1991

In the spring of 1989, I spent four months filming *The Last Samurai* in Transkei on the Wild Coast of the Indian Ocean. I traveled through South Africa and Lesotho, studing the art of various cultures.

The art of South Africa falls into two basic areas — social/political work, which focuses primarily on issues of apartheid, and art of the older concepts found in primitivism and spirituality. They are of course linked and much of the art explores crossover territory.

While on safari in the Drakensberg mountains I came across a number of rock walls filled with the stories and designs of the ancient bushmen. I also found inspiration in the masks produced by later tribes.

The patterns and designs used by the ancients are no different the world over and are the same used by us today. The formations in the beadwork of the Transvaal Ndebele, parallel those found in the beadwork of North America's Southwest Indians. Even symbols and metaphors are quite often identical in the art of cultures existing at opposite ends of the earth.

As part of a fund-raising drive for the building of a gymnasium, I was taken to the squatter's camp at Soweto just outside of Johannesberg. I was warned against going there, but contrary to predictions that I would be barbecued alive, I found the people welcoming and hospitable.

Their artwork spanned centuries. By applying primitive techniques and designs to modern Western objects and materials, they created not only a bridge connecting the past to the present but a perfect example of how one culture gradually blends with another to form the cultural path and heritage of the future.

In the same way that linear patterns in the palm of a hand describe the course of a life, so may the designs of art define and devine the destiny of humankind.

Through art, the sameness of our existence can be observed. The patterns that bind us, trace our history and our future as one.

Time present and time past
Are both perhaps present in time future,
And time future contained in time past.

—T.S. Elliot Four Quartets 1943

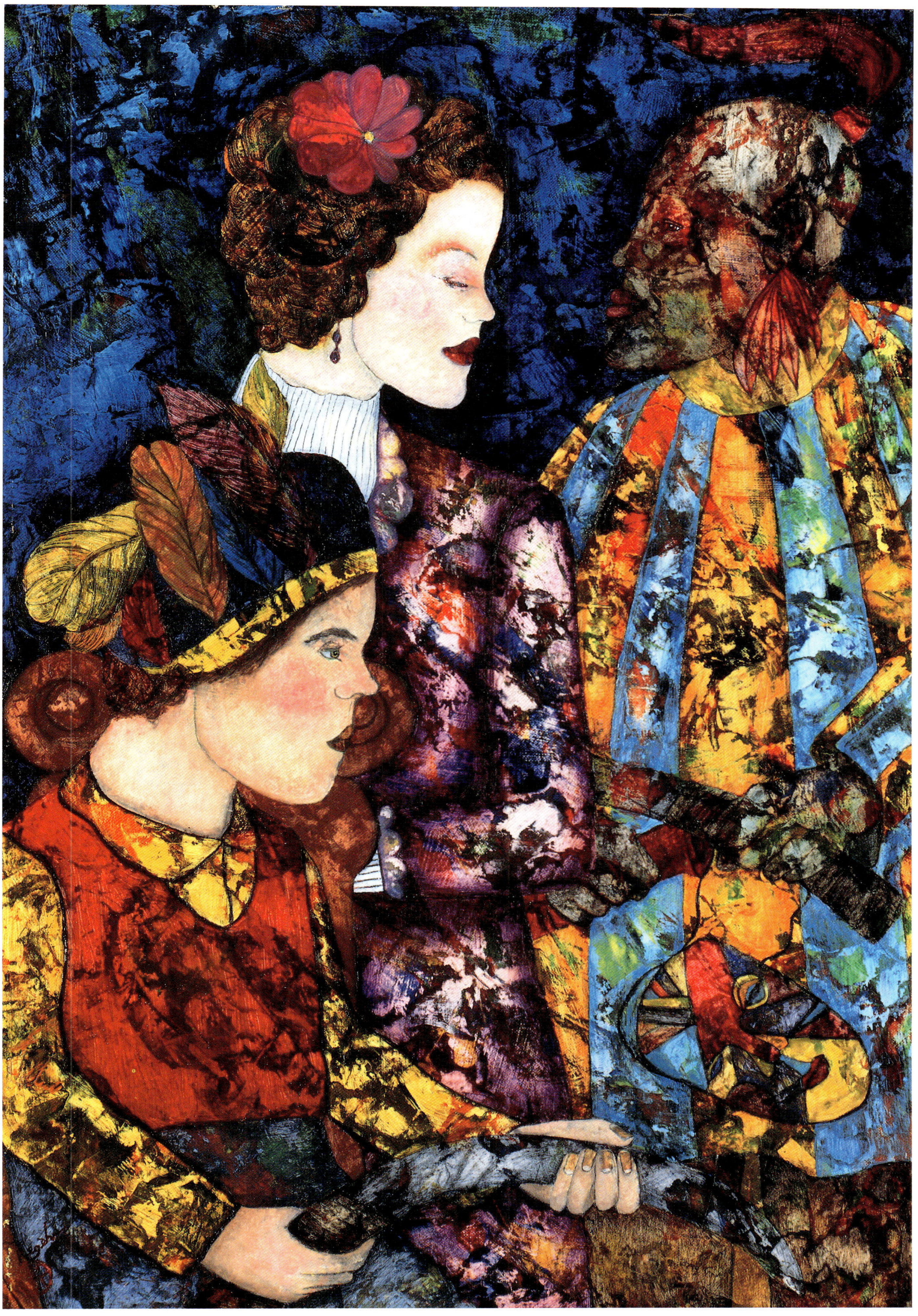

ARTIFACT

Poetic Imagery Series

Oil 20"x19 1/4" 1992

The Serpent's Tail

His cave is a hollow serpent,
A rib-cage within the earth,
That once breathed as the core of a saurian giant,
Now stone bones, now petrified stories
Of writhing travels never witnessed,
Are tunnel walls for the shaman.

He dips his brush in oxide to record another bison,
Another legend, another sediment,
The building up that shrinks the carcass walls,
He moves a little further down.

Meanwhile, on the terran crust
We rush to enter the serpent's mouth.

His day of night ends,
Slowly he collects his flint, his brushes,
The pigments wrapped in skins.
The lamp he holds, glows from the oil of fossils,
And lights the same on cavern ribs.
He shuffles down the narrowing tail.

He shuffles into dust,
As we arrive in the hall of bison,
The walls, still the same, are closer still,
As though the serpent breathed,
We sigh, relieved to be in time,
On time, to bear witness to the dust of dust.

We sigh in awe, and the motion releases
Our dust, the outside brought in.
Our contribution legacy falls upon the floor,
The stone thickens, our air grows small,
The serpent breathes again.

We move on swiftly,
There is barely time to glimpse the past.
We follow him, catching up his time,
Our time, our dust becoming his.
We follow him down the serpent's tail,
Coming ever swiftly towards us.

—DR

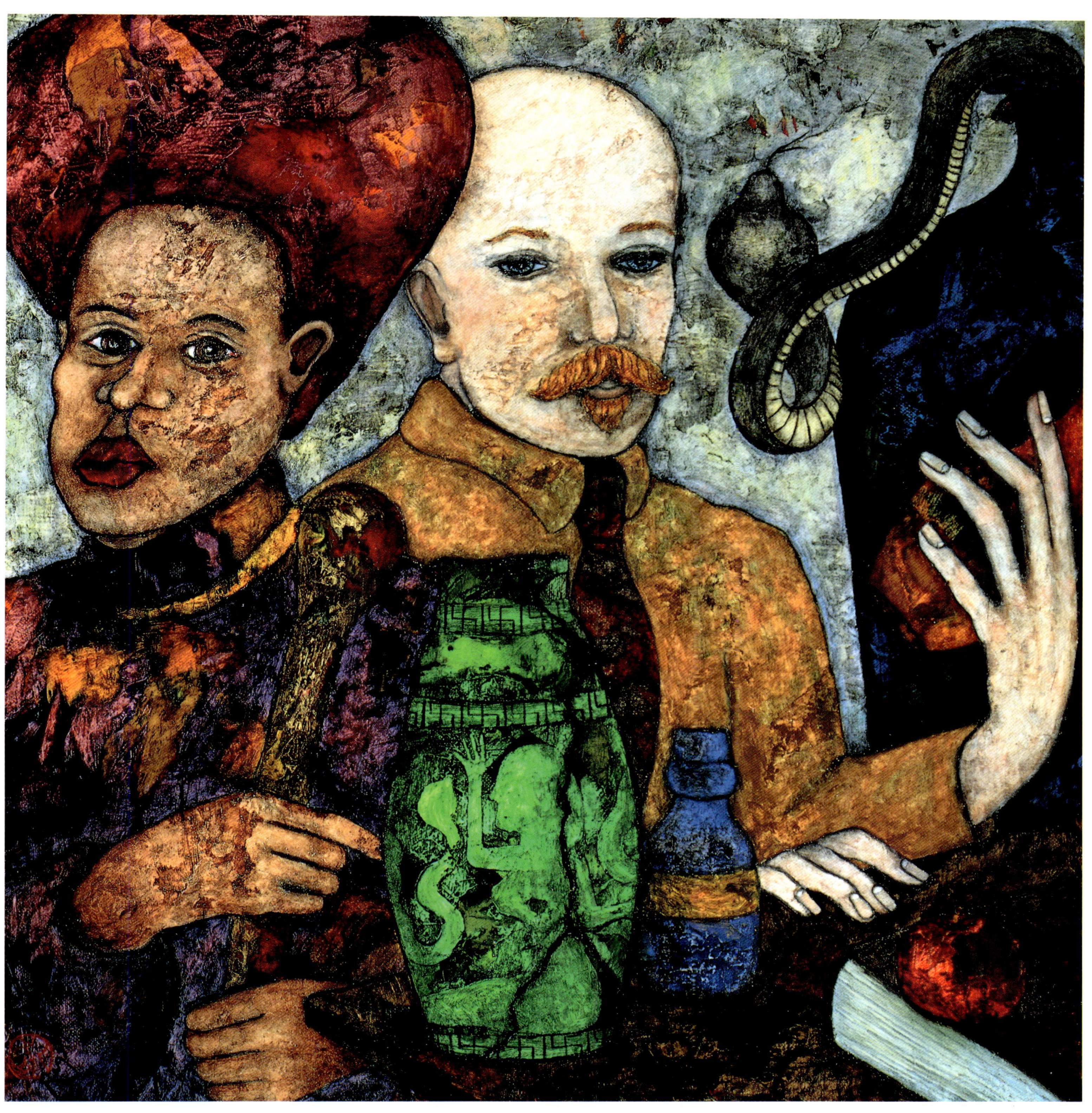

CORMORAN AND CORMELIAN

Henge Series

Oil on Shaped Canvas 31 1/2"x37 1/2" 1986

On the coast of Cornwall, England, long before the ocean had claimed Mount's Bay, a giant named Cormoran and his wife Cormelian lived in the woods.

Since the sea was gradually encroaching upon their domain, they decided to build a protective stronghold out of white granite.

They began to transport rocks to the place where St. Michael's Mount stands today. Cormelian used her apron to carry the huge white boulders, while Cormoran carried them on his back. It was heavy going, and they soon began to tire.

Cormoran, who was very lazy and bad-tempered, waited until his wife was out of sight before lying down for a quick snooze. When Cormelian returned, she was delighted to see her husband in a deep slumber, because it meant that she could collect the smaller, ordinary rocks closer to hand.

When Cormoran finally woke up, he was enraged to see his wife going by with an apron full of small green boulders, instead of the bigger white ones.

In a temper, he leapt to his feet and gave her a giant-sized kick so powerful, that it caused her apron to split apart. Both of them were swallowed up by the ensuing avalanche of rocks, which remain to this day as the causeway to St. Michael's Mount. It is said that the forms of the two giants can still be seen, caught inside the boulders.

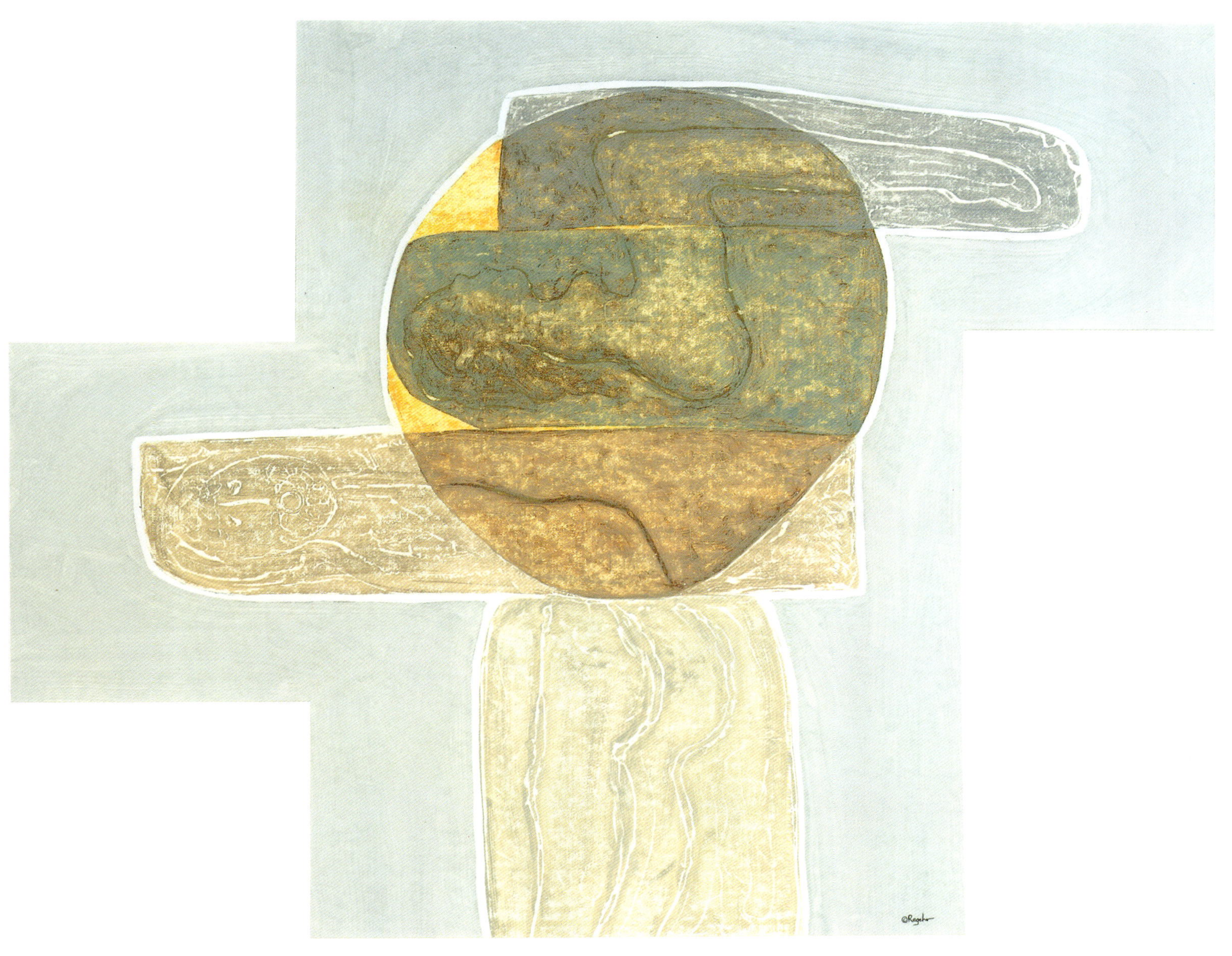

THE BLIND COCKATRICE

Poetic Imagery Series

Oil 30"x24" 1993

Hatched by a serpent from a cock's egg on top of a dunghill, the cockatrice is one of the deadliest creatures of British folklore, possessing the power to kill with its mere glance.

I once worked with a stage actress capable of the same feat. She would either glare mercilessly, or ignore one as though one were already dead. At the end of the run, the crew gave her a pair of Ray-Bans. Perhaps the cockatrice is responsible for the modern adage "If looks could kill..."

'sleeth folk by the venim of sighte'
—CHAUCER

'the death-darting eye of the cockatrice'
—SHAKESPEARE

A number of stories suggest that the way to destroy a cockatrice is to present it with its own reflection. One myth tells of a knight who put on a suit of highly polished armour before setting out to slay the local cockatrice. When the creature saw itself in the gleaming breastplate it dropped dead.

Traditionally, the creature has been described as having the head of a rooster and a long scaly form ending in a dragon's tail, sometimes with four legs and batlike pinions. My cockatrice is more human than ophidian or birdlike. He is also blind.

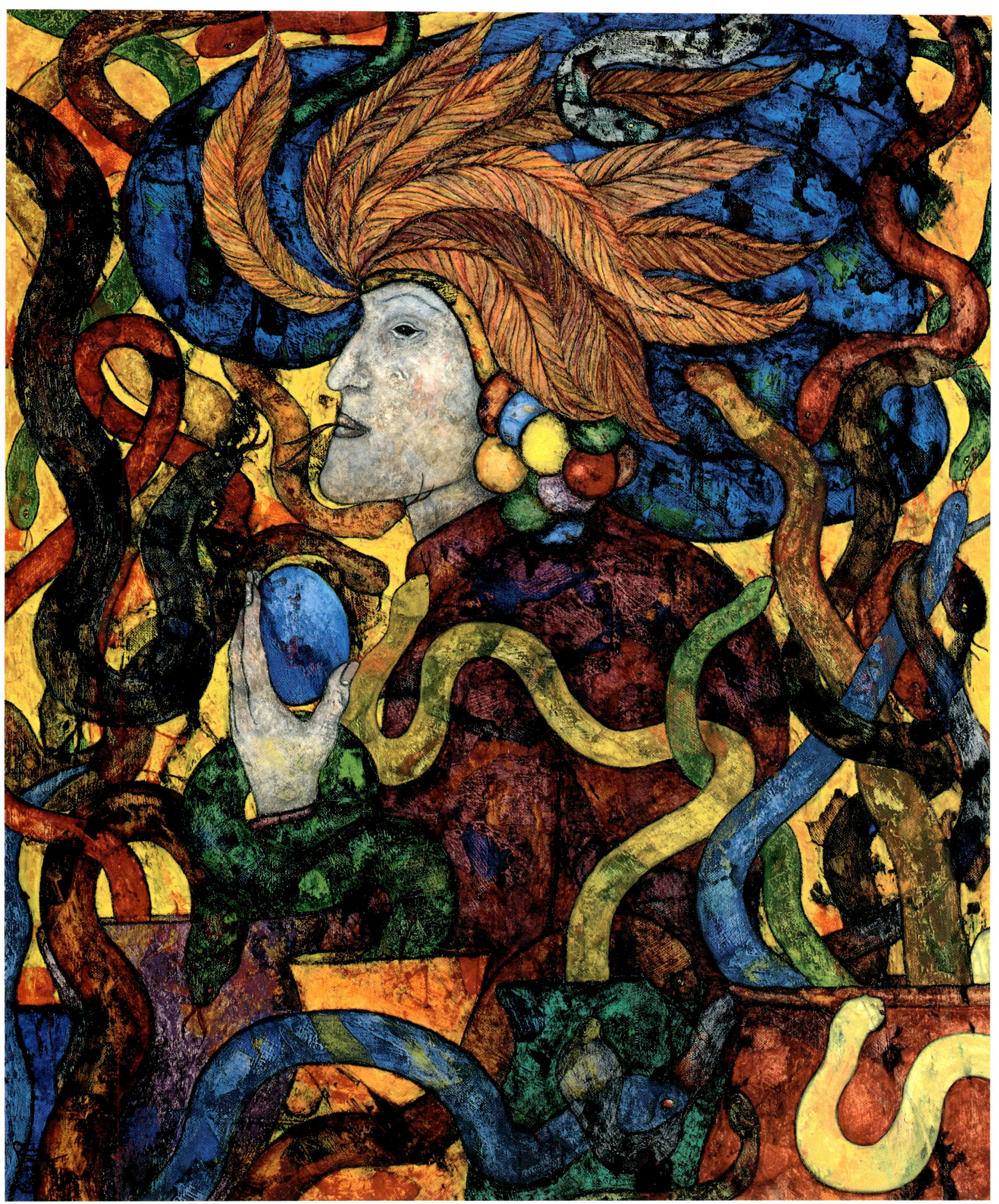

CARBON FAERIE

Coloured Pencil   24"x18"   1990

Coloured Rain

For awhile she floats by with everything in place:
Cartoons and Spring are filed together under
Volcano and Soaring Hearts,
They change flight with decaying totems or threat.

Because she is never the same,
You ponder the force behind, and why
It does not change or sleep.

Now she bids for coloured rain,
From golden deserts that were seas once,
Where fossils capered before suspension,
Before limestone,
Before carbon faeries in the petrified forest.

It could never be right here that you found fantasy.
Curated among molecules,
The spirit had to fall dried out,
Shaken and withered by stories.

All your scattered colours splash down
Hell-bent, through mud and the sediment of others,
Settling,
For comfortable cocoons in bedrock.

—DR

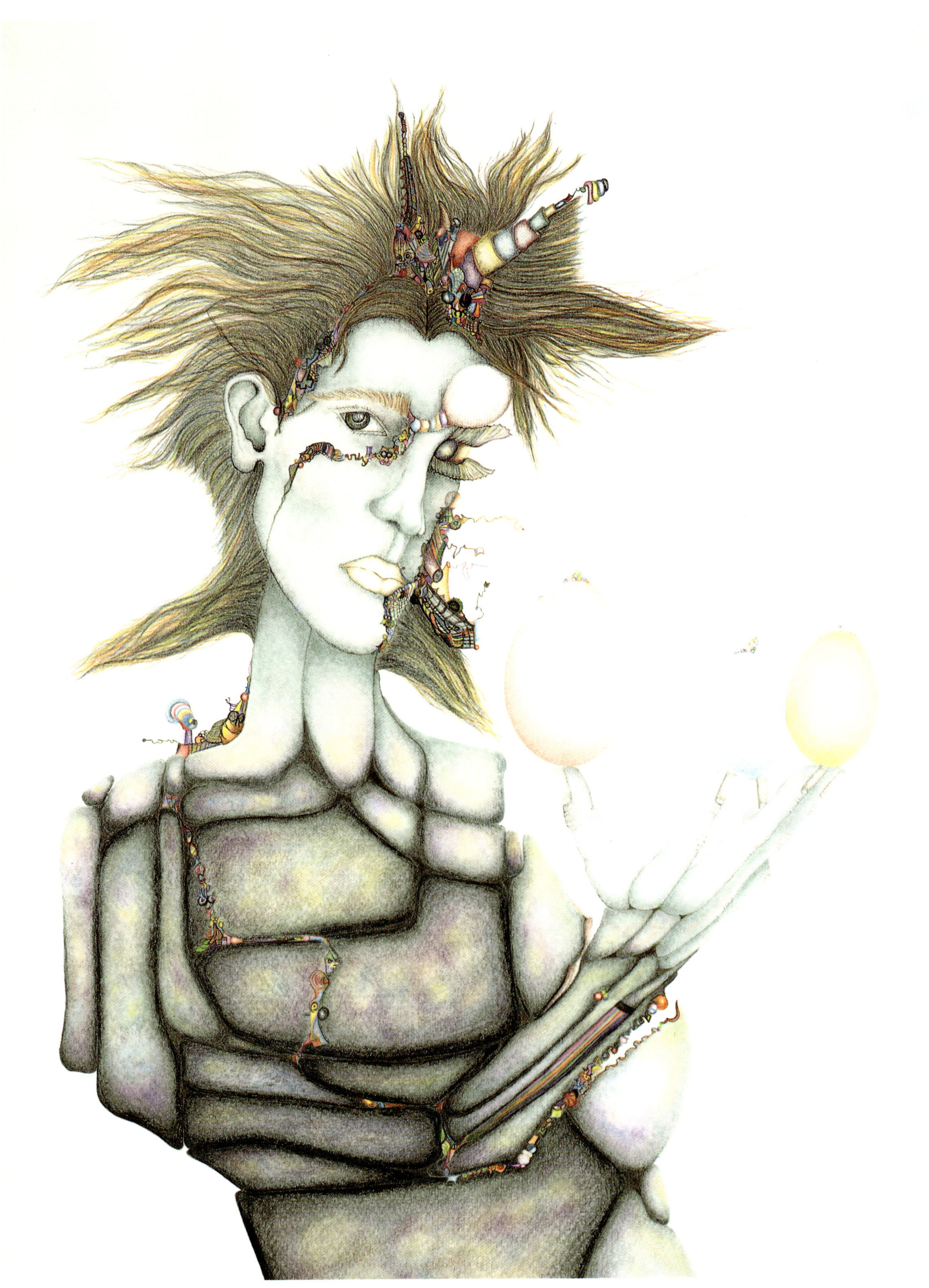

THE YARNSMAN

Poetic Imagery Series

Oil 30"x24" 1992

Weaver's Litany

Line up and recite after me...

Our daily routines are made up of habits
Which fit the patterns of a grand design

Inescapable,
Repeat please...

Our daily habits are made up of patterns
Which fit the design of a grand routine

Always,
Once more...

Daily patterns are made up of routines
Which grandly fit the habits of our design

Inevitable,
Carry on...

Our routines habitually fit a daily design
Which make up the grand pattern

Redundantly,
Again...

Routine patterns make up designs
Which fit our daily habits grandly

Relentlessly,
Continue...

Grand designs are made up daily to routinely
Fit the habits which our patterns make up

Endlessly,
Et cetera please...

—DR

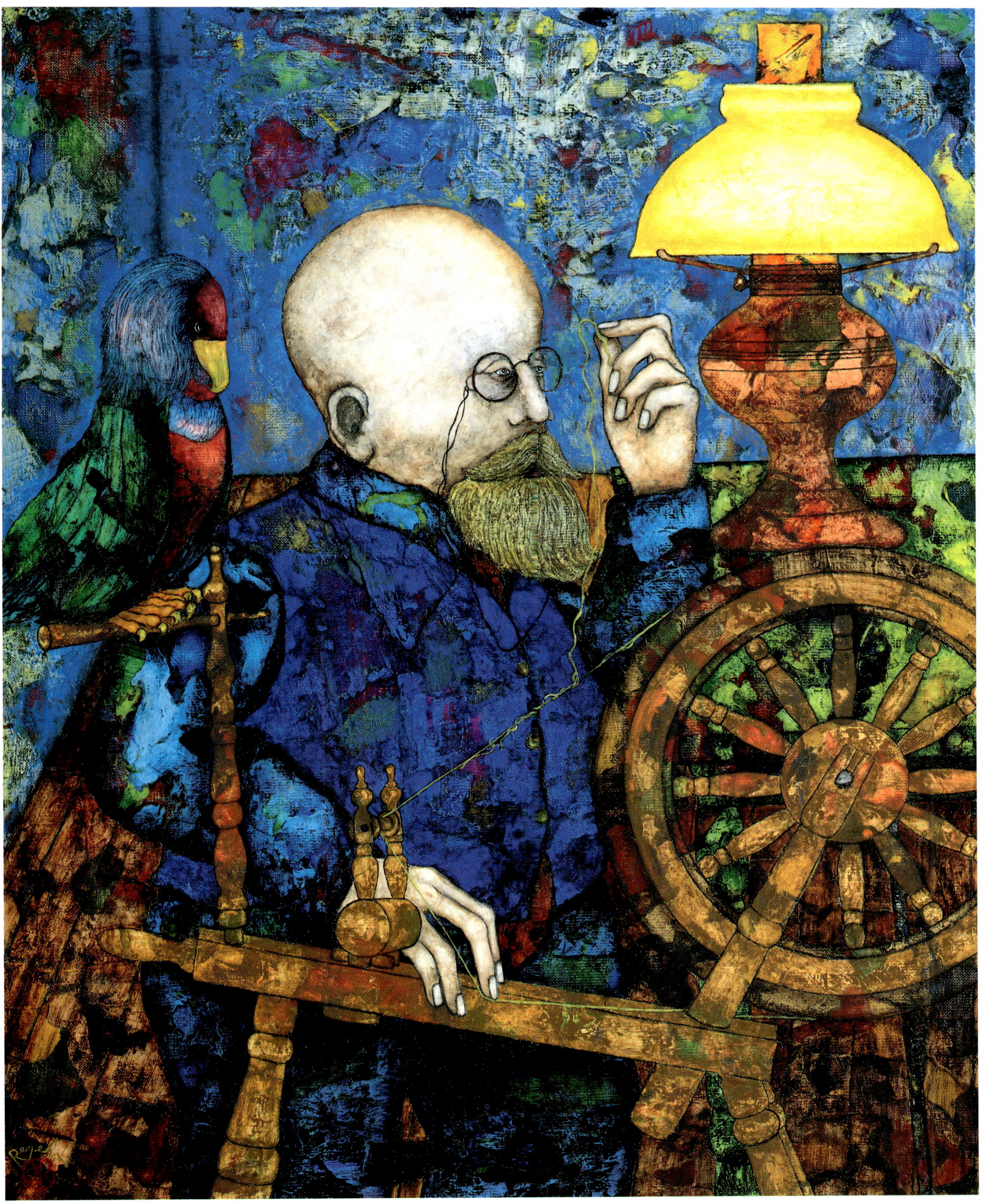

JACOB'S LAST DREAM

Poetic Imagery Series

Oil 30"x24" 1992

Cracks in the Fingers

Time and his memory swept away,
sharing a bottle on the shoreless sea.

For him all things became, at once.

And standing behind his hands
before the final sun he asked,

With these eyes covered,
does the ocean remain
beside, within the scent of backgarden honeysuckle
caught on the same breeze as mockingbird tunes
sung from swaying telephone wires
carrying the voices of cities?

Is that light(?)
shining through cracks in the fingers
to the darkness behind the hands
myself?

If it is,
do I (did I, will I)
shine on like a nova whose beacon reaches us,
after...

—DR

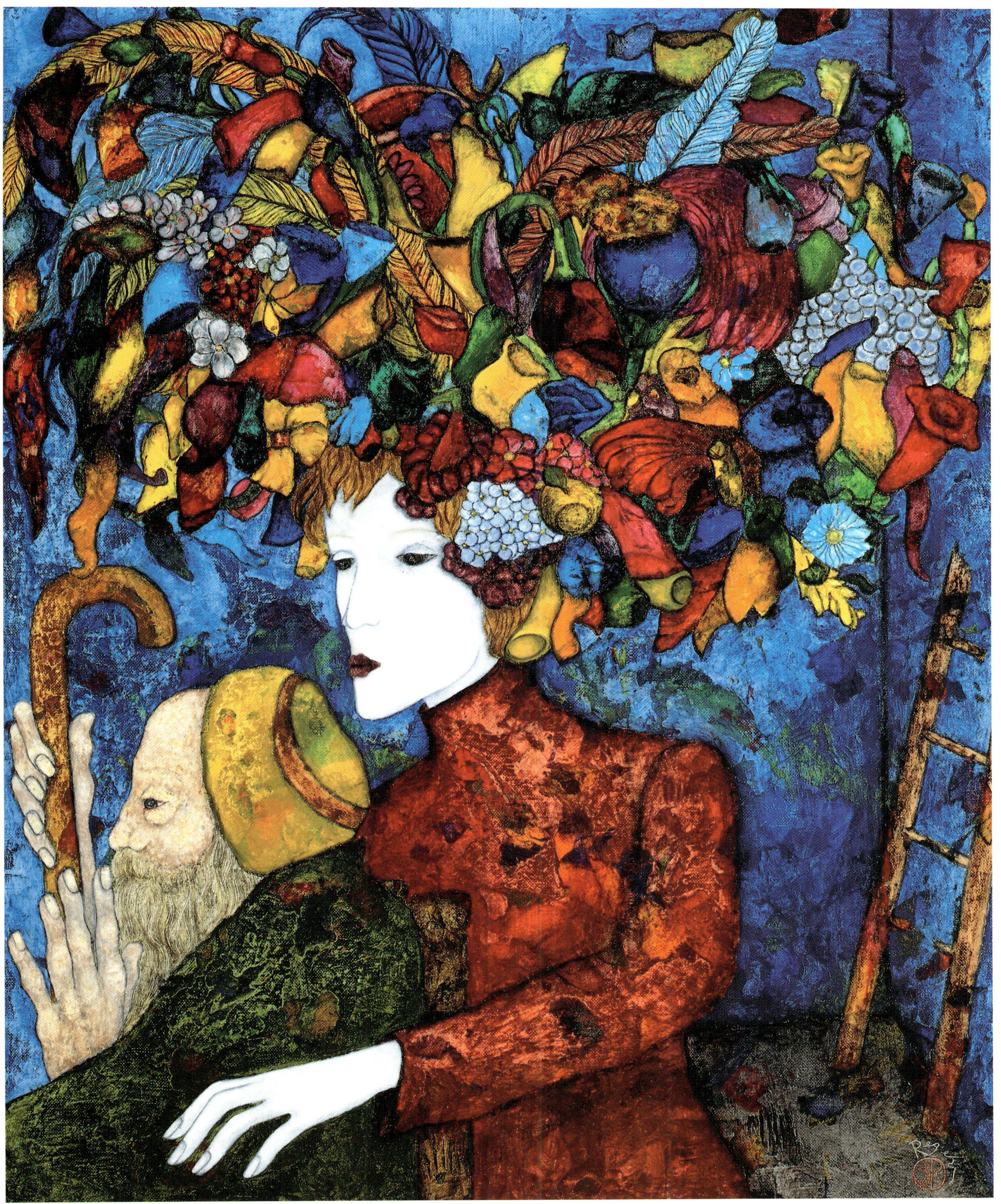

PROGENY

Poetic Imagery Series

Oil 16"x20" 1991

Widow's Prodigy

Look at my rose,
Fallen and broken by its own weight.

This is my son,
My leviathan, my talented one,
So famous from the plague.

When the follower's led his shadow away,
I grew him back from the ashes there.

Now his petals are like elephant ears,
Enfolded flaps of skin that slough,
That float again,
As ashes again,
To thunder down upon the grave.

—DR

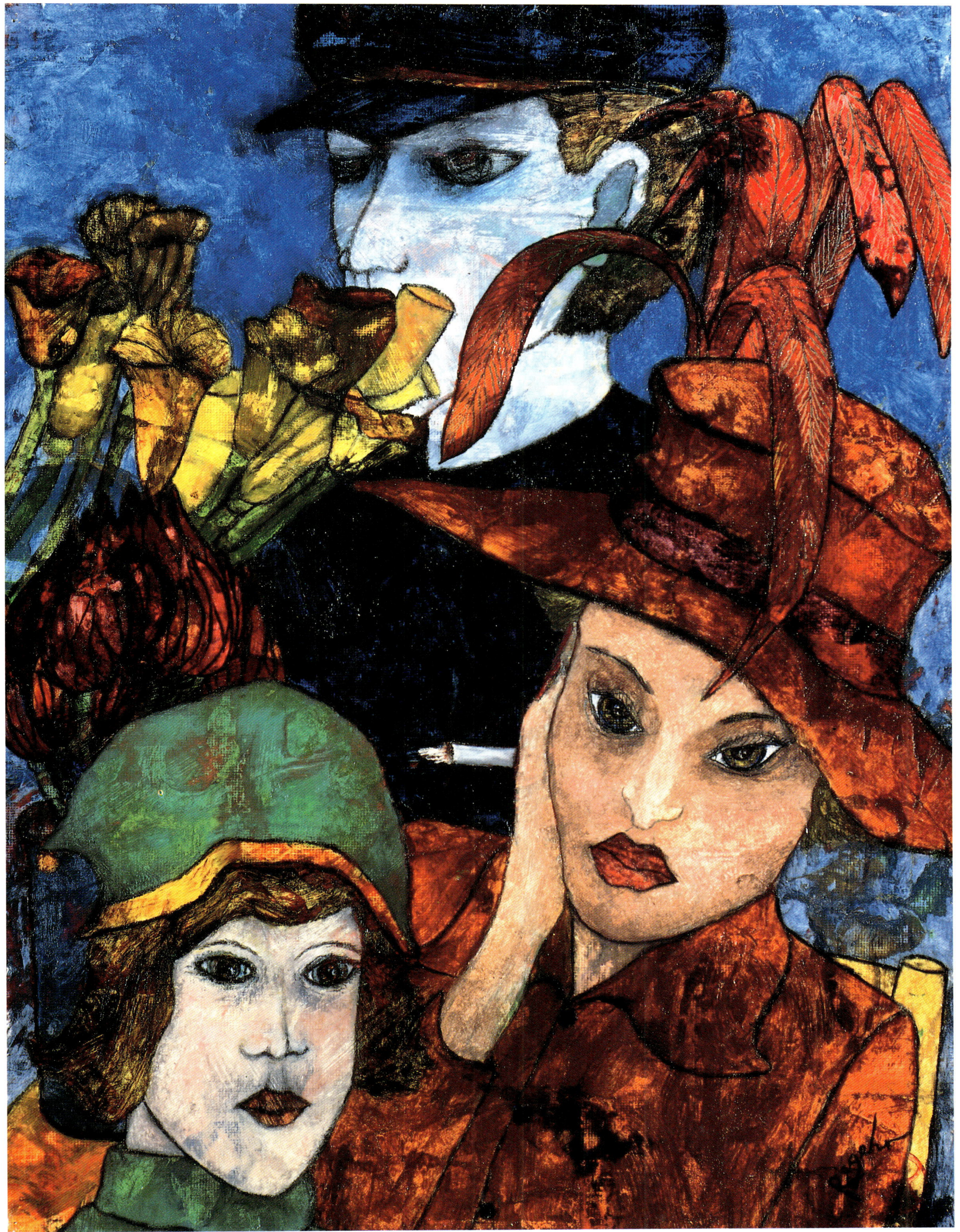

THE STROKE

Poetic Imagery Series

Oil 20"x11" 1992

The Final Stroke

Before going,
She listened to summer windchimes and teacups
Stirring in the hallway.
She wrapped herself with her friend,
The coat.
She closed the closet
Full of hangers without skins, names
Jostling in the dark.

Have I outlived everyone?

My cupboard is bare,
My thoughts repeat themselves
Like nursery rhymes,
They are old company.

Each dawn,
My walk in the woods reminds me that
I am not pretending
To be.
But I can be there,
From here.

Has confusion made a pattern?
Like my walk in the cemetery
Where the graves are scattered in order.

Surely I can be here,
From there.

—DR

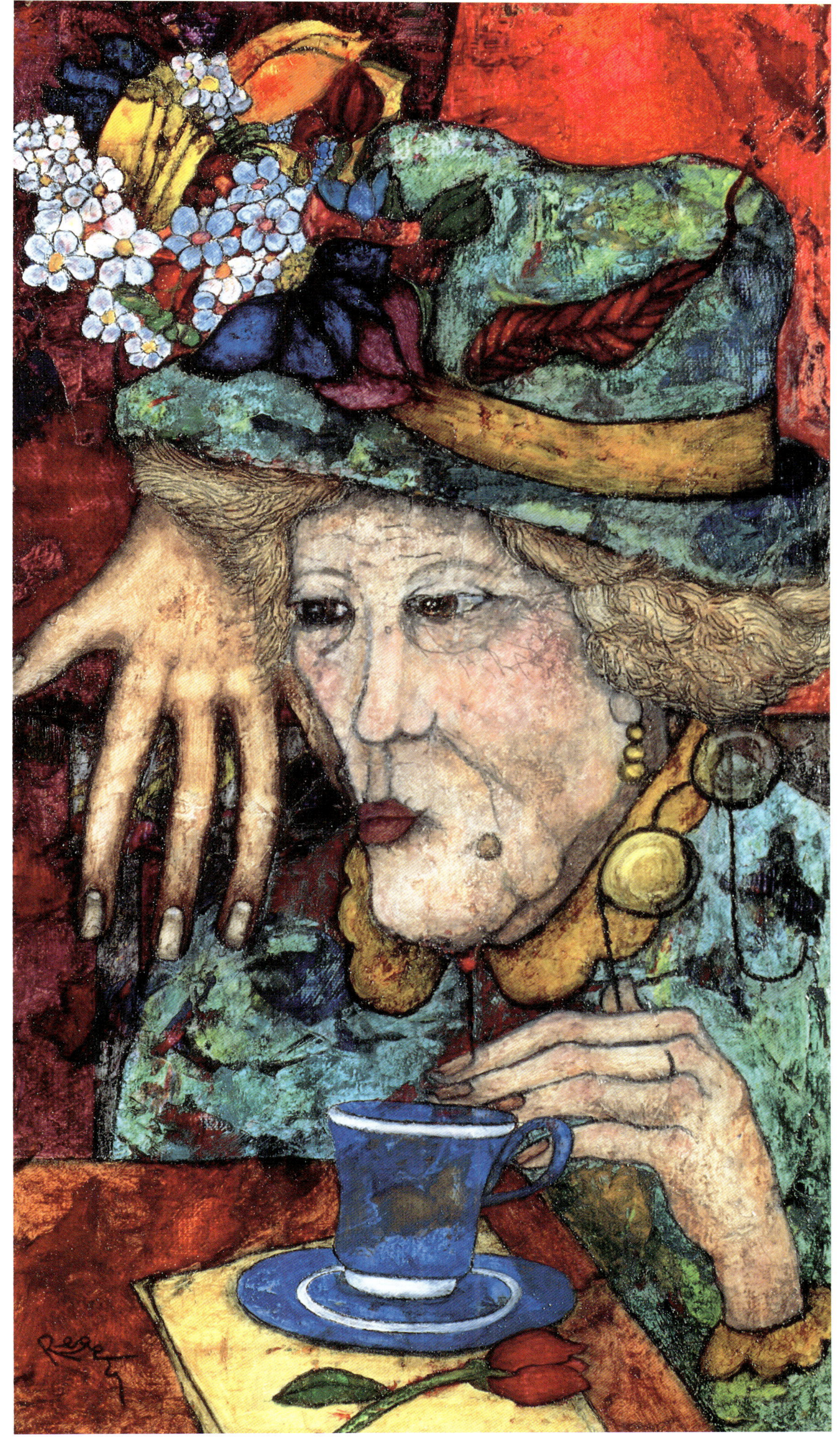

THE DWARF AND THE APPLE

Poetic Imagery Series

Oil 22" x 18" 1991

Kindred

Unaware that they know each other,
The dwarf and the apple know
The distance of the sky,
The nearness of the ground,
Know the swelling of the wind,
Exposure in the sun,
Know the jostling of a crowd
To be like rainfall.
That bruises are daily facts
That force them onward.
Know,
That hope raises purpose higher than life.
That growth ends
With a fall and a longing
That stirs the core of life to become.

Theirs is a shared knowledge,
Together no different.
Known unto itself
To be one.

Unbeknownst to the dwarf and the apple,
They are known to be the same.

—DR

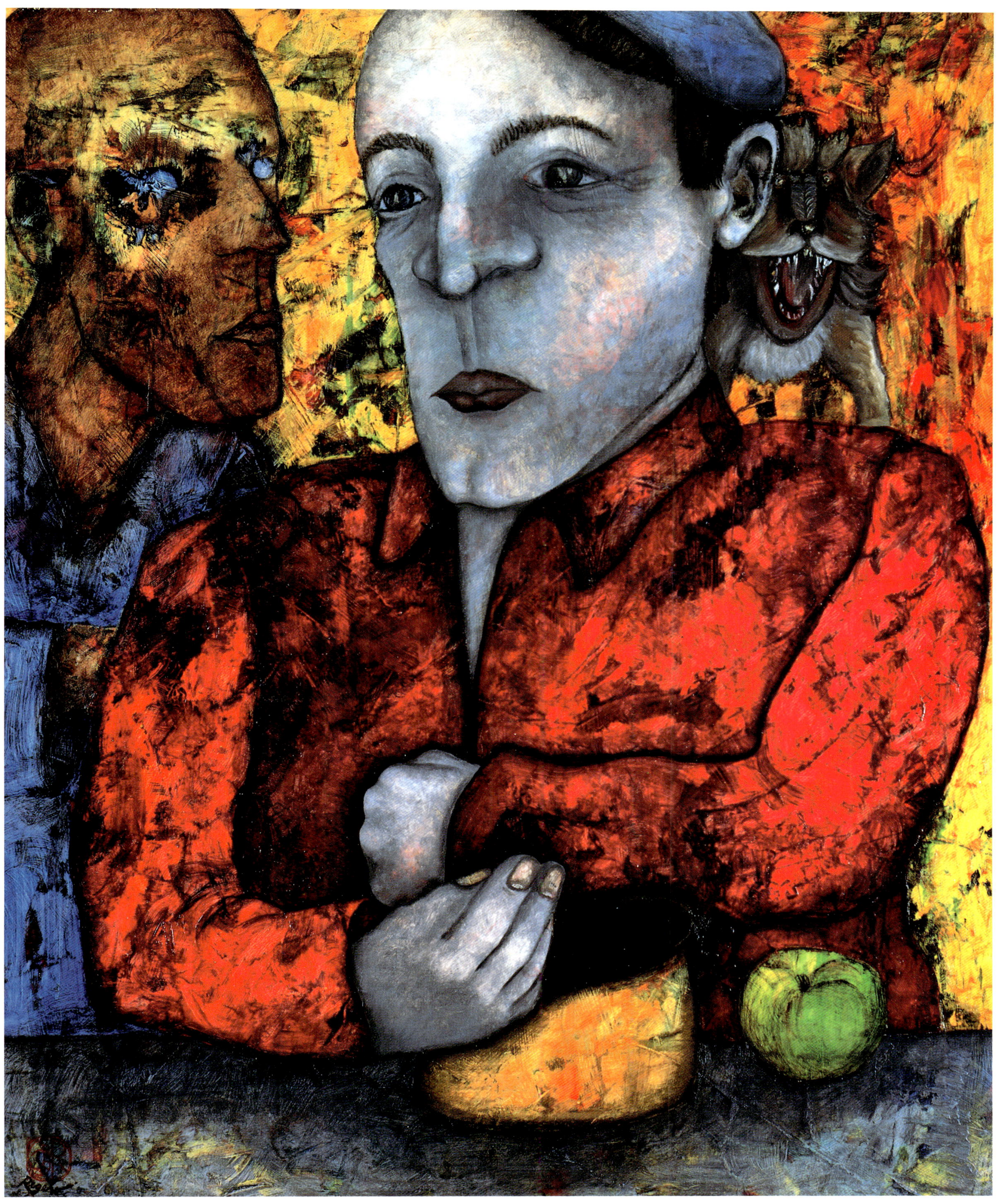

CREDO

Poetic Imagery Series

Oil 23¾" x 17½" 1991

"Print is the sharpest and strongest weapon of our party."

—Joseph Stalin

The Manifesto Line

The Credo is on the line again
Shouting invisible words, to be red
Shouting to be read between lines of the red book
Any book, has line upon line of marching words
Lines that are red, instead of read
Lines that are led, and lines that fled
Lines that bled, and lines that are fed
Line after line, said
Unheard
By the lines of marching dead.

—DR

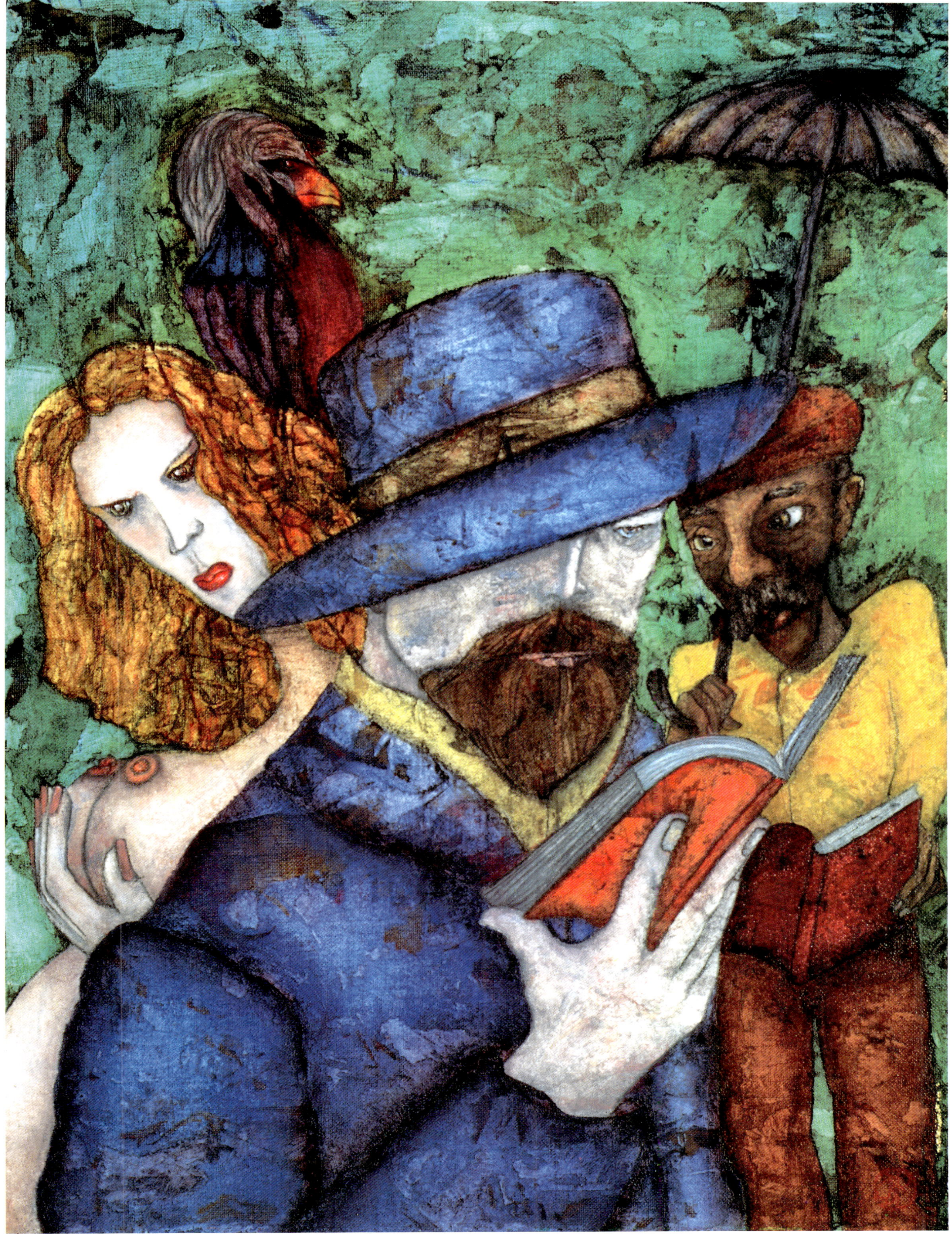

AMANUENSES

Line Drawing Series

Pen and Ink   24" x 18"   1989

The Fuller Circle

The eye blinks and waves crash.
From the milky way, poetry and geometry
Tumble with color and music,
Sighing into minds as one line.

Patterns settled upon the night owl's wing,
Refract with sunlight,
Into the stretch of a tabby cat's back,
Alike to the python's blaze.

And wrapped up in the skin of one leaf
Are the veins of a river, flowing
As lemming herds flow into the sea,
On the stream of a common will.

To a white lily, blows
The scent of blue sky and death,
While Spring bursts under a tide of ants,
Ploughing up the avalanche.

Nudged by imagination or the breath of a babe,
Come grains of sand in a cave wall,
Falling out as crystals and God drawings,
Fused to fossils by dragon's heat.

All this,
Joins air it knows well from a different time.
Rising to heaven or the milky way,
The spirit is a mote.

—DR

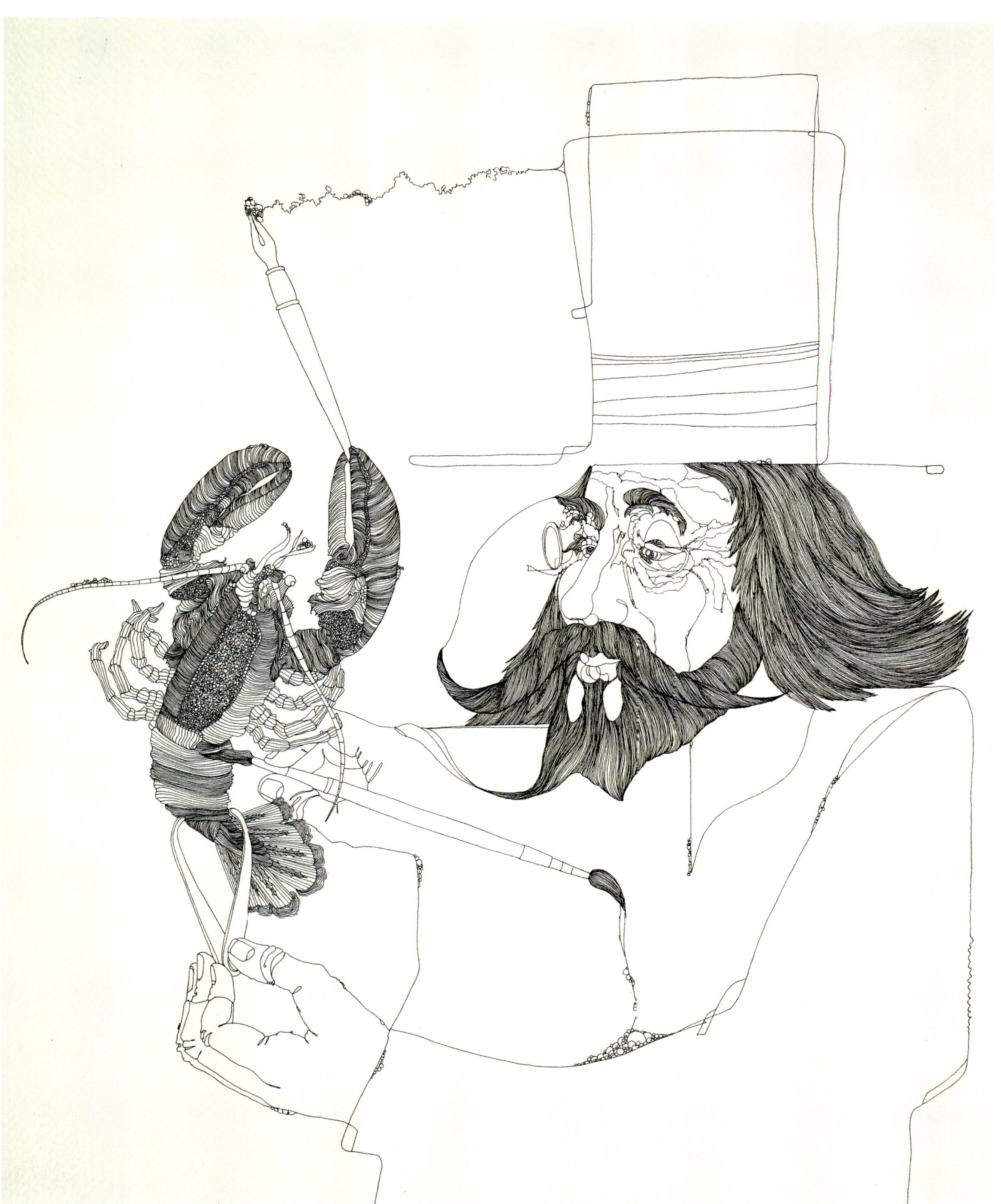

CONFESSIONS FROM THE EAVES

Poetic Imagery Series

Oil 25½" x 21¼" 1991

Peter Van Daan:
Confession from the Eaves

In a paneless attic room
We waltzed the borders of our frontier
On opposite sides swinging face to face
Wall to wall
Corner to corner
Backs to the foundation seams
. . . always

Later
The tiny paneless room turned itself inside out
We found ourselves perched
On the common ledge of distant walls

Lone gargoyles us
Addressing outward winds and the birds of prey.
Each of us a folly to separate balance
Our backs to the foundation seams
. . . always

Much later
Still clinging, still chafing at stone memories
We crept around the sill
Our sightless fingers met where the walls touch each other
Asking
Was it only hope when we were together?
Or were we just around the corner . . .

She sang so carefully then
A trembling hymn to the holiness of flying
Warning, that corners are the only mutual place
. . . all ways.

—DR

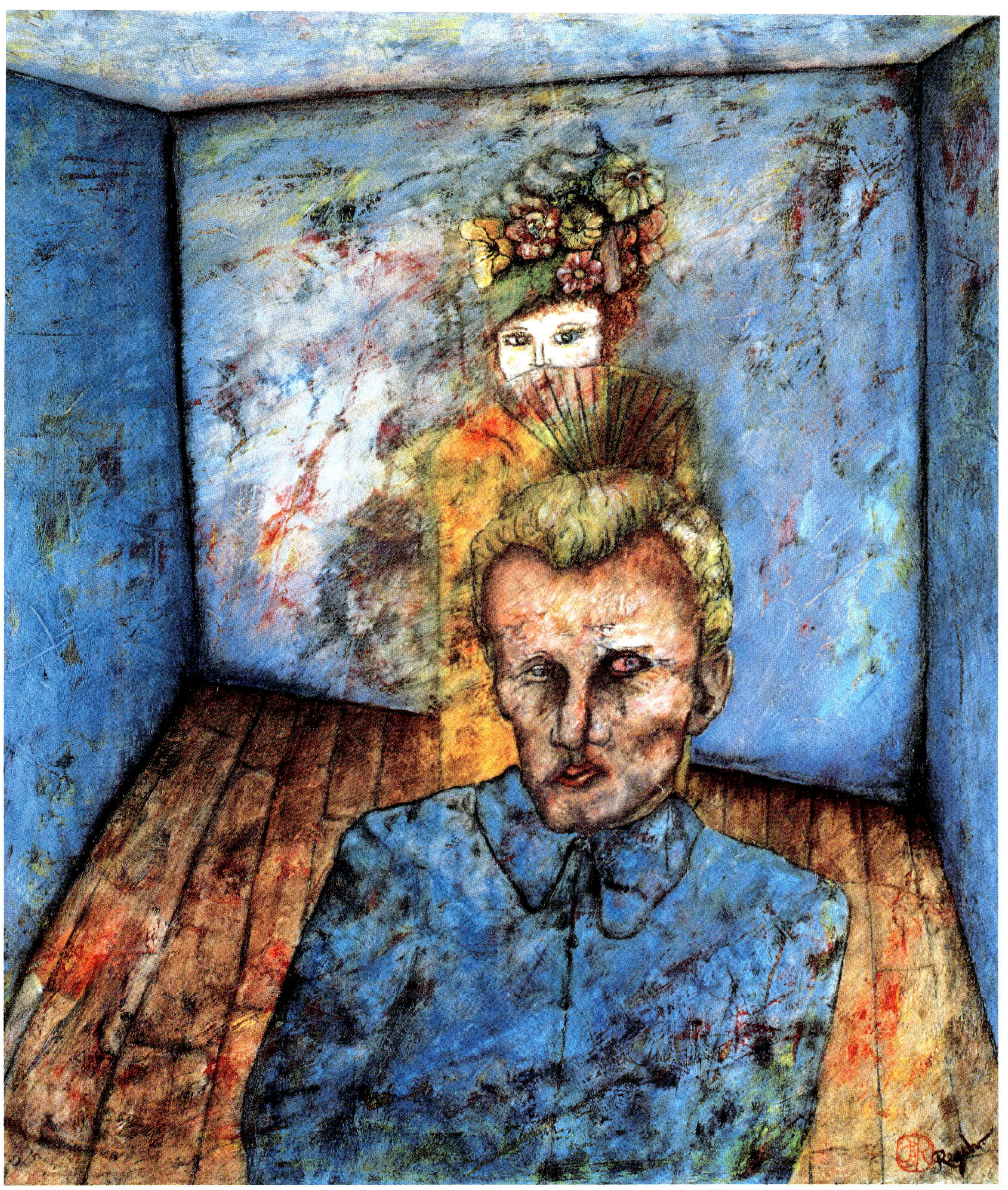

BIRDS OF PREY

Colored Pencil   14½" x 11"   1989

Brother Dragon and His Companion

We look into the eastern sky
and wonder if it is a hot sea that will rise
over us, above us

    in the heavy-bellied clouds
    our goblins fly with preying birds,
    with all the gifts in tow...

back to the glowing rim, the molten cave
where Brother Dragon seethes
a growing tide...

    From the other side, his companion
    breathes and broken ice
    stabs the fluttering Heartland.

Dry crystalline hands close the book of tales.
They shatter where the fossils lie,
melting in a cooling sun.

—DR

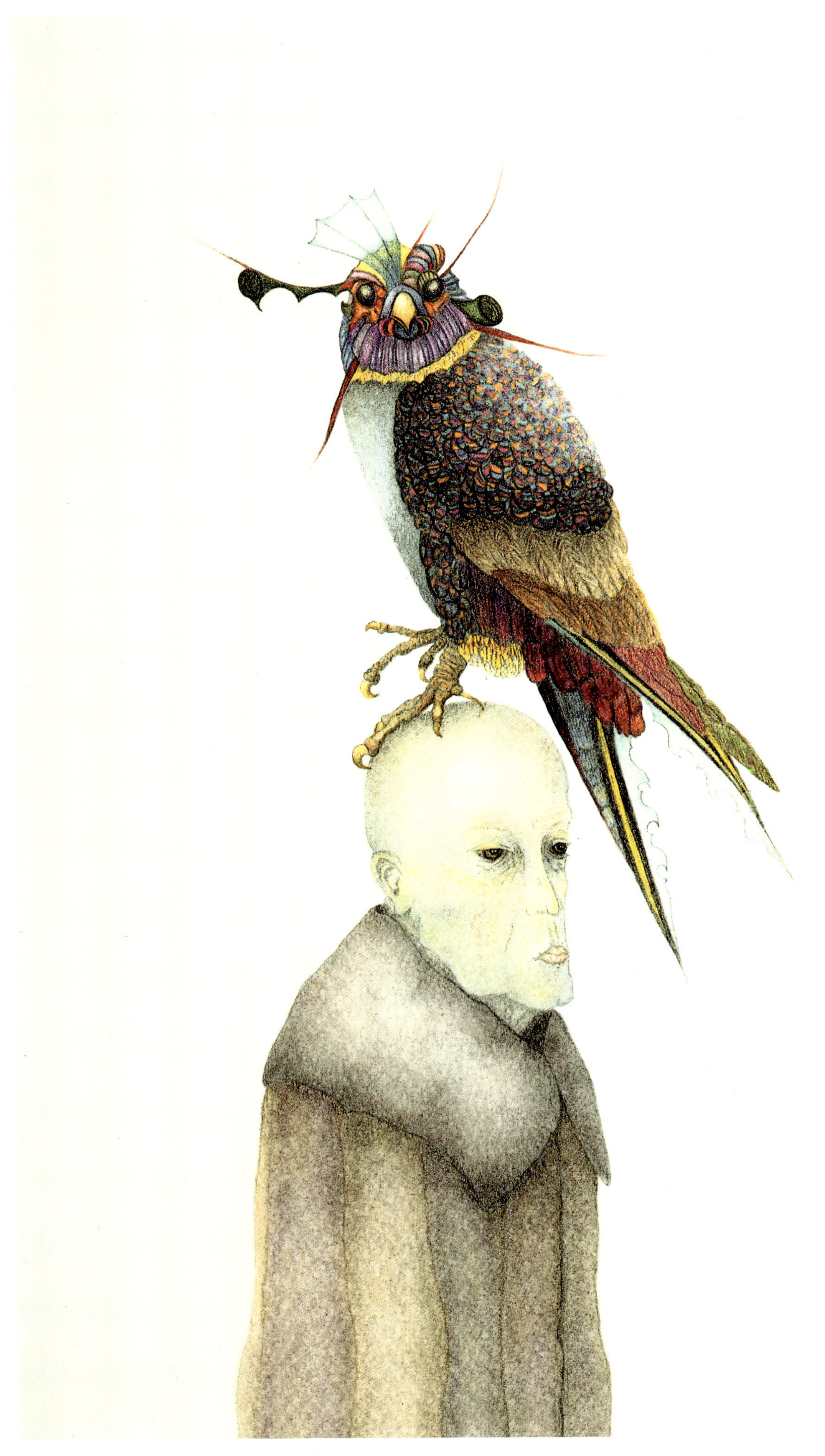

AFTER THE STILL LIFE

Poetic Imagery Series

Oil 18" x 14" 1991

Nature Morte

Sprout,
Watch closely,
As all the bouncing plums and rolling cherries
And snapping apples and popping grapes
And spraying spitting oranges
Flashing ripeness in color so rich, are
Stilled.

After the Still Life,
There is a stillness that swallows
All the living growing fruits.

In that very moment of after...
Time has eaten time.
All the times themselves are still.
Only the still, still are.

Sprout,
Grow before you eat,
Hold still before you live,
To watch closely, the time of life
Grow after...

—DR

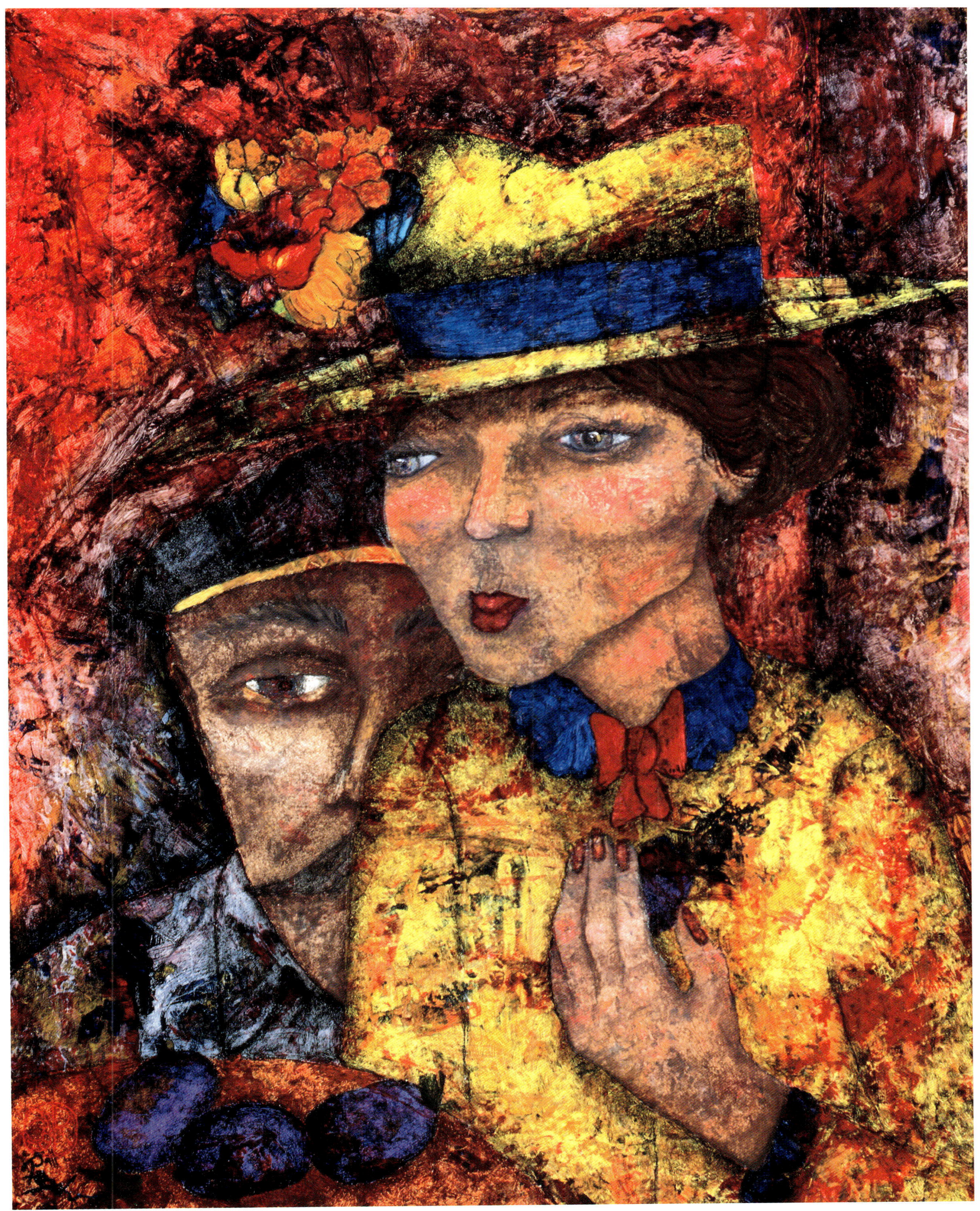

GABRIELLE 1910, THE SKINLESS WIRE

Poetic Imagery Series

Oil 12¾" x 10¾" 1991

The Skinless Wire

There is a period of waiting
When she longs for a window or her mother's womb.
She races to an imagined sky and back again,
To tears and the vomit on her bare legs.
Bare facts in this naked room.
She waits,
While her old clothes gossip behind the closet door.

Finally, she opens the closet door.
The clothes stop breathing.
Selection and decision from so much
That is exactly the same.

She reaches in with closet-eyes
And fate, finds the skinless wire.
No dusty life to shed in the gloom,
The old clothes close with a hiss.

She turns to the brilliant room,
Where love will hang as a bloody secret.
And fear and guilt hide the darkest acts
From a life,
That will never know.

—DR

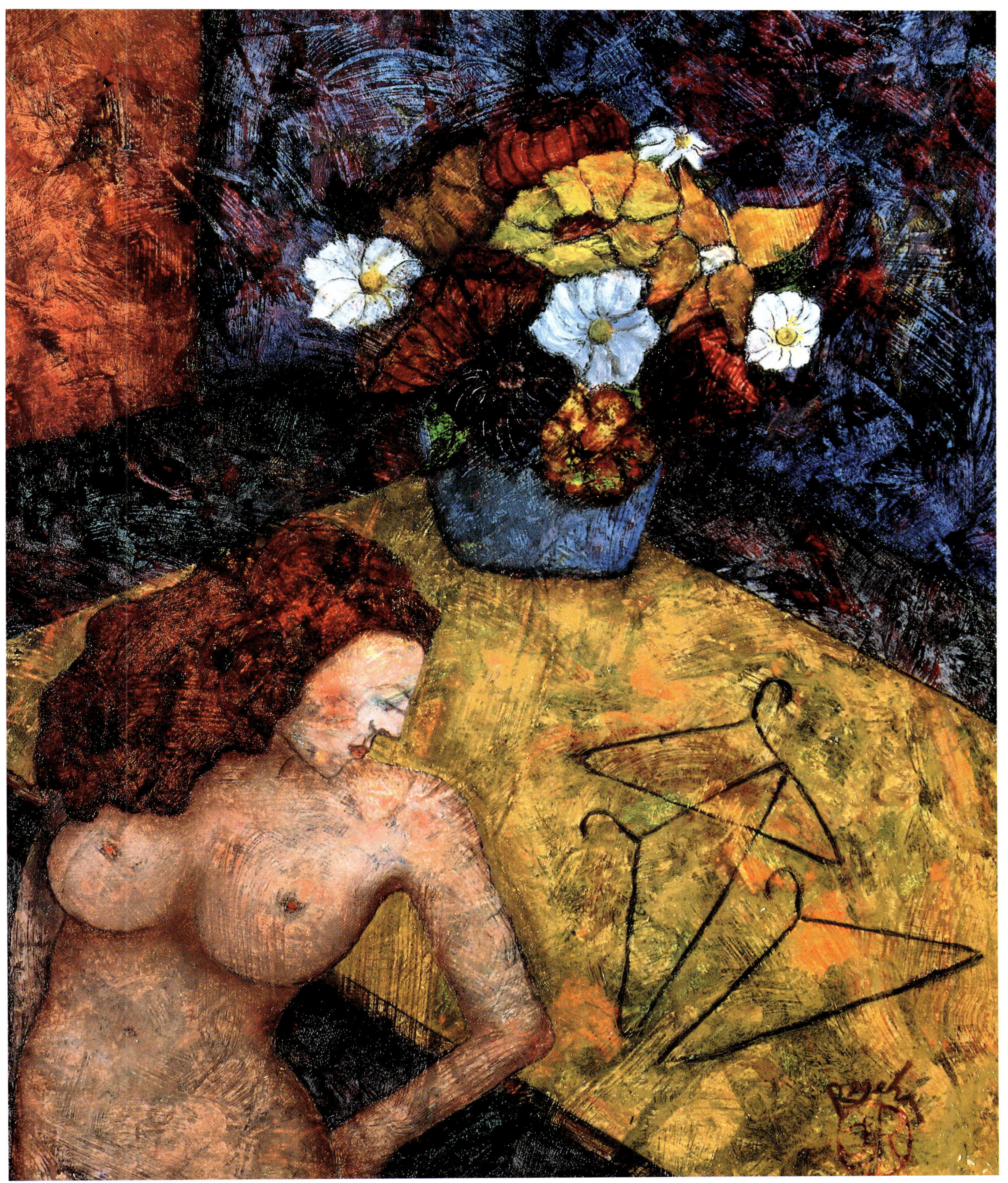

CASTING THE FEATHERMAN'S FATE

Poetic Imagery Series
Oil 35" x 27" 1992

The Featherman

Before the Featherman was blown away,
He used to say,
Those who stray to lose a pattern,
Will always find one anyway . . .

His sudden absence left a stain
And tore a hole in the sail cloth.
We stood and watched it expand, or unravel,
I forget which.
Just as we forgot that there was a far side
When we could no longer see it.

But we could always hear it,
A distant ripping.
The unmaking sound of the Featherman,
Or the Hole's creation,
I forget which.

I do remember queueing up
To play *double dare ya.*
We would rush to peer over the billowing edge,
Then scamper off giggling
As the fraying canvas chased
Our backward steps like beach surf, and

Always the hot drunken wind.
The Featherman's last breath yawning from below,
Snapping and chuckling the cloth like a flag.
We would clap our hands to the rhythm
And sway with the swell and roll, as one.
Then wave to the silent sea birds,
Or listen to the growing sky,
For an echo
A reminder
Or a sigh . . .
I forget which.

—DR

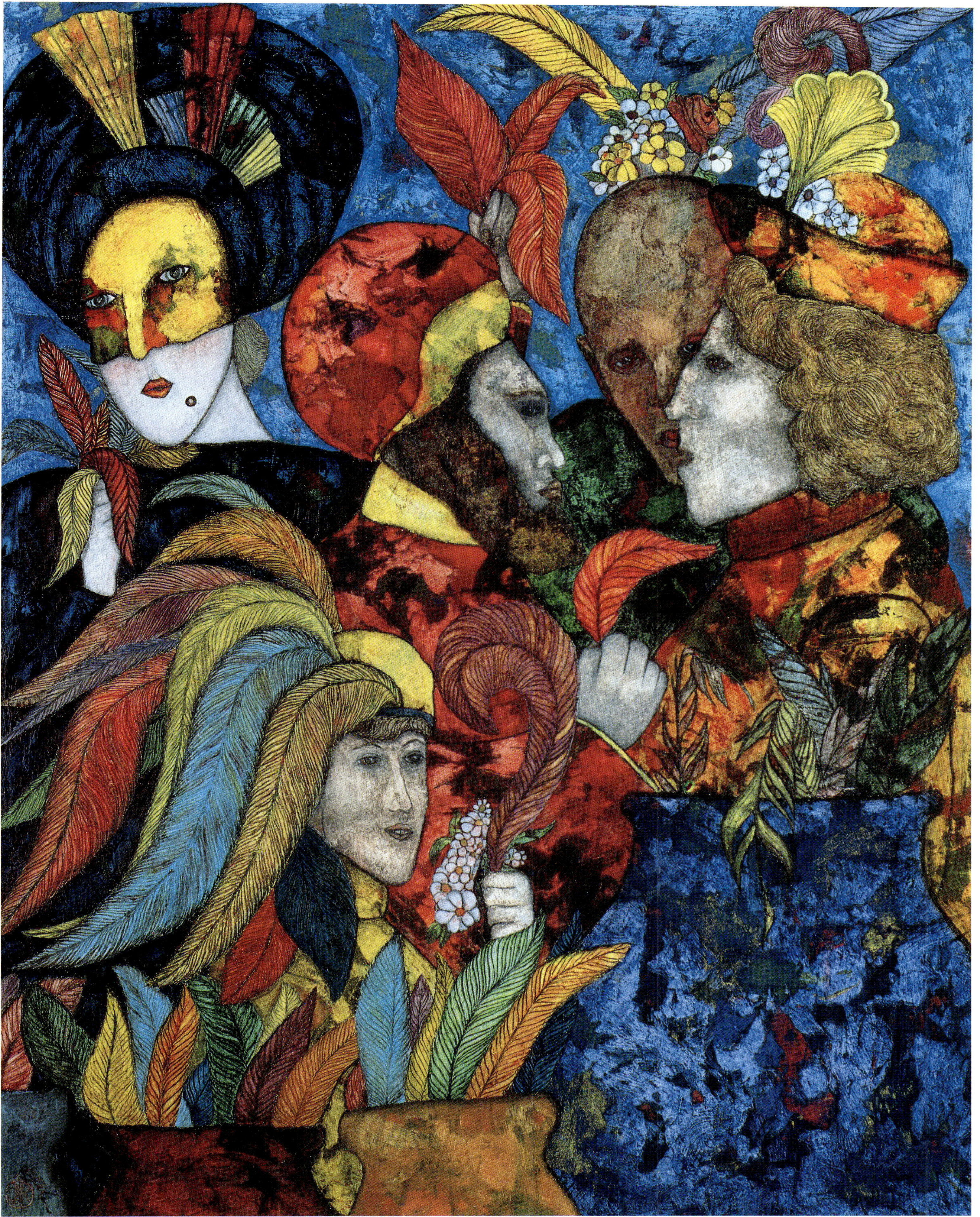

THE STONE PRINCE

Poetic Imagery Series
Oil 29" x 24" 1991

the stone prince

Like the laughing wind that cast you,
You have found what you wanted
By losing your way.

So,
You are the stone prince again.
Gloating under camouflage,
Bearing feathers in your cap,
Stolen flowers from the tomb.
Decorated like an ancient vampire,
Leaking at the seams.
You tread upon hourglass shards
While draining the poet's urn.

Yes,
You are stone again.
A rising pyramid,
Made from the great and small
Of other stones, that were
Grains and glass, and then stone
again.

Yes,
You are the shrine.
Dead before your death,
For the hyena wind devours the standing
And regurgitates in the barrens,
Where fallow dunes inter each other.

—DR

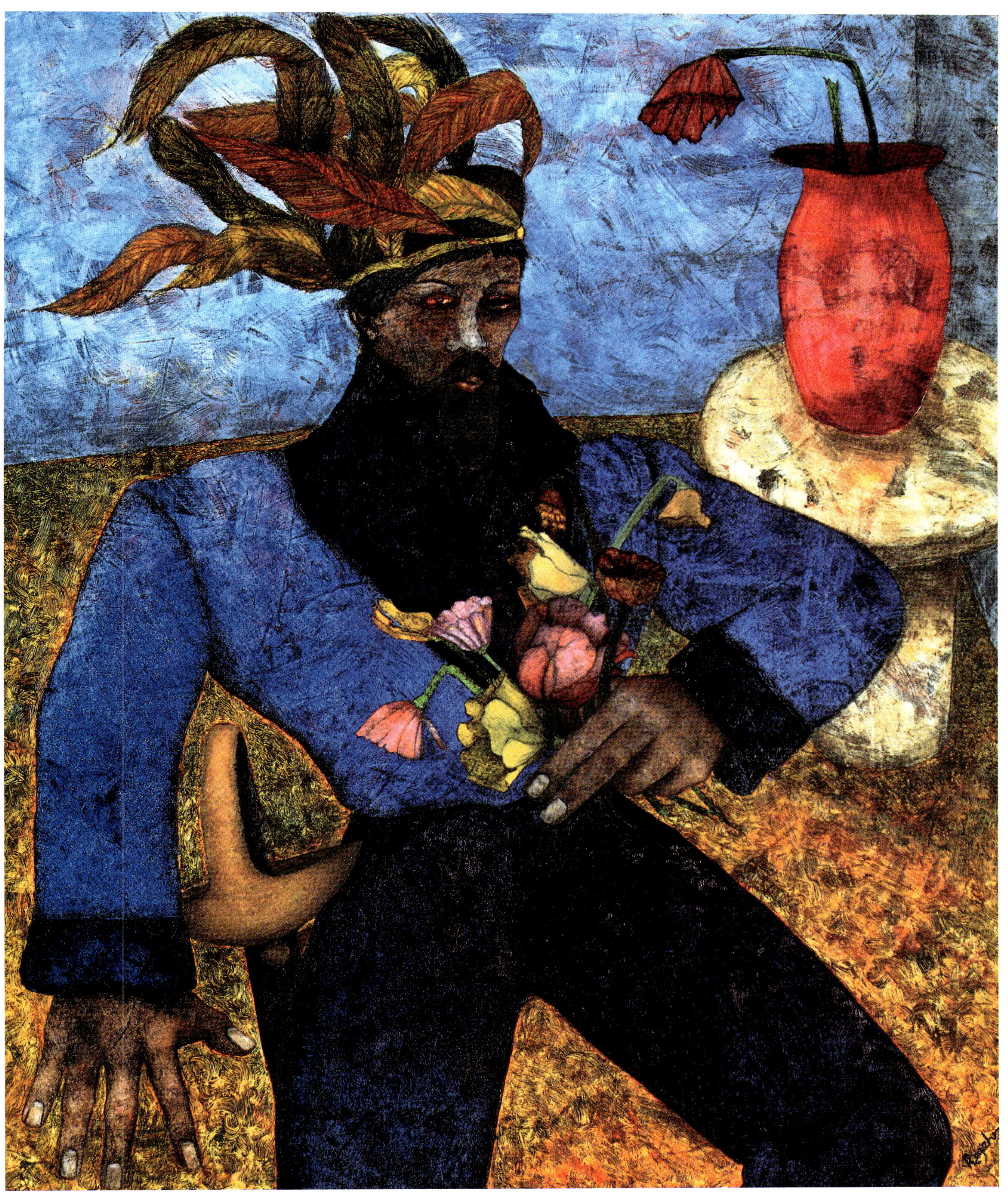

HEARTS

Smokin' Gun Series

Diptych – Pencil, Acrylic, Paper 36" x 48" 1988

The Bullet

From surface to surface, my destiny,
Like a carrion fly,
Now over here, my trust to there I abandon.
My allegiance, a ricochet kiss.

This flight path, my only faith,
Is a whining line,
A screaming bead of red,
A steady beam on a dead man's heart gauge.

So many lines crisscross,
So many lines shoot across and across,
And I have never wandered, never wondered,
Never pondered the zigzag left behind,

For there are no curves on a dead man's bead,
Only corners, bloody corners, broken corners . . .
So many corners off these walls,
This space could fill to black.

—DR

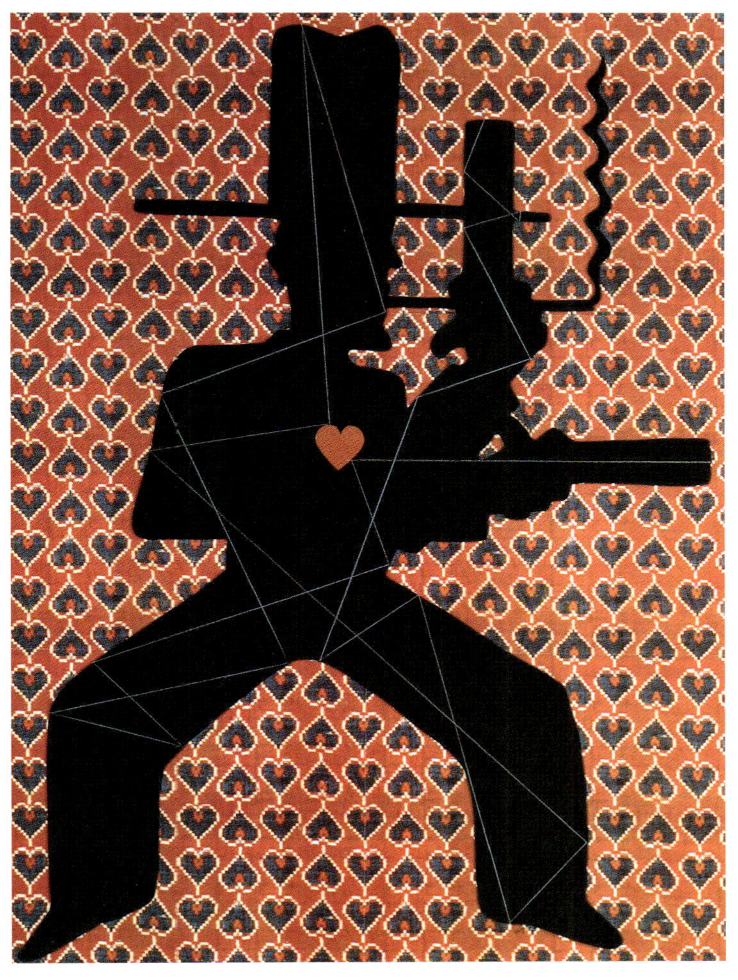

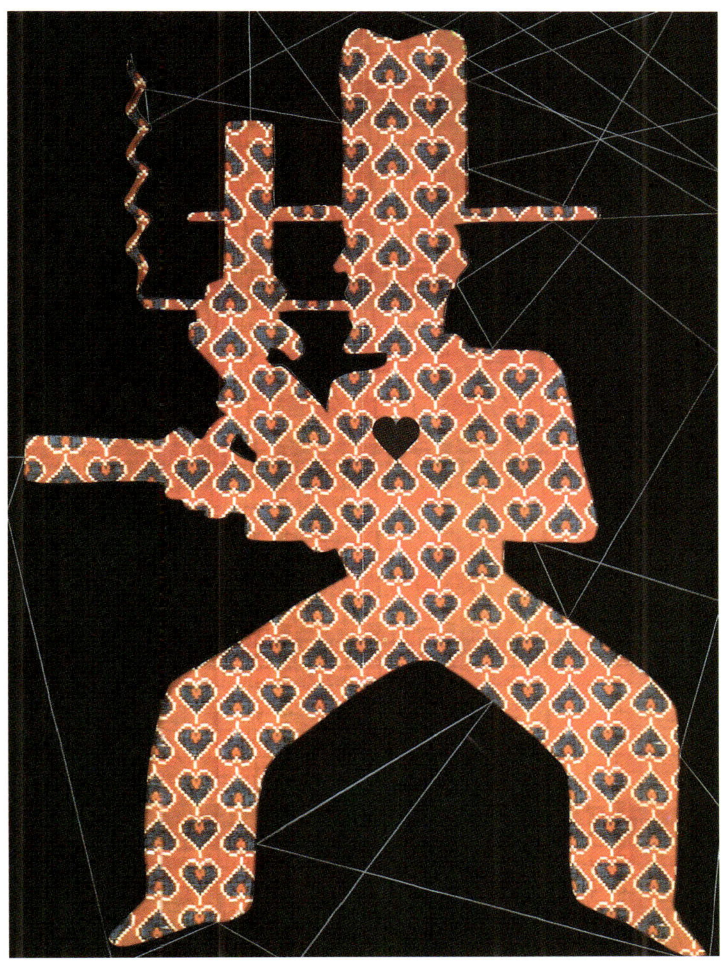

SMOKIN' GUN NO. 71
ANGEL OF THE WEST

Oil 36" x 24" 1988

Gaia's Daughter

The weeds of greed grow natural,
As nothing strange with the wild of things,
The seed is a grain in the grave again,
And the plague is a cyclical scourge.

So ran the course of the holy gunman,
Angel of the West, riding the wings of apocalypse,
With his blindman's code, his mercenary gold
And his legend lined with lead.

Back to the arms of the Scavenger's daughter,
She stretched his code to brittleness,
Powdered his gold to alchemic dust,
Threw salt on the slug of his conscience.

She straddled his faith on the altar stone.
And from her splintering thighs,
Pounded shards of wounded sacrifice,
Imbedding truth in his weakening fate.

And from her endless womb she spread
His plague beneath the weeds,
To cure as purist seed again, a grain again,
In her mother's tireless grave.

—DR

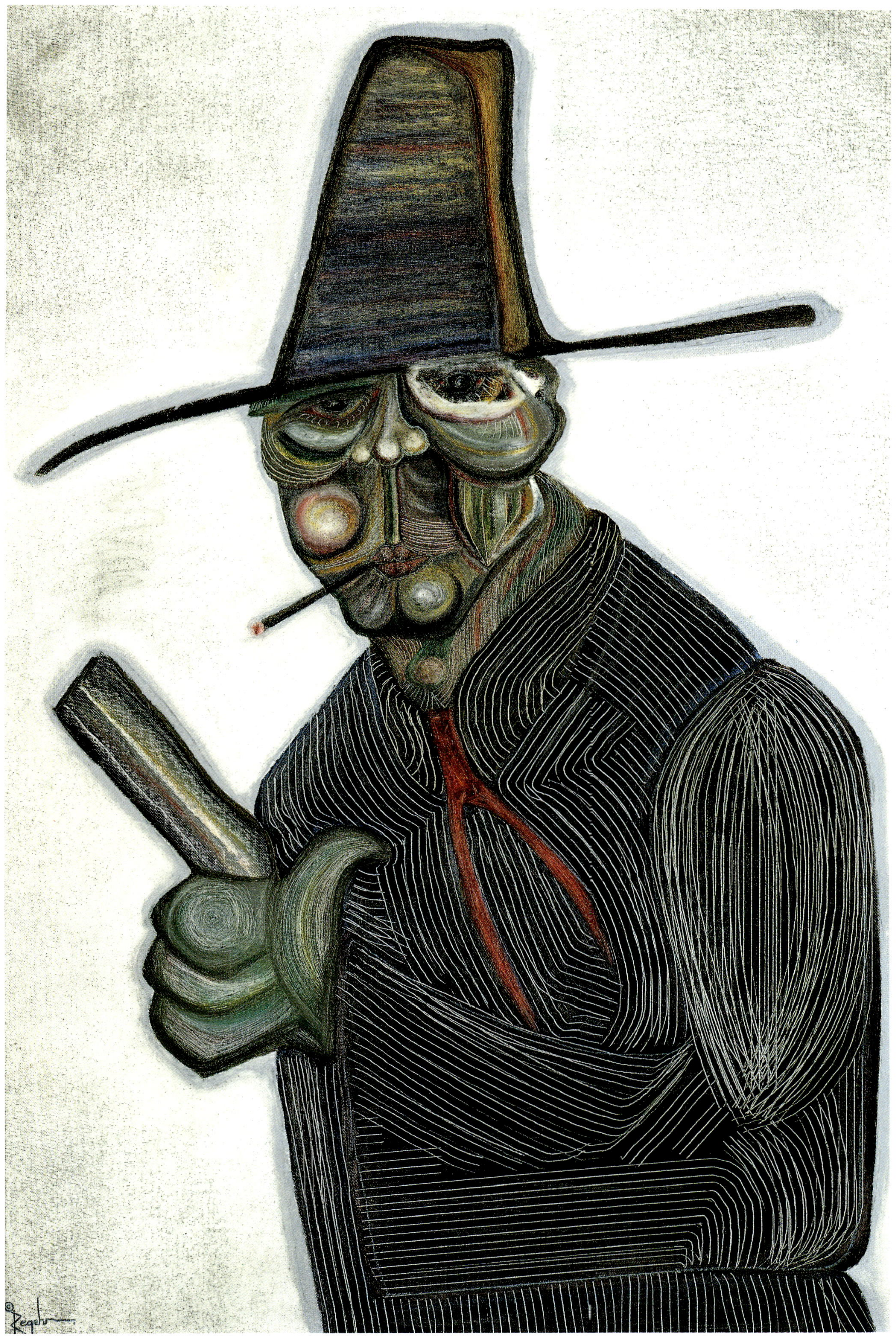

NO SECRETS

Poetic Imagery Series
Oil 36" x 24" 1994

Ghost Limb

I have gnawed away the captured part of me
That once knew the rest so perfectly as whole
The limb I leave to cure beneath your sun

I could rise again at dusk
But I will let myself flow with no tourniquet this night
No vessel to hold my life apart from earth's

And I will lie here on the forest floor
Staring up at a million island stars
That separated long ago now long for coalescence

And like a legless child writhing on its back
Inscribe the patterns of an angel's wings
Furrowed deep to fossilize in clay

And so preserve this place of rapture
With curing limb and flightless wings
Interred beneath your sun

Then I shall walk without standing first
Without design without rhythm to my stride
Having lost awareness of the part of me I leave behind for you

But you know well the vestige
Will call out for all it knows of me
Gone deep into forest shade

And I will walk apart from earth by the will of a ghost limb
That only knows itself as an ache
Yearning to be whole again.

—DR

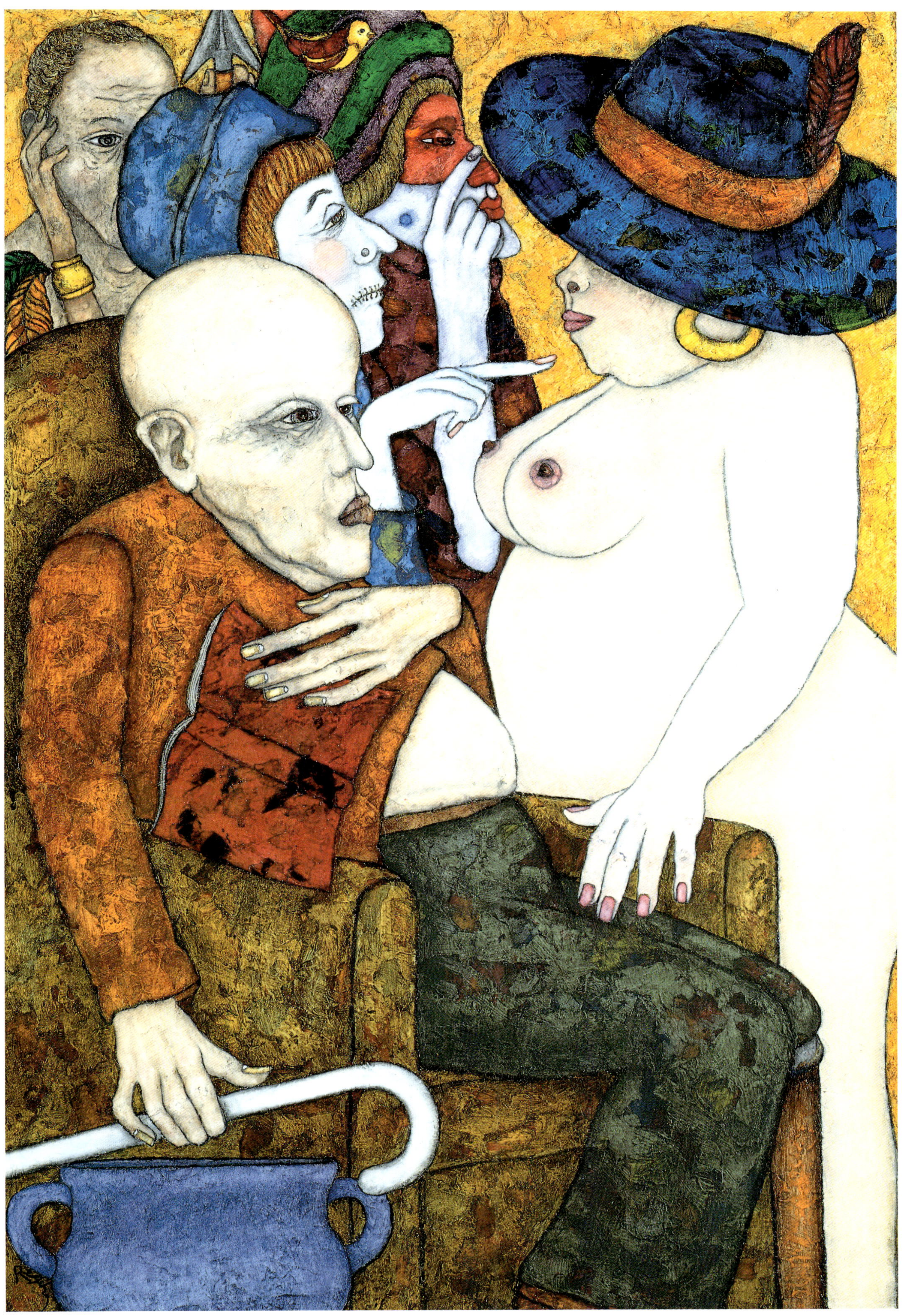

THE SPOILERS

Poetic Imagery Series
Oil 28" x 24" 1994

Old Seth is Spoilin'

After the life of day is lost,
you sit there rocking in the creeping dark,
your bonfire bottle on the window sill
glimmers deep red against a bleeding sky,

against your grit yellow teeth,
against your barbed-wire grin,
against a pane of black, reflects you back
to yourself old Seth,

but old Seth, you look out
and you look back when you look out,
watch out old Seth, you're out there
. . . and there's murder in your glass tonight

and there's poison in your spittle curse
against that ghost of a silo, goddamn you'll punish
who reaps the blame for those cast down cattle,
these broken down barns, this dead homestead!

Now there's an axe in the crippled shed Seth,
there's oil in the leaky drum
and branding coals beneath the boiler burn on,
while your world has fallen asleep . . .

You could torch the farm Seth,
or chop it fourteen ways,
anyway you cut it Seth
you blow it all away,

and you can sit right there in your rocking chair,
set back, lie back, drink back that bottle on the sill,
or you can start all over again,
but be sure to look back old Seth, look out old Seth

Old Seth? . . . there's murder in your glass tonight.
—DR

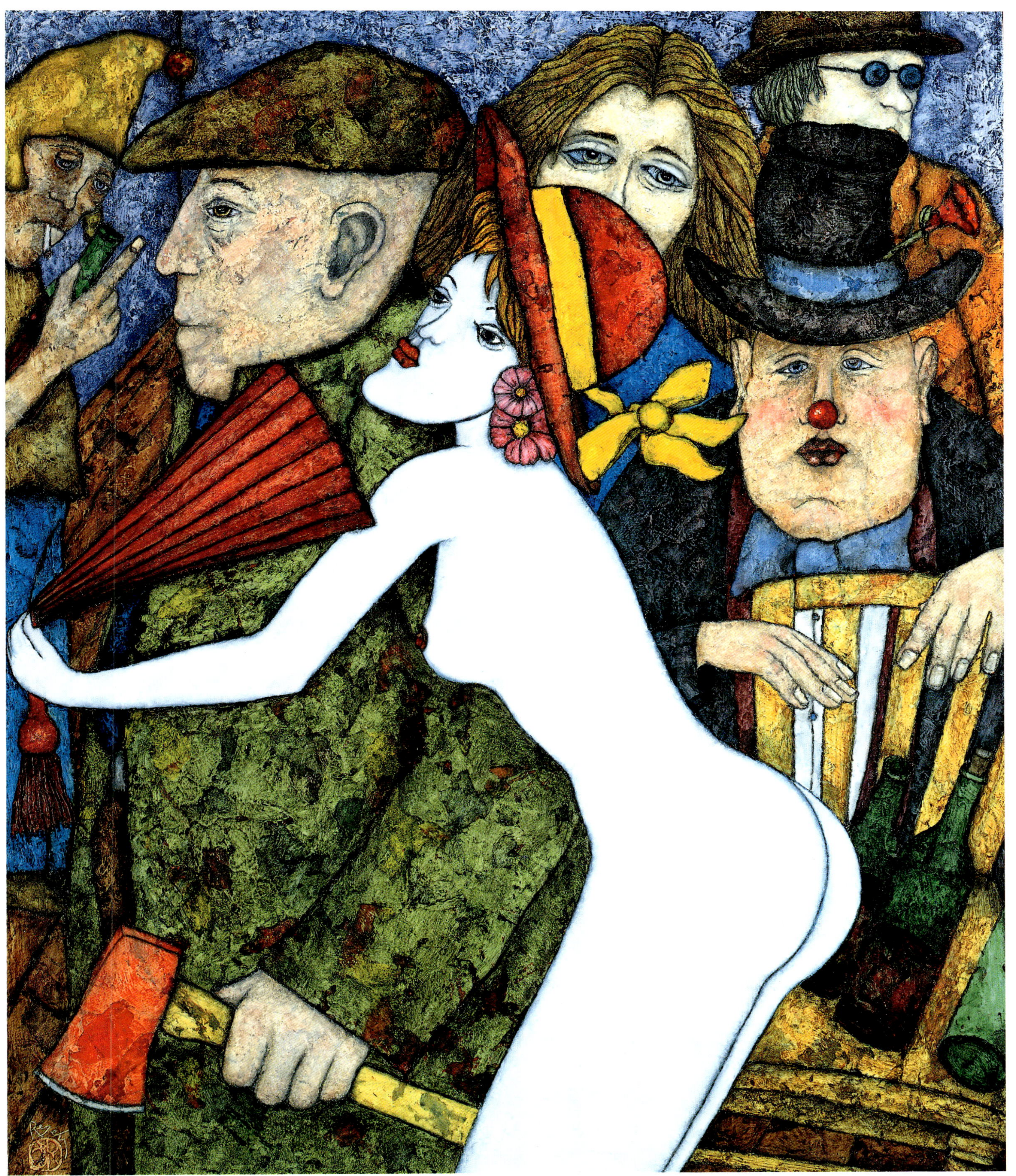

LEDA

Poetic Imagery Series

Oil 17" x 12" 1992

Stare

In Sunday stillness
By a sunlit window,
You are lying late and naked
On love and warm afternoon shadows

I am frozen by your cigarette
Spidering its smoke through your hair

Does this celebration escape
The way a tired balloon abandons circus litter . . .
Far below, tent lights echo the stars,
And without cause, we are between.
There is no more seeking, only floating.
We know the joy rides were never straightforward
And we realize the carousel is not magic, it plays
The axis trick,
Around and gone
Around and the same, around . . .
The colors are a stenciled rhythm
That the galloping stares of wooden ponies reflect.
Will we spiral?
Waiting faster and faster for some threshold
Or slow to pause a lifetime,
Angry with our tolerance

You stare,
I remain frozen,
As your cigarette retreats at dusk.

—DR

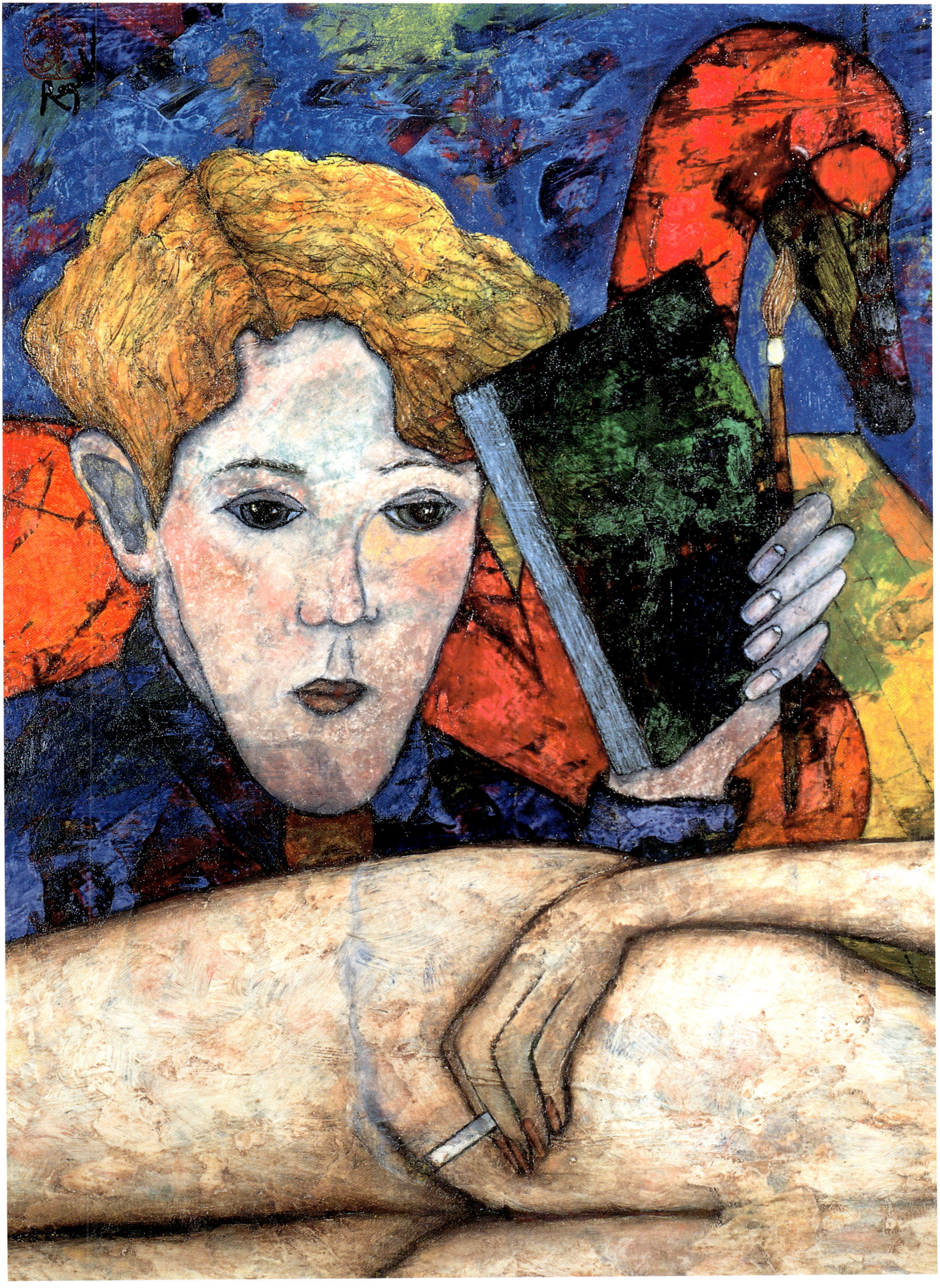

GLASS MEN

Poetic Imagery Series
Oil 12" x 9" 1992

The Jarless Genie

Time runs out of sand,
And glass men break along the shore,
Heaped beside shattered courier bottles,
All letters lost by storm.

Glittering shards tumble dull and smooth,
Cold rocks that were stars, are grit again, everywhere
Footprints race to etch a mark between erasing tides.

Now the house of glass has worn to a mote,
And the jarless genie wanders, wishing
For a magic lamp once more, before
Sand runs out of time.

—DR

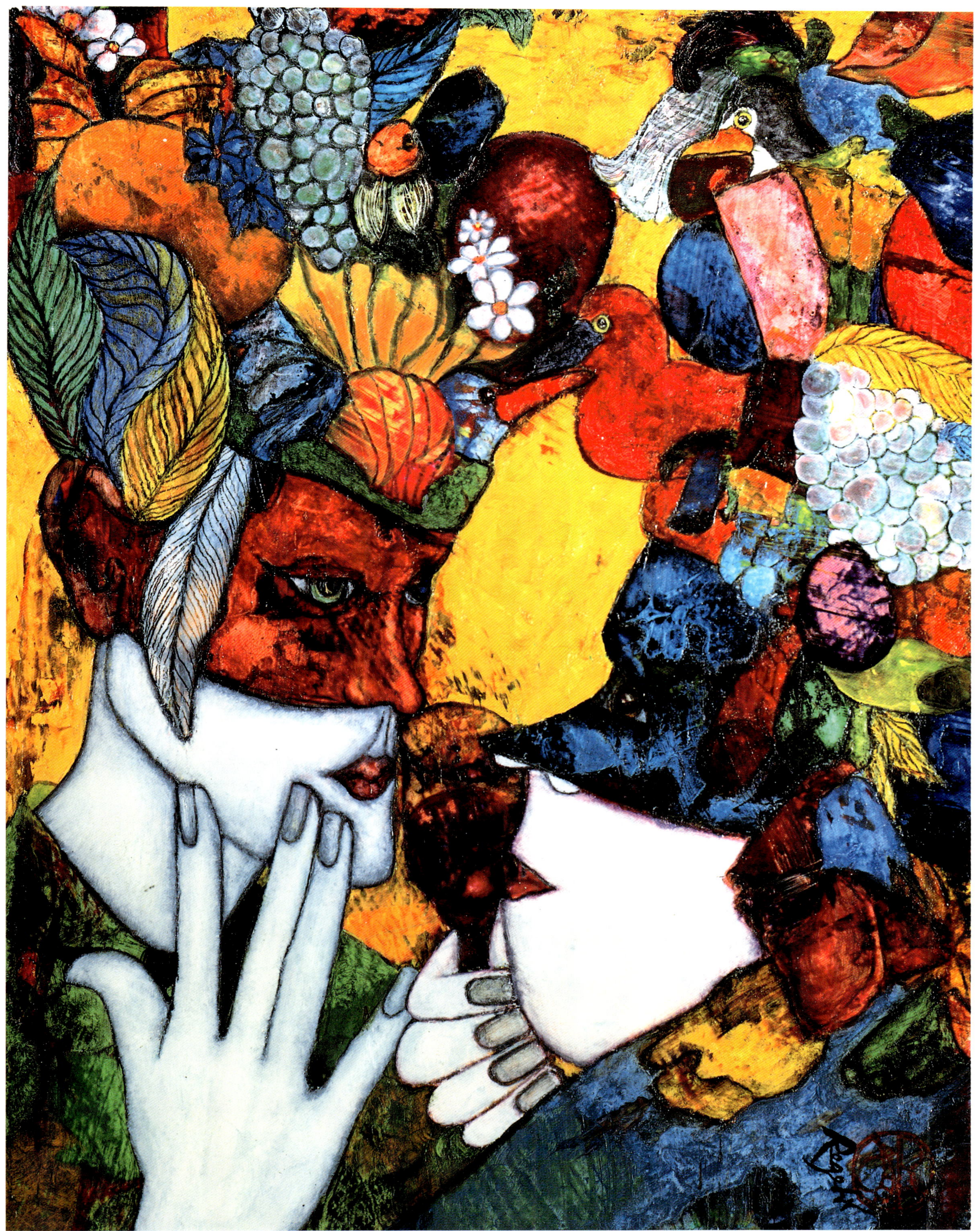

LIST OF ILLUSTRATIONS